DUQUESNE STUDIES

Psychological Series

1

PHENOMENOLOGY AND THE HUMAN SCIENCES

A Contribution to a New Scientific Ideal

DUQUESNE STUDIES
Psychological Series
1

PHENOMENOLOGY AND THE HUMAN SCIENCES
A Contribution to a New Scientific Ideal

by

STEPHAN STRASSER, Ph.D.

DUQUESNE UNIVERSITY PRESS, Pittsburgh, Pa.
Editions E. Nauwelaerts, Louvain
1963

DUQUESNE STUDIES

142.7

S89 p

PSYCHOLOGICAL SERIES

Adrian L. van Kaam, Ph.D., Anthony Barton, Ph.D., and Edward W. Hogan, Ph.D., editors.

Volume One—Stephan Strasser, PHENOMENOLOGY AND THE HUMAN SCIENCES. *A Contribution to a New Scientific Ideal.* XIII and 339 pages. Price: $6.00.

In preparation:

Aron Gurwitsch, FIELD OF CONSCIOUSNESS

Georges Gusdorf, INTRODUCTION TO THE HUMAN SCIENCES

DUQUESNE STUDIES are published in the following series:

Philological Series. Three volumes to date.

Philosophical Series. Fourteen volumes to date.

Psychological Series. One volume to date.

Spiritan Series. Five volumes to date.

Theological Series. One volume to date.

Catalog on request. Twenty percent discount on continuation orders for all series.

Periodicals published by Duquesne University Press:

Annuale Mediaevale. $4.00 per year.

Duquesne Hispanic Review. Three issues a year. $3.00 per year.

Duquesne Review. A Journal of the Social Sciences. Two issues a year. $2.25 per year.

Duquesne Science Counselor. Four issues a year. $3.00 (foreign $3.25) per year.

Review of Existential Psychology and Psychiatry. Three issues a year. $5.00 per year.

Library of Congress Catalog Card Number: 63-8143

©1963, by Duquesne University

Printed in the U.S.A. by
The Ad Press, Ltd., New York, N. Y.

TABLE OF CONTENTS

———

FIRST STUDY

THE SEARCH FOR A THIRD APPROACH

SECOND STUDY

THREEFOLD OBJECTIVITY

A. THE OBJECTIVITY OF THE EVERYDAY WORLD

vii

B. Universal Objectivity

THIRD STUDY

PHENOMENOLOGY AND EMPIRICAL HUMAN SCIENCE

PREFACE

During the defense of an historical dissertation a doctoral candidate was reproached for having neglected an important source. His defense consisted in a simple dismissal of the objection with the astonishing remark that he was following the "phenomenological method." A phenomenologist, so he said, had to analyse only a single representative case and did not have to waste time in carefully tracing and consulting sources. Shortly after this defense a prominent colleague asked us whether the standpoint of this student correctly expressed the fundamental principles of phenomenological philosophy. At that moment the plan of writing this work was born.

Inevitably this study will have a critical character. By being critical, however, we do not mean to disparage, to minimize or to make ridiculous. Our intention is to practice the art of *krinein,* in the original sense of this Greek term, as the art of discernment. The main idea is to distinguish three different cognitive attitudes without separating them—namely, the archaic-mythical, the scientific, and the philosophical attitude. It is our conviction that these essentially different attitudes cannot be arbitrarily and thoughtlessly chosen, exchanged or combined. By means of this distinction we hope to delineate a way out of the growing confusion which befuddles large numbers of students but not only students. At the same time we hope to absolve the phenomenological movement from a reproach which, *as such,* it does not deserve.

It is not possible to attain completeness in a study such as the present, in which philosophical and empirical insights have to be integrated into a synthesis to arrive at a theory of science, especially when one keeps in mind that the empirical insights are to be derived from different human sciences. First of all, every year hundreds of publications appear in the realm of each particular human science. Only a specialist in each area of research would be able to survey and evaluate this flood of books and articles. Secondly, completeness is not attainable also for personal reasons. An entire human life is needed to acquire solid knowledge in a single realm of the human sciences. Anyone, therefore, who would rigidly hold fast to an encyclopedic ideal would have to abandon the hope of ever arriving at a synthetic view of what it means to pursue science as such.

Such a completeness, however, is not required, for the purpose of this book is not to explore any particular realm of experience but to acquire essential insights. For this reason, whenever there was a choice between different examples, we have constantly given preference to the more *simple* over the more complex. This is one of the reasons why Künkel's characterology will be studied extensively. For the clarity of Künkel's methodic idea makes it possible to illustrate certain interconnections more appropriately.

We have, moreover, very deliberately used the *method of contrasting pictures*. "Classical" representatives of certain trends are compared with one another to show the results to which certain philosophical or epistemological presuppositions lead. We are very much aware of the fact that, for instance, there exist hundreds of intermediary positions between extreme existential philosophical views and extreme logical positivism.[1] Nevertheless, the various proposed compromises are less instructive than the attempts to think through a radical fundamental idea in the realm of scientific pursuits. Thus we have usually restricted ourselves to naming a single representative writer rather than the many who could have been enumerated. For, the adding of innumerable names and titles of publications would not have contributed anything to attaining the *insight* into human science which constitutes the goal of this book.

On the other hand, the fact that certain aspects of this study about a many-sided topic have not been very thoroughly elaborated gives us some qualms of conscience. This dissatisfaction applies especially to the question of what the essence of phenomenology is. It is our intention to devote a special work to the fundamental ideas of phenomenology and we trust that that work will give greater satisfaction to the professional philosopher.

While this book was being written, Sartre published the first volume of his *Critique de la raison dialectique*.[2] It has given us no reasons to modify our critical considerations. They are concerned

[1]Cf. pp. 10-55.
[2]Paris, 1960.

with Sartre the existentialist philosopher, who published his views in numerous earlier works, and not with Sartre the budding Marxist or half-Marxist. Sartre's earlier attempts to formulate an existential psychoanalysis remain instructive, even though the new Sartre does not continue along the same line.

It was impossible for us to take into account two recent important publications—namely, Herbert Spiegelberg's *The Phenomenological Movement*[3] and Georges Gusdorf's *Introduction aux sciences humaines*.[4] These two works are excellent complements to the ideas studied here in their more essential aspects. We would like to draw attention especially to Gusdorf's work, which is a grand attempt to present a topic which we ourselves wanted to avoid—a rather comprehensive historical picture of the origin of empirical human science.[5]

Stephan Strasser

The American edition of this book has been personally supervised by the author. I wish to thank Dr. John R. Kanda for his kind assistance in translating this book.

Duquesne University
Pittsburgh, Pa.

Henry J. Koren

---

[3]Two volumes, The Hague, 1960.
[4]Paris, 1960.
[5]Professor Gusdorf's work will appear in the DUQUESNE STUDIES, *Psychological Series*.

FIRST STUDY

THE SEARCH FOR A THIRD APPROACH

1. INTRODUCTION TO THE PROBLEM

What is Empirical Human Science? Contemporary thinkers are beginning to devote more and more attention to a certain group of sciences, in the broad sense of the term, which have a common characteristic. It consists in this that their students with the aid of empirical methods pursue the scientific investigation of man as a person. The qualification "as a person" is the crucial point of this description. In the realm of these sciences man is not studied as a conglomerate of albumen molecules, as a cellular state, or as a mammal, but studied in a way which, usually in an implicit fashion, takes into consideration man's specifically human character, i.e., his being a person. The historian, for instance, whether he mentions it or not, knows that only man is a being having a history. The linguist is aware of the fact that only man's behavior makes use of symbols.[1] The specialist in comparative religion is concerned only with man as *animal religiosum*. A similar situation exists in the scientific study of art, literature, culture, law, and economics. All these sciences could be conveniently classified under "positive anthropology," although in actual practice only the term "cultural anthropology" is customarily used when there is question of less civilized human beings. The possibility of this classification alone suffices to indicate that the sciences in question are interrelated. All of them, moreover, are closely connected with the science devoted to the existential orientation of man toward the cultural, historical, economic and religious world, i.e., *psychology*.[2] In addition, they are increasingly less capable of dispensing with the services of *sociology*,[3] the science which considers man as the bearer of typical social roles.

Accordingly, all these sciences constitute a single group. As a matter of fact, contemporary western thought is characterized by the increasing awareness which the various specialists have of the interconnection proper to their intellectual pursuits. We

---

[1]Cf. Maurice Merleau-Ponty, *La structure du comportement,* Paris, 1942, pp. 139-171.
[2]Cf. Stephan Strasser, *The Soul in Metaphysical and Empirical Psychology,* 2nd. impr., Pittsburgh, 1962, pp. 222-228.
[3]Cf. R. Dahrendorf, *Homo sociologicus,* Köln-Opladen, 1960.

3

may point to two symptoms to illustrate this assertion, viz., the constantly increasing difficulty to establish the respective boundaries of the various disciplines and the serious efforts to arrive at a synthesis. Clyde Kluckhohn, for example, speaks of "a comprehensive science of man" and remarks that "certain aspects of psychology, medicine and human biology, economics and human geography must be fused with anthropology in a general science which must likewise embrace the tools of historical and statistical methods and draw data from history and the other humanities."[4] John J. Honigman likewise connects culture and personality and states that "culture and personality is, as the name suggests, a synthetic or a cross-discipline and not an insulated department of social science. In the same way that present knowledge in the field reflects the work of psychologists, psychiatrists, sociologists and anthropologists, so future results will emerge from the continued integration of ideas from these and other specialists."[5]

"Sciences of the Mind" (Geisteswissenschaften) *or "Human Sciences"?* The group of sciences with which we are concerned here is indicated in French by the term *sciences humaines*. Commenting on this newly coined term, André Lalande says: "The term is of recent origin, but becomes more and more popular to indicate the sciences which used to be known as 'moral sciences.' The new term places more emphasis on the externally observable characteristics of the way in which human being behave whether individually or collectively."[6]

This remark is important. Why may the "human sciences" not be identified with the "sciences of the mind"? Why are they not "sciences which have the human mind as their object"?[7] The reason is that they study man precisely as a person, and not as a spirit, mind, consciousness, or soul which somehow resides in a body. Anyone who is familiar with the history of contemporary thinking knows that the substitution of "human sciences" for "mental sciences" must be viewed as indicative of an intellectual

---

[4]*Mirror for Man*, New York, 1949, p. 1.
[5]*Culture and Personality*, New York, 1956, p. IX.
[6]*Vocabulaire technique et critique de la philosophie*, 7th ed., Paris, 1956, p. 958.
[7]Lalande, *ibid.*

4

evolution. It means that the majority of thinkers have broken with the Cartesian idea of man as consisting of a "thinking substance" which is intimately connected with an "extended substance." It means also the elimination of Locke's theory that the "external world" is the object of experience in "perception" and that the "internal world" is the object of experience in "reflection." The rise of the new term "human sciences" is a result of this changed standpoint. It indicates that scientific research has to be devoted to man as a concrete spiritual-material unity, to his concrete behavior, his concrete way of living, his concrete realizations.

Human Science and Science of Nature. Viewed in this fashion, the sciences in question are essentially different from physical science. As Lalande remarks, "It is to be noted that 'the human sciences' do not include all the sciences concerned with man. For example, anatomy and physiology are not indicated by this term, which applies only to the sciences interested in that which is characteristic of man in opposition to nature."[8] Physical science, in the broadest sense, views man as a part of the cosmos, a part that is not essentially different from the rest. Human sciences, on the other hand, are concerned with that which is specifically human.[9]

Reserving the philosophical justification of this distinction for later, we want first to draw attention to a consequence flowing from the above-described antidualistic holistic viewpoint. The fact that man as a concrete totality, with his concrete behavior and his concrete realizations constitutes the object of scientific experience, means that all these branches of science allow the application of *empirical methods,* i.e., experience can be organized in such a way that it leads to inductive conclusions.[10] It implies, moreover, that in principle these conclusions are subject to the common critical appraisal of specialists and not accessible only to a single individual. It is in this sense that we speak here of *empirical experience,* with-

---

[8]*Ibid.*

[9]See, e.g., Frederick Buytendijk, "Das Menschliche in der menschlichen Bewegung," *Der Nervenarzt,* vol. 28 (1957), pp. 1-7.

[10]It would lead us to far afield to examine here the deviating view of Karl R. Popper, *The Logic of Scientific Discovery,* New York, 1959, pp. 106-111.

out in any way identifying it with human experience in general. The question, however, whether or not the results of inductive experience de facto constitute the *entire* substance of these sciences must be reserved for later. What has been said here is, at any rate, sufficient to justify the use of the term *empirical human science* in reference to the above-mentioned group of disciplines.

The human science based upon systematized experience agrees with physical science insofar as both make use of the empirical method. This agreement, however, should not make us forget that there is an essential difference between the two groups. The difference in question may perhaps be expressed in the following way. Physical science considers man as a being produced by nature. He appears to it as a link in a cosmic evolution, as an organism dependent on a biologically definable environment, as the result of a phylogenetic and ontogenetic evolution. *The empirical study of man,* on the other hand, *views man as the originator and worker of his own surrounding world (Umwelt).* It describes the rise, through man and for man, of a world possessing social, historical, cultural, and religious aspects.[11] *This distinction does not at all intend to cast doubt on the possibility that there are points of contact between the two groups of sciences.* On the contrary, we are quite willing to affirm this contact. In some sciences, such as medicine, social geography, and economics, the points of contact play an extremely important role. This contact, however, is not what concerns us at present, for our aim here is to describe empirical human science as an inter-connected group of sciences, to

---

[11]It is beyond the scope of this book to speak here extensively of the reasons why we cannot accept the division of the sciences into three groups, sciences of *logos,* of reality, and of nature, defended by Hans Freyer in his books, *Soziologie als Wirklichkeitswissenschaft,* Leipzig, 1930, and *Einleitung in die Soziologie,* Leipzig, 1931, pp. 124 ff. It seems to us that Freyer's "phenomenological" view is based upon a one-sided interpretation of one or two of Husserl's earlier works. The separation of the noematic ("objective") aspect of the human act from its noetic ("subjective") aspect is not in line with phenomenological philosophy. Secondly, it is not clear to us why the life of language and art should be reduced to the realm of the *logos,* and historical and social life to that of "reality." Most of all, we feel compelled to reject the concept of "objective spirit," which Freyer borrows from Litt, Spranger, Dilthey, and Hegel. Cf. our critique of "inhuman consciousness" on pp. 51 ff. and 281 ff.

6

investigate its proper character, and to explain the problems arising in this group.[12]

The Anthropological Dilemma. The crucial problem of empirical human science may be suitably expressed in the following question. *How can man as a person make man as a person the object of an empirical inquiry?* It is here that lies the core of the problem. Deliberately contradicting Auguste Comte, Kluckhohn points out that "the scientist of human affairs needs to know as much about the eye that sees as the object seen."[13] But, we may ask, how is it possible for the sociologist to describe human conflicts with empirical exactness while he himself is involved in such conflicts? The psychologist, likewise, has to characterize the behavior of human persons, but the pursuit itself of psychology is a typical behavior. There could be a psychology of the psychologist just as well as a sociology of the sociologist. Who, however, would be able to pursue such an investigation successfully—the psychologist or the non-psychologist? Both would appear to be eminently unqualified for such a task.

Another way of clarifying the "anthropological dilemma" lies in the above-mentioned description of empirical human science. The specialist in this science, who views individuals and groups as originators and organizers of their respective worlds, would be obliged, of course, to include the culture of science in these worlds, for no one would doubt that our society is decisively influenced, e.g., by Freud's psychological view and Marx's socio-economic ideas. Yet such an inclusion means that the man who studies

---

[12]If the question is asked exactly which sciences belong to the empirical human science, a twofold reply could be given. One could enumerate all intellectual disciplines in which the anthropological standpoint ought to play a role. The resulting list would become very long and the task of demarcating the boundaries between the sciences would be exceedingly difficult. The quotations from Lalande suffice to show that, e.g., certain parts of medical science require more anthropological thinking than others, i.e., more thinking from the viewpoint of man as man. To escape from this difficulty, we intend to limit our analyses to the sciences in which the anthropological viewpoint has already gained recognition, viz., psychology, psychiatry, sociology, history, positive an'hropology, and the comparative science of religion. In a future publication we hope to draw attention to the consequences this standpoint has for predominantly normative sciences, such as pedagogy.
[13]*Mirror for Man,* p. 11.

human science changes his object while he studies it and because he studies it. Consequently, we must ask, Where is the firm foundation which he needs in the pursuit of his supposedly empirical study?

The Problem of Freedom. Moreover, the creation and organization of a world is an expression of human freedom. The art, culture, religion, and political system of human groups reveal definite styles of existence. The Greeks, for instance, with their culture of the *polis* (city), and the empire-building Romans may not be compared with two kinds of spiders spinning respectively, a vertical and a horizontal web. The *polis* and the empire correspond to historically grown modes in which human groups pursued their freedom. The crucial question that arises here is whether or not there is a possibility empirically to investigate free activities. Does not to be free mean to be able to do whatever one wants? Is, therefore, a free being not as changeable as Proteus, the mythical sea-god, who constantly appeared in different shapes? Is he not able to assume any appearance? And if this is the case, how would it be possible to describe such changeable beings, to characterize their behavior, to compare their realizations, and to discover typical laws applying to them? A description which was true yesterday could tomorrow be rendered false by freedom. But what is needed, so it seems, in an empirical science are "fixed data," "facts" that can serve as a basis for conclusions. Otherwise, how would the man of science be able to justify the results of his work before the critical eyes of his colleagues?

Purpose as Problem. There is even more. Individual human beings as well as groups are sensitive to values, they are attracted by purposes, they sometimes make projects which refer not only to things and connections but also to their own way of life as individuals or as a group. All this causes the greatest trouble. Is it possible to measure values? Can they be compared and arranged in an objective fashion? True, people sometimes speak of a "hierarchy of values," but is not, e.g., an esthetic value really beyond comparison with a political value? And is it not true that a political value cannot be placed on the same line as a religious

8

1. *Introduction to the Problem*

value?[14]   The appreciation of values gives rise to the motives which determine man's actions.   But, is it possible to find rules enabling us to predict what the statesman will decide, what the artist will produce, what wife a man will choose?   Are all these things not influenced by "irrational factors"?   Are we not here fully in the realm of the subjective?

It is impossible to avoid the disturbing question about the *objectivity* of research that aims at man as a person.   How can there be real science of something as changeable, as ephemeral, as difficult to grasp as an inclination, an evaluation, a motive, a decision, a project?   Does not "to know" mean to let the object-to-be-known be the norm of the knower and does it not imply that the object should be relatively identifiable and relatively immutable?   If this is so, may human evaluations, motives and purposes still be referred to as "objects"?

All these questions indicate the reasons why we think that the empirical study of man as man is affected with a typical kind of problem.   Briefly put, this problem arises from a triple root. Firstly, it is connected with the reflective character of man's investigation of himself as a person; secondly, it arises from the impossibility of making an empirical approach to absolute freedom; thirdly, it springs from the difficulty of drawing inductive conclusions referring to evaluations, motivations, and purposes. The justification of an empirical human science stands or falls with the possibility of overcoming the problems enumerated in the preceding pages. Our first task, therefore, will be to subject this triple crucial point to a thorough examination.

---

[14]Cf. Paul Ricoeur, *Philosophie de la volonté,* Paris, n. d., pp. 100 ff.

2. THE "FIRST APPROACH": OBJECTIVISM

Technicians and Theorists. The misestimation of empirical human science as a special group of sciences is of fairly recent origin. Hence it should not surprise us that its students, who would seem called to supply the answers, usually fail to do so. As Georges Gusdorf points out, "a look at the present condition of the human sciences suffices to observe that they are in a state of utter disorganization. True, they develop, they multiply their work, but the technicians of the various disciplines usually do not know exactly what they want or what they are doing."[15] This complaint is certainly not without foundation. One of the consequences of modern specialization is the frequent restriction to a very limited realm of experience, a restriction which far too often is accompanied by a kind of narrow-mindedness in theoretical interest. One's whole energy is devoted to the technical organization of a tiny fraction of experience. Husserl complained that even in his time psychological research was degenerating into technique guided by instinct. Even mature and outstanding men of science are not always immune against the real or apparent fascination of successful research. It suffices to recall here the reply given by Alfred Binet to the question of what intelligence is: "Intelligence is that which is measured by my tests."[16]

Nevertheless, we should be on guard against generalizations, for every technique flows from a theoretical vision. There have always been theorists who have endeavored to disclose the implications contained in the concept of empirical research technique and who have developed these implications in the form of programs. Moreover, it would have been impossible to apply these techniques on a large scale if there had not been a fairly general conviction that in principle their application is justifiable. The above-mentioned difficulties, therefore, can be answered. The replies are supplied in a large number of textbooks, containing introductions to, and norms of research work, and in numerous publications of

---

[15]"Sur l'ambiguité des sciences humaines," *Diogène,* no. 26 (avril-juin 1959), pp. 57-81.

[16]Quoted by Paul Guillaume, *Introduction à la psychologie,* Paris, 1946, p. 303.

10

2. The "First Approach": Objectivism

theoretical science. It would not be feasible to analyze all of them here or even to enumerate them. All we are interested in here is to show the main line. Accordingly, it is only by way of illustration that we will introduce a few authors who have contributed to the justification of this "line" from the standpoint of scientific theory.

The "Scientific Apparatus." Despite divergences in many secondary respects, the theorists of objectivistic experience are in agreement about the important questions. Their reply to the triple problem discussed in the first part of this study is, leaving aside less important variations, as follows.

It is true that man as person can never make himself the object of an empirical inquiry. For this reason care should be taken to avoid such a situation, for it cannot lead to scientifically useful results. In principle it is necessary to make a clear distinction between the subject and the object of an investigation. *The subject of an investigation is he who organizes the experience* playing a role in the inquiry. This means that the subject must guide concrete experience along lines leading to empirically useful results. It means also that he introduces certain categories, concepts, and models, thereby producing a language enabling him to state the results of this experience. Thirdly, it means that the contents of these concepts, the meanings of the scientific "terms" are determined as accurately as possible. It is quite evident that the "language" of mathematics and logistics is very appropriate to this purpose, and it seems not subject to doubt that the experience in question can be made broader and more precise by means of instruments.

If we summarize all these elements—the system of concepts, the models, the instruments and the rules governing their use, the research techniques and the methods of interpretation and control —under the term *scientific apparatus,* we may propose the following principle: *the subject who organizes the experience cannot be at the same time the object of this experience.* The reason is that experience has to pass through the filter of the scientific apparatus if it wants to qualify as scientific experience.

11

Let us illustrate the point by means of a few examples. The eye-witness account of Napoleon's entry in Vienna will be accepted by the historian as a source of knowledge. His account, as such, however, is not "history," because he does not have at his disposal the necessary historical concepts and categories. Accordingly, he is an object and not a subject of history as science. The same applies to writers of classical antiquity who describe social changes or modifications in the religious sphere. They are not sociologists or historians of religion, but objects of, respectively, sociological or historico-religious research.

Wherever experimental methods are used, the scientific apparatus assumes an eminently technical character. A clear-cut distinction of subject and object seems to be the prime condition of research. "As an *experimental science,*" Wilhelm Wundt wrote, "physiological psychology aims at a reformation of psychological research, which in importance does not rank lower than the change which the introduction of the experiment caused in the thinking of physical science. . . . For so-called self-observation may be presented as observation only with certain essential restrictions and cannot at all lay claim to exactness."[17] This quotation shows that the ideal to equal the exactness of physical science in psychological research already played a role in the writings of Wundt. Behavioristic psychologists think that they have to go even farther. They distrust any interhuman verbal communication as source of scientific knowledge. For this reason they prefer to experiment with animals rather than with man. E. C. Tolman, for instance, did not hesitate to dedicate one of his works[18] to *Mus norvegicus albinus,* the white rat, with which he had experimented. A few years later, he wrote, "Personally . . . I am suspicious of . . . verbal reports. I prefer to try to work out psychology with the aid of more gross forms of behavior. My motto for the present is: 'Rats, no men.' "[19]

According to these psychologists, the ideal cognitive attitude would be that of the zoologist who observes the reactions of a

---

[17]*Grundzüge der physiologischen Psychologie,* Vol. 1, Leipzig, 6th ed., 1908, p. 4. Tr. as *Principles of Physiological Psychology,* New York, 1904.
[18]*Purposive Behavior in Animals and Man,* New York, 1932.
[19]"An Operational Analysis of Demands," *Erkenntnis,* vol. 6 (1936), p. 390.

strange organism or that of a chemist who watches the changes of certain chemical substances. Even a man like Paul Guillaume, who is more moderate in his views, asks, "Why would it be impossible to study the laws governing the behavior of a man or of an animal in the same way as one studies those controlling the physico-chemical behavior of any kind of a body? There appears to be no reason to doubt the possibility of such an inquiry."[20] Such an approach, he continues, would offer even certain advantages, for it guarantees the "duality of the observer and the observed," the exteriority of the subject with respect to the object of scientific knowledge.

These quotations allow us to determine the meaning of "objectivism" more accurately. Insofar as the interest of empirical human science remains deliberately limited to man as object, as seen through the scientific apparatus, we will from now on speak of an *objectivistic attitude* of knowledge. In other words, *objectivism* consists in the tendency systematically to eliminate man as subject from the totality of anthropological interest.

Freedom "Between Brackets." What about the second difficulty, the impossibility of describing a free being empirically? This difficulty can likewise be overcome. It is a question of not merely organizing the data of experience but of selecting them as well. Only those experiences are scientifically relevant which lead to the determination of facts. As the behaviorist B. F. Skinner tells us, "Science is first of all a set of attitudes. It is a disposition to deal with facts."[21] The fact may or may not be the result of a free deed, but the fact itself does not reveal this. Suppose, for example, that a person is left the choice of multiplying or subtracting two numbers and that he subtracts. In doing so, he has the "feeling" that he could just as well have chosen to multiply. This "vague feeling," however, is not a fact, for from the experiment it is not evident that this conviction corresponds with reality. What is a fact is that he subtracted and did not multiply. The experimenter is able to determine this fact with absolute certainty.

---

[20]*Op. cit.*, pp. 288 f.
[21]*Science and Human Behavior,* New York, 3rd ed., 1956, p. 12.

If the psychologist in question is an objectivist,[22] he does not have to "deny" freedom—which would be a "metaphysical" statement —but may limit himself to describe the human action in such a way that the aspect of freedom is wholly eliminated. In this way the objectivist is able to construct a descriptive system of concepts in which freedom plays no role and, to use Husserl's expression, is "placed between brackets." Once freedom has thus been sedulously excluded from the conceptual content of "fact," it is easy to speak of a "determinism of facts" (Guillaume[23]).

"Suspended" Purposes. In a similar way it is possible to avoid the embarrassing question regarding value judgments and purposes. Let us illustrate the point by means of a typical discussion. According to the sociologist R. M. MacIver, "there is an essential difference between a paper flying before the wind and a man flying from a pursuing crowd. The paper knows no fear and the wind no hate, but without fear and hate the man would not fly nor the crowd pursue." For MacIver there is explicitly question of emotional purposes, an anxiously tending toward safety and a hateful tendency to get rid of their opponent. There are likewise emotional determinations of value, for safety and, respectively, vengeance are experienced as "good."

George A. Lundberg, however, who is more positivistically orientated, does not agree with MacIver. He objects to the latter's description because "fear" and "hatred" are subjective terms. It is not absolutely certain that several independent observers would equally speak of "anxious flight" and "hateful pursuit" and for this reason the use of such terms harms the objectivity of the sociological investigation. Lundberg's conclusion is that only externally observable behavior leads to objective observations. All perceptible "facts" can be described in the same way by all observers—namely, in the way it is done in physical science. Unsurprisingly, Lundberg is convinced that physical science, in the broad sense of the term, should function as the model of science for sociology, for the simple reason that physical science possesses

---

[22]Michotte and Prüm, who performed these experiments, were neither objectivists nor behaviorists.
[23]*Op. cit.,* p. 318.

a superior method to determine objective facts. "It is my thesis," he emphasizes, "that if we follow this method as faithfully as we have followed it in physics, it may yield us a corresponding reward of control."[24]

The Objectivistic Reduction. What Lundberg proposes here is apparently a kind of reduction. For him, it is an objective fact that the fleeing man has gone from point A to point B. In addition, it is objectively observable that the velocity of the pursuing crowd has increased from V_1 to V_2. But when we speak of a "fleeing man" and a "pursuing crowd" we still use subjective terms. The fact, conceived in the sense of physical science, does not say anything at all about fleeing or pursuing. It is possible, of course, that the fact has arisen from a flight and pursuit, but this is something that cannot be determined through the methods of physical science.

All this shows that the term "reduction" is not used here by sheer coincidence. It has a philosophical meaning, which Husserl was the first among modern thinkers to describe. It refers to a kind of suspension of judgment, though not in the sense of the *epoché* of the old Greek sceptics[25] but in a modern methodic sense. The objectivist does not at all intend to doubt the reality of freedom, motivation, evaluation, or purpose. He would not even be able to do so, for this reality constitutes the basis of his entire "personal" life. However, he does not make use of this reality in his scientific descriptions. He places it "between brackets" and suspends all judgments referring to it. As Lundberg remarks, "I do not declare MacIver's analysis of the man and the crowd *false,* I merely point out that possibly I could analyze the situation in a frame of reference not involving the words 'fear' or 'hate' but in operationally defined terms."[26] The reduction of a description to that which can be expressed also in the language of physics leads not only to a typical "monism of method"[27] but also to a

---

[24]*Foundation of Sociology,* 2nd ed., 1953, pp. 12 f. and VII. Cf. also "The Natural Science Trend in Sociology," *American Journal of Sociology,* 1955, vol. 61, pp. 91 ff.

[25]Cf., e.g., Diogenes Laertius, 9, 107.

[26]*Op. cit.,* p. 13.

[27]Cf. P. J. Bouman, *Sociologie. Begrippen en Problemen,* Antwerpen-Amsterdam, 6th ed., 1958, p. 29.

certain habitual "intellectual attitude" on the part of the student of human science, the attitude which above we have characterized as objectivistic. For this reason we will use the term *objectivistic reduction* whenever there is question of methodically and systematically reducing all experience to the kind of experience that can be described accurately in the language of physical science.

What is "Objectivity"? If the question is asked why such a reduction is required, the almost unanimous reply is that it is necessary to safeguard the objectivity of the scientific investigation. Regarding the meaning of "objectivity" Guillaume states the following . "The term *objectivity* has a twofold meaning. On the one hand, it means the agreement of thought with its object and, on the other, it indicates the mutual agreement of individual thoughts. In the second sense of the term, science is objective because it is impersonal, universal truth. An observation is objective if all observers are in agreement about the observed fact."[28]

This twofold reply contains actually three different descriptions of what is meant by objectivity. The first, "agreement of thought with its object," does not differ from the age-old Aristotelian definition of truth. But, we may ask, are "truth" and "objectivity" the same? Is it not possible for a child to discover the truth by mere guessing without being in any way objective?[29] Secondly, is it true that the "mutual agreement of individual thoughts" safeguards objectivity? Let us have a look at the example of the crowd pursuing a man to lynch him. The individual thoughts of the pursuers are in perfect agreement. Yet we are not at all inclined to consider them "objective." There remains, therefore, only the third definition, which is borrowed from the actual pursuit of scientific research. This definition, however, is likewise unsatisfactory, for it simply begs the question. On the one hand, we are told that a fact is that which is observed by a plurality of observers who are in agreement about it on the basis of their objective attitude, on the other, this attitude is said to be objec-

---

[28] *Introduction à la psychologie*, p. 163.
[29] "Objective knowledge is not the same as true knowledge, objectivity is not the same as truth." F. J. Glastra van Loon, *Norm en handeling. Bijdrage tot een kentheoretische fundering der sociale wetenschappen*, Haarlem, 1957, p. 13.

tive because it enables the observers to observe the facts in such a way that they are in agreement.

A multitude of other authors writing about the theory of science could be quoted here. These quotations would show that their views are identical with those of Guillaume or at least very close to him. The result of such an investigation would merely serve to confirm the impression that the concepts "fact" and "objectivity" have not yet been sufficiently explored.

The Principle of Verifiability. A serious effort has been made by neo-positivists and logical positivists to justify the concept of scientific objectivity. This attempted justification is known as the principle of verifiability. According to Alfred Jules Ayer, who is more broad-minded and more prudent in this matter than is, e.g., Moritz Schlick, the principle is concerned with the following: "We say that the question that must be asked about any putative fact is . . . , 'Would any observation be relevant to the determination of its truth or falsehood?' And it is only if a negative answer is given to this question that we conclude that the statement under consideration is nonsensical." The judgment, "There are mountains on the other side of the moon," is, according to Ayer, meaningful, even though no astronomer would yet actually have observed mountains on that side of the moon. Bradley's assertion, however, that "the Absolute enters into, but is itself incapable of evolution and progress" must be rejected as a pseudo-proposition.[30] According to this criterion there are only three kinds of sciences in which meaningful propositions can be made—namely, empirical sciences, mathematics, and "philosophy." The philosophy, however, which Ayer refers to has only as its task "to clarify the propositions of science by exhibiting their logical relationship and by defining the symbols which occur in them."[31] Thus it appears that in Ayer's view man can be considered only as an object. He is the object of judgments of facts, based on experience, and these judgments constitute objects of logico-semantic analyses. To speak about man in any other way is "non-sensical."

---

[30]*Language, Truth and Logic,* 2nd ed., London, 1948, p. 36. Ayer does not classify himself as a neo-positivist but as a logical empiricist.
[31]*Op. cit.,* p. 32.

17

The Reduced Totality of the Sciences. Another result of this extreme objectivistic view is that the human disciplines are exiled from the whole of the sciences. The theory of science proposed by Rudolf Carnap, a prominent representative of the Vienna Circle, makes this very clear. If we ask the questions of how the edifice of the sciences must be constructed and what foundation underlies the whole, Carnap replies as follows.

To begin with, we should distinguish, on the one hand, the *formal sciences,* consisting of analytic judgments that are based upon a logico-mathematical foundation, and on the other, the *empirical sciences,* which contain synthetic judgments referring to the various realms of factual knowledge.[32] These empirical sciences are divided into three groups. *"Physical sciences"* are those which, in addition to the language of mathematics, use also the typical language of physics. The other experimental sciences fall under the heading of biology. However, a further differentiation is necessary, for biology itself must be divided. It is split into *biology in the narrower sense,* comprising general biology as well as botany and most of zoology, and *behavioristics.* The group of behavioral sciences, says Carnap, may be characterized as follows: "[It] deals with the behavior of individual organisms and groups of organisms within their environment, with the disposition of such behavior, with such features of processes in organisms as are relevant to the behavior, and with certain features of the environment which are characteristic of and relevant to the behavior, e.g., objects observed and work done by organisms."[33] Carnap calls the science of individual behavior *psychology,* which for him includes parts of physiology as well as some parts of the humanities. The science studying the collective behavior of organisms is *sociology,* which for Carnap includes also history and the greater part of the humanities. His table of the empirical sciences may be schematically presented in this way:

---

[32]"Logical Foundation of the Unity of Science," *International Encyclopedia of Unified Sciences,* vol. 1, no. 1, Chicago, 1938, p. 45.
[33]*Ibid.,* pp. 46 f.

2. The "First Approach": Objectivism

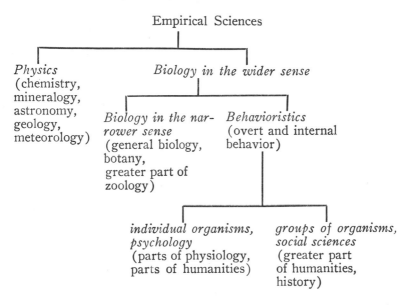

Empirical Sciences

Physics
(chemistry,
mineralogy,
astronomy,
geology,
meteorology)

Biology in the wider sense

Biology in the narrower sense
(general biology,
botany,
greater part of
zoology)

Behavioristics
(overt and internal
behavior)

individual organisms,
psychology
(parts of physiology,
parts of humanities)

groups of organisms,
social sciences
(greater part
of humanities,
history)

Carnap's division, however, is not quite clear. For example, it does not show which parts of zoology should be considered in biology and which parts in behavioristics. We suppose that the reactions of higher types of animals and those of man are to be studied in the behavioral sciences. At least it is certain that, in his view, man and human groups, their history, culture and forms of law are to be investigated on the level and within the horizon of biology in the wider sense.

We may be grateful to Carnap for his rigorous logic and clarity, for he shows very clearly what consequences are to be drawn from the objectivistic postulates. Let us indicate a few conclusions related to the concrete pursuit of the humanities. According to Carnap, the behavior of Napoleon must be placed on a par with that of Köhler's chimpanzee Sultan. Shakespeare's dramas belong to the "works done by organisms," just as the building of nests by birds. The Crusaders were a "group of organisms" whose behavior showed some relevant features with respect to their biological environment; consequently, they are to be studied in accordance with the same principles.

19

Carnap's theory of science actually amounts to a reduction of the human sciences to physical science. The proper character of everything human is neglected and deliberately so. Carnap admits this quite openly and demands that this sacrifice be made in the name of the unity of the sciences, for he is disturbed by the existence, side by side, of the most divergent sciences without any logical interconnection. To secure the unification of the sciences, man must see to it that he develop a universal scientific language. Because physical science is the most fundamental science of experience, this language can be only the language of physics. Whence he demands that all psychological propositions be changed into biological sentences, and all biological sentences into physical statements. The statement, for example that John Doe is excited, to be scientifically useful, has to be given the form of the following "super-proposition": "Whenever a person manifests the following bodily changes . . ., and executes the following motions . . ., we will call him 'excited.'" Such a definition can easily be "translated" into the language of physical science. For this reason the reduction of psychology to physics is a fixed point on Carnap's program.[34]

Guillaume, who is entirely independent of Carnap, arrives at similar conclusions, which he does not base on considerations belonging to logic and the theory of science but on methodology. "Physics," he says, "will be prolonged in a kind of physiology and of psychology," and he does not hesitate to speak about a "fundamental unity of the methods of objective psychology and physical sciences."[35]

---

[34]Cf. "Die physikalische Sprache als Universalsprache der Wissenschaft," *Erkenntnis*, vol. 2, 1931-32; and "Psychologie in physikalischer Sprache," *Erkenntnis*, vol. 3, 1932-33, pp. 107 ff.
[35]*Op. cit.*, pp. 170 and 319.

3. CRITIQUE OF OBJECTIVISM

The Unity of the Sciences as a Philosophical Problem. There are serious difficulties in the standpoint of objectivism. Undoubtedly, the unity of the sciences, the comprehensive interconnection between all kinds of research, is a great good. From Aristotle to Descartes, from Leibniz to Hegel, the greatest thinkers have made strenuous efforts to justify the unity of the scientific world view. But, why should anyone claim that this unity can be attained on the empirical level, by reducing all science of experience to a single empirical science? Similar objections arise in connection with the concepts "objectivity" and "verifiability." Again, it is undoubtedly true that the tendency to objectivity is a general characteristic of man's search for truth. One, however, who claims that, to safeguard the objectivity of all judgments, it suffices to stay on the level of physical science is satisfied with an easy but superficial reply. Regarding Ayer's criterion of empirical verifiability, can such a criterion be decisive with respect to verification in general? If the principle in question is to find meaningful application, does it not require thinking that goes beyond the realms of all particular areas of empirical experience? Does it not demand thinking which is neither empirical nor formal-logical but philosophical in the strict and proper sense of the term?

Language is Not a Neutral System of Symbols. Carnap would probably reply that he is primarily interested in the unity of scientific language, and that, if the judgments of various empirical investigators have to be formulated in the same "universal language," it would be possible to analyze these judgments critically, to arrange them in an orderly fashion, and to unify them in a logical synthesis. In other words, there would be no need of profound philosophical thinking but only of refined logic to safeguard the interconnection of the totality of the sciences. The idea behind such a reply is that the content of any datum can be expressed in any language.

First of all, however, this idea does not agree with our prescientific experience. Even in everyday life we spontaneously distinguish between, e.g., conversational, technical, official, and pulpit

21

forms of language. Anyone "knows" that what the lawyer carefully expresses in his legal idiom cannot be said in the teen-age jargon of a High School girl. The same applies even more stringently to the realm of scientific experience. For example, the ideas which the religious psychologist has to express in words cannot be compared with what the economist wants to state, and the economist's statements refer to an entirely different realm of theoretical interest than those of the physicist. Contrary to Carnap's assumption, human experience encompasses different realms and levels. It is for this reason that in the pursuit of the empirical sciences man has in the course of time created different languages, which are partially artificial, to put into words the different contents of his experience. It is not at all a coincidence that many generations of scholars and scientists have taken this trouble. There have to be different specialized languages because man's experiences reveal essential differences.

Secondly, by simply assuming that whatever is expressed in one language can be equally well stated in a different language, Carnap implies that everything that can be stated belongs to essentially the same level of being. This implication is, of course, a metaphysical thesis and not a proposition belonging to logic. It is connected with Carnap's logical positivism. This metaphysical thesis, moreover, does not agree with either pre-scientific or scientific experience.

No Dictatorship of Method. Similar objections may be made against the position of Guillaume. His methodological demands do not carry conviction. According to the original meaning of the Greek term, "method" means the road to be taken if one wants to reach the desired goal. In other words, the purpose determines which road should be taken. If, therefore, the aim pursued by human sciences differs from that of physical science, different methods have to be used in them. Guillaume, however, turns the matter around. On the basis of the excellence of the physical method, he demands that the standpoint be entirely changed in the realm of human science. "Man himself," he says, "will have to be studied in the light of things, and no longer things in the light of man."[36] It is possible, indeed, to study man from the viewpoint

[36] *Op. cit.,* p. 176.

22

of things—namely, insofar as man can be considered *also* as a thing. Or, to express it differently, questions of a physical nature may be directed to man. One, however, who asks such questions of man will, of course, receive physical replies, and this means that the characteristically human element will escape him. Briefly expressed, he who uses methods that are essentially the same as those of physics will remain in the sphere of physics and cannot even enter the realm of human science. In this respect it does not make any difference whatsoever that he calls his books and articles publications about psychology or sociology.

Accordingly, language, method and system of concepts are not neutral technical means that can be used to express everything. On the contrary, we would say rather that a definite scientific apparatus predisposes its user to a definite apperception of reality. Let us illustrate this contention in connection with Carnap's theory of science and more especially his concept of behavioristics.

The Ambiguity of Behavioristics. As we have noted above, according to Carnap, anything that can be scientifically affirmed of man is to be classified under behavioristics. The meaning of this term has to be seen in the light of the behavioristic psychology which has influenced Carnap. For this reason it is important to see here briefly what behaviorism ultimately wants. A look at the representative writings of this psychological trend shows that its proponents do not at all aim at the study of man as man. As John B. Watson declares emphatically, "throughout the preparation of this elementary text I have tried to write with the *human animal* in front of me."[37] The principal concepts and categories of behavioristic psychology are in accord with this aim. This applies in the first place to the fundamental concept "behavior." As Watson says, "If we look over the list of problems in human behavior . . ., we shall see that there are common factors running through all forms of human acts. In each adjustment there is always both a response or act and a stimulus or situation which call out that response."[38] Behavior, therefore, is always a response to a stim-

---

[37]*Psychology from the Standpoint of a Behaviorist*, Philadelphia, 1919, pp. VII f. Italics of author.
[38]*Op. cit.*, pp. 9 f.

ulus. In this sense every behavior is an adjustment to stimulating reality, and the term "stimulus" has here a biological-physiological meaning.[39] The situation is nothing else than a complex of physiological stimuli.[40] More accurately expressed, the situation is the whole of physiological stimuli which at a given moment act upon an organism; the adjustment is a reaction eliminating the stimulating action[41]; the organism is a being that adapts itself to the situation in the sense indicated above. In other words, *an organism, in the behavioristic sense, is a living being whose action consists exclusively of reacting in function of a given situation.* We may consider this description to be, as it were, the behavioristic definition of an organism.

Behavioristic literature replies to the questions concerning the objects to which this conceptual system applies, the situations which it characterizes, and the behavior that can be adequately described by means of it. Its "language" serves to describe the behavior of a rat which, placed in a maze, has to seek its access to food, of a cat which by means of trial and error must find its way out of a cage, of an amoeba which by fleeing attempts to escape the action of an acid. In all these cases the situation is artificially prearranged and the animal simply undergoes the situation's influence.

One, however, who uses the terms "situation," "reaction," and "organism" in the same sense with respect to man makes himself guilty of ambiguity. Unlike the rat in the artificial maze, man does not find himself in a situation that is strange-for-him and created by another being. It suffices to glance out of a window to convince myself of this point. The houses, street and traffic I see there are quite clearly man-made creations which I understand and appreciate as a good. As far as my vision reaches, there is not a single tree not planted by man, not a flower not cultivated by him, not a blade or grass for which he

---

[39] *Op. cit.,* p. 10: "We use the term *stimulus* in psychology as it is used in physiology."

[40] *Op. cit.,* p. 10: "A situation is, of course, upon final analysis, resolvable into a complex group of stimuli."

[41] Some psychologists speak here also of homeostasis, equilibrium, adaptation, reduction of tensions, etc.

3. Critique of Objectivism

did not care. Even the weeds on the sidewalk, the sparrows on the telephone wires, the flies on the window are there only as long as man tolerates them. I, too, this individual human being, who is looking now out of the window, am constantly involved in the preservation and modification of this specifically human world, and this involvement is an essential feature of me as an economic, social and cultural being. By doing my professional duties, by pursuing research, by writing, I am busily engaged in changing this surrounding world. Accordingly, this world is not at all a complex of stimuli undergone in a purely passive way.[42]

Thus it becomes evident that the behavioristic definition of organism does not apply to me. More generally expressed, man is not a being whose action is merely a reaction. He is not an organism in the behavioristic sense; his existence is not behavior in the behavioristic sense; his surrounding world is not a situation in the sense of behaviorism. In other words, within the framework of behavioristics there is and there can be no question of man as man. Accordingly, the system of the sciences described by Carnap leaves no room for human science.

Conclusion. There can no longer be any doubt about the reply to the question of what the "first approach" implies. Those who pursue it emphasize the *empirical* character of human science. They see physics as the model science *par excellence* and view the research of this science as the example to be followed in empirical research in general. For this reason they demand that the conceptual framework, method and scientific apparatus to be used do not essentially deviate from those of physics. They admit, of course, that accidental modifications are needed in the application of empirical methods, conceptual systems, etc. to the various realms pertaining to the study of man, but demand that in these accidental modifications attention be paid to the great line running from physics to chemistry, biology, physiology and to behavioristics. The preceding pages have shown what the

---

[42]A theory of human action would have to take this fact foremost into account. It is not sufficient that, driven by dislike, one substitutes "action" for "behavior." Cf. Richard C. Sheldon, "Some Observations on Theory in Social Science," *Toward a General Theory of Action,* ed. by T. Parsons and E. A. Shills, Cambridge, Mass., 1959, pp. 30 ff.

consequences are of this viewpoint. They consist in the sacrifice of human science to the empirical method. The goal is given up for the sake of the approach. The reply given by the proponents of the "first approach" to the question of how human science is possible consists in saying that this science is possible on the condition that it cease to be human. Thus it is hardly surprising that in the last two generations there has arisen a growing resistance to this so-called "objective reduction." The question to be considered next is whether or not there exists a fundamentally different idea about the possibility of human science.

4. THE "SECOND APPROACH": THE ABSOLUTISM OF FREEDOM

The Search for a "Second Approach" as Reaction. The idea of the "second approach" arose as a reaction to the one-sidedness, the blindness and the arrogance with which during a century the empirical method of physical science was imposed as the royal road to be trodden by all who wanted to obtain scientifically justified knowledge of man. This reaction resulted in a revaluation of all values, a veritable revolution and a complete change of course. As such, it could arise only in an entirely different intellectual climate. It would be an oversimplification of history to claim that the "first approach" belonged to the cultural mentality of the nineteenth century and that a new view of man's existence began to gain ground in the twentieth century. An historian would not fail to remark that the period from about 1880 to about 1930 constitutes an important period of transition characterized by such striking thinkers as Bergson, Dilthey, Spranger, Cassirer, Husserl and Scheler, to whom we may add also Freud and Nietzsche. However, it is not our intention to present here a history of Western thought but rather to draw attention to important interconnections of thought by means of contrasting pictures. In this way there can be no doubt about the question of where we must seek the counter-pole of objectivism, behaviorism, neo-positivism and logical positivism. The above-mentioned uneasiness over the purely physical picture of man has reached its summit in the trend of thinking usually called *philosophy of existence.*

It would be easy to show by means of typical expressions and principles that through existential philosophy a radical change has taken place in the way in which man sees himself. One could say, for example, that most thinkers of the nineteenth century saw man as a zoological species, a link in a process of biological evolution, or an element of a social process. Existential philosophers, on the other hand, draw attention to man as a unique individual who seizes control of his own existence and who, on the basis of his own peerless character, makes decisions which only he himself can justify.

Or, to give another example, in the old apperception borrowed from physical science man appears governed by universal determinism. According to this view, it would be possible in principle to describe everything in mathematical equations and to predict all changes of the cosmos, including human behavior. The philosophers of existence, on the other hand, view man as freedom. From their standpoint, man does not have an immutable essence, a fixed nature, essential characteristics, but every man makes a project of his own mode of being on the basis of a fundamental choice. He is that which he makes of himself. It is precisely this self-realization which constitutes man's existence.[43]

As a third example we may point out that for the student of man who is oriented by the mentality of natural science man is a fact, found in nature just like other organisms and studied by means of essentially the same methods. For the philosopher of existence, however, man is a being which chooses itself and through this choice at the same time "projects" his world. This world projected by man and his co-existing fellow-men is the only true and real world, so that the opposition of "world view" and "objective world" disappears.

It would be possible to continue in this fashion with theses and antitheses. Its disadvantage would be that it is inaccurate and not sufficiently differentiated, for it is very difficult to enumerate characteristics typical of all existential philosophers. Moreover, this method would not indicate in what the "second approach" consists. We face a real problem here. Most existential philosophers reveal an attitude that is anti-scientistic. They greatly despise all science in general and empirical human science in particular. For, what could be less suitable for helping us to understand the unique character of an existence than an investigation based upon inductive experience?

True, not all existential philosophers equally scorn empirical human science. We think here, e.g., of Karl Jaspers, who has seriously reflected on the question of "empirical universal sci-

---

[43] Cf. B. Delfgaauw, *Beknopte geschiedenis der wijsbegeerte,* Part III, Baarn, 1952, p. 68.

ences."[44] However, it is precisely Jaspers who doubts the possibility of a "second approach." He admits that the interest in "the existential" is the secret driving power of psychological and sociological research, but adds that it endangers the scientific character of this research. For this reason Jaspers calls psychology and sociology "plain boundary sciences" and asserts that, because they straddle the boundary of science, they will never get beyond the initial stage.[45] Accordingly, it would be evidently useless to expect that Jaspers would endeavor to make a synthesis of "world view" (*Weltorientierung*) and the "clarification of existence" (*Existenzerhellung*).[46]

Such an attempted synthesis, however, may be found in Jean-Paul Sartre. Although he rejects the study of man based upon the method of the physical sciences, or perhaps precisely because he rejects it, he proposes a new way to arrive at knowledge of man. He does not intend to exclude the existential vision but to make it perform useful services in the investigation. The very title which he gives to his new method shows this characteristically, for he calls it *existential psychoanalysis*.

In our critical study we will ask ourselves first upon which philosophical presuppositions Sartre's existential psychoanalysis is based and then whether it contains, at least in principle, any elements that can be considered as a philosophical clarification of the complex of problems arising in connection with the empirical study of man.

Sartre's Concept of Consciousness. The philosophy of Sartre is essentially a philosophy of consciousness.[47] Nevertheless, it deviates considerably from the philosophies of consciousness of Descartes, Leibniz, Berkeley, Hume, Brentano, or Husserl. It is neces-

---

[44]*Philosophie,* vol. I, *Philosophische Weltorientierung,* Berlin, 1932, pp. 200 ff.

[45]*Op. cit.,* pp. 201 and 204.

[46]*Philosophie,* vol. II, *Existenzerhellung,* Berlin, 1932.

[47]These words were written before the publication of Sartre's *Critique de la raison dialectique,* Vol. I, *Théorie des ensembles pratique,* Paris, 1960. This new work means a change in Sartre's thinking, but the full meaning of this change can be evaluated only after the publication of the second volume.

sary to emphasize this point at once because otherwise Sartre's view of man and his corresponding human science would be fundamentally misunderstood.

While everyone knows Franz Brentano's famous statement, "All consciousness is consciousness of something," less well-known is the way in which Husserl modified and enlarged Brentano's conception. Sartre's view in its turn deviates from that of the classical phenomenologists. For him, the statement "all consciousness is consciousness of something" means that consciousness "posits" a "transcendent" object, i.e., an object that is wholly "other" with respect to consciousness. Contrary to Brentano's view, therefore, the object of consciousness does not lie "in" consciousness, there is no question of an "intentional or mental inexistence of the object."[48] According to Sartre, consciousness does not have any contents, any data or "intimate facts"; it is not the bearer of "states of consciousness." The perceived table, for example, is not in any way "in consciousness. A thing, such as the perceived table, is a chunk of opaqueness for consciousness, for an infinite process would be needed to make the complete inventory of the table-thing. Consciousness, on the other hand, is perfectly clear to itself, it is wholly "translucid." To place a thing in consciousness, even in the form of an image, a representation, or a complex of data, would mean to deprive consciousness of its translucidity. A consciousness containing things or images of things itself would be a thing.

It is here that lies the reason for Sartre's totally different conception of the essence of consciousness. For him, consciousness is essentially a transcendent consciousness. Whatever intentionality it possesses is, as it were, directed "outwardly," to "the other," to the table of our example. This assertion applies not only to the cognitive intention but also to practical and emotional intentions, but insofar as consciousness is *also* cognitive consciousness, it is exclusively knowledge of its objects. If, then, the world is conceived as the totality of conscious objects, no matter in what way

---

[48]*Psychologie vom empirischen Standpunkt,* ed. by O. Kraus, Leipzig, 1925, p. 115.

we are conscious of them, one could say with Sartre that "consciousness is consciousness of the world."[49]

Self-Presence and Not Self-Knowledge. These assertions do not mean that Sartre is blind for the retro-directedness to itself of consciousness. In his view, however, this self-presence does not have the character of an explicitly cognitive reflection. It cannot be described as a knowing which knows that it knows, it is not an "idea of an idea." Sartre presents phenomenological arguments for this standpoint. Reflective consciousness, he points out, presupposes non-reflective consciousness. Let us take a simple case. I count the number of cigarettes in my pack and observe that there are twelve. By doing this, I reveal an objective property of these cigarettes—namely, that they form a group of twelve. It is quite possible that in counting I do not possess any thetic consciousness of my own counting activity, that I do not know myself as counting. Of course, if anyone would ask me what I am doing, I would reply: "I am counting." This reply shows that consciousness, as directly orientated to the objects, is the condition of reflective consciousness, that the "direct intention" is more original than the "indirect intention."

Accordingly, the original self-presence of consciousness does not have the character of reflective knowledge. It is not an explicit knowing of itself. Consciousness is not retro-directedness to one's own knowledge but to one's own existence. As Sartre remarks, "Every conscious existence exists as consciousness of existing."[50] In other words, consciousness is to be conscious.

Polarity. Accordingly, Sartre sees existence as a being-conscious-directed-to-the-world and at the same time as a being-conscious that is wholly transparent to itself. Thus it is evident that the mode of being of consciousness has to be wholly different from that of things. In this way Sartre is led to place in his ontology two modes of being as opposite poles—thing-like being or being-an-object (*être en soi*) and conscious being or being-a-

---

[49]*L'être et le néant. Essai d'ontologie phénoménologique*, Paris, 36th ed., 1950, p. 18. The complex of problems raised by this concept of the world will be considered in a different context on pp. 198 ff. and 214 ff.
[50]*Op. cit.*, p. 20.

subject (*être pour soi*). No positive relations are possible between these two ontological poles. Sartre denies, e.g., that a physical cause can ever have a psychical effect; for instance, it is a mistake to think that an organic lesion can ever give rise to awareness of pain. Otherwise the organic lesion would first be unconscious and then become conscious, which goes counter to the translucidity of consciousness. Moreover, what is caused by a thing can be only a thing. If pain were caused by an organic lesion, it would be a thing to which we later ascribe the "property" of being-conscious. For Sartre, such an idea is simply contradictory. Pain, for him, is identical with the painful consciousness, just as also lust is identical with the lustful consciousness and cannot even be logically distinguished from it. Concretely spoken, therefore, lust cannot exist prior to lustful consciousness.

Consciousness, then, cannot be motivated by anything else, i.e., by anything that is not consciousness itself. For, if consciousness were to undergo the influence of a thing or of a physical process, it would at once cease to be consciousness—even non-thematic consciousness—of its own existence. It would not be consciousness of itself but a kind of pre-consciousness, half-consciousness, un-consciousness which later becomes conscious. This again, however, would be against the perfect lucidity of consciousness.[51]

Negativity. If consciousness lies outside the causal influence of things, how can there be any relationship with things? Does not such a position imply that the universe of being is split into two parts: being-in-itself and being-for-itself, so that Sartre's ontology ends in an extreme form of dualism?

Sartre's reply is that consciousness has relationships with things but in a purely negative fashion. More accurately expressed, consciousness is characterized by this that it nihilates the being of things. The meaning of this strange term, "to nihilate" or "to noughten" (*néantiser*) may be best explained by means of an analysis of a human *question*.

Let us suppose that a physician struggles with the question whether or not there is a virus causing cancer. The reply to his

---

[51]We cannot enter here into a discussion of the dialectics of "motivum" and "mobile." Cf. *L'être et le néant*, pp. 522 ff.

question can be either the cancer-causing virus *is* or it *is not*. True, when the question is asked, the cancer virus is a certain mental idea of the physician. This idea has the peculiarity of floating, as it were, between being and non-being. To be able to form such an hypothetical idea, the physician has to remove himself from that which is given as such. But his placing himself at a distance from that which is positively, is not an act of logical negation nor an act of real annihilation. In Sartre's typical terminology, his transcendence of positive being is a *nihilating* act. The ability of consciousness to have nihilating relations to things appears to be a condition of the ability to ask questions. We should add that asking questions is a specifically human act, for man alone has the possibility of raising questions.[52]

"Notnesses." There are still other typical acts that disclose man as the being which introduces "nothingness" into being. Let us think of the numerous concepts implying a negation. Sartre offers many examples of such "notnesses" (*négatités*). A single one may suffice here. The notion of "distance" at first seems to be a positive determination of a spatial situation. Yet the observation that, e.g., a lamp is at a distance from me contains something negative. If I am ill and in bed, this negativity may make itself felt, for I cannot reach the lamp and have to remain in the dark. Nevertheless, the notion "distance" is an idea used all the time just like other "notnesses," such as "other," "possible," "later," "earlier," and "undecided." In a certain sense, therefore, it may be said that my world view cannot be formed without the typical introduction of such "notnesses." Sartre's conclusion from this point is that consciousness posits its world precisely because of its negativity.

Freedom. The preceding introductory analyses were necessary to understand the concept of freedom which plays such a crucial role in Sartre's philosophical anthropology. Freedom, for Sartre, is the essential capacity to transcend the concreteness of things. That being is free which does not let itself be determined by beings and relations that *de facto* are. Briefly, man's capacity to say im-

---

[52]Cf. E. Strauss, "Der Mensch als fragendes Wesesn," *Psychologie der menschlichen Welt*, Berlin, 1960, pp. 316 ff.

plicitly or explicitly "no" with respect to that which *de facto* is constitutes the essence of freedom.

Freedom, therefore, is not just another "property" pertaining to man, which together with all other properties would constitute his "essence" or "nature." In other words, man is not a mammal which builds houses and in addition is also free. Only a *thing* has a determined nature, capable of being expressed in a definition. Wherever this nature, in the sense of "essence," is realized, such things are. To-be-free, on the other hand, cannot be distinguished from being-man. Man is not first and then becomes free, rather to-be-as-man and to-be-free are one and the same.

The absolute character of this concept of freedom is, of course, decisive for the picture that Sartre draws of man and human life. In one of his minor works he expresses himself very forcefully on this point. "If man," he says, "as the existentialist conceives him, cannot be defined, the reason must be sought in this that he first is nothing. Next, he will be that which he makes of himself. There is, therefore, no human nature, because there is no God to think this nature."[53] As long, then, as man is not yet consciousness, he is nothing. Later he is his own project, his own choice, his own responsibility. But he does not have an essence, anything that would allow us to say: man is this or that. His being does not correspond to a divine thought or to an idea in the Platonic sense. To-be-man has neither *eidos* nor a human *morphē* or form in the Aristotelian sense, it has nothing which would allow us to assign a definite place to it in the cosmos. While existing, the individual man himself takes his place among beings. All this is expressed in Sartre's well-known but often misunderstood formula, "Existence precedes essence."[54]

Summarizing we may say that Sartre views human existence primarily as a world-positing consciousness which is perfectly translucid to itself but does not know itself thematically. As such, consciousness is the counter-pole of the being of things. For this reason its exercise of freedom cannot be determined or conditioned by any thing.

---

[53] *L'existentialisme est un humanisme,* Paris, 1954, p. 22.
[54] *Op. cit.,* p. 17.

4. The "Second Approach": The Absolutism of Freedom

Sartre's Idea of Existential Psychoanalysis. Such a view of man would seem to exclude any objectifying approach but, nevertheless, Sartre does not consider existential philosophy irreconcilably opposed to empirical research. What is needed, he claims, is a radical renewal of this research. In this way he is led to propose a plan for an entirely new kind of psychology. In this plan he speaks explicitly of a rigorously objective method, the number of explained cases needed to prove the truth of an hypothesis, and the classifications based on the results obtained.[55] Accordingly, it follows that Sartre thinks at least of a human science which is related to the psychological and psychoanalytic studies of man.

All this does not prevent him from making a sharp critique of the empirical science of psychology. He reproaches the psychologists for the neutral-descriptive character of their assertions. Their analysis, for example, of someone's life contains nothing else than a succession of fortuitous events,[56] so that they do not make clear why the individual's development has taken *this* course and not that one. As A. Chorus expressed it, they give "facts" but no "view."[57]

Another point of criticism is the analytic-synthetic mode of thinking adopted by a number of psychologists. Sartre rebukes them for analyzing the living person until they have reached so-called "ultimate data." These data, he says, play the same role in their psychology as "simple bodies" had in classical physics. After such an analysis these psychologists attempt to reconstruct the individual person from the building blocks resulting from their analytic work. Sartre wants to replace this analytic-synthetic psychology by an "understanding" (*verstehende*) psychology.[58] What he means, however, by this expression differs essentially from the meaning given to it by Wilhelm Dilthey, Heinrich Rickert and Eduard Spranger. It has to be seen within the framework of his philosophical anthropology.

---

[55] *L'être et le néant,* pp. 662 and 663.
[56] *Op. cit.,* p. 645.
[57] *Psychologie van de menselijke levensloop, Leiden,* 1959, p. 19.
[58] *Op. cit.,* pp. 646 f. In his *Critique de la raison dialectique,* p. 107, Sartre speaks again of "cette perpétuelle dissolution de l'intellection dans la compréhension."

"Verstehen" as Grasping the Transcendent End. According to Sartre, every man is full of a metaphysical desire, a "desire to be."[59] He wants to be "fully," and this means that he wants to possess being in both its fundamental forms. He desires to unite the self-sufficient mode of being proper to the thing with the perfect lucidity of consciousness; he wants to be a concrete substance and at the same time a "pure act"; he wants to be at rest with himself as an object is and also to stand out toward the others as a subject; he strives to be both "in itself" (*en soi*) and for itself (*pour soi*). In other words, man is man because he wants to be God. The secret desire to be like God is the driving force of all human existences. The ways, however, in which different persons want to execute their Promethean projects are fundamentally different, for the concrete projects are conceived in given situations, leading to different individual "lines of conduct." Concerning these "lines" we can say only that they are unknown, they are lived but not known. Only the "intermediary ends" are known but not the "ultimate end."

To illustrate the matter through an example, let us think of a Don Juan who is possessed by the desire to achieve erotic successes. Evidently, his desire has a more profound meaning, a meaning that cannot be grasped through such psychological notions as "need," "instinct," or "passion." The truth of this erotic desire does not lie in the desire itself but should be sought in a metaphysical dimension. Sartre bewails the fact that psychologists are blind to the transcendent character of human "lines of conduct," while certain "moralists" and writers, such as Pascal, Stendhal and Proust did not fail to pay attention to it.

Postulates of Existentialistic Anthropology. This critique is a first indication of the postulates formulated by Sartre in reference to his "existential psychonalysis." First of all, existential psychoanalysis must begin with that in which the unity of the individual person is rooted. Negatively, this postulate means that concepts such as "needs," "tendencies," "passions," "traits," and "disposition" must be rejected as ultimate data and building blocks of

---

[59]*L'être et le néant*, p. 652.

models. If the psychologist does not from the very beginning take into consideration that which accounts for the strictly personal unity of *this* man, he will never be able later to reconstruct this unity from the multiplicity of factors.

The second postulate consists in this that the act which is the foundation of this personal being must be meaningful also in itself. The fundamental choice has to show such an intelligibility that any attempt to clarify it through something else appears impossible. For this reason the psychologist must not hesitate to penetrate ever more profoundly in his analyses until he detects something that is evidently irreducible.[60] The act on which the person is founded, discovered in this way, obviously no longer refers to anything else.

Of course, that which the psychologist attempts to lay bare cannot be a general principle or idea, a primordial cosmic force or anything of the kind. For the psychologist endeavors to make *this* unique existence intelligible. The ultimate term of his inquiry, therefore, has to be something which itself is individual, unique and, consequently, also concrete. Sartre does not hesitate to speak in this connection of an "absolute concretion."[61]

The Existential Project. All this indicates that the starting point of Sartre's study of man will lie in *the existential project of the individual man,* for this starting point satisfies the three abovementioned postulates. First of all, it is that which justifies the unity of the concrete person. Every particular behavior, every particular disposition, every apparently capricious characteristic becomes intelligible as soon as the person's existential project is known. The important point is to determine in what way this concrete man has chosen himself, what direction his existential yearning takes, what he ultimately aims at.

The original project, moreover, is irreducible. It is "a yearning for being," and being is that which does not refer to anything else. Differently expressed, it is useless to try to find something else beyond being. This assertion applies also to the free project of

---

[60] *Op. cit.,* p. 651 : "irréductibilité évidente."
[61] *Op. cit.,* p. 660.

existence that man is, for this project is an attempt "to be more fully." If, then, Sartre says that "human reality is defined by the aims which it pursues,"[62] his words may not be interpreted in the sense of Alfred Adler. The aims referred to by Sartre cannot be described in terms of "superiority" and "society." Not social but metaphysical ends define man as man, they constitute his being-man.

In this way the third postulate is likewise satisfied. For, if the way in which an individual freedom is realized is absolutely unique, then it is also concrete. In such a case the choice man makes of himself does not correspond with any concept, idea or principle, but is a wholly irreducible, absolutely concrete act.

The big question, of course, is how the person's original project of existence can be discovered. With the possibility or impossibility of this discovery the whole idea of an existentialistic anthropology stands or falls. Sartre is under no illusions regarding the difficulty of this methodic problem. The person in question himself does not know which "line of conduct" he is following. Now he is attracted by *this* and then by *that,* and thus he is wholly lost in the fascinating spectacle of the world. It would be extremely naive to ask him about his original choice. At the same time, we are unable simply to read his fundamental orientation in his behavior. True, every concrete act, every concrete desire, every concrete behavior *in one way or in another* is connected with the original choice. But this fact does not mean that this connection is clear and still less that we can obtain an insight into it. On the contrary, every empirical datum is ambiguous and can be interpreted in different ways.

Existentialistic and Psychoanalytic Study of Man. A relationship reveals itself here between the existentialistic psychologist and the psychoanalyst. Their methods are analogous. Like the psychoanalyst, the existentialistic psychologist has to penetrate into the inner layers of personality through a comparative analysis of its apparently superficial manifestations. The relationship between the original project of existence and the empirical desires is that

---

[62]*Op. cit.,* p. 643. Cf. *Critique de la raison dialectique,* p. 64: "Man is defined by his project."

of the symbolized to the symbol. All concrete desires, all empirically observable behavior constitute, as it were, a cryptogram. The task of the existential psychologist as well as that of the psychoanalyst is to decipher this cryptogram. Both, therefore, are engaged in hermeneutics and aim at understanding man in his world, in his situation. The efforts, therefore, of the psychoanalyst to probe the traumatic experience of his patient are entirely justified. The aim is to reconstruct the decisive situation which makes the individual's subsequent life history intelligible as a "symbolic history."

The common fundamental idea, then, is that the "root" of existence must be laid bare. What the development of the libido is for the psychoanalyst, the project of existence is for the existentialistic psychologist. In this way both seek to discover an original choice (for the complex is a choice also) which defies all logic and consequently cannot be explained in a logical fashion. Both use likewise the same criterion of truth—namely, the patient's acknowledgment of his fundamental orientation.[63]

The Difference Between Psychoanalysis and Existentialistic Psychology. The main difference between psychoanalysis and individual psychology, on the one hand, and Sartre's psychology on the other, may be expressed in a single sentence: *for Sartre, "depth" does not mean "unconsciousness."* The patient "lives" his original choice and it is precisely for this reason that he does not know it. This point should be kept in mind, for otherwise assertions such as, "the complex is a choice," are simply meaningless.

In Sartre's view, with respect to the existential project the situation is in principle similar to that of the act of counting, viz., while I count my cigarettes, I do not know myself as counting.[64] In an analogous way, according to Sartre, I do not know my metaphysical desire precisely because I *am* this desire. The desire is "conscious" but not "known." It is only through the cathartic

---

[63]We may point out here that Sartre has modified his opinion about the psychoanalytic study of man. Cf. *Esquisse d'une théorie des émotions,* 1st ed., Paris, 1939; 2nd ed., Paris, 1948, pp. 28 ff.

[64]See above, p. 31.

influence of the existential analysis that I am able to reflect on this desire and to recognize it as my desire. Such a recognition, says Sartre, would not be possible if the fundamental choice lay buried under the unconscious "id."

Attention must be drawn also to another important difference, which refers to the method to be used. Freud provides the psychotherapist with various norms indicating how he has to interpret a mistake, a "faulty act" (*Fehlleistung*), a dream, a life history. He assigns fixed ways of understanding the symbols. According to Sartre, however, it is not possible to do this. He does not admit any universal "language of symbols." For the symbol "is nothing in itself. It operates only according to the way in which it is taken, and this very way of taking it expresses symbolically the individual's internal disposition."[65] In other words, the empirically observable behavior, representations, and desires are not simply ambiguous, in the literal sense, but can have an endless number of meanings. For this reason the interpretation of the symbols has to be made on a different basis from the one assigned by Freudian psychoanalysis.

Sartre emphasizes this point and indicates that existential psychoanalysis must be based on *man's pre-ontological comprehension of the human person.* Before all conceptual knowledge of beings, before their division into genera and species, before all reflective thinking there is something like an understanding of man by man. True, one may be mistaken about the meaning of a *particular* gesture, facial expression or word; nonetheless, each man is open to the expressive force of gesture and mimicry in general. In the realm of human science truth is no more discovered by accident than in any other realm, it is discovered only by virtue of a kind of pre-knowledge. For this reason the discoveries of the existential psychologist are not made by penetrating somewhere where he has not yet been, they cannot be compared with the discovery of the sources of the Nile. On the contrary, his discoveries are based on the firm foundation of a "human comprehension."[66]

---

[65] *L'être et le néant*, p. 657.
[66] *Op. cit.*, p. 656.

4. The "Second Approach": The Absolutism of Freedom

Summarizing, we may say that systematic analysis and comparison of empirically observable behavior and desires, according to Sartre, play only a preparatory role. The decisive psychological act is the intuitive grasp of the other's fundamental choice. The proper source of knowledge is the pre-ontological "human comprehension." The other's recognition of his existential project, hitherto hidden for him, provides the proof that the intuitive interpretation has been correct.

5. CRITIQUE OF THE "ABSOLUTISM OF FREEDOM"

Two Kinds of Critique. The existentialistic ideal of freedom finds its most authentic expression in the works of Jean-Paul Sartre. As we have seen, the same philosopher has also sketched what we may call a human science on an existentialistic basis. He has attempted to bridge the enormous gap separating empirical psychoanalysis from existential philosophy. His ambition was to present a grand synthesis. Aside from all the essential objections that will be mentioned presently, the synthesis itself has not been wholly successful. The passages referring to it contain many contradictions—so many, that they make it difficult to indicate what exactly Sartre has in mind. Their detailed analysis would require scores and scores of pages, which would lead us too far afield.

Moreover, such a critique would not be appropriate for the forceful synthesis presented by the French philosopher. It would be similar to reproaching a poet for having made mistakes in spelling. If the opus of the poet is a true poem, its misspellings are obviously of no importance and if, on the other hand, he has not succeeded in producing a true poem, then there is no point in mentioning also his bad spelling. We will therefore limit ourselves here to drawing attention to three difficulties connected with the master theses of Sartre's philosophical anthropology. Our critique will reveal at the same time that the possibility of an empirical human science is indissolubly connected with a certain philosophical vision of man.

What is a Situation? The concept "situation" is very important for existentialistic anthropology as conceived by Sartre. As we have seen, all human beings in the deeper layers of their personality are driven by a metaphysical desire. This metaphysical "appetite" or tendency constitutes their being-man in its proper sense. It is the reason why we can speak of man and not only of mutually incomparable human individuals.[67] On the other hand, the individual persons do not experience this metaphysical urge as such,

---

[67]Cf. *L'être et le néant,* p. 654.

5. Critique of the "Absolutism of Freedom"

for it assumes the form of a particular aim, and the choice of an aim is always made "in a particular *empirical situation.*"[68] Sartre admits that there is a limited usefulness in discovering the interconnection of various situations through observation, induction and experiment. He speaks explicitly of "experimentally defined 'situations.' "[69] The usefulness of such a definition flows from the fact that these situations are positive limitations of man's being-in-the-world in general.[70]

Although all this may seem to be clear enough, it is not easy to express what exactly Sartre has in mind, for he makes use also of a different concept of situation. "Situation" in this second sense is only that which the subject conceives as situation. It is true, of course, that the choice of concrete aims is made within the framework of empirically determinable surroundings, but Sartre adds that "it is precisely the pursuit [of an aim] that makes the surroundings a situation."[71] This Sartrian remark is in accordance with his philosophical conviction. A situation has always a definite meaning, and this meaning can never be ascribed to the objects but only to a giving of meaning by the subject. For this reason Sartre is forced to make a distinction between the concepts "milieu" and "situation." The milieu is what it is. As milieu, it cannot act on the subject, but it is only insofar as it is "comprehended" by man, i.e., insofar as it is transformed into a situation, that it can act on him.[72] A rock along the road, for example, may impress a quiet stroller as esthetic or as inesthetic, but for a mountain climber it is either scalable or unscalable. This being scalable or unscalable corresponds with a free project of the mountain climber in question. His decision ultimately depends not on one or the other "datum," but on the situation as *he* sees it. In this way Sartre is led to affirm that situation and motive are one and the same.[73]

---

[68]*Op. cit.,* p. 654. Italics of the author.

[69]*Op. cit.,* p. 655. Note Sartre's quotation marks around the term "situations."

[70]*Ibid.*

[71]*Op. cit.,* p. 654.

[72]*Op. cit.,* p. 660.

[73]*Op. cit.,* p. 568.

This second conception of the essence of situation also has a definite meaning for the person who pursues a human science and especially for the psychologist. He will say that there are empirically observable data which the subject may conceive in *this* way or in *that* way. The experimental psychologist will refer here perhaps to the well-known figures of Köhler and Wertheimer which can be perceived in two different ways. The developmental psychologist will point to certain ambivalent experiences, such as the father figure as object of emotional identification and as object of unconscious feelings of rivalry. A conflict, e.g., a war, the sociologist will say, may give rise in the interested parties to feelings of the greatest euphoria as well as of the deepest depression. In all these cases, however, there is question of empirically determinable data. The figures of the Gestalt psychologist, the father-son relationship, the war are identifiable realities. The question of how the human person will experience them, the question of the motivations to which they will lead can be raised only because it is possible to identify the "object" in question in an empirical way. If one wants to classify the whole of empirically determinable objects under "surroundings" or "milieu" and the whole as it is experienced under "situation," we could perhaps say that this proposal is a good way to make our terminology more precise. At any rate, the distinction between empirically identifiable reality and its divergent conceptions is essential with respect to the possibility of an empirical study of man.[74]

A question to be asked here is whether Sartre himself had such a thing in mind. The reply is again that his attitude is ambiguous in this respect. In another text he states explicity that the empirical description of the milieu cannot render any services to human science. When he says that "from the start the milieu refers to the choosing consciousness,"[75] he appears to abandon the distinction between "milieu" and "situation." A third conception of "situation" makes itself felt here. From the standpoint of this third view it is in principle impossible to arrive at general

[74]See below, the section, "The Twofold Track of Anthropological Research," pp. 137 ff.
[75]*Op. cit.*, p. 600.

interpretations of behavior, to observe regular successions or to discover a constantly recurrent connection between symbol and meaning. For this reason Sartre rejects any kind of general typology of symbolization, such as was given by Freud.[76] Everything can be the symbol of everything, for the choosing consciousness is an absolute. Its freedom is an *absolute freedom,* or more accurately expressed, it is an *absolutely creative freedom.*

This idea appears to harmonize with the fundamental thought of Sartre. In his view, human freedom cannot be motivated by anything else or anybody else, for it is pure negativity and, being negative, it does not listen to anything or anybody but is exercised "gratuitously," i.e., in an autonomous and wholly sovereign way.[77]

Sartre illustrates this position in one of his minor works, *L'existentialisme est un humanisme.* He describes there a young Frenchman who lives under German occupation and has to make a difficult choice: should he attempt to escape to England and join the Allied forces or stay at home to take care of his aging mother? He would like to consult a confessor. But among the priests some are patriots and others "collaborators." Before asking them, he would already know what their reply would be. It would be useless, likewise, to watch for "signs," for man himself freely decides what meaning these signs have. Thus Sartre is led to tell the young man: "You are free, choose, that is, invent."[78] In *L'être et le néant* also Sartre says, "Freedom is nothing else than a choice creating its own possibilities."[79] And because human freedom is creative, it does not essentially differ from divine freedom. According to Sartre, this thesis lies in the line of Cartesian philosophy.

The question to be asked here is whether these descriptions do not neutralize one another. Consider, e.g., the act of choosing. I choose, for instance, between three political parties. The characteristic feature of the situation, *as I experience it,* is that the terms of my choice are given to me. I did not invent them, they

---

[76]*Op. cit.,* pp. 600 f.
[77]*Op. cit.,* p. 648. The term "gratuit" of the original text should not be rendered by "arbitrary."
[78]*L'existentialisme est un humanisme,* Paris, 1954, p. 47.
[79]p. 654.

exist independently of me. This is the reason why certain choice-situations are dissatisfying. I have, e.g., to choose one of the three parties, though none of them has my sympathy. True, my evaluation of these parties is partly inspired by my view of man and society and by my history; nonetheless my judgment is not an "invention" but based on something. Insofar, therefore, as my choice is motivated by the characteristics of the political groups, one can think of an empirical contribution to clarify my choice. By means of empirical descriptions of the political situation in 1960, for instance, historians, sociologists and social psychologists are able to explain *to a certain extent* why the voter, who I then was, made this decision and not that one. We admit, of course, that their replies contain merely an *approximation*. Nevertheless, in principle, it must be said that the empirical description of the *milieu* in which freedom is exercised contributes to making the choice intelligible.

If, on the other hand, I am in a position to *invent* the terms between which I have to choose, then my choice is a pseudo-choice. I resemble a chess player who is allowed to move both the black and the white pieces. Such a play is nothing but a mock-fight. If one goes even further and supposes that by choosing I "create" my own possibilities, that I myself make them, there can no longer be any question of choice. It would no longer be meaningful to speak here of choosing "oneself." For the choice of oneself always contains an element of acceptance, e.g., the acceptance of my body, of my sex, of my socio-historical environment.[80] Freedom which does not have to accept anything cannot make a choice.

The important point here is to see that the concept "creative situation"[81] implies a contradiction. Human creativity is always exercised in a milieu which is not created but given.[82] This implies that man's creative activity is always channeled by this milieu. Man's genius may be able to change the given situation into *this* or into *that*, but he cannot make everything of it. The expression

---

[80] See the description of this point in Maurice Merleau-Ponty, *Sens et non-sens*, Paris 1948, pp. 15 ff. (le doute de Sézanne).
[81] Cf. Sartre, *L'existentialisme est un humanisme*, p. 77.
[82] Cf. pp. 281 ff.

"creative situation" could perhaps be used in reference to God to indicate that for God there is no situation. But such a way of speaking would be theological and no longer philosophical.

What is Meant by Pre-ontological Knowledge? Undoubtedly, there is such a thing as an intuitive knowing of man by man. We may think here of the mutual recognition of human beings, of the original understanding of certain human gestures, such as threatening, irate and loving gestures, and of certain "attitudes," such as desire, rivalry, aggression, joy and sadness. This understanding precedes conceptual thinking and cannot be deduced from it. Sartre himself discloses this point when he speaks about the phenomenon of shame.[83] For this reason we may justifiably speak of "pre-scientific" and in a sense "pre-ontological" knowing. It is moreover, as we shall show, beyond dispute that this pre-scientific knowing has a definite importance for the study of man.

First, however, we must raise a critical question with a different aim—namely, *how far this pre-ontological knowing of man by man can go*. This question arises in connection with the human science proposed by Sartre. According to him, the "pre-ontological comprehension" is the method *par excellence* of existential psychoanalysis. True, the knowledge of men is prepared through an analysis and comparison of empirically observable behavior, drives and desires; nonetheless, the decisive step is the immediate grasp of the existential project of the human being under consideration. As a mood is understood on the basis of an expression, so likewise the existential choice is grasped on the basis of observable psychical phenomena. Thus in a single intuitive grasp an "individual fullness" is seized.[84] There is question here of intuition in the sense described by Henri Bergson. As he wrote in 1903, "the term *'intuition'* indicates that kind of *intellectual sympathy* through which one is transported into the interior of an object to merge with what is unique and consequently ineffable in it."[85] Because Bergson's "intellectual sympathy" refers to a spiritual feeling-

---

[83] *L'être et le néant,* pp. 275 ff.
[84] *Op. cit.,* p. 650.
[85] "Introduction à la métaphysique," *Revue de métaphysique et de morale,* Jan. 1903, quoted in Lalande, *op. cit.,* p. 541.

with-the-other and understanding of him, his description applies fully to Sartre's conception of "pre-ontological knowing." The question, then, is: what may be expected of such an intuition for the study of man?

As we have noted before, the fundamental choice which determines the orientation of an existence is always made in particular circumstances. As Sartre himself says, "This project itself . . . expresses my original choice in particular circumstances"[86] and he even speaks of a "particular empirical situation."[87] If this is so, it means that the fundamental choice cannot be understood outside this empirical situation. The assertion that "the situation is empirical" implies that it can be known, and normally will be known, *by means of experience*. No matter how one wishes to define "experience," it does not mean suddenly to enter into the most intimate being of another and to merge with it. If, then, it is true that knowledge of the situation is indispensable for understanding the existential choice which has orientated a person's life in a certain direction, it follows that *no study of man can be based upon intuition alone,* and that the "pre-ontological comprehension" has very definite limits.

Let us clarify the matter by means of Sartre's own works.[88] He has written two studies devoted to, respectively, Baudelaire and Jean Genet[89] which deserve to be called "existential psychoanalyses." There are hundreds of passages in both works showing that their scope corresponds with the great lines of Sartre's study of man. We will limit ourselves to a few quotations. In his Preface to *Baudelaire* Michel Leiris explains what Sartre had in mind in this study: "to relive from within . . . what Baudelaire, experience was, instead of merely considering its externals."[90] The last conclusion drawn by Sartre himself from his analyses is: "The free choice which man makes of himself is absolutely identified with what is called his destiny."[91] There is no fate in Baudelaire's

---

[86]*Op. cit.,* p. 651.
[87]*Op. cit.,* p. 654.
[88]*Baudelaire,* Paris, 22nd ed., 1947.
[89]*Saint Genet, comédien et martyr,* Paris, 15th ed., 1952.
[90]*Baudelaire,* pp. VII f.
[91]*Op. cit.,* p. 224.

life, no unfortunate family or social conditions. There is only one destiny, and this destiny is identical with the original "guide line" chosen by Baudelaire himself. Such is the thesis which Sartre endeavors to establish by means of this study. This thesis is in agreement with the fundamental idea of his existential anthropology. It is an "existential psychoanalysis."

It is interesting to watch how Sartre proceeds in his study. After the preceding considerations no one will be surprised to hear that he endeavors above all to reconstruct the situation in which Baudelaire's decisive choice was made. Right at the beginning of the book the reader hears that young Baudelaire's father had died prematurely, that for six years the boy had been his mother's confidant, that his passionately loved mother remarried in 1828 with a soldier, that the boy was then placed in a boarding school, etc.[92] All these items are undoubtedly facts, empirically observed facts having the same meaning for all readers. Alongside these explicitly mentioned facts there are all kinds of implicit facts known to the readers, such as that a French soldier of 1828 was something else than a Greek hoplite of Xenophon's time. All these explicitly mentioned or implicitly present facts contribute to create an atmosphere, the atmosphere in which the "Baudelaire experience" occurs. Note that they do not automatically contribute to it. It is Sartre's *skill* which makes these little stones form a mosaic, but he is able to join them into a picture only because they have a definite color and a definite shape.

In *Saint Genet* Sartre likewise wants to make us understand the decisive choice of the principal character. He is not able to do so without telling us that Jean Genet had known neither his father nor his mother, that the authorities entrusted him to a farmer's family in the Morvan, that for many years he was considered a "good boy." We learn also that he was caught doing something which grown-ups called "stealing," and that this stigma became the occasion of a kind of psychical transformation: the "good boy" became a juvenile delinquent.[93] In his story Sartre makes use of empirical concepts to explain the psychical event, which would

---

[92] *Op. cit.*, pp. 17 ff.
[93] *Saint Genet*, pp. 9-15.

49

probably be characterized as a psychotrauma in the technical language of psychologists. The fact that the whole story of Genet is fiction does not diminish but increase its value as an example. From the very start the author appeals to facts, fictitious facts, of course, but facts which make us ask why the author would have introduced them if he did not really need them. The way in which these facts are arranged in groups is very skilful and betrays the presence of a vision of man. This vision, however, is not at all the elementary intuitive knowledge of man by man. It does not deserve the qualifier "pre-ontological comprehension," but rather flows from an extensive study of man. The author of *Saint Genet* reveals himself well-informed about child psychology, adolescent psychology, social psychology, sexual psychology, and religious psychology. His knowledge is not pure book knowledge but based on the experience of human beings, social conditions, psychical conflicts and needs. We doubt very much that Sartre could have written his analysis of Baudelaire or of Jean Genet without his psychological knowledge and experience. His experience acts, as it were, as a spring-board, making it possible for him to leap toward his vision. Moreover, the vision would remain unintelligible and unjustified for the readers if it were not embodied in facts. It is only by creating an atmosphere and the reconstruction of situations that the vision of a psychologist, a litterateur, an historian, or a sociologist acquires convincing power; only that which constitutes the substance of all genuinely human science, the *meaningful fact*,[94] makes his vision valuable. *When hereafter we will speak of "vision," the term should be understood as referring to a synthetizing conception which endows a number of experiences with a meaning that transcends these experiences.* As understood in this sense, vision cannot be identified, therefore, with a pre-predicative intuition or a pre-ontological comprehension.

At the same time it becomes clear that there is no such thing as an "a priori description"[95] in the realm of human science. It is true, of course, that since the time of Kant the concept of "a priori"

---

[94]Cf. A. Chorus, *Psychologie van de menselijke levensloop*, p. 118.
[95]*L'être et le néant*, p. 652.

5. Critique of the "Absolutism of Freedom"

has been considerably enlarged.[96] Nevertheless, a vision of a human existence, of a man's life may not at all be identified with an a priori in the philosophical sense. The concept "a priori description" is a contradiction and, by using it, Sartre displays a lack of intellectual self-discipline.

All this leads us to a few *provisional conclusions,* for endless confusion would result unless certain distinctions are kept in mind. They are the following:

1. Man's pre-predicative intuitive knowledge of man is not to be confused with the vision taken by the historian, the litterateur, the psychologist or psychiatrist with respect to certain human beings, groups of men or cultural products.

2. On the other hand, a description may not be identified with the a priori which, in the view of certain philosophers, makes the description possible.

3. Only a negative reply has *thus far* been given to the question of how far man's pre-predicative knowing of man can go: it does not go far enough to make this concrete character, this concrete life immediately intelligible. For its understanding experience and facts are needed in addition to intuition.

As to the positive value of pre-predicative intuitive knowledge for the study of man, it will be discussed later in this book.

Inhuman Consciousness. If human freedom is a situated freedom, human consciousness is a situated consciousness. This is a viewpoint that is currently defended by many phenomenological philosophers. They speak more and more of a consciousness dwelling in the world, communicating with men and things and having a reciprocal relationship to other conscious existences. Maurice Merleau-Ponty, for example, emphasizes that "the world is not constituted by consciousness but, on the contrary, consciousness is always already at work in the world."[97] One who accepts this standpoint should be willing to draw from it the necessary consequences. Nevertheless, not all self-styled phenomenologists are

---

[96]Cf. M. Dufrenne, *La notion d' "a priori,"* Paris, 1959.
[97]*Phénoménologie de la perception,* p. 494.

51

ready to do so. To illustrate the point, let us revert to Sartre's case, which is unusually instructive.

One who admits a consciousness that is really in communion with other conscious existences, living beings and things has to drop at once the postulate that consciousness is of a negative nature. For it is abundantly evident that such negativity would eliminate any possible connection between consciousness and the world of men and things. It leaves room only for an inhuman consciousness, i.e., a consciousness "that can be limited only by itself."[98] We are almost spontaneously reminded here of Fichte's famous "self" (*Ich*) and his no less famous "original deed" (*Tathandlung*).[99] One who does not want to get lost in fancies has no other recourse than to reject at once such an impossible position.

There are other anomalies. In his book, *L'être et le néant,* Sartre displays great ingenuity and persuasive powers to prove all kind of things, save the main point. From the standpoint of a philosophical anthropology undoubtedly the following axiom will be considered to be the crucial point: consciousness (*la conscience*) = a consciousness (*une conscience*) = a human existence (*une existence humaine*). This axiom is the basis of Sartre's entire system, yet nowhere does he examine its truth.

The very transition from consciousness to a consciousness causes the greatest difficulties. Sartre's proposed solution consists in the assertion that consciousness is "finitized" by being negated by another consciousness. According to Sartre, two conscious monads are related to each other in a reciprocal absolute negation and "cannot be reunited by any synthesis."[100] The two obvious objections arising here are, Does not mutual negation presuppose the existence of several conscious monads? and, Is not a relationship of absolute negation without any reuniting synthesis an absolutely negative relationship, i.e., no relationship at all? Briefly put, the transition from consciousness (as an absolute) to a (finite) consciousness is a

---

[98]*L'être et le néant*, p. 22.
[99]"Das Entgegengesetztsein überhaupt ist schlechthin durch das Ich gesetzt. *Grundlagen der gesamten Wissenschaftslehre* (1794), Hamburg, 1956, p. 23.
[100]*L'être et le néant*, p. 362.

5. Critique of the "Absolutism of Freedom"

particularly weak point in Sartre's philosophy. Small wonder that he sighs: "The ecstatic totality of the mind . . . appears to us as a shattered being."[101]

Sartre's "deduction" of *a* consciousness from consciousness, as an absolute, appears a failure. As for the second part of his axiom, the assertion that "*a* consciousness" = "a human *existence,*" he does not even attempt to establish this point. He simply asserts that man is consciousness, that he is a *finite* consciousness because there are other conscious beings which negate him as subject, and that he is nonetheless essentially consciousness, "consciousness through and through."

All this disagrees with very elementary evidence. While I am writing these lines, I am suddenly seized by a slight fatigue. I can no longer concentrate easily, the logic of my thought does not proceed in orderly fashion, and I have trouble in remembering. When later I have recovered, I observe in an act of reflection that, willy-nilly, I had withdrawn somewhat from the world. We like to draw attention to this point. *That* this withdrawal did occur and *in what* it consisted are things I know only as a conscious being. Only because I have knowledge of my intentional achievements, I am able to observe the deficiency and the absence of these achievements. But this does not take away from the fact that I am fully justified in speaking of a diminished consciousness. Dreams, sleep and unconsciousness likewise provide opportunities for phenomenological considerations. A constantly recurrent flaring-up and burning-low of the natural light known as "consciousness" appears to be characteristic of existence as human existence. Husserl was careful enough to take this characteristic somewhat into account by making a distinction between "functioning intentionality" (*fungierende Intentionalität*) and "act-intentionality" (*Akt-Intentionalität*).[102] His unpublished manuscripts bear witness to the fact that

---

[101] *Op. cit.*, p. 363.
[102] See, e.g., E. Fink, "Beilage zum Problem des Unbewuszten," in E. Husserl. *Die Krisis der europäischen Wissenschaften und die transzendentale Phänomenologie,* The Hague, 1954, pp. 473 ff.; A. de Waehlens, "Réflexions sur une problématique Husserlienne de l'inconscient. Husserl et Hegel," in *Edmund Husserl, 1859-1959,* pp. 221 ff.; Stephan Strasser, *The Soul in Metaphysical and Empirical Psychology,* Pittsburgh, 2nd impr., 1961, pp. 169 ff.

he did not cease to meditate on the meaning which insanity, unconsciousness, and "breaks by sleeping" have for the stream of consciousness. Sartre, on the contrary, shows no such preoccupations. Even though human consciousness is finite, it is, he thinks, perfectly translucid. In this way he loses sight of an entire dimension of human consciousness, the dimension of *depth,* i.e., the dimension in which man's labile and frail consciousness goes through phases of sinking and rising.

It goes without saying that this neglect diminishes the value of Sartre's descriptions. What he describes as consciousness (as an absolute) is not a human consciousness but, in the words of Buytendijk, "a transcendence that is not determined by anything, unlimited and without direction."[103] Unsurprisingly, comparisons between consciousness (as an absolute) and divine consciousness, between freedom (unqualified) and the creative freedom of God are constantly made in Sartre's work. They are characteristically in harmony with the Promethean aspirations of Sartre's philosophy, but they are wholly unrealistic and unphenomenological.

An important decision has to be made here. If there is an absolute consciousness, endowed with a creative freedom, it is of necessity beyond the reach of any form of experience. Such a consciousness is not motivated by anything, not bound by any laws, not conditioned by any past. It does not have any "structures." It can be known only to the extent that it communicates itself. In other words, a consciousness which "posits" a world can be understood only to the extent that it is willing to reveal itself in its world.[104] Such a revelation is a sovereign act, it is fully "gratuitous." One could conceive of a science which would have such a revelation of sovereign Consciousness as its object—namely, the science of *theology.* Differently expressed, there is a theology of absolute creative Freedom but not a phenomenology, there is a theology of sovereign Consciousness but not a psychoanalysis. Anyone, however, who wants to make a contribution to an existential science of man should abstain from beginning by describing man as

---

103 Frederick J. J. Buytendijk, *De vrouw,* Utrecht, 1952, p. 274.
104 In this sentence we use the term "world" in the Sartrian sense. Cf. pp. 198 ff. and 214 ff.

5. Critique of the "Absolutism of Freedom"

a God and then asking himself how this God "finitizes" himself, but should begin with man as he experiences himself.

Conclusion. When the representatives of the "second approach" are asked how an empirical human science is possible, their reply ultimately appears to imply a rejection of all authentically scientific experience. According to them, the danger of objectivism is inherent in the empirical approach and in the methodic selection of experiences. On the other hand, however, existentialistic thinkers of Sartre's type make such a selection. They abstract certain experiences from the whole of human existence and transpose them into the realm of the absolute; for instance, the experience of one's own being-conscious, of being-free, of the uniqueness of one's own individuality. Other experiences are simply discarded; for example, the bond of being-conscious with other forms of being or that of one's own consciousness with other conscious beings. The picture resulting from this procedure can hardly be accepted as representing man. The "absolutists of freedom" do not even make any effort to justify their one-sided vision, they do not attempt any verification. With respect to their "a priori description" one simply has "to take it or leave it."

Later we will have to revert to the question of their method, which they themselves call "phenomenological."[105] For the present we may be satisfied with the remark that the "second approach" leads to a human science which is essentially based upon suggestive descriptions of a few carefully selected human experiences. It should be evident that we must consider this reply just as unsatisfactory as that proposed by the proponents of the "first approach."

---

[105]Cf. the third study, pp. 245 ff.

6. PROVISIONAL DETERMINATION OF A
NEW DIRECTION

The "Broken World" of Philosophy. The two groups of thinkers of whom the preceding pages have analyzed a few leading thoughts are irreconcilably opposed to each other in the intellectual life of our time. For the sake of easy reference we may indicate the two groups as, respectively, the "scientists" and the "existentialists." We realize, of course, that the historian of philosophy would be inclined to make corrections in the use of these popular terms and to differentiate their application. Nonetheless, they have been chosen intentionally to express the general impression made by the philosophical life of our time. Gabriel Marcel voices this impression faithfully when he observes that there is question here of two disparate attitudes of mind which make any philosophical dialogue impossible. To philosophy also applies the assertion that "the world is 'broken' as it has perhaps never been before in any known period of history."[106] Whence, we must ask, comes this unyielding attitude? What motive if any, is given in support of it?

Typical Polemics. The "scientists" reproach the "existentialists" with projecting their emotional states into reality. These states, they argue, at most could serve to offer artistic visions, fascinating descriptions and original thoughts, but they do not contain anything that imposes itself upon the knowing mind. It may be interesting, for example, to make a thought experiment about the "nihilating" power of consciousness, but it contains nothing obliging us to take this asserted power seriously. On the other hand, the "scientists" are proud of the fact that they can support their own assertions through "well-established methods." Their judgments are based either on empirical insights, such as induction, formulation of an hypothesis and reply to the question raised by the hypothesis, or on formal acts of thinking, i.e., on logical, logistical or mathematical procedures. Even their hypotheses are supported by arguments borrowed from their various special sciences. While the "scientists" are perhaps willing to listen with

---

[106]Marcel, *Le monde cassé*, Paris, 1954, pp. 104 f.

kind patience to the tale told by the "existentialist," they often end by declaring that they do not feel competent to evaluate "poetry." Others will declare that the view elaborated by the "existentialist" is not "objective," not "scientific," but purely "subjective."

The attitude of the group conveniently indicated by the term "existentialists" is precisely the opposite. They make no effort to prove their assertions through scientific arguments. On the contrary, they want to see their suggestive descriptions of—usually well-chosen—phenomena accepted as *the* description of *the* phenomena. They reveal themselves strong in polemics. In their view, the "scientists" in their suits of methodological armor are unwieldy characters. The opening in the visor of these knights of exactness, so they wittily declare, is too narrow and allows them only a small range of sight. The most obvious human phenomena simply escape these knights. Specifically human phenomena cannot be approached by means of induction, but require a "vision." A "vision" speaks for itself and makes further arguments superfluous. Demonstrating something is a hopelessly outdated procedure, for the important point is "intuition."

Discussion Without Intellectual Effort. For the past few decades discussions like the above-mentioned example have been going on without resulting in any inclination among the proponents of one trend to consider their antagonists serious participants in a dialogue. Yet the stubbornness of the debate shows that both parties believe that they have to defend certain "truths." Obviously, the mutual distrust and contempt can hardly be said to contribute to placing the discussion on a high level. What strikes anyone trained in philosophy is the fact that neither party shows much willingness to come to grips with the fundamental philosophical issues behind the disputed questions. Let us mention a few of these issues.

The "scientists" do not ask themselves what is meant by "experience," "knowledge," "objective knowledge," and "scientific knowledge." Sadly enough, there is no inclination to make a searching analysis of the ontological status of science. Yet it is only when one knows what knowledge *is,* what experience *is,* that scientific knowledge can be compared with the "vision" which, according to the "existentialists," likewise flows from experience. The "scientists" are far too easily inclined to argue in this fashion: there are physical sciences, whose constant progress brooks no doubt. Their success reveals itself in their technical realizations, such as rockets and atomic energy. For this reason any other attempt to reach truth is a wrong approach, it is "unscientific" and nothing else needs to be added to this condemning epithet.[107]

The "existentialists," on the other hand, likewise do not ask themselves what the meaning is of their most-used slogans. Speaking about Sartre, for example, we had to ask in what exactly the role of intuition consists. Is it the same as "vision"? Do they both lead to "a priori descriptions"? Is there no essential difference between artistic and scientific vision? What exactly is meant by such an expression as "consciousness posits"? What is a "world" and what is a "situation"?

It should be evident that the discussion is bound to remain sterile as long as both parties do not want to make any effort to reflect profoundly upon their most important fundamental concepts.

Typical Ambiguities. We may offer here a first modest contribution toward disentangling the affair by pointing out a few typical ambiguities.

1. As we have mentioned, the term *scientific* plays an important role in the discussion. It has a twofold meaning, which is not always realized by those who use it. The first meaning of "a 'scientific' proposition" is that the proposition has been proved in accord with certain rules. In modern English usage, however, the term "sciences" refers to mathematics and natural science, and this usage has resulted in a secondary meaning. In this secondary sense something is "scientific" only if it has been established in accord with the methods of mathematics and natural sciences. Nevertheless, it should be evident that there exist other methodic-critical forms of thinking which differ essentially from those used in the "sciences."

---

[107]Lundberg provides a typical example of such an attitude. Cf. above, p. 15.

6. Provisional Determination of a New Direction

2. A similar misunderstanding arises in connection with the term *objective*. In certain empirical sciences methods are called "objective" if they do not appeal to the self-experience of the subject. The subject is considered as an "object" of empirical research in exactly the same sense as a chemical substance, a crystal or a micro-organism. Yet the same term "objective" applies also to the intellectual attitude of someone who pursues his study in an unprejudiced fashion and allows his judgment to be determined by that which really presents itself.

3. The opposite of the "objective" attitude of mind is supposed to be the "subjective" attitude. A judgment is subjective if it flows from a mood, an impression, an emotion. One who makes a subjective judgment is not ready to submit to the norms imposed by reality. So far, however, as the "scientist" (in the narrow sense) is concerned, any statement is "merely subjective" if it expresses a pre-scientific experience. The remark, for instance, that this room is hot is merely subjective in this sense. On the other hand, in everyday life we speak of "subjective opinions" when there is no possibility or no inclination to form a well-founded judgment. When, for example, a student is introduced to a professor and the latter at once evaluates the former as "he will never amount to anything," his judgment is subjective in the second sense because it is based merely upon an impression. When someone does not make any effort to justify his assertions either to himself or to others, he is reproached for his "lack of objectivity." Finally, we brand as *subjectivism* any theory conceived by reason of sheer preference or emotional need without regard for the demands of reality. According to Lalande, "subjectivism" is "the tendency of the individual to lock himself up in his own ideas and feelings, the inability to consider things from the objective viewpoint."[108]

Provisional Distinctions. An important distinction imposes itself here. It is very well possible that in the study of man one will reject upon perfectly objective grounds the dictatorship of the so-called "objective methods" demanded, e.g., by the behaviorists. In other words, one may combat the views of Carnap and

---

[108]*Vocabulaire technique* . . . , p. 1040.

Watson without becoming a "subjectivist," i.e., without giving in to emotional needs. Without locking himself up in the narrow world of his own thoughts and feelings, but on the contrary, on the basis of that which really presents itself, one may reject the opinion that only the method of the "sciences" (in the narrow sense) leads to an intellectually justified knowledge of man.

Our conceptual analysis allows us to draw conclusions of greater scope in the realm of the theories of knowledge and science. Firstly, *it is possible to deny that the "sciences" (in the narrow sense) are models for the study of man, without becoming "unscientific,"* i.e., unjustifiable, unmethodical, uncritical. Secondly, without lapsing into subjectivism, one may observe that *the dictatorship of objectivity, in the sense of the behaviorists and the logical positivists, leads to an objectivistic attitude of mind.*[109] Thirdly, it must be admitted that *objectivism is a degenerative phenomenon of the otherwise laudable tendency to intersubjectively valid truth,* i.e., to objectivity in the sense of being free from prejudices.

Basic Principles of a New Program. The preceding distinctions, however, are not sufficient. For a theory of science (in the broad sense) must evidently be based on a certain conception of human knowledge, and the theory of knowledge in its turn has to be rooted in a general philosophy of man. For this reason we will introduce here as a kind of program and prelude two philosophical-anthropological basic ideas, which later will receive a more extensive justification.

In the discussion sketched above the concepts "subject" and "object" play rather an enigmatic role. According to the "scientists," the object determines the subject's act of knowing, but in the view of the "existentialists" the conscious subject posits a world of objects. As we have seen above, both views lead to impossible consequences. We want therefore to oppose to these views a position that deviates fundamentally from both and claim that *"the object" is a discovery made by human subjects and that objectivity is the result of a certain subjective approach.* This twofold assertion implies a definite conception of man and his

---

[109]"Objectivistic" is understood here in the sense explained on p. 13.

subjectivity. It excludes, on the one hand, that man's knowing would amount to a purely passive being-determined,[110] and on the other, it disagrees fundamentally with the idea that man's consciousness "posits" the world of objects, is "creative" in the absolute sense of the term. Knowledge always requires a certain activity of human consciousness, which we may call *un-veiling* or *dis-covering*. But only that can be unveiled which lets itself be unveiled from a certain standpoint and in a certain way; hence what is discovered in this way is not reality unqualified but an aspect of reality. Accordingly, our first fundamental principle may be formulated also as follows: *human subjects discover the objectivity aspect of reality by means of an objectifying approach*.

Object and objectivity may now appear to owe their being-for-us to a free project. This sounds very strange to the "scientists" and seems to resemble the well-known slogans of the "existentialists." To prevent the latter from offering premature congratulations, let us quickly add a second proposition. The project of objectivity is a discovery and not an invention, it is not a "gratuitous project" of a sovereign freedom, but rather *a necessary project for mankind on the road to consciousness and liberation*. This assertion contains a conviction in the realm of the philosophical view of man— namely, that human freedom does not exclude but includes certain kinds of bonds. It is only when this concept of freedom has been clarified that it will become clear why it is meaningful to speak of a project which is both free and necessary.

Toward a Phenomenological Philosophy. These remarks delineate the direction taken by the "third approach." Anyone acquainted with contemporary thinking knows that by going in this direction we will enter into the realm of *phenomenological philosophy*. For the conviction that objectivity results primarily from certain intentional activities of a subject is a typically phenemenological conviction. Yet great prudence remains necessary. Questions such as, What is an intentional activity? what is the

---

[110] D. M. de Petter calls this kind of view "passivism." Cf. *Metaphysiek en phenomenologie*, lezing gehouden voor de "Vereniging van thomistische Wijsbegeerte" November 20, 1960, p. 6.

meaning of "primarily"? what is subjectivity?, arise here and have to be faced, for the phenomenological terms may have a meaning that deviates somewhat from the sense given to them by other phenomenologists. Fortunately the realm of phenomenological philosophy is rather large and leaves room for the task of clearing a suitable road. More accurately expressed, our task will be to outline a philosophical anthropology on a phenomenological basis, showing how man makes a project of objectivity and scientific objectivity. We propose to proceed here in the opposite direction from the customary procedure. Instead of "explaining" man by means of the sciences, we hope to make the sciences intelligible by way of man.

SECOND STUDY

THREEFOLD OBJECTIVITY

A. THE OBJECTIVITY OF THE "EVERYDAY WORLD"

1. THE "EVERYDAY WORLD" AS THE FOUNDATION OF SCIENTIFIC THOUGHT

Husserl's "Lebenswelt." None of Husserl's ideas has been more enthusiastically received by the "existentialists" than the so-called *"Lebenswelt,"* the "everyday world."[1] Some of them, however, have interpreted this idea so one-sidedly that one may legitimately question whether they have understood what Husserl had in mind. For this reason it will not be amiss to recall here briefly what the Father of phenomenological philosophy meant by this term.

In his book, *Die Krisis der europäischen Wissenschaften,* Husserl wanted to show that anyone pursuing science, even so-called "exact science," makes an extremely naive use of certain "obvious data" of everyday life. Husserl used several examples to emphasize his point. While, for instance, Einstein repeats Michelson's experiments in his laboratory by means of instruments copied from those of Michelson, he knows exactly what an instrument is, what the human use of an instrument is, what a science institute is, etc. He knows all this not on the basis of his physico-mathematical knowledge but because of his prescientific experience. Yet this naive knowledge of human achievements, human cultural products, and human institutions is the foundation of his scientific pursuits.[2] Let us next pay attention to Michelson's instruments. They are constructed in such a way that the crucial observation is reduced to a "pointer reading" (Eddington). Ultimately, therefore, that which is observed, the pointer on the scale, is nothing else than a figure against a background. Its observation takes place in a "subjectively relative way," and the resulting observational judgment in its turn becomes the premise of further physico-mathematical conclusions.[3]

---

[1]"Lebenswelt," literally "life world," indicates the world of immediate experience in which everyday life runs its course. (Tr.)

[2]*Die Krisis der europäischen Wissenschaften,* p. 128.

[3]Husserl, *op. cit.,* p. 129.

Along the line suggested by Husserl other facts may be put forward. Let us suppose that one and the same instrument is first used to measure A and then B. To execute this double measurement, the physicist has to identify the instrument. But this act of identification does not essentially differ from the one enabling a housewife first to put a pot on the fire and then to remove the same pot from the fire. Secondly, let us assume that Einstein is visited by a fellow professor who does not understand the symbolic language of modern physics, but nonetheless would like to know what the meaning is of the physicist's investigations. In that case Einstein will be forced to explain the meaning of his symbols, he will be obliged to have recourse to the ordinary language of everyday life as it is spoken in Germany, France or the United States.

All this shows that the world of immediate experience, of the obvious, may not be neglected by the philosopher and especially not by the philosopher who wants to conceive a theory of science (in the broad sense of the term). For this world, the "world of everyday life," is the *"forgotten sense foundation of physical science."*[4]

A Subjectivistic Interpretation of Husserl. This whole train of thought has not been followed with sufficient attention by some "existentialists." As elsewhere, so here also they have seized a few words, cut loose from their context. In this case the words "subjectively relative" are viewed as a subjectivistic individualistic confession of faith. Husserl's emphasis on the original sujectively relative givenness of things is conceived as a rejection of every form of objectivity. Thus they are led to the following conclusions:

1. That which is relative to the subject appears differently to every subject. For this reason it is entirely individual.

2. The phenomena perceived by one individual are never wholly the same as those perceived by another. For this reason the sense attributed to these phenomena differs from individual to individual. Thus it will be of decisive importance that every philosopher describe his individual impressions as accurately and

---

[4]Husserl, *op. cit.,* p. 48. Italics are his.

as clearly as possible. Some go even so far as to claim that phenomenology is nothing else than the art of describing impressions.[5]

3. Because the impressions and the "givings of meaning" by distinct individuals are ultimately just as incomparable as these individuals themselves, any tendency toward objectivity amounts to a falsification of man's most original experiences. French philosophers of existence especially like to emphasize this point. They crusade against what they call "objective thought." In their view, *"objective thought"* prevents man from discovering that which is fundamental, genuine and authentic. They appear unaware of the distinction between objectivity and objectivism.

Jeanson's Rejection of Objectivity. A single example may serve to illustrate this view. A motorcar, Francis Jeanson says, is a material thing. It has a certain mass, volume, degree of elasticity, etc. It is, moreover, a car of a certain make, say, a 4 CV Renault. So far as these points are concerned, there is no difference of opinion. Nonetheless, they do not at all reveal to us how the individual sees the car. Let us assume that its owner suffers from an inferiority complex and is under the domineering influence of his wife. The only thing that allows him some superiority is the fact that *he* alone in the whole family knows how to drive. What, then, Jeanson asks, is this car really? A 4 CV Renault or a means to escape a woman's domineering influence? True, all individuals agree that it is a 4 CV Renault, but precisely this objective truth is wholly unimportant and without any value, it has no "validity" for anybody.[6]

Subjectivism as Skepticism. Undoubtedly, if Husserl himself had seen this quotation from Jeanson, he would justifiedly have branded it as a *skeptical* argument. For "all genuine skepticism, no matter to what kind or trend it belongs, manifests itself through the internal contradiction which makes its arguments implicitly presuppose, as a condition of their possible validity, precisely that

---

[5]Concerning this "impressionistic" phenomenology, see pp. 296 ff.
[6]"Cette objectivité, valable et vraie pour tout le monde, c'est à dire pour n'importe qui, *ne 'vaut' précisément rien et n'est 'réelle' pour personne.*" *La phénoménologie,* Paris, n. d., pp. 14 f. Italics of Jeanson.

which it denies in its theses."⁷ This Husserlian statement applies to the skepticism of certain existential philosophers.

Let us demonstrate the point with respect to the case under consideration. Jeanson makes the following distinction. The judgment that the gentleman's car is a 4 CV Renault refers to an objective datum and as such is valueless. The remark, however, that for the gentleman in question the car is a means to escape from his wife's domineering influence and to compensate for his inferiority complex corresponds solely with his strictly subjective view and therefore is meaningful. The question that arises here at once is, How is it possible that we, who do not even know the gentleman who owns the car, understand the terms "domineering influence," "inferiority complex," "escape," etc., and that we perfectly grasp the situation even though it is concerned with very intimate conditions? Or, to reverse the question, How is it possible that, if no one sees the car in the same way as this gentleman, Jeanson is able to know this view, to describe and express it? We may even add, Why does Jeanson have his description printed and published? Why does he bring it to the attention of "anybody" (*n'importe qui*)?

Somewhere Jeanson makes the remark: "Through our words and in our speech we are unfaithful to our experience of ourselves and of the other."⁸ But he makes use of language and of speech to characterize the intimate experiences of the car owner. Accordingly, isn't is true that Husserl's words apply to him, that he presupposes as a validating condition precisely that which he denies in his assertions? He presupposes specifically that it is possible to make the strictly individual accessible to some extent to people speaking the same language by means of objectifying expressions. For objectifying language, as the embodiment of objectifying thought, does not destroy the individual experience but raises it to a higher level, to a level on which concepts such as "domineering," "inferiority complex," and "escape" have meaning-for-us, a meaning even which, horrible as it may seem, is the same

---

⁷Husserl, *Ideen zu einer reinen Phänomenologie und phänomenologischen Philosophie*, Part One, edited by W. Biemel, The Hague, 1950, p. 189. Hereafter we will quote this work as *Ideen I*.
⁸*Op. cit.*, p. 16.

for each one of us. By making implicit use of that which he explicitly rejects as impossible, Jeanson's radical subjectivism reveals him as a genuine skeptic.[9]

Objectivism and Objectivity. Thus it is apparent that this crusade against "objective thought" is a quixotic enterprise. For anyone who enters into communication with others to start an action, anyone who speaks, writes, and publishes books presupposes and makes use of some form of objectivity. The only world which is unconditionally determined by "subjective relative" elements is the world of the schizophrenic and perhaps also that of the autist. Without the slightest doubt, however, Husserl did not intend to describe an insane asylum when he spoke of the "everyday world."

Beyond Scientism and Antiscientism. What Husserl wanted to combat was exactly the same as we have rejected above—namely, *scientistic objectivism.* "From the very beginning," he points out, "the entire meaning of the idea of objective truth is determined in opposition to the idea of truth in prescientific and extra-scientific life."[10] According to Husserl, therefore, there is truth also in prescientific life, a truth which is a truth-for-us. The fault of the scientistic attitude lies precisely in its scorn for, and neglect of this prescientific truth. For this reason he emphatically refers to the "everyday world" as the forgotten foundation of all scientific giving of meaning. This statement, however, should not be mis understood. One who emphasizes the importance of the foundation does not mean to minimize the house that is to be built on this foundation. He does not claim that it will be useless, unimportant and unfit to live in. True, the everyday world is the realm of the most primary evidence,[11] but this admission does not lead Husserl to conclude that scientific evidence, based on this primary evidence, would not have any value of its own. Briefly, he was just as much against reviling the sciences as against idolizing them.

---

[9]In all fairness it should be pointed out that in his latest work, *Critique de la raison dialectique,* pp. 106 f., Sartre at least shows an awareness of this problem. However, his proposed solution is not at all acceptable to us.
[10]*Die Krisis der europäischen Wissenschaften,* p. 127.
[11]*Op. cit.,* p. 130.

He belongs neither to the camp of antiscientism nor to that of scientism. It is perhaps for this reason that it is not so easy to understand his standpoint.

The Two Meanings of the "Everyday World." A careful analysis of Husserl's works shows that the "everyday world" contains two elements which may not be simply identified. The everyday world is first of all the world of prescientific life in which everyone participates to a greater or lesser extent. As such, it is a wholly non-historic concept, which is always there for everyone. In this sense Husserl says, "The everyday world is the world which is always pre-given, which is always accepted in advance as being."[12] Accordingly, one would be inclined to characterize the prescientific sector of our everyday world as the "prescientific world."

The second element of the "everyday world" manifiests itself less clearly in Husserl but nonetheless is present in the background. It is the idea that the everyday world is the human world prior to the origin of a universal theory of *scientia*. As a matter of fact, Husserl speaks also of man in the "prescientific period" and in this connection he uses the term *"Lebensumwelt,"* i.e., the surrounding world as given in our immediate experience.[13] Scarce as Husserl's statements about this point are, they make the phenomenological philosopher pause to reflect. Perhaps it would be commendable to reserve the term "everyday world" for certain historically and anthropologically discernible phenomena—namely, the typical phenomena of periods in the life of peoples in which they are guided by *doxa,* by traditional belief, and not, not yet, by *epistēmē,* by the critical knowledge which, by virtue of its critical self-awareness, lays claim to universal validity.

"Prescientific World" or "Prescientific Level"? On second thought, doubt may arise about the question whether or not the concept of "prescientific world" is free from contradiction. "World," as is generally known, means an horizon encompassing an interconnected whole of beings. The question to be asked here

---

[12]*Op. cit.,* Beilage XVII, p. 461.
[13]*Op. cit.,* Beilage XXV, p. 491.

is whether the reality given to us in a prescientific fashion is so clearly distinguished from scientific reality that it constitutes a whole. We may think here of man's perceptive and apperceptive cognitive life. For instance, it is not possible for us to see the setting sun as a thing as big as an orange, for we know that the sun is a sphere of gas whose size is far greater than that of the earth and this knowledge influences also our perception. Likewise, the simple country dwellers who witnessed the first steam-driven train rush by saw the locomotive as a "fire-wagon" moved by demonic forces. We, however, who know more or less what happens in the interior of a locomotive see the engine simply as a mechanism.

What we want to say is that prescientific experience does not constitute a world in itself but refers to a certain level of our personal cognitive life. Yet even this term "level" has to be used carefully. It should not be understood as if the prescientific level is "low" and the scientific level "high." As we will have ample opportunity to point out later, the realm of original evidences is very important for the discovery of scientific evidences. For this reason it is better to compare the prescientific level with a fertile soil in which critical and systematic knowledge produces ample fruit. Like such a soil, it is penetrated by numerous roots, some of which remain close to the surface while others go down deeply. Like such a soil, therefore, the prescientific level is fully of "holes"; it undergoes many changes just as the physical and chemical properties of the soil are modified by the vegetation it supports. To drop the metaphor, not only is there no sharp boundary between prescientific and scientific life, but there exist also static and dynamic relationships between the two. With this twofold proviso it will be permissible to maintain the expression "prescientific level."

The Problems Presented by the Sphere of Ownness (Eigenheitsphäre). It is not a mere coincidence that we have made this tiny correction of Husserl's philosophical thinking. This correction was concerned with Husserl's tendency to construct or reconstruct certain "layers" of intentional life by means of thought experiments. The way in which he developed the concept of "everyday world," in the first sense of the term, provides an example of this tendency. The subtraction of scientific experience from the whole of human experience results, he thinks, in the "everyday world." The question, however, is whether the remainder may still be called a world.

There is another famous example of this questionable procedure in Husserl's fifth *Cartesian Meditation*. This meditation is devoted to the derivation of intersubjectivity from the experience of the solitary ego. Husserl proceeds here in a peculiar way. First he reduces total experience to the sphere of "ownness," i.e., the realm of transcendental experience which remains after I have systematically abstracted from the existence of other human subjects. This abstraction implies that I have to abstract also from all spiritual and cultural predicates of things as well as from the property of the surrounding world (*Umwelt*) of being the surrounding world-for-everyone. Only then does the world cease to be objective world. What is it that remains after this systematic abstraction? "From the phenomenon world, from the world appearing with an objective sense, a substratum becomes separated, as the nature included in my ownness."[14] The sphere of ownness, therefore, is nature-for-me and nothing else. Note that nature-for-me does not correspond with a phenomenological datum. That which appears is the world, and the world, even according to Husserl, always has an objective sense. Nature-for-me is merely a construct. It shows us the ultimate consequence to be drawn from the idea of relative-to-the-subject and relative-to-the-individual. The world without objectivity is "pure nature," as it would appear to a wholly solitary ego. To this extent Husserl's thought experiment is instructive.

The question, however, is whether the cultural predicates and meanings of things are based on a "substratum" of nature-for-me simply perceived as such. Husserl himself defends this view, when he says that a thing is first a perceived fragment of nature and then a fragment of nature endowed also with value, practical importance,

[14]*Cartesianische Meditationen und Pariser Vorträge*, The Hague, 1950, p. 127; English translation, *Cartesian Meditations*, The Hague, 1960, p. 96.

emotional significance and intersubjective meaning.[15] It would seem to us, however, that this is not an adequate description of the perceptive act.

A concrete analysis may serve best to demonstrate the point. What would correspond with nature perceived by me alone? Let us assume that during a walk I arrive at a rock. There is here, of course, no question of cultural predicates or spiritual symbols. The rock is a piece of virgin granite, devoid of any ornaments or inscriptions; moreover, I am alone in the neighborhood. Nevertheless, I "know" that the rock has different sides, so that it will appear differently to imaginary other persons. In a faithful description of my act of perception I would, therefore, have to say that I see the rock as differently seen by possible other persons. As Paul Ricoeur remarks, "My percept is at once perceived also as perceived by others."[16] Accordingly, there exists no perceived nature for me alone and there exists no "sphere of ownness" as a "layer" which is the bearer of intersubjective meanings.[17]

To "Perceive" and to "Perceive as." Someone who is familiar with certain basic ideas of a trend of psychology which is already somewhat antiquated will be inclined to remark that we confuse perception and apperception. Consequently, our analysis would be "unpsychological." That which is perceived is one side of the rock and that which is associated with the percept are the other sides as they could be seen by possible other persons. The same critic will add that the other analyses suffer from the same confusion. He will say that everyone will perceive the locomotive in the same way, but one associates this perception with the "devil" and the other with a certain kind of "mechanism." In this way there are different apperceptions of the same object.

Our reply to this objection can be very simple. For us to perceive is to have an immediately communicating experience in time

---

[15]See, e.g., *Ideen I*, par. 95, p. .
[16]"Sympathie et respect," *Revue de métaphysique et de morale,* 1954, (pp. 380-397), p. 381.
[17]For a critique of Husserl's derivation of intersubjectivity see, in addition to the above-quoted article of Ricoeur, Alfred Schutz, "Le problème de l'intersubjectivité chez Husserl, *Husserl, Cahiers de Royaumount,* Paris, 1959, pp. 334-381.

and space of a concrete reality. In this communicating experience there is no awareness of the distinction between the percept and its association. In other words, there is no experience in three successive moments of time. The subject does not first perceive the locomotive, then imagine a devil, and finally associate the two, but rather *sees* the locomotive at once as a "fire wagon" moved by demonic forces. We do not question here that the distinction between perception and apperception may have a solid foundation, for it may be made on the occasion of the question of *how* this immediate experience arises. Nevertheless, when it is a matter of expressing *that which* is immediately experienced, the distinction between "perception" and "perception as" is irrelevant.

Let us illustrate the point by means of an example. When my working day is over and I hungrily walk beside the house on the corner, I smell "something delicious." That it is delicious and desirable I experience in the most direct fashion. What this delicious thing is, steak or roast, I do not know, but I experience it as a value to be pursued and therefore I hurry home. Accordingly, there is no question of a substratum, constituted by a value-free and merely perceived nature, which would be the bearer of value predicates, emotional predicates, intersubjective predicates. On the contrary, I perceive reality with its values, and these values are always intersubjective meanings. This is the reason why we reject the concept "pure nature-for-me-alone" not only as a descriptive concept but also as a fundamental theoretical concept.

2. OBJECTIFICATION AND OBJECTIVITY

The Origin of the Thing-Object. To see, as Buytendijk says, is always to see meanings. This "seeing of meanings" is not at all an intellectual process, an introjection, or reasoning through analogy, but there is really question of perceiving meanings. Any child is capable of such a perception. When he plays hide and seek, he sees his hiding place, the rock or lamp-post, as it will appear to his seeking companions. In playing tag, he runs in such a way that the thing (the lamp-post or rock) will be between him and his pursuer. To add another example, for Mother fire is something which she can handle very easily, but for the child fire is a frightful "biting" thing.

Accordingly, the child experiences that one and the same thing is for the one a hide-out and for the other a trick, for one something safe and for the other a dangerous obstacle. What for grown-ups is "manipulatable equipment"[18] may not at all be manipulatable for a child. One and the same thing, therefore, may protect or betray, help or hinder, be useful, troublesome or dangerous, because it has literally and figuratively several "sides"; and because it has several sides, it appears differently to distinct persons. This observation is the general and necessary result of a general and necessary experience. The experience in question does not have the character of a solitary experiment, but arises when several subjects do things together, explore their environment together and act together. It is only in the communication with others that it becomes clear what a thing is.

Specifically human communication in the full sense of the term is, of course, communication by means of speech. Even as speech is the intermediary between the "I" that becomes conscious and the "I" that is conscious, so also is the spoken dialog the intermediary between the "we" that becomes conscious and the "we" that is conscious. For, as we will see later, only experiences which are given a name receive a permanent place and function in the structures of our consciousness, only these experiences are at our free

---

[18]Cf. Heidegger's *Sein und Zeit,* pp. 68 f. (zuhandenes Zeug), English translation, *Being and Time,* New York, 1962, pp. 97 f.

disposal as contents of consciousness. In this way speech and dialog increase our own consciousness. As Marcel remarks, only where there is a dialog is it possible to think of an object. He asks himself when we used the second person and replies that we have recourse to it when we address ourselves to something judged capable of replying in one way or another. When no answer can be expected, we are reduced to using the impersonal "it."[19]

This important statement may be rendered more complete by three supplementary remarks. First of all, the "object" is a wholly abstract concept, a "being of reason." According to Lalande, it is "that which is thought or represented insofar as it is distinguished from the act by which it is thought."[20] Taken in this sense, the "object" evidently belongs to the sphere of scientific and philosophical thinking. Secondly, insofar as a thing is the object of prescientific thinking and doing, it may be called the *thing-object*. Accordingly, the thing-object is the concrete *insofar as* it can be determined by means of speaking to one another and acting together. Finally, as is evidenced by the preceding analyses, in addition to the dialog, the communicating praxis of speaking and acting as "we" is of decisive importance. For it is also characteristic of the thing that it has different "sides" giving rise to different "aspects," "ways of seeing" and ways of acting. *The thing-object, then, is, first, that which is spoken of but itself does not speak; secondly, from a practical standpoint, that with which one can do something but which of itself does not do anything;* thirdly, *the same thing which can be spoken of in different senses* because it has different "sides."

Opinions may differ as to *what*, concretely speaking, is a thing-object and what is not a thing-object. Meanwhile it is certain that in the mythical everyday world there is no sharp boundary between subjects and thing-objects. We will have to revert to this point later in this work.

Three Objectifying Achievements. Nevertheless, both on the prescientific level and in the everyday worlds there exists something

---

[19]*Journal métaphysique*, Paris, 1927, p. 138.
[20]*Op. cit.*, p. 702.

2. Objectification and Objectivity

like objectivity. Husserl was not a complete stranger to this truth. As we have just seen, he held that only the "sphere of owness" is wholly divested of the world's objective sense.[21] Elsewhere Husserl emphasizes that "this everyday world is nothing else than the world of mere . . . *doxa* [belief]. Of course, in life outside science this everyday world is not so devaluated at all; there it indicates a *sphere* of good confirmations."[22] "Confirmation," proving to be good or true, presupposes a certain objectivity, albeit an objectivity which differs essentially from scientific objectivity. How does this minimal objectivity arise? What intentional achievements are required to safeguard a valid minimum of understanding? Why is it that prescientific life and historically observable everyday worlds do not at all resemble an insane asylum?

To be able to speak with other existent subjects about a certain "something," to be able to act together with the others in orderly and purposive fashion, appears to require *three fundamental intentional achievements—namely, isolation, identification, and name-giving.*

With respect to isolation, the crucial point is to distinguish one definite person from other persons, one thing from other things, one situation from other situations. This distinction may be *implied* in the act of perception, in a deed, in a subject's behavior, but it is not identical with them. There exists, for example, also a form of perception in which no distinct object-thing in particular is fixed in the field of perception. As long as *A* is not distinguished from *B,* it is not possible to make *A* the theme of cognitive or practical actions. True, one could take the *A-B* group from the whole, but this also would presuppose an achievement—namely, the distinction of this group from other groups. *Isolation,* therefore, is a first intentional achievement and at the same time a condition making other achievements possible.

Identification is a second fundamental achievement. It should not be confused with isolation. The perceived thing-object, says Husserl, is "an identical pole of multiple acts of comprehension

---

[21]*Cartesian Meditations,* p. 96.
[22]*Die Krisis der europäischen Wissenschaften,* Beilage XVII, p. 465.

referring to this pole"; it is on a higher level—the level which we would call that of the dialog—something "identical as the unity of predicative actions."[23] The way in which this achievement of identification is brought about has been repeatedly and extensively described by Husserl and does not need to be reconsidered here. Nevertheless, we want to draw attention again to the important concept of "making-true," of confirmation (*Bewährung*). No matter how my exploring acts develop, that which I have grasped as a definite "something" must always continue to reveal itself as the same "something." For instance, from whatever side I look at the rock, it always rises before me as one and the same mass of rough granite. "It 'makes itself true,' " i.e., it reveals itself as real and the same.

In a different respect, however, Husserl's descriptions need to be complemented. The decisive confirmation-for-me exists in this that my fellow subjects experience the same "something" as I. A little boy, for example, who makes his first visit to a mountain region "does not believe his eyes" and will ask his mother whether she sees the same as he. Only when Mother affirms it, do the mountain tops, shrouded in clouds, become real for him and not a product of his imagination. Adults act in the same way. A pilot who thinks that he perceives an "unidentified flying object" is not absolutely certain but, when other reports come in and fully agree with his, then the "unidentified flying object" has become a reality.

With the last two analyses we have reached the realm of *naming*. For, on the level of the dialog, identification takes place by giving a name to the "something" in question and subsequently always indicating it by the same name. Name-giving differs essentially from isolation and identification. It must always be done explicitly, but isolation and identification may be implicit in perception and action. A simple example may serve to illustrate the point. For a child a pair of scissors is the thing to cut paper with. Because it can cut paper with the scissors and not with something else, the child's doings make it spontaneously distinguish

---

[23]*Erfahrung und Urteil,* edited by L. Landgrebe, Hamburg, 1948, p. 279.

2. Objectification and Objectivity

the scissors-thing from other things and identify it. The fact that adults constantly name the thing "scissors" does not merely serve to confirm the result of its practical experience but also raises this result to a higher level. It is now possible to make such a judgment as, "scissors are dangerous; be careful with them." Such judgments go beyond the realm of the factual and express a kind of "ought." Through name-giving the thing-object is pushed into the open, an openness which provisionally is that of a concrete we-community. But this giving of names requires an explicit act, an act that is characteristic of man as man.

Skepticism About Language. Name-giving is literally the apex and the crown of experience. It means that for the child a "locomotive" and "mountain tops" are not real if other persons did not indicate them by means of sound symbols. Speaking about the thing confirms and, as it were, ratifies its reality. In this sense words render secure the minimum order that is required for speaking of a world.

This point is important. Rather frequently one may hear the fearful or ironic question whether or not the use of certain words refers to the same phenomena. Do all of us think of the same when, for example, we speak of "shame" or "love"?

The reply to this objection must distinguish between what is essential and what is accidental in this point. It is not certain that we always mean exactly the same when we use the same words. There is a possibility of divergences in the use of sound symbols within one and the same linguistic community. Often such divergences are observable and they may be laid bare by empirical-linguistic, socio-psychological and anthropological research. On the other hand, however, it is not possible that we, as members of one and the same linguistic community, would continue to refer to radically different realities by means of the same terms. For otherwise we would not be able to communicate with one another, our linguistic community would fall apart. Moreover, if there were no similar situations which my fellow-men consistently called "shameful" and "loving," shame and love would not exist for me. For my experiences about the shameful and the loving owe their unity and consistency also to the fact that my fellow subjects always

79

refer to them by means of the same sound symbol. By doing this, they have placed my experiences in certain categories of practical, social, ethical and even religious life. No matter how volatile and variable these experiences may have been, the understanding I have gathered of their surpra-individual meaning has withdrawn them from the discontinuity of my personal adventures. Here lies the reason why I co-exist with others in a world in which "shame" and "love" are realities.

Importance of Objectification. Accordingly, name-giving is a specifically human achievement. The correct description of this achievement is of paramount importance. As we have already emphasized, the verbal expression does not destroy the individual, the variable, the personal character of my experiences. My experience of shame remains my individual experience, my experience of love does not cease to be a highly personal affair. Everything remains the same and, nonetheless, everything becomes different, for through the verbal expression the experience is rescued from its solitude. Love no longer remains limited to me and "my intentional poles." I now see love in its interconnection with supraindividual realities of the social, ethical and religious orders, and in this way only it becomes fully *my* love. Where previously I *experienced* love, I now *know* love and recognize it also in others. I know now something about love unqualified.

With Kant one could call this view of the more encompassing spiritual whole a "synthesis." However, with Ernst Cassirer, we prefer to speak here of *objectification.*[24] By means of this objectification man removes the opposition between the individual and the universal, between the variable and the permanent, between the "I" and the "we."

Jeanson, therefore, is wrong when he asserts that "by means of language and in the 'universe of discourse' we are unfaithful to our experience of ourselves, by constantly substituting for it abstractions which disguise or betray it while we think that they give expression to it."[25] In truth, it is precisely language and "dis-

---

[24]*Philosophie der symbolischen Formen,* Part One, *Die Sprache,* Berlin, 1923.
[25]*La phénoménologie,* p. 15.

2. Objectification and Objectivity

course" which to a certain extent make it possible for us "to exchange experiences." Without "language," in the broadest sense of the term, every subject would be locked up in the cocoon of his own little world as, we may repeat it, happens in certain abnormal psychical conditions. The subject would be centered on himself and his situation, so that no genuine interhuman relationship would be possible. Verbal expression mediates between subjects, not despite but precisely because of its objectifying force. It gives rise to the dialog and it is only in the dialog that a world-for-us becomes a reality.

Unveiling Experience, Disclosing Dialog. In the preceding pages we have used such expressions as: the thing-object "originates" and something "becomes for us reality." The important point is, of course, the question of how these expressions must be understood. Does the thing "originate" for us because by way of a sense stimulus, neural traces and cerebral cortex it evokes in our consciousness a representative? Must we conceive its "origin" as if consciousness "constitutes" its objects in the sense of "positing" them?

At present we will give only a provisional reply to this crucial question. This reply has a positive as well as a negative aspect. So far as this negative aspect is concerned, it should be sufficiently clear that we reject both empiricist objectivism and idealistic subjectivism. Using Gordon W. Allport's terminology, we could say that we consider the "Lockean tradition" just as unsatisfactory as the "Leibnitzian tradition."[26] The reasons have been given above. They show that the stimulus myth no more agrees with the genuine data of experience than does the myth of a world-positing consciousness.

For the positive aspect of the reply we would like to begin with experience, more specifically with perceiving experience, described in non-empiricist terms. Perception is by its very nature *sui generis*. If nonetheless we want to typify this act, paying attention to what we really experience, I would prefer to compare it with a

---

[26]*Becoming. Basic Considerations for a Psychology of Personality*, New Haven, 1955, pp. 7-17.

81

question. Every glance is, as it were, a question, which, verbally expressed, asks, "Won't there be something to see?" Note that a question is not a reaction. One who asks a question knows already what he is asking about. A question, therefore, as Plato already emphasized,[27] implies a kind of knowing. In an analogous way, we must say that one who looks assumes that there is something to see. One who gropes, likewise, is ahead of that which is actually experienced. Every motion of groping may be compared with the question, "Won't there be something to touch?" When such a question meets something that can be seen or touched, the visible or the touchable collaborates, as it were, with the perceiver. There arises an interplay between the one who sees and that which is seen, the one who touches and that which can be touched. This interplay can be described in the language of phenomenological psychology.

Analogous observations apply to man's way of acting. He acts spontaneously but not without there being something which "collaborates" with him in his different activities. He is able to hide, for example, only when something offers a hiding place. His technical work supposes the presence of things that lend themselves as suitable materials or tools. Accordingly, we do not say that real is what "acts" upon us. Likewise, we do not want to assert that reality is "constituted" by man, but we rather claim that for us *reality is that which* replies to our theoretical and practical questions and in this way *collaborates with us.* We *unveil* it and it *reveals* itself to us. In other words, the thing-object acts primarily as a *partner* in our cognitive and practical life. It is on our interplay with such partners that our experience is based.

On a higher level, that of the specifically human, things are related in an analogous fashion. The difference is that the speechless interplay becomes here an explicit giving of names and speaking. Yet there is again an assumption. By speaking, we presuppose that experienced reality can be indicated by means of symbols. And this presupposition appears to be justified. The word seizes the experienced reality and it is only in the word that this reality

---

[27]E. Strauss. "Der Mensch ein fragendes Wesen," *Psychologie der menschlichen Welt, Göttingen-Heidelberg,* 1960, p. 319.

2. Objectification and Objectivity

fully becomes human reality, is dis-covered for us, dis-closed for us. "The symbol," says Cassirer, "is not the fortuitous wrapping of thought but its indispensable and essential organ. It does not merely serve to communicate the completed content of a thought, but is an instrument through which this content forms itself."[28] Heidegger has given this idea an ontological meaning by emphasizing that "while speech first names being, it is only this naming that makes being speak and appear."[29] We "make being speak" by interrogating it correctly. By speaking and to the extent that it speaks, it makes its appearance, it is *un-veiled,* dis-closed for us.

It should be noted that not everything lends itself to the same kind of questions. Fire may be "questioned" by means of visual perceptions but not through touch. Practical questions also must be adapted to the nature of the being that is supposed to "collaborate." The thing, for example, which serves as a tool does not lend itself to being a shelter, it does not offer its collaboration for this purpose. Most of all, however, it must be kept in mind that we cannot speak of all beings in the same sense. Of course, it remains possible to ask whether a table is true and a judgment is brown, but such questions are merely empty sounds, for the beings in question cannot be interrogated in this way. The question does not "touch" them, the words are meaningless for them, as the silence of the beings in question "tells" us. Accordingly, the dialog of fellow-existents is not a kind of magic dialectics, through which everything can become everything else. Being determines what we may speak about and in what sense. It is the norm both through its silence and through its replies, and this norm applies also to dialectics.

Orientation. All this would need to be more fully developed in a philosophical way. However, here we will limit ourselves to a single and apparently simple conclusion—namely, that *man's essence is an orientation to others.* Negatively this conclusion means that man is not a sovereign consciousness, that his acts

---

[28]*Die Sprache, op. cit.,* I, p. 18.
[29]*Holzwege,* Frankfurt, 2nd ed., 1952, p. 16: "Indem die Sprache erstmals das Seienden nennt, bringt solches Nennen das Seiende erst zum Wort und Erscheinung."

are not based on arbitrary projects, that his free acts do not originate anything. He is "dependent," in the strong sense of the term,[30] i.e., he cannot exist as a conscious being without the others. His consciousness is a needy consciousness.

From the preceding considerations the positive implications of this need should be clear. Man depends on something which he is not and which is his norm in a *twofold* way. To acquire experiences, his finite consciousness has to address itself to "something." In doing so, it opens itself and lets itself be determined by that which it experiences. Its questions are given replies which contain a norm for its knowledge.

Secondly, man's needy consciousness depends on other conscious beings. Listening to the others, man compares his experiences with those of others. The dialog unveils the common experience as identically the same being having several "sides." Moreover, through the verbal embodiment of the common experience the individual human being learns principles enabling him to arrange his experiences in an orderly fashion. At the same time these experiences receive a new dimension. The individual's love, for example, is given an ethical and social meaning through the dialog and this meaning is a norm for his cognitive and practical life.

Accordingly, the orientation to others assumes of necessity the form of opening-oneself-to and listening-to. In other words, it has a normative character. However, this normative character should not be understood in a "deterministic" sense. There is no question of a foreign law imposed on man "from without." On the contrary, man desires this law on the ground of the law which his nature is. His finite freedom is not merely reconcilable with this but demands meaningful bonds. Although they are neglected by existential philosophers of Sartre's type, these bonds are the foundation underlying the order and continuous orientation proper to the normal life of the "I" and the "we." It is only because of his free acceptance of norms and principles safeguarding continuity and lasting orientation that man can become the founder and developer of his surrounding world.

---

[30]Cf. Heidegger, *Sein und Zeit*, p. 137; *Being and Time*, p. 176.

2. Objectification and Objectivity

The Fundamental Concept of Objectivity. We have now reached the stage where a first contribution can be made toward the clarification of the concept "objectivity." *Objectivity, as a human attitude,*[31] *is free man's recognition of his orientation to, and being normalized by something which is not himself,* insofar as this recognition finds expression, usually in an implicit fashion, in his words and deeds. It is the opposite of arbitrariness, prejudice, and self-sufficient subjectivism.

Objectivity as a human attitude gives rise to that which is objective, and not vice versa. "Objective" here means the same for us as for Kant—namely, that which is necessarily and universally valid for us.[32] Accordingly, that which is objective is not the mode of being of things, it is not the mode of being of "the fact," it is not something which can be laid down by technical approaches or guaranteed through instruments.[33] On the contrary, one would rather have to say that the concept "fact" as well as the scientific apparatus have arisen from the desire for objectivity, a desire, moreover, that was limited to a very special form of objectivity. Briefly put, neither in us nor outside us does there exist any mechanism safeguarding objectivity. Sensitivity, the appeal to sense experience, is not such a mechanism. Nothing is objective before it is unveiled by us as real being. In other words, *nothing is objective for us without us.* On the other hand, we may not neglect the correlated truth that *nothing is objective through us,* we do not make anything objective, for whatever has been un veiled by us or will ever be unveiled by us was already there.[34]

Being contains within itself every possible meaning which we are able to discover. All our discoveries together will not succeed in exhausting its wealth. This thought induces us to assume the attitude of humbleness, respect and prudence which is usually indicated by the term "objectivity."

[31]See above, pp. 16f. and 59.
[32]*Prolegomena to Any Future Metaphysics,* paragraph 18.
[33]Concerning this modern superstition, see the amusing satire of Erwin Strauss, "Ojektivität," *Psychologie der menschlichen Welt,* pp. 409 ff.
[34]Our term "unveiling" corresponds with the Heideggerian *"volbringen,"* to bring to fullness: "To bring to fullness means to unfold something into the fullness of its being, to bring it to this (fullness), *producere.* Accordingly, properly speaking, only that can be brought to fullness that is already." *Über den Humanismus,* Frankfurt, 1949, p. 5.

The preceding ideas indicate the fundamental concept of objectivity. Objectivity, as attitude, is the, at least implicit, recognition of man's finiteness and want with respect to being. However, this concept is still very abstract and general, so that there can be a great divergence regarding that which is explicitly recognized and the way in which this recognition is experienced by men. In the subsequent pages we will speak of three essentially different levels of objectivity. We will describe each of them separately and then endeavor to throw some light on the interconnection of these three forms of objectivity.

Objectifying Praxis. As we have sufficiently shown, the everyday world is a world for us and prescientific life is the life of a "we." As Husserl himself admits, no phenomenologically demonstrable reality corresponds with existence in the "sphere of ownness." The everyday world as well as prescientific life have their own language, their own concepts, their own ways of "making true," their own truths. They possess their own values, purposes and norms. These values, purposes and norms are supra-individual, valid for all and consequently objective. Without objectivity the everyday world would not be a human world but would correspond with the surrounding world of an animal or of the psychically abnormal.

A question that remains to be answered is why we speak of an objectifying *praxis*. Has there not been question of "knowing" and even of "understanding"? Such terms would appear to indicate that we are here in the realm of theory and no longer in that of mere *praxis*. Yet, we would not unqualifiedly want to affirm this statement. Theory, in the narrow sense, usually means fully conscious and explicit knowledge through principles. In this sense there is no question of theory in the everyday world and in prescientific life, in which the technique of isolating, identifying and name-giving is pursued in a naive way. Words and concepts are present here in a simple and ready fashion, without becoming an occasion of reflection and especially of critical reflection. There exists no need for explicit theory, explicit principles and methods of knowledge and activity. The available concepts allow man to

2. Objectification and Objectivity

grasp things but do not yet lead an independent existence. In Aristotelian-Scholastic terms, they do not lead to "second intentions." For this reason we may correctly speak of the objectifying praxis of the everyday world.

We may terminate by drawing attention to another typical characteristic which is connected with the above-described essential feature of objectifying praxis. As we have pointed out, on this level concepts, representations and views do not exist for the one who conceives, represents to himself and views things. They are a *quo* but not a *quod*, i.e., they are merely means through which he conceives, represents, etc., but they themselves are not considered. For this reason man does not place himself critically at a distance from them on this level. Consequently, on this level of knowledge there is no difference between appearance and being. In other words, *things, living beings and men are as they are "seen,"* in the broad sense in which we have used this term. On the other hand, *this "seeing" is such that it is in agreement with the experiences of everyday praxis.*

For this reason one may say that the objectifying praxis of prescientific life is *naive.* The meaning, however, of this term is not always the same. Primitive man is naive because there is no room in his life for reflection, doubt and critique. The civilized man who remains satisfied with prescientific obviousness is naive because he does not consider it necessary to doubt and to be critical. The thesis that things are as they are "seen" and that this "seeing" is normalized also by a successful intersubjective praxis is typical in both cases for what presently we will call *first objectivity.* At first, the standpoint of this "first objectivity" does not seem to be very profound; nevertheless, it could very well be that "first objectivity" and its inevitably naive character are the first and necessary beginning of all possible science and wisdom.

3. THE EVERYDAY WORLD AS PRIMITIVE WORLD

The Objectivity of Primitive Man. The point has now been reached at which the description of the prescientific life of civilized man no longer runs parallel with that of primitive man. Essential differences need to be pointed out here and the anthropological advances of the past few decades demand that these differences be emphasized.

Let us begin by pointing out that it does not exactly appear reasonable to us to criticize the primitive everyday world from the standpoint of modern Western civilization. Such a critique would remain wholly restricted to externals. As we have seen above, primitive man does not and cannot make any difference between appearance and being, between phenomenon and noumenon. If, then, we want to describe the reality of his everyday world, we must endeavor to see what he "sees." Following the example of numerous modern anthropologists, we will therefore try to approach the archaic world "from within" for the purpose of arriving at an understanding of its nature.

The fact that we want to take this approach indicates that we do not share the deeply rooted prejudice which makes civilized man "objective" and "savages" merely "subjective." If objectivity manifests itself in the recognition that man is oriented to, and normalized by something he is not, it must be admitted that such recognition is found nowhere more spontaneously, more artlessly and more totally than in primitive man. For he feels himself, both as individual and as member of a group, wholly dependent on the powers and forces ruling the cosmos. Their law is also his law. The thought that he would be able to dominate nature and use it in accord with his whims and desires does not arise in him. A comparison, borrowed from G. van der Leeuw, may clarify the point. When modern man says that he is "at the mercy of wind and waves," he does not mean this literally, but uses a more or less poetic expression to say that he does not yet dispose of the technical means to control the ocean. Only other human beings are not simply objects for him. "Primitive man, however, sees all that is given as the Other. Not only plants and animals but also the non-living are for him the world together with which he is. He tries, of course, to take a standpoint toward this fellow-world, . . . but he does not attempt to do so by making it an object or raw material."[35] Accordingly, primitive man feels himself wholly oriented and dependent on the Other. The possibility of "subjectivism," in the sense of soverign arbitrariness and "gratuitous" self-determination, simply does not exist for him.

The fact that he has magical convictions and customs does not militate against this statement. Let us take, for instance, the case of a primitive Melanesian who, after making a canoe, considers it necessary to perform certain rites so that "the canoe makes up its mind to run quickly."[36] If it is true that the canoe is "inhabited" by forces which are independent of its maker and user, then the Melanesian acts correctly and purposively even from a practical and business-like standpoint. The existence of such forces seems evident from his experience. For his ancestors and his fellow tribesmen have always performed such rites before making use of their canoes and their canoes have always been able to cruise around rapidly. Thus our Melanesian has no reason to doubt the existence of these magical forces or the efficacy of the magic rites. Within the horizon of his primitive everyday world his attitude is wholly intelligent. This example shows that "objectivity" and "scientific objectivity" do not at all coincide. Their differences are profound and manifest themselves even in a comparison with the prescientific life of civilized man. In the following pages we will limit ourselves to emphasizing a few important and fundamental points of difference.

Differences in Objectifying Praxis. Primitive man also pursues a *kind* of objectification. Without abstraction, says van der Leeuw,[37] life would assume an animal or vegetative character, and any kind of abstraction is necessarily objectifying. Nevertheless, his objectification differs from that of civilized man. The latter knows the

---

[35]G. van der Leeuw, *De primitive mens en de religie*, Groningen, 2nd ed., 1952, pp.. 25 f.

[36]B. Malinowsky, *Argonauts of the Western Pacific*, London, 2nd ed., 1932, p. 133.

[37]*Op. cit.*, p. 140.

possibility and the necessity of critically justifying his concepts. As we will see, this critique and self-criticism are typical of scientific life. We must add again, however, that in civilized man the spheres of prescientific and scientific knowledge are not divided by airtight compartments. Just as his knowledge of the sun's size influences his perception of the sun, so also his knowledge of a subjective error in the giving of names exercises influence on his objectifying acts. The result is that even on the prescientific level his isolation, identification and name-giving are more logical and more analytical than is the case with primitive man.

In primitive man there is no knowledge of concepts as such and this absence has repercussions on his entire cognitive life. He "sees" things differently. "The contours of phenomena in the primitive world are diffuse. There are no fixed boundaries between the various beings of the world. Man lives in the world without objectifying it in the 'modern' way."[38] In primitive man the analytic conception of reality is replaced by a different "fundamental apperception"—namely, that of *participation*. According to this view one being participates in the existence of the other, it shares in the working of the other.[39] The fundamental apperception of participation necessarily presupposes a *kind* of objectification, for the participating beings must be distinguished before they can be seen as participating. However, they are not first separated through an abstract analysis and then put together again by means of an even more abstract synthesis, but everything comes about in a much more simple fashion. The fundamental apperception of participation itself influences the perception. Perception and apperception fuse here also. The result is that primitive man sees reality differently from a civilized man even if the latter does not pursue science. Primitive man is attuned primarily to *situations*. This orientation manifests itself, for instance, in his language which, according to anthropologists, has a "holophrastic" character. To give an example, certain Bantu languages use a

---

[38]van der Leeuw, *op. cit.*, p. 38. See also H. Werner, *Einführung in die Entwicklungspsychologie*, München, 3rd ed., 1953, pp. 317 ff., 331 ff. Tr. as *Comparative Psychology of Mental Development*, New York, 1940.

[39]L. Lévy-Bruhl, *Fonctions mentales dans les sociétés primitives*, Paris 1928, p. 6.

single word to express the idea of "going through a field whose surface has cracked wide open through drought."[40] The globalizing character of this holophrastic name-giving clearly expresses that the isolation and identification of distinct beings have not gone very far.

No Thing-Objects. The fundamental apperception of participation exercises influence on the conception of the distinction between subject and thing-object. As we have pointed out before, even adult civilized man sometimes experiences difficulties when he wants to apply this distinction consistently. For instance, he will not hesitate to classify certain self-governing mechanisms (so-called cybernetics) simply among thing-objects, i.e., in the class of beings "with which one can do something but which of themselves do not do anything." As appears from our preceding analyses, a child possesses only the germ of this distinction. Is fire, for instance, a biting animal, or a manipulatable tool? Is the locomotive a fiery monster or a mechanism? According to their age, sex and environment, children will give different answers to these questions.

In primitive man the fundamental apperception of participation extends also to the relationship of subject and thing. Subjects participate in the being of things and vice versa. A striking example is provided by Lévy-Bruhl's study of the Papuans. The Dobu tribe uses the word *tomot,* which means, "that which pertains essentially to man." They apply the word to themselves but also to yams, for they participate in the being of the yams by consuming them as food. On the other hand, these Papuans do not call white man *tomot,* for white man and the primitive have nothing in common, they do not share in the same existential situation.[41] From this single example it is apparent that in reference to primitive mentality it is meaningless to speak of thing-objects. We may add that the distance between man and thing is small. As van der Leeuw very emphatically points out, "The primitive men-

---

[40]van der Leeuw, *op cit.,* p. 36.

[41]*La mythologie primitive. Le monde antique des Australiens et des Papous,* Paris, 1935, p. 65.

tality differs from modern mentality by this that there is *very clearly less distance between subject and objects.*"[42]

Mythical World-Apperception. Undoubtedly, the most typical characteristic of the primitive mentality is its *mythical apperception of the world.* Husserl was not entirely unaware of this characteristic, as appears from the following quotation: "Philosophy designs the logos of the world, which is pre-given, historically pre-given and prescientific. The mythical world is the surrounding world of life, which in this historical situation of mythical mankind (and concretely of *this* mythical mankind) possesses its mythical reality in its confirmation."[43]

Husserl's words point to something which, strictly speaking, should have found its place in a later stage of our inquiry. Just as in philosophy, so also in the myth the chief concern is directed to the *logos of the world.* The big difference, however, is that in the primitive world this logos is everywhere present. It dwells in things, in living beings and in man; it lives in the tribes, the sib, the individuals; it collaborates with man in all important human actions. "For primitive man everything is connected with everything. His thinking is always directed to the totality. For him, to think is to make the whole his own."[44] Georges Gusdorf explains the difference between the modern and mythical apperceptions of the world in the following way. In the modern apperception metaphysics is based on physics, but the same is not true for primitive man. His physics is metaphysical through and through, and his metaphysics assumes at once the form of physics.[45] We would be inclined to go even farther. To explain in modern terms what mythical apperception of the world means, one would

---

[42]*Op. cit.,* p. 31. Italics of author.

[43]*Die Krisis der europäische Wissenschaften,* Beilage XXV, p. 491: "Die Philosophie entwirft den Logos der Welt, der vorgegeben ist, historisch vorgegeben—vorwissenschaftlich mythische Welt als Lebensumwelt, die in dieser historischen Situation des mythischen Menschtum (und concret *dieses* mythischen Menschtum) in Selbstbewährung ihre Wirklichkait hat."

[44]van der Leeuw, *op. cit.,* p. 32. This quotation shows that what we, more or less in imitation of Husserl, have called "the mythical logos of the world" differs fundamentally from the modern concept of logos. From the modern standpoint it would be necessary to make a distinction between logos, in the narrow sense, and myth. Cf. below, pp. 104 f.

[45]*Mythe et métaphysique,* Paris, 1950, p. 40.

have to say that it is physics, metaphysics and religion at the same time. For the "metaphysical physics" spoken of by Gusdorf is not for ancient man a "world view" which he is free to "choose" or to "reject." The myth implies a "being-held-back by the bonds" of man to his sib, his tribe, nature, primeval age and symbols. Thus it is religion (re-ligio=binding back) *par excellence.* This bond is so strong that within the framework of the mythical world-apperception everything is religious in a certain limited sense.

This characteristic manifests itself especially in connection with the distinction between the world and the logos of the world. Primitive man does not make a clear distinction between the meaning of the cosmos and the cosmos as symbol of this meaning or, expressed in more religious terms, between the sacred and the profane which points to the sacred but is not itself sacred. The "symbol" is more a "sign" for him than it is for us. "For the mentality of the primitive . . . 'symbol' is exactly that which this term expresses—namely the co-inciding of two realities. 'It means' from the primitive standpoint equals 'it is.' "[46] True, for primitive man there are certain focal points of the "numinous," such as objects, events, men, and places in which the beneficial or destructive force is condensed. However, this force is able to assume the most divergent forms. Mischa Titiev compares this force with electricity, which is everywhere and nowhere, which is capable of striking a man down but also of bringing him well-being.[47] Claude Lévi-Strauss offers an illustration of this point by means of the Melanesian "concept" of *Mana,* which corresponds to similar "concepts" discovered among other primitive tribes. The relationship of man to *Mana* cannot unqualifiedly be described as an intentional relationship. *Mana* is both the desire of full life and its "symbolical" realization. For this reason, says Lévi-Strauss, it may be described in different and apparently contradictory ways as force and as action, as a noun and as a verb, as abstract and concrete, as omnipresent and localized, as beneficial but also as dangerous. In this way he is led to con-

---

[46]van der Leeuw, *op. cit.,* p. 41.
[47]*Introduction to Cultural Anthropology,* New York, 1959, pp. 334 ff.

sider *Mana* as a kind of floating meaningfulness which oppresses any finite thinking.[48]

Mythical Time. The peculiar unity of mythical time is in harmony with this insufficient—for us—distinction between symbol and meaning, between religious intention and the intended salvation. A mythical story refers to an indefinite past, a past that is at the same time present. "The myth takes place in primeval time, i.e., a time that lives in our time. . . . We are inclined to see primeval time as a time outside all time or at least on the border of time. However, this is not so. Primeval time is the time which gives meaning to every other time."[49] For this reason primitive man sees events as well as his own actions as a repetition and a continuation of the primeval happening. As van der Leeuw expresses it, "Both culture and nature are subject to the necessity of the primeval. I cannot sow, reap, eat or fight unless I do it as it was done in primeval times. . . . In other words, an event, whether it belongs to nature or culture, is nothing in itself but *exclusively and solely a repetition of what has happened. All happenings are mythical.*"[50]

Accordingly the everyday world in which man lives and works possesses its own objectivity. Obviously, however, this objectivity differs considerably from both scientific objectivity and any theoretical objectivity. It has certain limits which may not be neglected.

Firstly, the general validity of this pre-theoretical objectivity is limited. It actually holds only within the sphere of a *concrete* "*we.*" This *we* may be a sib or a tribe, a people, a nation or a cultural community, it may have many members or only a few. Yet it pertains to the proper nature of this objectivity to be rooted in a certain nature, in a number of typical situations, in a closed little world.[51]

Secondly, in the archaic world, *tradition* plays a dominant role. This role is not connected with conservatism, in the sense of trying

---

[48]Signifiant flottant, qui est la servitude de toute pensée finie." Preface to Marcel Mauss, *Sociologie et anthropologie*, Paris, 1950, p. XLIX.
[49]van der Leeuw, *op. cit.*, p. 87.
[50]*Op. cit.*, p. 91. Author's italics. Cf. M. Eliade, *Le mythe de l'éternel retour*, Paris, 1949.
[51]Cf. Gusdorf, *Mythe et métaphysique*, p. 105.

to retain the past, but rather with the above-mentioned mythical conception of time. What happened in primeval times is an example and an exemplar for all times. Anyone, therefore, who wants to perform a sacred action or to execute an important work has to repeat the exemplary event of primeval times. For this reason primitive man is bound to hold fast obstinately to the traditional way of life. Traditional convictions and practices function more or less in his world as science and technology in ours. As Varagnac expresses it, "Until man acquires intellectual, logical and finally scientific apparatus, tradition offers him the sole safeguard and the first rudiments of intelligibility."[52]

Thirdly, the pre-theoretical convictions are united by an *unbreakable bond* precisely because they refer to reality in its totality. Different world views are impossible within the framework of primitive societies. In the words of Gusdorf, "The bond of primitive man with his community remains an inflexible bond. . . . The individual does not know himself as the center of a universe or as the source of value. All truth that is necessary and sufficient for him is found written in reality in a definitive fashion. The absolute is identical with the very structure of the human community, established in reality, which at the same time expresses the truth of the world."[53] Accordingly, the members of the primitive *we*-community possess a common style of living, which simply binds them together. They understand one another because of their common mythical apperception of the world in a universal and necessary fashion. The same realities exist for all, and these realities can be known, grasped and influenced through magical practices by all or at least by some common representatives. What we meet here is the objectivity of the everyday world or, as we will say hereafter, the *first objectivity*.

The "Meeting of Opposites." Accordingly, the objectivity of the everyday world remains limited to a concrete *we*, it is based on an uncritical tradition, rooted in an inflexible social order which is meant to be one with the cosmic order. Nevertheless, the three

---

[52]*Civilisations traditionelles et genres de vie,* Paris, 1948, p. 355, quoted by Gusdorf, *op. cit.,* p. 79.
[53]*Op. cit.,* p. 104.

above-mentioned restrictions are "accidental." They do not permeate the essence of objectivity. As always, the proper and farther-reaching limitation arises from within. From the preceding descriptions it should be clear where this inner limitation is to be sought.

Primitive man, as we have pointed out, does not distinguish himself from the situation of which he is a part. He does not conceives himself as a unique individual, he does not consider himself as a source of values, he does not know himself as the pursuer of free deeds. For this reason subjectivism, in the above-described sense, is not possible for him. For a subjectivistic attitude demands reflexive knowledge of one's own being-a-subject, being-an-individual, being-free, and primitive man is not able to have such acts of knowing.

The objection could be raised that, if subjectivism is not a real possibility for a person, it would not seem appropriate to speak of objectivism with respect to such an individual. Is not, one could argue, the situation of primitive man like that of a little child, which cannot yet really obey because it does not yet have the power to be disobedient? Is not the primordial identification of oneself with all-deciding Reality comparable with the emotional self-identification of the little child with its parents? Is such an identification a free deed? Is the little child capable of avoiding this identification? Let us recall our description of objectivity as a human attitude. There was question there of man's *free* recognition of his being orientated to and normalized by something which he is not. The question must be raised whether one can exercise freedom if there is no alternative course of action. Or, to put it even more strikingly, can there be question of genuine recognition with respect to one who cannot do otherwise than recognize?

We face here a remarkable "meeting of opposites." Primitive man, whom from a certain standpoint we have called the most objective of all, appears to be not at all objective from another and higher point of view. For he has not rejected subjectivism, he has never consented to let himself be governed by Reality instead of by himself. And the same line of thought applies also to other realms. It is very tempting to characterize the primitive man as a profound metaphysician, but anyone who does so forgets one important point. Because in the primitive's mind physics and metaphysics constitute a single undivided whole, he is unable to apperceive reality in any other way than as metaphysics. He has no alternative; therefore, he is a "metaphysical animal" but not a metaphysical thinker.

In an analogous way we must say that primitive man is objective of necessity. This assertion implies that he has not yet reached objectivity as a human attitude. In order that the "first objectivity" be able to play a role as a thesis in knowledge of reality there has to be an alternative, which means a negation. First objectivity has to be divested of its unfreedom, it has to be taken out of the strait jacket of rigid traditionalism. This liberation, however, can be brought about only through a radical crisis, a crisis which is nothing less than an existential negation of the historical everyday worlds of life in their totality.

This crisis may be compared with an explosion. Three elements which in the myth were fused so wonderfully and yet so simply into a single truth—"the" truth—have been torn asunder as by an explosion. The pieces have been hurled into the "space" of history, flying off in different directions. Physics grew and developed into a science, metaphysics became systematic philosophical metaphysics, and religion assumed the form of worship based on theological thinking and expression.

Are the three elements of this one truth now definitively separated from one another? Have they to remain separate? Is modern mankind doomed to remain confused, disturbed and frightened by this separation? And if the answer is in the negative, can the disruption of human truth be overcome by a simple return to the "natural condition"? In the following pages we will attempt to reply to this question with respect to the first two of these elements—namely, physical and metaphysical truth.

SECTION B. UNIVERSAL OBJECTIVITY

1. THE SCIENTIFIC ILLUMINATION

The Disintegration of the Everyday Worlds of Life. Everyday worlds perish because they are a plurality of worlds. If any development of history gives rise to the impression of being a "Hegelian" necessity, it surely is so with the evolution of the everyday world. Sooner or later the historical moment arrives when the traditionally developed original society comes in contact with another society which lives in a fundamentally different way. The inevitable result is a crisis, for the structure of a primitive society claims to be one with the absolute order, the cosmic order. It is irrelevant whether or not the contact with an essentially different everyday world is peaceful, and it is not of crucial importance whether one's own group is politically or militarily victorious or defeated. The disturbing and shocking aspect of the encounter lies in the experience that for the "foreigners" decisive reality lies in something which for one's own group does not even exist and that, reversely, one's own we-group recognizes realities that are wholly unknown to the other we-community. The "foreigners" have other myths, another mythical origin, a different mythical time, and for them things are ruled by different laws. Yet their everyday world is not doomed to perish. It preserves its own existence and functions in such a way that all human relationships are taken care of. This everyday world is just as "naturally" normalizing for the members of the other we-group as one's own world is for our we-community. Inevitably the realization of this point means that for both groups the evident character of their world ceases to be evident. At least in a transitory fashion this evident naturalness gives way to doubt, confusion and a feeling of being uprooted. The naive thesis of the everyday world changes, temporarily at least, into the antithesis of critique, skepticism and nihilism. Here lies the starting point of the great evolution of mankind, the beginning of its conscious struggle for freedom.

1. The Scientific Illumination

History Versus Prehistory. Two replies can be given to the question of when this decisive evolution began, but both are bound to be disappointing to the historian. Nevertheless, we believe that, no matter how general our considerations may be and how much they may lack precision, they are, relatively speaking, as justified as any reply could be, even from the historical standpoint.

First of all, it is necessary to point out that primitive man must be called "prehistoric" in a strict sense, a sense which, incidentally, is more profound than the one we usually attach to this term. For his time, the mythical era, is not the temporal dimension in which history unrolls, in which events can be dated and facts can be observed. For this reason the starting point leading to the disintegration of the everyday worlds lies in this that the stream of dramatic events which are currently known as "history" disturbs the traditional stability and continuity of these worlds. As Gusdorf says, "The end of the mythical era and the beginning of history constitute one of the decisive turns in the development of mankind. It is a phase of its evolution rather than a date of history."[54]

Accordingly, it is useless to look for a precise date. Nonetheless, one could ask when this great change assumed for the first time a clearly distinguishable form in the history of the world. From this viewpoint Gusdorf thinks that we should refer especially to the second and third millennia before Christ. For in this era huge empires and high cultures arose in Egypt, Mesopotamia and China. The foundation, expansion and preservation of these empires would not have been possible without a *universal plan,* a plan which had also religious-cultural and moral implications. For this reason these empires made such a tremendous impression in the world of Antiquity. These first "imperialists" did not merely abolish the particularism of the clans and tribes from the political and social viewpoint. By subjecting the members of the most diverse groups to a single power, they withdrew them also from the exclusive influence of local traditions and local convictions, they forced them to accept, at least in part, the infinitely richer and wider horizon of the empire.

---

[54]*Op. cit.,* p. 93.

Such is the hypothesis of Gusdorf.[55] No matter how one may evaluate this position, it is certain that everyday worlds could continue to exist in the strictly primitive sense only in places where they were removed from the scene of great historical events, viz., on islands, in inaccessible forests, in limitless prairies and endless deserts. For in such places they escaped from the leveling influence of the great civilizations. This fact pleads in favor of Gusdorf's view.

The Process of Universalization. The second reason why it is difficult to describe the starting point and the development of the great universalistic revolution lies in the fact that concepts such as "everyday world," "primitive," and "mythical" can be used only in a dialectic fashion. If this fact is kept in mind, one can understand why different authors evaluate certain historical data of culture so divergently. For instance, should astrology, as it was pursued in Egypt, Chaldea, India, China, Hellas and even in Europe until the seventeenth century, be considered as "myth" or as "science"? A reply is possible only from a dialectic standpoint. To the extent that there was question of systematically observing celestial bodies, of discovering universally valid laws, of formulating these laws through numbers, astrology was a beginning of thinking in terms of the universal. Insofar, however, as astrology was based on the conviction that man's life participates in that of celestial bodies, it was a typical example of a mythical attitude.

For this reason we are inclined to present the historical situation somewhat differently from the usual interpretation. We are convinced that *the disintegration of the everyday world is an evolution which,* at least in the realm of western civilization, *has not yet reached its term,* and that the process of universalization still continues. Such a "process" can be described, of course, only by dividing it as meaningfully as possible into phases. In each of these phases the concepts of "prescientific," "primitive" and "mythical" have a different content, but their dialectic function remains the same. For example, one may say that the astrology of the ancients was a beginning of scientific thought in comparison with the think-

---

[55] *Op. cit.,* pp. 93-106.

ing of prehistoric people, but, from the standpoint of modern astronomy, it was full of mythical ideas. There is no contradiction here if the two statements are viewed as characterizations of an element of dialectic development.

The process of universalization took place wherever great empires were founded, great civilizations arose or supranational cultures created. For example, the ancient wisdom of India or that of China laid likewise claim to universal validity. On the other hand, in none of these cultures did the dissolution of the mythical convictions assume such a radical form as in the world of the West. For this reason our attention will be restricted here to the development of western thought.

The Scientific Illumination. The crisis of the everyday worlds gives birth to *scientific illumination.* This term needs to be explained. As we have seen in the preceding pages, the evolution which still continues gradually makes the primitive, or relatively primitive, everyday worlds merge in more comprehensive political and social wholes. This evolution has as a result that regional mores and customs give way to a morality and law which lay claim to a rational basis and therefore are obligatory for all. Finally, and this is most important for us now, the traditional *doxa,* the unproved "opinion" of the everyday world, is replaced by a scientific[57] *epistēmē,* the demonstrable intellectual view, which likewise claims to be based on intellectual grounds and therefore to be valid for all.

Above we have characterized this entire process of development as "universalization." The transition from the uncritical convictions of the everyday world to scientific knowledge, capable of withstanding close scrutiny, is merely one of the aspects of this universalization. This transition also takes place in a gradual and continuous fashion. It may be compared with a mighty river which makes all the waters of a continent flow in a certain direction. Usually this stream runs so slowly that the current is barely perceptible. Here and there, however, there are "rapids," which make the continuous process of enormous change suddenly so clear that it be-

---

[57]It should be evident that the term "scientific" is used here in this section in its classical or broad sense and not in its contemporary restricted meaning, applicable only to systematic empirical disciplines. Tr.

comes easily observable. From now on we will consider such historically demonstrable "rapids" in the process of universalizing theoretical convictions as belonging to the above-mentioned "scientific illumination."

Accordingly, when we speak here of "scientific illumination" we are not referring solely to the European movement of the eighteenth century known as the *"Aufklärung"* or "Illumination," for Socratic, Platonic and Aristotelian philosophy, rationalism, Kantianism and positivism likewise fall under this term.[58] These intellectual currents may be compared with spectacular landslides; nonetheless, the historian of culture knows that each of them had been prepared by a preceding series of small and unobtrusive shifts of equilibrium. This shows that the concept of "illumination" itself is also a dialectic notion. A single example may serve to illustrate this. The famous *daimon* of Socrates is undoubtedly a mythical element of thought. Nevertheless, his philosophy is characterized by the fact that it placed itself at a distance from the traditional fossilized moral and religious convictions of his contemporaries. Viewed within the framework of its era, his philosophy exhibits an "illuminated" character in spite of some remnants of mythical thinking. Accordingly, the concept of "illumination," as a dialectic notion, may have a different content in different phases of mankind's history without becoming an ambiguous or equivocal concept.

The Twofold Dialectic Function of "Illumination." A typical feature of illumination in the above-described sense is the way in which it makes myths relative and devalues them. All myths, so it is usually said, are equally limited, equally inadequate, they have to be replaced by a universal *theory* which is valid for all everyday worlds and for any of the closed little worlds. The same remark applies to the praxis of the various everyday worlds. It is not always wrong, it may contain "something good," but it has to be complemented, perfected and purified in the light of the universal theory. In this way the traditional praxis of the everyday world becomes a *technical praxis* in the modern sense, a praxis which

---

[58]By referring to these trends as "scientific illuminations" we do not at all want to characterize the content of these systems but merely their function in the process of universalization.

1. The Scientific Illumination

makes systematic use of universally true knowledge of nature for the purpose of dominating nature and making it subservient to man.

However, the illumination has also another aspect, which is sometimes neglected by its critics. The dissolution of the everyday world, as we have pointed out, first results in disorientation, crisis and skepticism. This mental condition is not the effect of the illumination but one of its motives. On the contrary, we should say that every illumination is a grand attempt to transcend the disintegration of ideas. A few examples may serve to illustrate the point.

As is well-known, the Athenian society found itself in a state of crisis at the end of the fifth century and the beginning of the fourth century B.C., perhaps as a result of the Persian wars. There was great uncertainty in the realm of morals, politics and religion. The procedures of the Sophists, no matter how one may want to interpret them from other standpoints, could only serve to increase the confusion. Their method of subjecting established opinion to dispute favored relativism and skepticism. The "illuminated" philosophical thinking of Socrates, on the other hand, was driven by the desire to overcome the moral and religious crisis of society. Descartes reacted in an analogous fashion against the shortcomings of late scholasticism but also against the insufficiently mature and unsystematic philosophy of the Renaissance. His passionate search for an "unshakeable foundation" of universal science was typical in this context. Kant likewise did not hesitate to say that Hume's skepticism had awakened him from his dogmatic slumbers. Finally, positivism is an attempt to transcend the confusion caused by a plurality of idealistic systems claiming to be sciences.

Later we will examine whether and to what extent all such endeavors must be considered to have been successful. For the present we may limit ourselves to observe that "illumination" exhibits also a *positive aspect*. It does not merely aim at destroying the old myths, magical practices and the norms implied in the everyday world. It aims also at substituting something better for them—namely, a universally valid theory and a praxis that is effective anywhere in the world. It wants to replace the "first" objectivity by a scientific objectivity. And this objectivity must be such that it can withstand all subsequent critique.

The Withdrawal of the Doxa. In spite of the various waves of "illumination," certain traditional convictions and magical representations have not yet been eradicated in Western man. They continue to exist and still exercise a limited influence, they constitute, as it were, a counter-current on the bottom of the stream of universalization. However, such convictions have lost their generally obligatory character, their role is limited to being prejudices or superstitions of primitive, naive or backward people. Their *doxa* is constantly more and more replaced by the *epistēmē* of the educated, the intelligentsia, the *"évolués."*

Scientific knowledge and power triumph. True, the victory is not absolute, for remnants of *doxa* manage to maintain themselves even in the twentieth century. Quite a few civilized people, for example, who are disappointed in their physicians go to quacks using magical methods. Many civilized human beings place their first trust in the skill of the engineers who have constructed their motorcar, but add a little mascot, which is really nothing else than a fetish. Such examples show that the struggle between *doxa* and *epistēmē* is not yet finished. Nevertheless, those who hold fast to the *doxa* resemble a rear guard, withdrawing while it continues to fight. Twentieth century man usually is aware of the fact that in our era it is *"norm*al" to trust scientific medicine and technology; magic is for him only a little back door enabling him to escape from his *own* norms. Thus it is evident that magic has lost its normalizing power for him.

Myth, Religion, Mythology. *Logos* is not myth. *"Logos* is distinct from myth in this that it knows *method,* we may even say that it *is* a method, a road to be followed rather than an image that is seen."[59] Yet this statement needs to be rendered more precise. First of all, the *logos* could not be a "road" if it were not able to distinguish itself from its goal. The *logos,* therefore, knows that it exists as a concept, as a grasp of something, for the sake of laying hold on something; it knows that it is a concept for the sake of something that has to be conceived; it knows that it is thought for the purpose of thinking of that which is worthy of thought. There

---

[59]van der Leeuw, *op. cit.,* p. 42 f.

exists, moreover, between the road and the goal that typical tension which modern thinkers call *intentionality*. Finally, the *logos* would not be able to distinguish itself from its goal if it did not know itself. Thus to know about itself pertains to the essence of the *logos*. It knows itself as word, language, story, as concept, judgment, reasoning and logico-scientific method, as artistic technique, motive and style. And because the *logos* exists for itself, it is no longer naive in the typically philosophical sense of this term.

This distinction is rich in consequences, two of which we will mention here explicitly. First, it is now evident that the *logos* which aims at the Sacred—even if only to formulate it dogmatically —*is* not the Sacred. Because modern religious man is aware of this distinction, his attitude differs essentially from that of mythical primitive man. However, so far as the problem of the religious element is concerned, we will systematically abstain from considering it and will limit ourselves to indicating the point at which religion originates from the myth and draws away from it.

A second consequence is directly concerned with the problems at stake in this inquiry. As appears from the preceding pages, *the logos which aims intentionally at the myth is essentially different from the myth itself.* This assertion applies equally to philosophical and anthropological considerations as well as to poetic and epic "mythologies." Such mythologies may be profound, original, fascinating, interesting, instructive and beautiful, their authors may be filled with admiration and longing for the virginal integrity of the everyday world. All this, however, does not bring them one step closer to this world. For the scientific illumination is not an event that can be undone, but is a destiny. The entire Western world has undergone this destiny and its entire culture is permeated with it. No one can act in a bona fide way as if this "mutation" (Gusdorf) had not taken place. A return to the naive attitude and the myth is impossible for the simple reason that history does not run backward. The naive attitude is not something that can be put together again. True, this assertion is a philosophical intuition, yet it is also an historical experience. No "renaissance" has ever given rise to the actual rebirth of the old, but the result of every renaissance movement has always been the rise of something new. For this reason we think it possible that the myth may be a source of inspiration for poets and a fountain head of insight for philosophers and anthropologists, but all this will never take away the distance which separates mythologies from the original myths. We may add that we quite willingly leave the glorification of the Golden Age to others. A firm orientation to the future appears more meaningful to us. In our view, "being illuminated" is not a curse but a destiny and at the same time a task which twentieth century man has to accept soberly and courageously, it is an "existentiale" (Heidegger) of modern mankind. Perhaps mankind will be able to go beyond the "illumination," but only on condition of first passing through it. We must therefore endeavor to understand the essence of scientific illumination, its possibilities and its limitations.

Universal Theory Versus the Perspectivism of the Everyday Worlds. The objectifying praxis of prescienitfic life aims at transcending individual perspectives and modes of appearance. A single example should suffice to illustrate this point. Is the mountain which "in our valley" appears with gentle slopes the same high ground which descends precipitously in the other valley? Such a question is typical of the prescientific level. It can be solved through isolation, identification and name-giving. The identification is in principle possible by means of "seeing" and can be confirmed through a judgment of perception. It can become intersubjectively valid through an act of name-giving. Once it is evident that the towering rock is the same high ground as the mountain with the gentle slopes, it becomes possible to act in accord with this evidence and to seek, e.g., a way to the other valley.

In the life of science, broadly conceived, the negative aspect of the aim pursued is likewise to overcome a kind of perspectivism, but the perspectivism in question belongs to a higher order. A famous example of Aristotle may serve to illustrate the point. Is it true that a falling stone tends to its "natural place"? Aristotle's view is connected with his conception of God and *physis,* nature,

1. The Scientific Illumination

whose operations are ordered in a teleological fashion.[60] This conception of nature as a principle of teleological operation and teleological coming-to-be is typical of Aristotle. Other nations did not know the idea of a cosmic teleology; moreover, other times made a sharper distinction between God and nature. A moment arrived at which representatives of other nations and cultures raised critical questions, because they found Aristotle's explanation "naïve" and "primitive." A theory had to be found which was not based on remnants of mythical and everyday world convictions.

No matter how rich and beautiful the perspectives of a given national and historical culture may have been, they have to be transcended. The new theory must be able to withstand the objections which people from the most divergent everyday worlds of life may raise against it and, positively, it must be based on proofs possessing universal convincing force.

Scientific "Fact" and Verification. Where can such proofs find their convincing power? On the one hand, they may be based on the formal laws of thought in general, which leads to the construction of formal-idealized sciences,[61] such as logic and mathematics; on the other hand, they may have their foundation in experience. However, experiences which depend on the nature of a particular everyday world and on the ways in which this nature is "seen" in them do not qualify, for they cannot be compared with experiences obtained in a different everyday world. A universally valid empirical science can be constructed only when it is possible to identify certain experiences or kinds of experiences. This identification requires that the experiences can be selected and channelized by means of an intersubjectively determined "scientific apparatus."[62] For in this way any representative of any everyday world is able to verify the result of experience. The most obvious way is, of course, to use formal-idealized concepts derived from logic and mathematics for the purpose of describing experience in a way

---

[60]"God and nature create nothing that has not its use." *De caelo*, bk. I, ch. 4, 271a 33.

[61]In the next section we will inquire further into the meaning of "idealization."

[62]Cf. above p. 11.

that everyone can understand. As we will have ample opportunity to see, this idea lies at the basis of modern scientific experience.

The result of an experience, obtained by means of a predetermined method, is generally called a *fact*. Modern empirical sciences owe their universal convincing power to this that their results are "facts." There is hardly anyone who doubts this point. However, very little reflection has been devoted to the way in which the "fact" arises. In the subsequent pages, therefore we will ask two questions. How are facts arrived at in physical science? And, In what way do we arrive at facts in the realm of the human sciences? These two questions will lead us inevitably to the question whether or not the fact in the realm of the human sciences is of essentially the same nature as the fact pertaining to physical science.

2. FACT AND METHOD IN PHYSICAL SCIENCE

The Method of Idealization. In the oft-quoted work, *Die Krisis der europäischen Wissenschaften,* Husserl attempted to reconstruct the long road by which man in the Western world went from primitive measuring of the earth to the "pure geometry" known by the Greeks. He analyzes also the view of Galileo, which we twentieth century human beings find so obvious but which, considered in itself, may justly be called astonishing. In the above-mentioned terminology we would say that what Galileo succeeded in doing was to construct the scientific fact in the modern sense. For this reason it appears necessary to follow here in outline Husserl's analyses in order to penetrate to the heart of the problems facing us here.[63]

The difficulty encountered by the first geometers was, of course, practical. It may be described as follows. The various configurations of the earth's surface do not at all correspond to the concepts of geometric thought. In daily life we may be satisfied with characterizing these configurations by means of comparisons. We say, e.g., that this mountain resembles a roof and that this river curves like an *S*. But we are unable to determine their forms with anything approaching exactness. Moreover, concrete things constantly change, so that their typical features are likewise continually modified. The river with the *S*-curve, for example, in the course of years becomes almost straight. A branch which at first was a separate stream has now joined the main stream and has entirely lost its identity. The first task of the geometer was to find orientation points that are independent of one another and relatively unchangeable. For this reason our geodesist introduced a principle of spatial orientation into the Heraclitian stream of concrete reality, in which "everything is in a state of flux." On the basis of his fixed points of orientation he was able to strictly identify *this* and accurately distinguish it from *that*. This first activity of the geometer was still fully

---

[63]Cf. Husserl, *op. cit.,* pp. 18 ff. We abstract here from the question whether some of the ideas which Husserl attributes to Galileo are not really of a later date.

in line with what we have called "the objectifying praxis of the everyday world."

However, the geometer could not be satisfied with this first result. He had to apply a new method—namely, the method of approximation. While it is true that concrete nature does not contain anything like geometric figures or mathematical bodies, there are things which remind us of such figures and bodies. These things, as it were, "invite" us to conceive geometric ideas and help us to form them. Looking at such things, we think that we perceive straight lines, planes or circles. Thus the geodesist was led to construct models. True, the ruler or the measuring tape is not a straight line and the wooden triangle is not the ideal triangle spoken of by Euclid, yet they make us think of these figures. By perfecting the models, the geodesist would perhaps acquire a more correct picture of the ideal geometric figures. But here the question of exactness became a technical problem. It meant making straighter that which is almost straight, more circular that which is almost circular. But all we can really do is to represent the ideal figures as the ultimate limit cases[64] of an unending process of approximation.

Ultimately, of course, the concreto-real praxis of *homo faber* was replaced by an ideal praxis of *homo sapiens*. Here man's thinking no longer worked with models but only with "ultimate limit figures." The ideal figures became for him beings of reason, which were at his disposal in an habitual fashion as permanent acquisitions of his mind. Any such "being of reason" is, of course, wholly identical with itself and perfectly distinct from all others. As soon as man had learned to make use of these beings of reason he was no longer a geo-meter but a geometrician.

Idealization of Nature. Through these successive stages man arrived at a "pure" geometry. If, next, we ask about the new viewpoint introduced by Galileo, the reply is that he was the first to see the possibility of exiling the subject from nature by means of mathematical methods. By measuring, counting and calculating, the physicist is able to overcome the relativity of sub-

---

[64]"Limes-Gestalten," as Husserl calls them, *op. cit.,* p. 23.

jective perception. He is enabled not only to correct the one-sidedness of individual perceptions but also to overcome the limited way of "seeing" that is typical of the various everyday worlds, which is, of course, the avowed aim of the physicist. The most important means at his disposal is the above-mentioned method of idealization. Wherever the physicist can appeal to "ultimate limit figures" there is a possibility of absolute identification and, consequently, also of exactly determining the inter-relationships. By rigorously adhering to this method and apply-ing it consistently, he transcends all possible perspectives. He eliminates the perceiving subject and groups of perceiving sub-jects and ends up by retaining only that which is proper to nature itself. In this way the physicist arrives at an objective picture of reality, a picture which can serve as the foundation of a uni-versal scientific theory.

Forms and "Contents" ("Füllen"). There remains, however, a difficulty. Through mathematics the physicist is able to grasp the extended character and the quantity of things, but their per-ceptible contents escape him. These contents do not seem to lend themselves to an idealizing approach. Colors, sounds, odors and taste impressions do not have any ultimate limit figures. These "sense contents," as Husserl calls them,[65] are and remain subjective data. Accordingly, it seems impossible to identify them in a rigorous fashion.

However, this difficulty did not deter Galileo. He saw in principle a possibility of overcoming it. Even the old Pythagorians knew that there was a fixed relationship between the length of a vibrating cord and the pitch of the tone produced by it. But Galileo went far beyond this. He found his starting point in the postulate of an all-encompassing interconnection. Everything that is at the same time, this postulate claims, is subject to causal laws because of its co-existence. Galileo knew that the effects of causal operations can be predicted by means of mathematical calculations; he knew also that the method of the idealizing approach could be applied just as well to dynamic reality as to static reality; therefore,

---

[65] *Op. cit.,* p. 27.

would it not be possible to make accurate predictions with respect to the *whole* of nature?

The mathematical method constitutes a unity. It has a universal character because it offers a possibility to construct not only all real but also all possible forms and spatial configurations. Anything which cannot be directly approached in a mathematical fashion allows perhaps an indirect approach, for evidently there are no qualitative contents without forms and no forms without contents. Moreover, if it is true that all events in the material cosmos are causally related, qualities also have to be subject to causal laws.

Once these positions have been accepted as true, it is tempting to go even further and to formulate a new postulate. The theory will be proposed that *any change of qualitative content is somehow caused by changes of forms.* Let it be noted that we are dealing here with a *postulate;* what it states is neither self-evident nor proved in any other way. Nevertheless, nowadays this postulate is accepted without question. We find it quite natural that that which is perceived as color, sound, temperature or weight is "in reality" respectively vibration of ether, air, molecules or the effect of gravitational fields. Through Galileo the perceived world has been given a mathematical index; he discovered a method to give an exact description of universal causality. Thus Galileo has, as it were, vested the everyday world, the world of prescientific experience, with a well-fitting garment. Saying that this garment "fits well" means that *physical nature lends itself to a mathematical description.* The successes of the physical sciences prove the point very strikingly. On the other hand, these successes make us forget that we are dealing merely with a method and a consistent description based on this method. Again, this description may be suitably compared with a garment, woven from concepts and beings of reason. As Husserl expresses it, the description given by physical science is a "garment of ideas."[66] However, since the time of the Renaissance and the Illumination we have become accustomed to identify the garment with the person wearing it, i.e., we call an ingenious scientific construct "true nature" and "objective reality."

---

[66] *Op. cit.,* p. 51.

2. Fact and Method in Physical Science

This identification is a mistake, and it is this mistake which lies at the root of the mentality which we have characterized as the "objectivistic attitude."

The Construction of the Scientific Fact. We must now return from Husserl's interpretation of the history of mankind and of the sciences to the question which was our starting point. We are now sufficiently prepared to reply to it. To what extent and by what right do we say that the physical sciences construct facts? First of all, the general characterization of fact, given above, applies undoubtedly to physical science. For in this science "factual knowledge" is obtained only by means of those experiences which follow a previously established method. However, and this brings us to the second point, this very broad characterization of fact needs to be complemented in the light of the preceding analyses. What is the character of the previously established method or road to be followed? An experience becomes scientific (in the narrow sense of physical science) only when it is concerned with a regular succession[67] of phenomena, capable of being described in the language of formal-idealized sciences, such as logic, logistics and mathematics. For this reason scientific experience has to be organized and cannot dispense with a scientific apparatus, for it is only within the framework of this sharply delineated and structured realm that the physicist can observe "facts."

Accordingly, Moritz Schlick is wrong when he asserts that "knowledge in life and in research begins *in one sense or another* with the observation of facts and that 'protocol sentences,' in which precisely this observation is made, lie in the same sense at the *beginning* of science."[68] The entire fruitless discussion of Schlick, Carnap, Neurath and Popper[69] about the essence of the "protocol

---

[67]Intentionally we avoid here the use of "causal connection."

[68]"Über das Fundament der Erkenntnis," *Erkenntnis,* vol. 4 (1934), p. 80.

[69]Apart from the just-quoted article of Schlick, see O. Neurath, "Soziologie im Physikalismus," *Erkenntnis,* vol. 2 (1931), "Protokollsätze," *ibid.,* vol. 3 (1932) ; "Radikaler Physikalismus und 'wirkliche Welt'," *ibid.,* vol. 4 (1934) ; Rudolph Carnap, "Über Protokollsätze," ibid., vol. 2 (1931) and vol. 3 (1932) ; "Testability and Meaning," *Philosophy of Science,* vol. III (1936) and vol. IV (1937) ; K. Popper, *Logik der Forschung,* Vienna 1953, pp. 53 ff. and *The Logic of Scientific Discovery,* London, 2nd ed., 1960, pp. 95 ff.

sentences" shows that the representatives of the Vienna Circle have neglected an important datum. To use Schlick's terminology, we could say that first one has to determine *in what sense* one wishes to speak and that only then there is question of an *observation,* an *ascertainment* and not merely a perception, only then can there be question of setting up a *"protocol,"* in the sense of making a "scientific record."

Many empirical scientists are quite willing to concede this point today. Helen Peak, for example, formulates six critical questions to be raised in connection with a scientific observation. The first of these questions is, "What *behavior* is to be *selected* and recorded in order to obtain the information required?"[70] It should be evident that as long as one does not know what kind of information is desired, it is impossible to make the necessary selection, so that it is likewise impossible to arrive at a "statement" or a "record."

From our analyses of experience in the everyday world[71] we may conclude that the "fact" plays no role whatsoever in naive knowledge because there is no need there to defend one's own experiences against critical objections. We may add now that the "fact" is not the first thing encountered by the scientist and that on the contrary a scientific question must already have been raised before the scientist can observe facts.

The Magic Lure of Numbers. Helen Peak's fourth question in connection with observation is, "Has an attempt been made to summarize what is observed in quantitative terms? Can a *score* be assigned . . . ?"[72] Anyone who is familiar with the problems encountered in human research will appreciate the prudent way in which the authoress formulates her question. She asks whether an *attempt* has been made to express the result of the observation in quantitative terms, in the form of a quantitative idealization, but is not *a priori* certain that it is possible to formalize the observed data. This reserve sets her apart from the attitude of those

---

[70]"Problems of Objective Observation," *Research Methods in the Behavioral Sciences,* ed. by L. Festinger and D. Katz, New York, 1953, pp. 243 ff. See especially p. 245.
[71]Cf. above, section A, pp. 85 ff.
[72]*loc. cit.*

2. Fact and Method in Physical Science

"scientists" who think that any research in which numbers, mathematical and logistical symbols occur is by the very fact superior to research which does not assign any role to these signs. In their mind an observation becomes scientific only when its result can be expressed in the language of physical science, and any observation that fails to reach this standard is "subjective," inexact. In our view this quasi-religious worship of numbers is a veritable superstition.

Pseudo-Exactness. The effort to arrive at all cost at quantitative data sometimes leads to results which are scientifically irresponsible. The example which follows has been taken from Hans L. Zetterberg's well-known book, *On Theory and Verification in Sociology.*[73] Zetterberg wants to change the nominal concept of "the degree of rejection of deviates from society norms" into operational definitions. He calls a definition "operational" when it refers to measurements and counting. As to how this change is to be brought about, Zetterberg sees no difficulties. "We may select the proportion of laws requiring the death penalty, deportation and long prison terms (but not fines) to stand for the degree of rejection of deviates from society norms."[74] Briefly put, the number of laws providing the death penalty, deportation and long prison terms, divided by the total number of laws determining the society in question, indicates the degree of repression and severity ruling this society. Undoubtedly, there is question here of counting, resulting in a number. But is there any certainty that this number really indicates the degree of rejection? Is it not possible that a lawgiver who surrounds these penalties with many restrictions will arrive at a greater number of laws imposing such punishments than another lawgiver who wants his judges to make broad use of harsh punishments? Is it not possible that an age-old code of law with a venerable tradition of gradually becoming milder and more human would contain a greater number of laws naming severe penalties than that of a new nation emerging from a revolution and still governed with an iron hand?

---

[73]Stockholm and New York, 1954.
[74]*Op. cit.,* p. 19. For Zetterberg the concept "operational" has a meaning that differs considerably from that of Bridgman. Cf. pp. 159 ff.

These questions name two possibilities, and undoubtedly there could be others. Actually the relationship investigated by Zetterberg is determined by a whole of conditions so complex that no one can say anything about the actually existing "degree of rejection" by means of a Zetterberg number. All he succeeds in doing is to raise an appearance of exactness, but this appearance has no foundation. Gusdorf is right when he remarks that "this superstition of numbers, endowed with exclusive explanatory power represents a modern form of magic."[75] We would like to go even further and say that *within the framework of certain interchanges of ideas the mathematical idealization may be superfluous or insufficient.* Two simple analyses may suffice to illustrate this point.

A child's remark, "Mom, you have again put *so much* on my plate!" is unqualifiedly understandable and meaningful on the prescientific level. There exist on this level also intuitive criteria enabling "Mom" to determine whether the quantity of food is actually more than average. She does not have to measure it. However, the remark in question cannot be accepted as a scientific judgment, for no observation can decide the truth or falsity of the child's judgment. Ayer would not hesitate to speak here of a "nonsensical statement." One and the same judgment which is unqualifiedly meaningful within the surroundings of a family lacks the necessary universal meaning needed to make it scientific knowledge. If the child had said, "Mom, you have put x grams of this food on my plate and this equals y calories," the scientist would have been satisfied, for this judgment refers to a fact in the sense in which this term is used in physical science.

The assertion, "It is hot here," will not satisfy the physicist. He will remark that what one calls "hot" is "merely warm" for the other and "mild" for a third. However, the perceived heat is a quality which can be transposed into quantity in an indirect way. If the present heat makes quicksilver rise in the thermometer to 85° F, then we are dealing with a "fact." Only such "factual judgments" are relevant and meaningful for the physicist.

---

[75]"Sur l'ambiguité des sciences humaines," *Diogène*, no. 26 (1959), p. 68.

2. Fact and Method in Physical Science

Let us go a step further and assume that the child's remark, "Mom, you have again put *so much* on my plate," is made in the form of a tearful protest. Let us assume further that the quantity of food is small, not as determined absolutely in grams and calories but in relationship to what is customary in this particular family. In such a case the remark in question may be scientifically relevant. A child psychologist will not hesitate to draw conclusions from this and other similar phenomena. He will observe facts, but these facts are not facts of physical science.

The second example, "It is hot here," is also full of meaning if it comes from a student sitting in a crowded auditorium and suffering from claustrophobia. The statement is particularly meaningful if the temperature is rather low, not in degrees but as compared with what is customary for the way of life proper to the student's world. However, the meaning in question is not identical with the content expressed in the judgment, it can be revealed only within the framework of a psychopathological and psychiatric realm of thought. In this realm this meaning gives rise to observations and to the establishment of facts.

Apparently the situation here is not as simple as Ayer and other representatives of scientism proclaim. First, the question whether a judgment is meaningful or meaningless depends also on the context of the realm of thought in which it is asked. The interchange of ideas, in its turn, does not take place in a vacuum but occurs on a certain level of human dialog. In addition, it is not so easy to determine which phenomena lead to observation. One and the same phenomenon may be unimportant for the specialist in one particular science but extremely important for the specialist in another science; consequently, it may be neglected by the former but lead to the observation of important facts by the latter. Thirdly, the possibility or impossibility of formalizing a scientific judgment is not a norm governing its importance. The diagnosis, "This student suffers from claustrophobia," is more important than the observation that the temperature in the lecture hall is 65° F, even though the first-named judgment does not use any algebraic symbols. Accordingly, it is not right to think that a dissertation assumes a scientific character only when it is full of numbers, statistics, tables and calculations. This mathematical and statistical apparatus may be useful and even indispensable, but on the level of human science its function will usually be purely subservient.

From all this we consider ourselves justified in drawing a fourth conclusion—namely, that *the "fact" in the realm of human science differs essentially from the "fact" of physical science.* One may ask why this is so, to what extent, and how this essential difference should be explained. Before a reply can be given to these questions, we must first reflect more profoundly on the concept of "fact" as it is used in human science.

3. FACT AND METHODIC IDEA IN EMPIRICAL HUMAN SCIENCE

Intuitive Typologies in Physical Science. At first the tendency to be as radical as possible in the mathematization and formalization of all judgments may seem characteristic of modern scientific life in its entirety. For mathematical-logistical methods are used today in many disciplines which at the turn of the century were called "descriptive natural science." Nevertheless, this impression is not wholly correct. On closer inspection it becomes apparent that formalization and mathematization are used only when they are considered useful. A botanist, for example, does not hesitate to describe the structure of a plant as having pulpy fruits or clusters of flowers. It would not do to ask him for the mathematical formula of a cluster, for he does not know it and does not even care. He can be satisfied with an intuitive typology. What he is interested in is to understand and to be understood by specialists in a certain "universe of discourse," viz., that of botanists.

Similar remarks may be made with respect to other boundary areas of physical science. Clinicians, for example, speak of a "purulent exudate," a "motoric ataxia," and a "Parkinson-tremor." Of course, an academic discussion would be possible whether or not there exists a complex of mathematical formulae which allows us to exactly determine the typical Parkinson-tremors. But it is characteristic that physicians in their clinical practice do not have recourse to such monstrous equations. Nevertheless, the occurrence of the above-mentioned symptoms is an important scientific *fact* for them.

Accordingly, it is true that the representatives of natural science prefer to use the method of mathematical idealization. The road discovered by Galileo is and remains for them the "royal road." However, if we take the term "natural science" in the broad sense, we see that even in this realm there exist facts that are not described by means of formalization and mathematization.

Orientation Points in Anthropological Research. In the realm of empirical sciences of man as man the situation is not identical with, but analogous to that of natural science in the broad sense. The sociologist speaks of a "group," the psychologist of an "emotion," and the historian of a "revolutionary movement." None of them tries to determine the content of his fundamental concepts in a mathematical fashion. It is even rare that efforts are made to arrive at strict definitions of these terms. What is important for these men of science is the mutual understanding which must prevail among the members of a research community in the use of their technical language. True, this mutual understanding is far from perfect. There remains much more to be desired in this respect among the specialists in the human sciences than among those who pursue physical science. While we may safely assume that two botanists mean exactly the same by "clusters of flowers" and that two physicians are in perfect agreement about the meaning of "purulent exudate," the same is not so certain with respect to two psychologists speaking about an "emotion."[76] In the realm of human science a confusing influence is often exercised by certain intellectual trends, by "schools," national traditions, and systems of concepts devised by individuals in connection with a particular set of problems.[77] On the other hand, however, these annoying misunderstandings are not essential but only of an accidental nature. In principle the possibility of constructing facts exists just as well in the realm of empirical human science as in that of natural science. The specialist in human science is driven by a desire that may be compared with that of the first geo-meter. He, too, feels the need to create order in the Heraclitian stream of phenomena. He can succeed only by discovering relatively identical points of orientation and by comparing as accurately as possible how other data are related to these points of orientation.

Because of this fundamental tendency it is permissible to say that empirical science manifests a universal form in all its branches. For the empirical theory is based on the typical correlation between the two fundamental concepts of *method* and *fact*.

[76]Cf. Stefan Strasser, *Das Gemüt*. Utrecht, 1956, pp. 161-216.
[77]Cf., e.g., A. Chorus, "Wijsgerige en nationale krachtlijnen in de ontwikkeling der psychologie," *Ned. Tijdschrift v.d. Psychologie*, vol. 15 (1960), pp. 85 ff.

3. Fact and Methodic Idea in Empirical Human Science

The "Fact"—a Fundamental Notion. Let us begin with the investigation of the concept *fact*. The influence of this notion on modern mankind can hardly be overestimated. For the average European and American the two expressions, "to know the truth" and "to know the facts" are simply synonymous. The enormous influence of the scientific Illumination, especially of positivism, makes itself clearly felt here. As Auguste Comte exclaimed, "Since Bacon all clear minds repeat that there is no real knowledge save that which is based on observed facts."[78] The very concept "positive" is intimately connected with that of "actually observed" in Comte's philosophy. Among the neo-positivists and the logical positivists the situation is much more complex, but among them also it remains true that the notion of "fact" plays at least implicitly a decisive role. We may refer here again to the discussion of "protocol sentences" by the more prominent representatives of the Vienna Circle,[79] and to the well-known aphorisms of Ludwig Wittgenstein:

"The world is everything that is the case."
"The world is the totality of facts, not of things."
"Facts in logical space are the world."
"The world divides into facts."[80]

Popper also, who rejects any appeal to inner evidence, proves unable to avoid such assertions as, "the system of basic sentences [contains] . . ., so to speak, all conceivable observations of *facts*."[81] In other words, one has to know what a "fact" is before one can speak of "basic sentences." Because of the enormous importance which these thinkers attached to the concept "fact," it is, we repeat, most disconcerting to see that they did not attempt to give a more accurate description of this fundamental notion.

---

[78]*Principes de philosophie positive,* Paris, 1896, p. 92.

[79]See above, p.   .

[80]*Tractatus Logico-Philosophicus,* New York, 3rd ed., 1947, 1; 1, 1; 1, 13; 1, 2.

[81]*Logik der Forschung,* Vienna 1935, p. 45. Author's italics. Cf. *The Logic of Scientific Discovery,* London, 2nd ed., 1960, p. 84.

Let us try, therefore, to indicate the characteristics of the "fact." It appears clear that the fact has to correspond to the following fundamental needs of the human mind.

1. Isolability of the "Fact." A fact always refers to something that is clearly distinguishable as such. This distinction may be based on an observation, but it may also be arrived at in a different way. The important point is that that which has to be "observed" is isolated from the concrete situation or the abstract context to which it belongs. One who describes Roman architectural elements must begin by separating and identifying his object just as well as one who wants to investigate Shakespeare's use of the particle "and."

Isolability is a typical postulate demanded in reference to the "fact." Take, for example, the research of an historian. Anyone will consider it a fact that Napoleon I was born in 1769. On the other hand, the assertion that Napoleon was the greatest genius or the greatest criminal ever produced by France will not be able to pose as the observation of a fact. What is the difference between the first and the second judgment? The first refers to an isolable temporal relationship. The second would have to be prepared by means of hundreds of observations before it could be explicitly defended as a thesis at the end of an historical dissertation. For this reason it cannot be presented as a "fact."

2. Immutability of the Fact. Another requirement of the fact is that it may not change, become different, or undergo development. The term "fact," as well as its French equivalent *fait,* is derived from the Latin *factum,* a past participle meaning "done." The German *Tatsache,* as well as the English "case" (from *cadere,* to fall), likewise refer to something that has happened in the past and the effect of which is irrevocable. The verbs "to establish," *feststellen* and *constater* also have the original sense of placing something in such a way that it does not move.

The opposite of a fact would be a reality which evolves, which is still in a process of becoming that has not yet reached its term. As long as we are in doubt about the development of a process, an event or an act, we are unable to establish the facts. For ex-

3. Fact and Methodic Idea in Empirical Human Science

ample, it is a fact that the United States' economy entered a recession in the year 1958. Our opinion, however, that this economy is healthy and will enter a period of boom does not refer to a fact. For this boom of the economy is still in the process of development, it has not yet manifested itself very clearly, it cannot yet point to definite results. Once, of course, such results become evident, they can serve as arguments to demonstrate the healthy state of the economy "by means of facts."

3. The "*Standing Apart*" of the Fact. Accordingly, we speak of a "fact" only when we co-exist in a very special way with the real being in question. A "statement of fact" always refers to a being or a situation with which we are *confronted.* We place ourselves *opposite* a whole to distinguish facts in it. This relationship of being-placed-opposite-something-else we used to call, following Husserl, "objectity," but to avoid confusion it is better simply to say that the fact "stands apart." It is because of this very special relationship that a real being can become for us a *datum,* something "given." When the situation is essentially different, it is not possible for us to arrive at *data.* Let us assume, for example, that I am not confronted with beings as a disinterested spectator but that I am involved in a passionate struggle with a *You.* As long as this combat lasts, it will be impossible for me to establish facts.

It is again the historian who has the best opportunity to realize this aspect of the "fact." Why does he find it relatively much easier to write the history of the Punic Wars than to sketch a justified picture of contemporary political events? Why is it that we consider ourselves able to enumerate the great poets of the seventeenth century, but make only hesitant judgments of contemporary poets? The apparent reason is that we—you and I—together "make" the history of our time. We make this history by struggling and disputing with one another, for one another, and against one another. Here lies the reason preventing us from assuming the attitude needed for judging persons, events, and works of arts. Apparently a certain inner distance is needed before we are able to apply historical categories. The same applies also in a properly modified way to the use of psychological, sociological and anthropological categories. Wherever it is impossible to place oneself opposite "human reality," there it is also very difficult to judge this reality, to isolate facts, compare relationships, and to unite the resulting data into a systematic synthesis.

The question may be asked whether there are not different forms of "standing apart" and whether being-placed-opposite-to in human science is not essentially different from its counterpart in physical science. We will consider this point later and restrict ourselves here to the conclusion that *standing apart* is a necessary, though insufficient, condition for the establishment of facts.

"Fact" and "Methodic Idea." Do we know now what a fact is? Not yet, at least, not yet completely. It is clear nonetheless that the fact is not the same as a sensation. The view that these two are the same is based on sensualistic and atomistic ideas which modern psychologists have long since abandoned. Likewise, a fact is not the same as a perception. For example, to perceive a flower is not the same as to establish botanical facts. It is true, of course, that in certain cases a fact is established in the course of an observation. However, even so it should not be forgotten that every empirical science determines for itself what is meant by an observation. The observation of an astronomer, for instance, has to satisfy quite different demands from that of a psychologist. There exist, moreover, important empirical methods other than observation. Finally, there are facts which do not refer to anything that is directly observable; for example, the date of Napoleon's birth.

Thus our characterization of the "fact" appears to be incomplete. The reason has already been indicated in a passing way. It is that we are unable to dissociate the concept "scientific fact" from another equally important notion—namely, that of "methodic idea." The most unprejudiced witnesses testify to the truth of this statement. Claude Bernard, for example, affirms that "facts are the only reality which can give the formula to the experimental

3. Fact and Methodic Idea in Empirical Human Science

idea,"[82] and Auguste Comte emphasizes, "If in contemplating phenomena we do not at once attach them to some principles, it would not only be impossible for us to combine these isolated observations . . . but . . . also most of the time the facts would remain unobserved before our very eyes."[83] What these authors call an "experimental idea" and "principle" and what others would perhaps call a "methodic plan" is precisely that which we have indicated as a previously established method or road. Claude Bernard's notion of an "experimental idea" seems somewhat narrow to us and for this reason we will hereafter speak of a "methodic idea." Without such a guiding principle produced by the mind it would be impossible to assemble an orderly whole of facts and to incorporate every particular fact into a whole of factual knowledge. This assertion is valid with respect to human science as well as physical science. The "fact" is always an aspect of reality seized in accordance with a definite methodic idea; reversely, a methodic idea is that which enables us to discover certain features of reality.

Accordingly, it is just as true that without methodic ideas there would be no facts as that without facts no methodic ideas would be devised by the human mind. Asking which of these two is prior to the other seems just as useless as asking the age-old question whether the chicken is prior to the egg or vice versa. The two concepts are *correlated*, i.e., one cannot be thought of in an adequate fashion without at least implicitly referring to the other.

The Fact, as Artificially Obtained Evidence. Because of its harmony with a methodic idea, factual knowledge is distinct from our prescientific knowledge. For now we understand that the three above-mentioned characteristics of the "fact"—namely, isolability, immutability and "standing apart"—lie still fully in line with the so-called "praxis of the everyday world." They correspond, albeit on a higher level, to the "isolation and identification" of prescientific life. However, determining something in accordance with a methodic idea is different from, and more than

[82]*Introduction à la médicine expérimentale,* Paris, 1900, p. 85
[83]*Cours de philosophie positive,* Paris, 5th ed., 1907, vol. 1, p. 5.

mere name-giving. It is here that the specifically scientific character of knowledge manifests itself.

A single example, taken from the sociological research of C. G. Homans, may serve to illustrate the point. He characterizes the sociological "fact" in an indirect but nonetheless very instructive fashion. "The basic characteristics of social life," he says, "are well known in the sense that everyone has some intuitive familiarity with them, but they are not well known in another, and more important sense. They have not been stated in such a way that a body of scientific knowledge can be built on them. Above all, the links between the different aspects of social behavior have not been made clear. A fact is commonplace or not according to its connection with other facts. The fact that an apple would fall was the dreariest fact in the world until Newton showed that an apple and a planet obeyed the same laws of motion. The theoretical synthesis in this book will attempt to state some perfectly familiar ideas about social behavior . . . in such a way that their relation to other equally familiar ideas will become clear. We will make the commonplace strange by showing it in new connections."[84] It should be evident that the "theoretical synthesis" through which Homans wants to change familiar prescientific knowledge into sociological facts is based on a "methodic idea." His comparison with Newton is very illuminating in this connection.

By means of the methodic idea the fact is *demonstrable*. It can withstand critical reflection because it can be made manifest in a certain way. For this reason it is an "evident fact" for all who are willing to adopt the methodic idea in question. And because the methodic principle presents itself as a universally open road to truth, every "fact" lays claim to being universally true. Or more accurately expressed, the fact is unqualifiedly true for all who are able and willing to make use of the methodic idea; it is verifiable by all who are willing to acquire the experiences demanded by the methodic principles.

The Fact in Natural Science Versus the Fact in Human Science. We are now in a position to clarify the essential difference between

---

[84] *The Human Group*, London 2nd ed., 1957, pp. 5 f.

3. Fact and Methodic Idea in Empirical Human Science

the fact in physical science and the fact in human science. In the preceding section we have seen, following Husserl, what the fundamental methodic idea of natural science is since the time of Galileo. Its purpose is to fix an experience in a network of mathematical, logical and logistical ideas. More philosophically expressed, experiences have to be translated as much as possible into the language of *formal idealization*. This "as much as possible" applies also to human science, but here there is only a limited possibility, because *in the realm of human science content-ideas play a decisive role alongside formal ideas*. Three analyses may serve to illustrate and clarify this assertion.

Formal Methodic Ideas in the Realm of Human Science. Let us take the sociological and socio-geographical fact that the Dutch city of Nijmegen has 125,000 inhabitants. What exactly does this mean? It implies that in the mind of the sociologist or the socio-geographer somewhere an ideal line is drawn separating the city from its environs. Actually this line is drawn in such a way that some outskirts, such as Hees, are counted as Nijmegen. Yet the people of Hees are primarily rural. Obviously, therefore, one could dispute the correctness of this line. However, any dispute will be ultimately settled by the argument that a boundary never agrees completely with the concrete situation and that *somewhere* there has to be a boundary. Note this "somewhere," for it shows that not *this* boundary is judged necessary but *a* boundary. *A* boundary is needed as a formal instrument of thinking not only by the sociologist and the geographer but also by anyone who pursues practical sciences, e.g., the practice of law, administration and fiscal matters. Because of this methodic idea it is a fact that the city in question has 125,000 inhabitants.

Max Weber and the Religious-Sociological Fact. In his essays on the sociology of religion Max Weber says, "The Protestant asceticism pursued in the world . . . brought its full weight to bear against untrammeled enjoyment of possessions, it restricted *consumption* and especially the consumption of luxuries. On the other hand, from the psychological standpoint it *unburdened* the *acquisition of possessions* from the restrictions of traditionalistic ethics."[85]   It is very difficult to analyze this important thesis. Let us assume that the sociologist bases himself directly on the experiences of economic and social life when he forms the concepts of "consumption," "enjoyment of possessions," and "acquisition of possessions." In that case the notions in question may be considered to be "empirical concepts."[86]   Their content is, in principle, subject to a descriptive definition. Let us assume, furthermore, that it is possible to draw somewhere a line between "consumption" and "consumption of luxuries," between "untrammeled" and "trammeled" enjoyment. (This line will of necessity have to be an ideal boundary which at the same time has also a definite content.)   There remain now two most substantial ideas in the quoted passage—namely, "the Protestant asceticism pursued in the world" and "the restrictions of traditionalistic ethics." These concepts can hardly be called empirical concepts. They do not immediately flow from the experience of, respectively, Protestant and Catholic religious life. Their contents cannot be simply described in the form of a definition. Max Weber himself needs 190 pages to develop the content of these concepts. Anyone who wants to know what "exactly" these notions mean has no alternative but to study Weber's essays. And even in the above-quoted passage the author uses figurative language, apparently for the purpose of clarifying what he means by the two notions playing a fundamental role in his inquiry.

What is a Content-Idea?   If we ask what these fundamental notions are, there is no way of avoiding the term *ideas.* Max Weber himself speaks of " 'ideas' of historical phenomena" which, according to him, are "a kind of formation of concepts, which are proper to the sciences of human culture and which to a certain extent are indispensable."[87]   The term "idea," however, has many

---

[85]*Gesammelte Aufsätze zur Religionssoziologie,* Tübingen, 4th ed., 1947, p. 190.   Partly translated as *The Protestant Ethic and the Spirit of Capitalism,* New York, 1930.

[86]Cf. Lalande, *op. cit.,* p. 160: "Empirical concepts . . . [are] general notions defining classes of given objects."

[87]"Die 'Objektivität' sozialwissenschaftlicher und sozial-politischer Erkenntnis," *Gesammelte Aufsätze zur Wissenschaftslehre,* Tübingen, 2nd ed., 1951, pp. 189 f.

3. Fact and Methodic Idea in Empirical Human Science

meanings and should not be misunderstood. We should not simply think here of an idea in the Kantian sense, of a "concept [formed] from notions which transcends the possibility of experience,"[88] or of a Platonic idea, which can be contemplated only by one who fastens his spiritual gaze on the eternal, the pure and the immutable, without being influenced by changeable bodily impressions.[89]

Perhaps it may be useful to clarify here the *phenomenological concept of "idea"* by means of Husserl's analyses presented in the preceding section. Let us take the ideal "limit figures" of geometry. The "triangle in general" is not an arbitrary figment of the mind or a fancy which the mathematician projects into reality. The "triangle in general" arises from man's practical experience with concrete extended things, from the idealization of imperfect models, from the creation of "limit figures," from his transition from purely practical skill to the art of thinking. In an analogous fashion the historian is able to use his familiarity with certain historical, social, economic and religious phenomena to form more fundamental concepts by means of *idealization*. These concepts are for him both principles of order and methodic ideas.

The example of Max Weber illustrates the point. He thinks that the economic history of the sixteenth and seventeenth centuries can be best understood if the economic evolution is connected with certain changes occurring in the religious sphere of that period. This is his methodic idea. In these centuries the medieval Catholic ethics, which allowed the enjoyment of earthly goods but not their accumulation, was replaced by a Puritan morality, which disapproved of luxuries but saw wealth as a sign of the individual's divine predestination. From this standpoint, according to Weber, it is possible not only to describe the origin of modern economic life but also to *understand* it.

It is to be noted here that the idea "restrictions of traditionalistic ethics" cannot be found as such in historical facts, and the same applies to the idea "Protestant asceticism pursued in the world." Both notions are derived from experience, but they transcend this

---

[88]*Kritik der reinen Vernunft, Werke* ed. by A. Buchenau and E. Cassirer, vol. III, p. 260. Note that according to Kant a "notion" is a "pure" concept to which no "contemplation" (*Anschauung*) corresponds.
[89]Cf. *Phaedo,* 78b ff.

experience, and it is for this reason that they make experience intelligible and provide principles for arranging it in orderly fashion—just as "the triangle in general" does with respect to spatial experiences.

However, an essential difference manifests itself here. The historian's idealizations are concerned with contents, but those of the mathematician are formal. The latter refer to all conceivable spatial configurations while the former refer "merely" to certain fundamental human attitudes which were relatively general in a certain culture. The term "merely" should not be taken to mean that content-ideas are of less value, but is used to indicate that these ideas do not possess a universal compelling force because of their content-character. Anyone who does not know what Protestantism is, asceticism, traditionalistic ethics, etc., will understand nothing at all of Weber's fundamental idea, and no power can force him to see what Weber sees.

Accordingly, content-ideas possess only a relatively general and relatively necessary validity. They are not based on "notions" in the Kantian sense (on concepts which can be formed only by thinking) but on *views*. They are not connected with "forms" but with "contents." On the basis of Weber's methodic idea one is able to *establish* certain religious-sociological facts and at the same time to *understand* these facts; e.g., the fact *that* the economic history in Catholic countries took another course than in regions which were dominated by Puritan morality can be established and one can see *why* this was so. Thus Max Weber has opened a pathway which other historians may be able to follow fruitfully. The question, of course, is whether they are willing to enter into the "universe of meaning" created by this author's view of the period and his idealizing thought. We will return later to this point.

Künkel and the Characterological Fact. A third analysis may serve to complement these considerations. It is concerned with Fritz Künkel's attempt to describe and understand the structure of the human character by distinguishing two fundamental functions in it. He calls them the *"sachliche"* and the *"ichhafte"* functions, which we may translate as the "objective" and the "egocentric" functions.[90] The "objective" function, says Künkel, is at the service of the object and aims at the realization of objective values. The egocentric function, on the other hand, is subservient to the individual's own ego and aims at increasing his own value. Künkel describes a long series of cases to illustrate the meaning of these functions. They show how a person acts who is preponderantly "objective" and what the behavior is of an individual whose character is preponderantly "egocentric."

Note that the author says "preponderantly." According to Künkel, both functions are present in every normal human being. There is a definite relationship between them—namely, the greater a person's "egocentricity" is, the smaller his "objectivity." And the more an "egocentric" person has a feeling of inferiority, the more he feels the need to impose himself in order to increase his value. The "objective" man, on the other hand, does not suffer from such fluctuations of his self-esteem.[91]

Künkel has never met *the* "egocentricity" in his office and he has likewise no experience of *the* "objectivity." On the other hand, one cannot say that egocentricity and objectivity are simple abstractions from concrete data of experience; they cannot be compared, e.g., with the color or form of a thing. So we must ask, What are they? Inevitably, the term *idea* presents itself again. Of course, such ideas are not exemplars existing somewhere in a kind of metaphysical heaven. What happened is that Künkel's psychiatric and psychological practice gave him an opportunity to form such ideas. Starting from his experience with "egocentric" patients and through idealization, Künkel arrived at the "boundary idea" of *the* egocentricity. Because of his familiarity with "objective" people he was enabled to form the boundary concept of *the* "objectivity." Both ideas are closely connected with his psychological and psychiatric experiences, but they transcend the level of experience.

The fundamental methodic thought of Künkel consists in this that every character can be conceived as composed of an "ego-

---

[90]*Einführung in die Charakterkunde,* Leipzig, 2nd ed., 1929, pp. 13-27.
[91]*Op cit.,* p. 15. The author mentions the saint as 100% "objective" and the wholly insane as exclusively "egocentric" only as boundary cases.

centric" and an "objective" function. In Kantian language one could say that according to Künkel egocentricity and objectivity constitute a priori's of every possible character. For this reason every conceivable character and every possible change of self-evaluation can be described by means of the above-mentioned schema. Note however, that the a priori's in question are not formal but material,[92] and consequently do not possess a universally binding power. While man is bound to conceive the algebraic number "three" as consisting of three units and the circumference of a circle as the geometric place of all points situated at the same distance from the center, he is merely *able* to conceive character as composed of the two functions in question. This possibility means no more and no less than that every character can be described in Künkel's "language." In the practical pursuit of psychology it means that for those who are accustomed to work with Künkel's ideas, these ideas are useful principles of order. The psychologists in question form a group which, in Husserl's language, is a "research society." For the members of this group it is a *fact* that patient *X* has a strongly egocentric character. And within the framework of this "research society" there exist methods to confirm or refute the diagnosis in question.

Overestimation of the "Orthodoxies." We are touching here a weak point in the empirical human sciences. In most of them use is made of several, more or less divergent, methodic ideas and the various "research societies" speak different "languages" and apply different material a priori's. None of these possesses an absolutely binding character.

This situation results sometimes in unnecessary sharp oppositions. An orthodox Marxist, for example, will refuse to accept the methodic idea of Max Weber's sociology of religion. An orthodox psychoanalyst will show little respect for Künkel's fundamental characterological ideas. This rigid adherence to such "orthodoxies" is regrettable. It is based on an overevaluation of one's own methodic ideas, which are viewed as the only scientific

---

[92]The concept of "material a priori" disagrees with Kant's thinking. For this reason we do not consider the use of this terminology very satisfactory. See below, p. 291.

approach. Such a view forgets that any methodic principle is merely an *attempt* to comprehend the inexhaustible wealth of forms in which human life manifests itself. It considers as *the* human reality that which is merely a means to grasp *something* of this reality in a network of ideas.

In opposition to this narrow-mindedness we recommend that anyone who studies man as man become familiar with several divergent approaches and with the corresponding systems of concepts. Such a change of methodic standpoint broadens and refines anyone who pursues scientific endeavors. It may be compared with the wholesome influence which the study of several languages exercises on man in a more general sense. By broadening and refining his view in this fashion, man sees with increasing clarity that methodic ideas are neither "true" nor "false" but only "fruitful" or "unfruitful." As Max Weber emphasizes, "Whether there is question of a mere playing with thoughts or of a scientifically fruitful formation of concepts can never be decided a priori. There is only one norm here—namely, the norm of the result it has for our knowledge of concrete cultural phenomena."[93] We may add that a methodic idea may be "useful" in one realm and "useless" in another. For example, the "experimental idea" of behaviorism is useful as long as there is question of experiments with animals in artificial surroundings, but it is insufficient for the investigation of specifically human forms of behavior.

Of course, it is not possible to make a judgment about the usefulness or uselessness of a methodic idea unless one is willing to make a profound study of it and to accept it provisionally as a guide in one's research. This condition, however, presupposes a certain scientific broad-mindedness and thus stands in contrast with the blind zeal displayed by certain proponents of "orthodox" theories.

Rejection of Idealism and Conventionalism. There are all kinds of possible misunderstandings regarding our view of the essence of the "fact." We find it necessary to make explicit mention of two.

---

[93]*Art.cit.* (footnote 87), p. 193.

Phenomenology and the Human Sciences

First of all, our view could be interpreted in the spirit of *idealistic philosophy*. The very term "methodic idea" could give rise to such an interpretation. For, according to Kant, a "transcendental idea" is a regulatory principle safeguarding the consistent and thoroughly radical empirical use of reason. Nevertheless, he admits, transcendental ideas have something good in this that they lead reason "in the direction in which its use, while becoming as broad as possible, is at the same time made to harmonize constantly with itself."[94] One could point here also to a few neo-Kantians who assign a higher rank to thought than to experience. They view reality merely as an hypothesis, a scientific hypothesis, devised by creative thinking. When, for example, we speak of the "construction of a fact" this expression could bring to mind the concept "product of thinking" that was so dear to Hermann Cohen.[95]

Secondly, our view could be interpreted also in the sense of *conventionalism*. It could be compared, for example with Henri Poincaré's question, "Is science artificial?"[96] It reminds one of Kasimir Ajdukiewicz assertion: "We can say of the judgments which we accept and which constitute our world-view that the data of experience do not unambiguously determine any of them. Rather, they depend on the choice of the conceptual apparatus by means of which we describe these data."[97] Ajdukiewicz's notion of "conceptual apparatus" seems to be related to our concepts "universe of discourse," "methodic ideas," and "scientific apparatus."

Let us begin by stating emphatically that we cannot agree with these interpretations. The conventionalistic interpretation of our view would be justifiable if we had offered the following simplistic explanation: the "methodic idea" is a thought construct, the "fact" a content that can be conceived in accord with this thought construct, and the "research society" is a group of people who have accepted the convention of conceiving certain contents in accord

---

[94]*Kritik der reinen Vernunft, Werke, loc. cit.,* p. 262.
[95]*Logik der reinen Erkenntnis,* Berlin, 2nd ed., 1922, *passim.*
[96]*La valeur de la science,* Paris, 1929, pp. 221 ff.
[97]"Das Weltbild und die Begriffsapparatur," *Erkenntnis,* vol. 4 (1934), p. 259.

with certain thought constructs. Our view, however, is far from being so simplistic. We started from human experience, an experience which we have never qualified empiricistically as a mosaic of "data of experience." Moreover, it should be evident that that which we have called "methodic idea" and "scientific apparatus" must show itself useful. Even as nature lends itself to a description in the style of mathematical idealization, so also must the phenomena of social and cultural life let themselves be grasped in a network of sociological and cultural-anthropological ideas. True, the methodic idea cannot be directly tested by means of "facts," because it is the matrix of all facts. Nevertheless, it has to show its usefulness by offering the possibility of establishing facts and seeing a connection between them. The factual character of these facts and the intelligibility of this interconnection are subject, of course, to the critique of a "research society." Accordingly, the methodic idea and the scientific apparatus can never be based on convention.

It remains true that we have emphasized the role of productive thought for all forms of scientific life, even for purely empirical forms. The "mechanism of sensitivity," even if it existed, could not suffice to create an "objective picture of reality." For this reason we spoke, somewhat too suggestively perhaps, of the "construction of facts." This construction, however, in our view is not an arbitrary structure, a capricious invention of the mind, a fanciful combination. On the contrary, the constructive idea has to offer the possibility of comprehending a given sector of experience. Insofar as it provides this possibility, it has been "made true," veri-fied, and if it does not do so, it is rejected or discarded.

Our entire argument concerning the connection between "fact" and "methodic idea" lies in line with what we have said about the fundamental concept of experience. The methodic idea is an intellectual organ enabling the man of research to disclose, unveil certain types of beings as beings-for-us. Once this unveiling has taken place, these beings *factually* exist for a research society, a nation, a cultural group, or mankind itself. The methodic idea, therefore, is *productive* in the original sense of the Latin *pro-*

135

ducere, it "brings forward" that which first was hidden. But it is not productive in the sense of idealism, it is not *creative,* for "whatever has been unveiled by us, or will ever be unveiled by us, was already there."[98]

Accordingly, our standpoint is neither idealistic nor conventionalistic nor even empiricist. It is, in a sense that remains to be further clarified, *phenomenological.*

Conclusion. In the light of the preceding considerations we may complement our analysis of the concept "fact." To the three above-mentioned characteristics of the "fact," viz., its isolability, immutability and "standing apart," we must add two others:

4. *Every fact corresponds with a methodic idea.* In physical science the methodic ideas are mainly of a formal nature, and in human science content-ideas play a role alongside formal ideas.

5. *Every fact is verifiable for those who are willing and able to use the corresponding methodic idea.* We think that this sentence correctly formulates the *principle of verifiability* in a way which is in harmony with the reality of scientific life.

---

[98]Cf. above, p. 85.

4. THE PROPER CHARACTER OF EMPIRICAL HUMAN SCIENCE: THE TWOFOLD TRACK OF ANTHROPOLOGICAL RESEARCH

Analysis of a Test Situation. Let us start with a clear case and think of a psycho-diagnostic investigation in which the psychologist makes use of the well-known Rorschach test. It is hardly necessary to indicate what this test involves. The subject is offered one by one a series of ten pictures, representing ink blots, some in black and white, others in color, which do not picture anything in particular. Nevertheless, the psychologist asks the subject to tell him what the blots could be. In his reply therefore the subject is obliged to *interpret* what the forms and colors happen to be for him. From the way in which he "sees" the forms and colors the trained psycho-diagnostician is able to draw certain conclusions.

What is important here for us is that in this test we are dealing with a double series of facts. The first is formed by the ten Rorschach blots, which are exactly the same in any Rorschach set. Any psychologist knows what is meant when, for instance, there is question of blot no. 8 of the series. This rigid identifiability and immutability of the blots is of decisive importance for the application of the test, as Herman Rorschach himself emphasizes very strongly.[99] In contrast with the constant character of the testing material we find the variability of interpretations. These interpretations also are identified—in the form of a so-called Rorschach protocol—but they vary with respect to their contents. The interpretation possibilities of the forms are theoretically unlimited, although there is a great probability that certain interpretations will occur in a plurality of protocols. The replies of the subject taking the test, laid down in the protocol, constitute the second series of facts.

The judgments of the test subjects are, of course, "nonsensical statements" in the sense of Ayer. There is no possibility of any observation which could determine whether the blot of card no. 1 is or is not a butterfly. From the standpoint of the physical scientist, therefore, the judgment of the test subject is without

---

[99]*Psychodiagnostik, Textband,* Bern, 6th ed., 1948, p. 20.

any importance. However, within the "universe of discourse" of psycho-diagnosticians the reply, "it is a butterfly," is relevant. It is, e.g., an interpretation that has reference to the totality of the figure, is in harmony with its shape, and "sees" this shape as the form of an animal. From the whole of similar data the psycho-diagnostician will be able to form a mental image of the subject's psychical dispositions.

Rorschach's Methodic Idea. If the question is asked of how these data can lead to a psychological image of the subject, the reply has to be based on the following foundation. Because the Rorschach blots are intersubjectively identifiable, all subjective attempts to interpret one and the same blot can be compared with one another, and because they can be compared, it is possible to discover in the plurality of subjective interpretations typical regularities which have an intersubjective, scientific value. It is in this that the methodic idea of Rorschach consists. The way in which a subject "sees" a blot, conceives and names it, unconsciously expresses his intelligence, his sociability, his affectivity, his imagination, his attitude toward the world (*"Erlebnistypus"*), etc. For this reason the empirical typology of the interpretations may be prudently translated into an empirical typology of persons.

It is to be noted that this new idea was based on a previously established science of psychology and psychiatry. Rorschach had at his disposal certain fundamental concepts of psychology, such as intelligence, social contact and affectivity. His discovery consisted in this that he saw a connection and the possibility of translating certain specifically human actions, the interpretation of ink blots, into the language of psychological ideas. In this way he was able to construct a universe of new facts which today under the name of "Rorschach psycho-diagnostics" have become familiar to every empirical psychologist.

From our analyses it becomes apparent that specifically human intentions, attitudes, and behaviors can be scientifically compared only when they are first made comparable. They become comparable when they are called forth in a carefully determined situation. The scientific apparatus itself of the empirical human sciences is destined in part to discover and/or create comparable situations.

In this way the two above-mentioned series of facts arise. The first series is artificially created by acting and thinking and is concerned with the framework. In the case of the Rorschach test these facts are concerned with the ten blots, the way in which these blots are offered, the way in which the replies are interpreted, etc. These facts are intersubjectively determined in a precise fashion, for they have to be rigorously identical for a research society. Otherwise there would not be any possiblity of mutual understanding and critique in this society.

The second series of facts refers to the behavior of human individuals in a previously discovered and/or created situation. In the Rorschach situation the last-named facts are the interpretations of the test subject, recorded in the Rorschach protocol. Because the individual behavior take place within an intersubjective framework, it ceases to be strictly individual. Something general can be said about them and typical connections may be discovered. Opinions may differ about the question whether or not the situation was really the same in concrete cases. However, this possibility does not jeopardize the correctness of the principle underlying the procedure. This principle may be formulated in this way. Without a firm foundation for systematic comparison it is not possible to predicate anything of a subject in a scientifically justified fashion. There would even be a danger that without such a firm basis the evaluation of human intentions, behavior and attitudes will assume the character of more or less fortuitous impressions.

Case History as Method. Experiments and tests are not the only methods offering possibilities of systematic comparison. Künkel, for example, makes use of case history, i.e., the description of typical cases, to make his characterological views acceptable. To clarify the essense of the "egocentric" and "objective" character, he describes a number of typical ways of behavior. He speaks, for example, about two persons A and B who wanted to go on a trip. When they arrived at the station, they heard that their train had been cancelled. A became furious and considered it an insult to his personal dignity, but *B* simply decided that they would have to take the next train. Before this train could leave, however, a violent thunderstorm suddenly broke out. *A* viewed this new development as a mean trick inflicted on him by heaven. *B* went home and spent a quiet day absorbed in reading an interesting book.[100] Two forms of behavior thus are characterized in a well-chosen methodic fashion. For Künkel describes the subjective ways in which two persons have experienced an intersubjectively known situation. Anyone is familiar with the situation that a train he wants to take does not run and anyone likewise has sometimes experienced that the weather refuses to cooperate. Thus the familiarity with these situations provides a first series of facts. The second series is constituted by the way the two persons behave. Because the two series are brought to bear on each other, the behaviors become comparable, albeit not in an exact fashion.

This comparability is the basis of the scientific value proper to an enumeration of cases. Such an enumeration would not warrant any progress of knowledge if it dealt with wholly incomparable phenomena. But because human intentions and ways of behaving are connected with known situations, the intentions and behaviors become comparable. It is for this reason that certain conclusions may be drawn from psychiatric and psychological case histories.

Making Situations Comparable. One who pursues empirical human science, we have said, will attempt to discover and/or create comparable situations. The historian who investigates the past of human groups has to rely, of course, on the discovery of such situations. He also needs a scientific apparatus for this purpose, but it consists of historical ideas and concepts. Almost any of the fundamental historical concepts and categories may be used in this context. Max Weber, for example, applies the comparative method to economic history in the following way. Toward the end of the Middle Ages, he observes, the actual condition of the commoners in a number of European countries was more or

---

[100]*Op. cit.*, pp. 17 f.

4. Twofold Track of Anthropological Research

less the same. Next we see that among some peoples there begins an early development in the direction of what later will be called "capitalism," while other peoples do not follow this example or follow it only later and hesitantly. His comparison, therefore, refers to the behavior of certain human groups with respect to a known historical initial situation. Weber now tries to find a connection between the two series of facts. His well-known religious-sociological theory provides him with an hermeneutics which makes the divergent attitude of the human groups in question intelligible.

Meaningful Facts. It should be apparent now why remarks that in themselves seem to be wholly unimportant may become scientifically relevant. They become important only when they fit in like a key with a known situation described within the framework of a certain human science. For example, there exists an attitude which child psychologists describe as "stubborn through overindulgence." The situation of the child who has to empty his plate is an intersubjectively known situation, and the tearful protest, "Mom, you have put so much on my plate again," could characterize a typical attitude of the child toward this situation.

The second example, mentioned above, should be interpreted in an analogous way. The situation is the same for all gathered in the lecture hall. One student, however, feels it is hot and the others don't. If, then, there exists an idea of the illness called "claustrophobia," and if other symptoms are present pertaining to the same idea, the psychologist or psychiatrist may attach importance to the casual remark, "It is warm in here."

Generally speaking, precisely the most subjective phenomenon will be most relevant for the study of man as man. However, it is not sufficient to record the phenomenon. Observing, tape recording, filming, studying cultural objects and documents, establishing statistical frequencies and significant connections are not enough. The phenomenon has to be placed within the framework of a possible intersubjective giving of meaning. This alone is the decisive step. The twofold track of anthropological research is in harmony with this demand. It makes it possible *to discover*

141

facts on the basis of their meaning. The words "on the basis of their meaning" are not an ornamental addition, something accidental or superadded but, on the contrary, the very possibility of an empirical human science stands or falls with these words. For, if it is true, that man is a being which unveils the meaning of things, then the facts which refer to this being have to be meaningful facts.

5. THE PROPER CHARACTER OF EMPIRICAL HUMAN SCIENCE: ANTHROPOLOGICAL RESEARCH AS ENCOUNTER

Subject—Object or Subject—Subject? The concept "meaningful fact" needs to be more carefully examined. This examination will show once again that the situation in the realm of physical science differs essentially from that in human science.

When, for example, a mineralogist observes that a diamond has the tenth grade of hardness and that kitchen salt crystallizes in the form of cubes, this observation has a certain meaning for him. He makes use of ordering principles that are suitable for a description of the material world. That which is arranged in an orderly fashion, by the very fact of being thusly arranged, cannot be said to be wholly meaningless. In the case under consideration all giving of meaning originates, at least so it seems, with man as pursuing physical science. Material reality *allows* itself to be "vested" in the physicist's ideas.

In anthropological research, however, the situation is much more complex. The "object" here is man, as the fountainhead of meaningful intentions, and the purpose of the research is to discover the meaning of these intentions. But there is more. The investigator himself is a human being with intentions, scientific intentions. His interest is of a theoretical nature. He wants to know, to see interconnections, to understand. What he desires to see is the orientation of other, individual and collective, human intentions. This aim implies that the concept "subject-object relationship" does not apply to this situation and that it would be misleading to speak of it here. Nevertheless, as we have pointed out, even within the framework of research about man as man there is question of a *certain* objectivity, but this objectivity differs from that which is typical of physical research. If the relation of the atomic physicist to the atom is called a subject-object relationship, then the relationship of a child psychologist to a child may not be considered a subject-object relationship. If the relation of a biologist to a cell is a subject-object relationship, we may not call the relation of a psychiatrist to his patient likewise a subject-object relationship. Such a careless use of terms would lead to misunderstandings and contradictions. In investigating man as man we are dealing with an *encounter* of human beings, animated by different intentions. This encounter may be direct, as in the case of a cultural anthropologist, or indirect, as in the case of an historian; it may take place within the fixed framework of an experimental situation, during consultation hours, or in an interview. No matter, however, in what way the encounter takes place, it is always based on a *subject to subject relationship.*

Subjects or Automata? The reader will be aware of the fact that our view deviates from the standpoint obtaining in certain research groups. To clarify the difference, we will offer here the example of the Dutch sociologist E.V.W. Vercruysse. According to this author, there is no essential difference between a physicist examining the solubility of a substance and a sociologist investigating to what extent a certain population group has lost contact with every religious denomination. "There is no question," the author says, "of a purely apparent similarity, but there is an essential similarity between the attitudes of the physicist and of the sociologist with respect to the facts which they study. Just as the physicist treats his substances, so likewise the sociologist endeavors to treat the investigated subjects and their reactions as *objects.* Both work for the avowed aim of attaining the highest possible degree of objectivity. Both endeavor to reach their aim by standardizing the necessary research activity as much as possible. . . . For this reason the sociologist treats his subjects as much as possible as automata which, according to their mechanism, reply "Yes" or "No."[101]

Like innumerable other authors, Vercruysse thinks that the objectivity of an investigation depends on the willingness of the man of research to treat his subjects as objects. The question, of course, is whether the sociologist is really able to do so consistently. In addition, one could doubt whether the author's recommended *objectivistic* attitude promotes the objectivity of the investigation.

Vercruysse is honest enough to recognize at least implicitly that the sociologist soon runs into difficulties with his objectivism. As

[101]*Het ontwerpen van een sociologisch onderzoek,* Assen, 1960, p. 9.

5. *Anthropological Research as Encounter*

an example he refers to the study of J. P. Kruyt about non-denomi-nationalism in the Netherlands.[102] It was striking that this study revealed a very high percentage of unchurched people in prepon-derantly Baptist areas. Subsequent inquiry showed the following. The organizers of the census had decided that the denomination of under-age children should be considered to be the same as that of the father as long as these minors had not personally given adherence to one or the other denomination. The Baptists, how-ever, interpreted these instructions in the light of their doctrine of "adult baptism." The result was that numerous under-age chil-dren were reported as not belonging to any denomination. Vercruysse draws an important conclusion from this study when he says: "Although the sociologist may have the same aim as the physicist, . . . in order to be able to arrange *social* phenomena in this fashion, he must first know their meaning, i.e., *their meaning as seen from the perspective of those who participate in social life.*"[103]

If this conclusion is correct—and we are convinced that it is— the question arises whether it can be reconciled with Vercruysse's starting point. In the light of the conclusion, can it be asserted that the sociologist has a purely subject-object relationship to the human beings whom he questions? The author himself admits that these human beings "rarely if ever interpret" the questions asked in the same sense.[104] But if this is true, what possible meaning could the term "object" have here? We realize, of course, that the concept "object" has undergone great changes in western thought from Duns Scotus to Sartre.[105] Nevertheless, we cannot see any pos-sible meaning in speaking about *objects* which view things in a cer-tain perspective, which attach to social phenomena now this sense and then that sense, and which interpret questions. Even if abstraction is made from all philosophical implications, one will have to admit that the substances investigated by the physicist do *not interpret* the liquid in which they are dissolved, but always

---

[102]*Onkerkelijkheid in Nederland. Haar verbreiding and haar oorzaken,* Groningen, 1933.
[103]*Op. cit.,* pp. 10 f. Author's italics.
[104]*Op. cit.,* p. 10.
[105]Cf. Stephen Strasser, *Objectiviteit en Objectivisme,* Nijmegen, 1947.

react by dissolving or not dissolving in the same way. If the terms "objects" and "reactions" apply to these substances and processes, then it has to be admitted that questioned human beings are not objects and that their replies are not reactions.

Vercruysse's comparison with automata is very much to the point here. The human beings, investigated by the sociologist, he says, have to be considered as automata which according to their mechanism reply "Yes" or "No."[106] But now it appears that the Baptist automata view the questions differently from the Dutch Reformed, the Reformed, and the Catholic automata. Moreover, quite obviously, the mechanism of these automata would undergo great changes if their theological understanding of the essence of the Sacrament of Baptism would be modified. All this leads us to conclude that Vercruysse's model of *man as an automaton* is not as innocent as he himself would like us to believe.[107] The model is misleading rather than clarifying.

We also, however, would like to ask the important question of *how the sociologist can ascertain the meaning which is ascribed to a certain phenomenon by one who takes part in social life.* Regarding the case quoted above, how can he find an explanation for the fact that in Baptist areas so many people report that they do not belong to any denomination? The fundamental reply is that he has to enter into a closer subject-subject relationship with the people questioned in the inquiry. This subject to subject relationship may be arrived at directly or indirectly—directly, by means of conversation and spontaneous or guided interviews, indirectly, by becoming acquainted with the theological literature, the origin and history of the Baptist movement. All these means may be included in the broad sense which we attribute to the term *encounter*.

What is an "Encounter"? It was Buytendijk's important publication, *Zur Phänomenologie der Begegnung,*[108] which stressed the value of this concept and made it fashionable to speak about "encounter." Numerous authors now use the term, but nearly

---

[106]Vercruysse's idea is based on P. F. Lazarsfeld's article, "A Conceptual Introduction to Latent Structure Analysis," *Mathematical Thinking in the Social Sciences,* ed. by the same, Glencoe, Ill., 1954, pp. 349-388.

[107]*Op. cit.,* p. 9, footnote 1.

[108]See *Eranos-Jahrbuch,* vol. 19 (1951), pp. 431-486.

everyone of them in a different sense. A whole booklet could be filled with a comparative analysis of these divergent meanings. I will limit myself, however, to state as clearly as possible what I mean by it. By encounter I mean *the communication of persons with each other in a situation that is meaningful for both of them.*[109] This description implies that the encounter does not at all have to be a unique and unintentional event. Romano Guardini, who claims the opposite,[110] thinks too exclusively of man's encounter with God and disregards the meaning which the term "encounter" or "meeting" has in everyday speech. For example, we speak quite frequently about the meetings of statesmen and how carefully they should be prepared, we try to encounter influential people, and lovers are proverbially ingenious in seeking to meet each other.

On the other hand, it is not necessary that the situation should have the *same* meaning for the persons meeting. While Friedrich Otto Bollnow correctly emphasizes that encounter implies reciprocity because it is based on a subject to subject relationship, the intentions of the persons who meet do not have to be the same. In other words, reciprocity does not mean symmetry. Everyday language may serve here to exemplify the point. Let us say that John goes to a certain restaurant to eat. Peter knows this and goes to the same restaurant to speak with John. The encounter is not a chance meeting but arranged by one of the partners. The resulting situation is meaningful for both, but has an additional meaning for Peter.

To Encounter and to Allow Oneself to be Encountered. Such an additional meaning is likely to be always present when there is question of research about man as man. For the one who makes the encounter possible, who prepares and organizes it, is man as pursuing science, and the one who allows himself to be encountered, either directly or by way of documents, cultural products, statistics and test results, is simply man. For this reason the situation will always have a different meaning for the former than for the latter. This difference is an essential aspect of the

---

[109]For the concept "communication" see the author's, "Het wezen van de mens," *De Mens,* Utrecht, 1958, pp. 1-31, on pp. 8 ff. and 14 ff.
[110]Guardini, O. F. Bollnow, *Begegnung und Bildung,* Würzberg, 1959.

research situation. The human being who is being investigated does not know the system of ideas in which the investigator places him.

We may refer here again to the above-mentioned test situation. For the subject tested the interpretation of the Rorschach blots is a meaningful activity. However, he seeks its meaning elsewhere than does the psychologist. As Rorschach remarks, "Nearly all subjects view the test as an examination of their imagination."[111] Moreover, attention has to be paid also to the *indirect encounter*. As we have pointed out in passing, there exists a possibility to meet spiritually with persons or groups of persons who are no longer alive by studying their works of art, their autobiographies, life-stories, and documents. In such cases also the meaning which the esthetic, social, political or scientific projects, performances and acts have had for the historical subject or subjects differs of necessity from that which they have for an historian.

Let us take an extreme case and consider a Catholic historian who endeavors to ascertain the course taken by the Council of Trent. While he will agree, of course, with the dogmatic decisions of the Council, their historical value will differ for him from the value they had for the assembled members of the Council whose mentality he endeavors to understand. The reason is that our historian evaluates the acts of the Council in the light of three centuries of history, centuries that are filled with the conflicting currents of Reformation and Counter Reformation, rationalism, Jansenism, "Illumination," etc. He is familiar with the enthusiastic reception of the Council's decisions as well as with their outspoken rejection. He not only *knows* these reactions but, by virtue of his fundamental historical concepts, he is able also to *understand* and *comprehend* them. Accordingly, on the human level he knows more than the members of the Council who were active in it. In this way the historical situation has another meaning for him than for the historical persons whose motives he endeavors to understand.

Our conception of encounter deviates considerably from that of those who view the encounter as a purely personal relationship

---

[111]*Psychodiagnostik,* p. 17.

5. Anthropological Research as Encounter

which gives rise to intuitive knowledge of the other's existential project. In their view, the encounter would lead us to discover the other "in the heart of his existence." This view, it seems to us, is related to Sartre's "preontological comprehension." We are quite willing to concede, of course, that the ultimate goal of any study of man as man is to discover the other "in the heart of his existence." However, to reach this goal, it is not sufficient to go to the encounter of the other in a personal, trust-inviting and purely human way. For encounter is always also communication, i.e., communications are given and received, questions are asked and replies are understood. The communication does not have to be direct and it does not have to be verbal. Nevertheless, on the specifically human level a moment will arrive when recourse must be had to speech. When this happens, concepts are used and, because concepts are always interconnected, there is no escape from a system of ideas. One who wants to discover the other "in the heart of his existence" is already in possession of a system of ideas, he has already a certain scientifically-founded plan of how he will be able to reach his cognitive goal. This statement does not mean that the investigator will obstinately hold fast to a limited number of "pictures," in the firm conviction that one or the other picture *has to* fit the subject of his investigation. It does mean, however, that it is *he* who determines in what spirit the dialog will take place. On the basis of his knowledge and experience he manages to lead the dialog in such a fashion that it is clarifying, even from a scientific standpoint. For this reason we agree with D. J. van Lennep when he emphasizes that encounter "to be scientifically justified, must include both methods of approach [the statistical-inductive method and the interpretative method of "Verstehen"] and humanize both."[112] Accordingly, the encounter, as a scientific attitude, is more than a friendly acceptance of the other which would offer an opportunity for acquiring infallible intuitive insights into the other.

Two Languages. The difference of mental horizon affecting the investigator and the subject investigated has certain conse-

---

[112]*Gewogen-bekeken-ontmoet in het psychologisch onderzoek.* The Hague, 1949, p. 28.

149

quences with respect to what above we have called the "direct encounter." One of these is that those who pursue certain human sciences are forced to speak two languages. The test situation, mentioned above, may serve again to illustrate the point. The language in which the psychiatrist-psychologist communicates with his patient is wholly different from the Rorschach jargon in which he communicates with his colleagues about the interpretation of the test. Calling the jargon the *scientific* or *technical language,* we may describe it as the verbalization of the whole system of methodic ideas and of the concepts and classifications flowing from this system which characterize a "research society." The language used in the communication with the test subject, on the other hand, we will call the *interview language.* The interview that is uppermost in our mind here is the type which social psychologists and sociologists use methodically in our time. In this kind of interview the investigator endeavors to speak a language understood by the subject interviewed. For, if the investigator's language is not intelligible for this subject, the situation will be meaningless for him, so that the interview does not lead to an encounter. The technical scientific language in which psychologists and sociologists express and interpret the results of their research differs greatly from the idiom used in the interviews.

When we speak here of "interview language," this term should be understood very broadly, for it indicates a complex of verbal communications of which interviewing is only a part. It applies also to other forms of linguistic contact, e.g., the conversations of an anthropologist with primitive tribes, the careful questions asked by a religious psychologist seeking to ascertain the religious attitude of a person, the words by which a child psychologist encourages children to play so that he can arrive at a diagnosis of their playing, and many other forms. Moreover, it should be evident that the bi-lingual approach used in some empirical human sciences has nothing in common with duplicity, but is a simple necessity flowing from the two surrounding worlds in which the man of science has to move—viz., the world of the child, the primitive and the patient and, on the other hand, the world of specialized science.

5. Anthropological Research as Encounter

Artificial but Not Inhuman. All this shows that the intention of the one who wants to know cannot be the same as that of the one who is to be known. To this extent there is a kind of *"standing apart"* also in the research of the human sciences— namely, the "standing apart" of two intentionalities with different orientations. More figuratively expressed, two human beings walking in the same direction do not meet each other, just as they likewise fail to meet by walking in opposite directions. If they are to meet, it is necessary that the directions converge, and such a convergence does not come about automatically. At least one of the two has to want the meeting, not merely abstractly but concretely, i.e., *he must want to realize the meeting in a certain fashion.* Such a realization demands that his intentions are attuned to those of his "partner." For this reason the "standing apart" of anthropological research is limited and cannot unqualifiedly be compared with that commonly found in the research of physical science.

For the pursuit of research in human science this limited "standing apart" implies that the investigator will attempt to encounter primitive man differently from civilized man, the child differently from the adult, the psychically normal differently from the psychically abnormal. At the same time he will endeavor to discover or produce comparable situations. All this flows from the nature of his theoretical interest. For encountering someone to get to know him is not the same as encountering him to help him, whether externally or internally. The latter may flow from the former, but it is not the same.

Summarizing, we may say that human science, the complex of the empirical sciences of man as man, is an *artful* edifice. It is also *artificial* in a certain sense, so that an affirmative reply must be given to Henri Poincaré's question whether science is artificial. All science, including human science is artificial. This artificiality, however, should not be understood as if it meant pure conventionality or an absence of authenticity. It does not at all mean that human science is inhuman, for the very *foundation* on which it is based lies in *man's understanding of the specifically human.*

151

6. THE PROBLEMS OF "VERSTEHEN": PRESCIENTIFIC INTUITION

The Disappearance of the Disinterested Spectator. There still remains a glaring gap in the way in which we have thus far characterized the nature of the human sciences. One could be led to deduce from our descriptions that only pure theory has value for one who pursues science. The subjects whom he is to investigate would be interested in all kinds of value realms, such as friendship and love, gracefulness and beauty, wealth and power, purity and sanctity. Yet all this would have to be literally valueless for the investigator himself, who would and should be no more and no less than a lynx-eyed observer. The ideal man of research would consist of a pair of sharp eyes connected with a powerful brain. As a matter of fact, such was the ideal pursued in the era of scientism. Husserl's expression, "the disinterested spectator," is a relic of this era. Such a "spectator" is characterized by his attitude of "non-participation" (*Nicht-mitmachen*).[113]

It should be evident that the disinterested spectator is indeed the ideal investigator as long as one considers the cognitive connection as a subject-object relationship. For in that case one silently assumes that human beings who love each other, struggle for power, or are religiously moved are nothing else for the man of science than mere cognitive *objects*. Provisionally leaving aside the question whether such an assumption is *capable* of ever being justified, we will consider here only the most important question: Does the ideal of knowledge *force* us to make this assumption? May the disinterested spectator still be viewed as the ideal knower now that we are aware of it that human science aims at understanding subject to subject relationships? From the standpoint of human science, is it really an advantage if the investigator manifests purely theoretical interest and remains insensible for all other human values? We doubt it very much.

For example, it is conceivable that someone would write a Hölderin biography while he is wholly indifferent to the esthetic

---

[113]*Cartesian Meditations,* p. 34 (German ed., p. 72).

values contained in Hölderin's poetry. The biographist could be, for instance, a psychiatrist-psychologist who is solely interested in the personality development and the origin of Hölderin's psychical illness. Yet this onesided theoretical interest would not improve the biography. For Hölderin's life was filled with a passion for poetry, so that anyone who wants to communicate with him will have to do so primarily by way of his poetic works. Reversely, he who does not understand the spirit of Hölderin's poetry will have no access to the most important source of knowledge concerning Hölderin's person, and this will be a disadvantage in his psychological and psychiatric analysis.

Accordingly, it is useless to attempt a scientifically justified biography about a poet if one is utterly without feeling for the esthetic. In an analogous way it will be impossible to understand the history of the religious wars of the sixteenth and seventeenth centuries if one does not know or does not want to know anything about the religious values pursued at the time by the Christian world with its Catholic and Protestant forms of piety. For the areligious or antireligious historian the deeds of the leading characters of the time, the reformers, the popes, emperors and princes, will appear as meaningless as the behavior of a number of madmen. Of course, he will be able to gather data and arrange them into an exact chronicle, but his research is similar to painstakingly charting the façade of a building whose doors and windows are kept locked. What is happening inside the building escapes him entirely, he does not know anything about the motives, aims and values of the inhabitants.

Accordingly, the attitude of the disinterested observer, so characteristic of physical science, cannot be proposed as an obligatory example to be followed in the pursuit of human science. The difference of cognitive attitude in these two realms is very sharply characterized by Helmuth Plessner, who writes, "The [physicist's] object and method allow him to make use of a reduction which retains nothing but the bare minimum of the observer's existence. He, however, who pursues human science is required to bring into play all the soundboards of his entire personality. Although he must keep them under control, he must allow them

153

to play their role in order to let the material appear to him, in order to see it."[114]

For this reason the historian, for example, will generally endeavor to become familiar with the "sphere" of an era before he attempts to characterize this era. However, his endeavor will be successful only insofar as he shows himself sensitive to the great ideals which at the time inspired the thoughts and deeds of man. An historian who would see nothing but phantoms in the decisive values of an epoch would not be able to describe the period in any other way than as a phantasmagoria. Obviously, such a description would not deserve the name of history.

The Understanding Witness. These critical remarks should not be misunderstood. It is undoubtedly true that one who pursues science is driven by other intentions than the persons whom he wants to know. As the preceding section has shown very clearly, different intentions are needed. For the investigator may not interfere in the events but must limit himself to understanding them. He cannot become a participant without ceasing to be a man of theory. The values animating the persons whom he scrutinizes are not unqualifiedly decisive for himself. Perhaps the best way of characterizing his specific function would be to call him an *understanding witness.*

In this way we arrive again at the category of *"Verstehen,"* the fundamental importance of which has been stressed in the preceding pages. In our view, man's understanding of the human is fundamental for all human sciences. This assertion is, of course, neither new nor very original. As early as 1883 Wilhelm Dilthey characterized the task of the biographer as a function which makes us understand the unity of a life by means of anthropology and psychology.[115] He classified these two sciences as *"verstehende"* sciences.[116] However, even Dilthey was not quite original here, for in 1829 Schleiermacher gave a lecture to the Berlin Academy

---
[114]"Mit anderen Augen," *Zwischen Philosophie und Gesellschaft,* Bern, 1953, p. 205.
[115]*Einleitung in die Geisteswissenschaften,* vol. 1, Stuttgart, 4th ed., 1959, p. 34.
[116]Cf., e.g., his article, "Ideen über eine beschreibende und zergliedernde Psychologie," *Sitzungsberichte der Berliner Akademie,* 1894.

about "hermeneutic theory." Moreover, Joachim Wach's[117] research has shown that even Schleiermacher had his precursors. Wach's monumental three volumes consider only the older theories of *"Verstehen"* or understanding as a scientific method. Anyone who today would want to write a critical synthesis of all publications that have appeared for or against *"Verstehen"* would need not three but six volumes. Without fear of exaggerating, one may say that at least since Dilthey there have been constant discussions and arguments about the cognitive value of *"Verstehen."* The sad point in these discussions is not the difference of opinion but the absence of argumentation which is willing to take the opponents seriously. What has been said above about the "broken world of philosophy"[118] applies just as stringently to the problem considered here.

The reason why there is so much misconception about "understanding" is not far to seek. Without any doubt the one-sidedness of the debaters' starting point is one of the causes. While the older protagonists of *"Verstehen"* (Friedrich Ast, F. A. Wolf, Friedrich Schleiermacher) were almost exclusively concerned with philology, the modern opponents are interested in natural science. Another cause of endless misunderstandings lies in the aprioristic programmatic slogans which set down what should happen in this or that particular pursuit of science and close the mind to that which actually occurs. In other words, there exists *no phenomenology of the life of science.* Thus it may happen that certain authors most emphatically deny something which they vigorously pursue in the practice of their science. Likewise, it often happens that two men of science argue about a term, without realizing that they use the same term to indicate distinct phenomena. It goes without saying that in this way there is no possibility of a fruitful discussion.

Phenomenological analysis will show that the slogan-like term *"Verstehen"* or "understanding" is made to refer to three distinct intentional achievements, which we will call *prescientific intuition, hypothesis* or *interpretation* and *vision.* In the following pages we

---

[117]*Das Verstehen,* 3 vols., Tübingen, 1926-1933.
[118]Cf. pp. 56 ff.

will present a brief sketch of each of these three modes of knowing that are indispensable in the human sciences.

What is Prescientific Intuition? There exists something which we may call "prescientific intuition" and it is a source of genuine knowledge. Without this intuition there would be no explanation why the praxis of the everyday world keeps functioning and why on the prescientific level things run their orderly course. As we have seen, the praxis of the everyday world in which we live has its own way of "making-true," of confirmation. These "confirmations" are, of course, intuitive.[119]

Although the assertion that there exists a prescientific intuition may seem rather simple, it needs to be explained. For the notion of intuition is ambiguous and not everyone takes the trouble to indicate what he means by it. As a Louvain professor expressed it rather wittily, "When philosophers speak of intuition, the one means that he sees what he sees and the other that he sees what he does not see." This statement is literally true, as appears from a comparison of Kant and Bergson. According to Kant's simple description, intuition (*Anschauung*) is "immediately directed to an object and is unique,"[120] but according to Bergson's above-quoted definition, the intuitive knowner through a kind of spiritual sympathy coincides with that which is most intimate and unique in his cognitive object.[121] For Kant, "intuition" is sense perception, so that through intuition one sees what he sees. Bergson's definition, on the other hand, applies, for instance, to the ingenious commander general who by "intuition" sees the weak point of the enemy's army without seeing it.

The idea of intuition defended here is closer to Kant than to Bergson, although it does not share Kant's conception of the essence of sense perception. *We use the term "intuitive" to refer to the cognitive attitude of one who is confident that things are as he "sees" them.* More philosophically expressed, *for the intuitive knower the being of beings is evident, manifest*; it can simply be grasped, and this grasping is intuition. The intuitive act, more-

---

[119]Cf. pp. 76 ff.
[120]*Kritik der reinen Vernunft, loc. cit.* p. 260.
[121]See above, p. 47.

over, is an *immediate* knowing, for it is not based on inductive or deductive mental processes. It is immediate also in another equally important sense—namely, insofar as it takes place without reflection and especially without critical reflection. On the level of intuition, therefore, no distinction is made between "being" and "appearance." The truth of the beings that are grasped immediately is evident from the success of the praxis based on this intuition. If this praxis is successful, it does not give rise to a critical reflection. Accordingly, it is in the successful praxis that consists the verification, the "making-true," of prescientific intuition. This verification, therefore, is likewise of an intuitive nature.

On the other hand, our concept of intuition is not identical with that of sense perception, for relationships also can be grasped intuitively. The judgment, for example, that one of two moments of time is before the other is based on an intuitive evidence which cannot be explained by sense perception in the usual sense of this term. Finally, intuition is not a solipsistic way of knowing. There exists an intersubjective understanding, based on an intuitive foundation, which we have called "first objectivity."[122] For this reason we speak of a *"prescientific"* and not of a "pre-predicative" intuition.

The existence of intuitive knowledge is hardly subject to doubt, for any explicit act of reflection presupposes something that first is grasped without reflection. "Reflex intention" without "direct intention" is simply inconceivable. On this point there is a fairly general agreement among the thinkers of the past and present. The difference of opinion begins only with the appreciation of intuitive knowledge and especially with the question whether or not this knowledge has value for science. While some attempt to exclude the content of intuitions from scientific discourse as wholly unscientific, others think that intuitive knowledge cannot be dispensed with even on the level of science. In the following pages we will first let the opponents of intuition explain their view. Only when it becomes evident that they neglect forms of knowledge which are fundamental in reference to man as a person, will

---

[122]See above, pp. 75 ff.

we continue our analysis by investigating the importance of pre-scientific intuition for science.

The Deficiency of the Empirical Reduction. In a preceding section we have already met a convinced protagonist of radical empiricism in the person of George A. Lundberg.[123] Arguing against MacIver, Lundberg rejects such concepts as "anxious flight" and "hateful pursuit" because they cannot be defined "operationally," so that different observers do not necessarily arrive at the same results. Positively, as we have seen, Lundberg endeavors to establish facts in the sense of the physical sciences and this positive pursuit leads to the negation of all notions based on intuition, such as "anxious," "hateful," "flight" and "pursuit." According to Lundberg, these "subjective" terms must be reduced to "objective" terms, i.e., terms pertaining to physical science.

The first question to arise here is whether or not this reduction really leads to the elimination of *all* intuitive elements. The reply is somewhat disappointing. Even if in the description of the above-mentioned pursuit one would speak only of a plurality of organisms which at a given time move with different velocities through space, there would still be question of intuitive concepts. For it is primarily on the basis of our prescientific experience that we know what is meant by "living beings," "motion," "time" and "space." Moreover, Lundberg himself in the justification of his *Foundations* speaks about "concreteness," "tangibility," "reality" and "symbolic representation."[124] Is there any possibility of defining a concept such as "concreteness" in mathematico-physical terms? Lundberg does not attempt it and he does not even envision the endeavor to arrive at such a definition.

Of course, it is possible to go beyond the foregoing description of the event and to use more formalizing abstractions. The space, Lundberg tells us, of which he speaks is not the space of everyday experience or that of geographers and ecologists. "Space," he says, "in mathematics (and in sociology) merely means a mani-

---

123See above, pp. 14 ff.
124*Foundations of Sociology,* 2nd ed., New York, 1953, p. 105.

6. Prescientific Intuition

fold (a number of entities related under a system) in which *positional relationships* of many kinds may be expressed."[125] However, even this description makes explicit use of fundamental notions such as "plurality," "relationship," "positional," "expressed," and "entity." These explicitly used concepts, moreover, imply many others. Without "unity" it is not possible to speak of plurality, and without "identification" one cannot speak of unity. Do empiricists really think, then, that such notions can be defined by means of physicalistic terms?

Operationalistic Pseudo-Definitions. Operationalism may seem to offer a way out. As a matter of fact, Lundberg speaks somewhere about "operationally defined terms."[126] If we ask how identity is to be defined in operational terms, P. W. Bridgman, the founder of operationalism, supplies us with a long reply. "One of the most fundamental concepts," he says, "with which we describe the external world is that of identity; in fact thinking would be almost inconceivable without such a concept. By this concept we bridge the passage of time; it enables us to say that a particular object in our present experience is the same as an object of our past experience. From the point of view of operations the meaning of identity is determined by the operations by which we make the judgment that this object is the *same* as that one of my past experience."[127] This definition is very instructive. It shows that, in order to be able to perform these operations, one must already have intuitive knowledge of that which is to be defined. For example, to recognize a thing as the same at different moments of time and to determine its identical reality, one must already possess a certain notion of identity. The same line of thought applies to other operationalistic definitions. When Bridgman says, e.g., that "the concept of length is . . . fixed when the operations by which length is measured are fixed,"[128] he disregards the phenomenological relationship, for an intuitive fa-

---

[125]*Op. cit.*, p. 104.
[126]*Op. cit.*, p. 13.
[127]*The Logic of Modern Physics*, New York, 7th ed., 1954, pp. 91 f.
[128]*Op. cit.*, p. 5.

miliarity with "length" is needed before one can undertake spatial measurements.

Similar examples may be found in the works of other operationalists. S. S. Stevens, for example, writes, "Few concepts have proved as troublesome to psychology as the concept of *existence,* and yet this concept is fundamental to the notion of definition itself. We might have avoided this embarrassment if we had recognized that *existence* is used in two senses: 1. to denote the presence, as opposed to the absence of a certain object or event, and 2. to affirm the adequacy of a definition."[129] All we can say about such descriptions is that they are naive. Stevens forgets that the operational establishment of a presence requires knowledge of the present as existent, and that, in order to evaluate the adequacy of a definition, one will have to deal with an existent definition. (Stevens himself tells us that the concept of existence is fundamental to the notion of definition.)

Briefly put, all such operational definitions are pseudo-definitions. First "identity" is explained by means of "sameness" and then "sameness" can be explained through "identity." "Presence" is used to clarify "existence," although "presence" implicitly contains "existence." "Existence" is defined by means of "adequacy" or "being-adequate," yet any one knows that "being" is more fundamental than "being-adequate." It is obvious that such a playing with words does not mean any progress whatsoever.

While it may be true that the operationalistic approach offers certain advantages in the realm of physical science, the system should not be proposed as a general theory of knowledge. Bridgman himself carefully abstained from making any such claim. "What we are here concerned with," he says, "is an observation and description of methods which at least some physicists had already, perhaps unconsciously, adopted and found successful— the practice of the methods already existed. What I have attempted to do is to analyze these successful methods, not to set up a philosophical system and a theory of properties that any method

---

129"Operational Definitions of Psychological Concepts," *Psychological Review,* vol. 42 (1935), p. 517.

must have if it hopes to be successful."[130]   Accordingly, sociologists and psychologists who think that their theories *must* be constructed operationalistically cannot at all appeal to Bridgman.

Summarizing, we may say that the empiricist reduction cannot be carried through radically, for ultimately one has always to presuppose primary experiences and the knowledge and practical familiarity flowing from them, which can no longer be circumscribed in terms of empirical and formal-idealizing sciences, but are understood intuitively.   Lundberg's proposed road is a blind alley.

Is the Empiricist Reduction Successful? If, next, we consider the usefulness of the empiricist reduction for the human sciences, we may ask whether or not it is "successful" in Bridgman's sense. With Theodor Litt one could point out that as a consequence of the reduction man disappears as an impression.   While we are willing to agree with this statement, we fail to see any decisive value in it. In the equation expressing the working of a lever this lever disappears likewise as an impression; nevertheless this equation is a source of knowledge about the mechanics of the lever.   As Lundberg correctly remarks, "All symbolic representation is 'artificial' in exactly the same way,"[131] so that the artificial and symbolic character of expression resulting from the empiricist reduction alone cannot be put forward as an argument against its scientific value with respect to man.

The decisive question is whether or not the symbolic language expresses really that which the man of research wants to attain. For it could happen that he is primarily interested in something which does not at all reveal itself in the systems of symbols.   One could, for example, be interested in a human science, a science of man as man and of things human.   If, then, reality is pressed into a system of ideas in which the human element as such disappears, it follows that this system is unsuitable for the scientific purpose which he pursues.   Motion, for instance, can be described in a way that is equally applicable to an electron and to a human being.

---

[130]"Operational Analysis," *Philosophy of Science,* vol. 5 (1948), pp. 114 f.

[131]*Op. cit.,* p. 106.

Such a description is useful for a man of science who is interested in "locomotion,"[132] but it is meaningless with respect to a man fleeing from a pursuing crowd.

Accordingly, human science will have to speak another language than physical science. If we inquire about the difference between the two languages, the reply has to be that this difference appears to lie in this that the language of human science has to make use of more intuitive notions than is the case with physical science. The appeal to more frequent use of intuitive notions does not at all mean that the human sciences have to abandon the strictly scientific attitude, but just the opposite. The human sciences cannot attain their aim if they do not make use of a broad range of fundamental experiences. This use is wholly in harmony with a strict and rigorous pursuit of science, as we will show in the following pages.

Fundamental Forms of Prescientific Intuition. One who knows intuitively, we have said, is confident that things are as he sees them. This description of intuition has the advantage of divesting the concept of romantic, pseudo-romantic and neo-Platonic appendages. Described in this way, intuition is a clearly demonstrable and frequently occuring phenomenon, for it is the way in which knowledge is had on the level of the everyday world. We leave out of consideration here how this intuition takes place and we do not have to determine the role played in it by instinct, tradition, social milieu and physical environment. We merely observe phenomenologically that, for example, certain primitive Melanesians "see" their canoes inhabited by magic forces. The reply to the difficult question of how this "seeing" takes place may be left to cultural anthropologists and cultural psychologists who, undoubtedly, will be able to answer it only on the basis of empirical research.

The primitive Melanesian sees his canoe as inhabited by magic forces, but the half-civilized or wholly civilized Melanesian sees it as a wooden vessel. Apparently the mythical way of seeing things and living beings is not general and necessary. However, there are other intuitions which do possess this character of being

---

132Lundberg, *op. cit.*, p. 13.

general and necessary for man. From now on we will use the term *fundamental intuition* to refer to that intuition without which human existence is inconceivable. Although there exists a method to distinguish fundamental intuitions from others, this method is of a philosophical nature and may be provisionally[134] left out of consideration. At present we merely wish to observe that in the pursuit of science it is not possible to avoid making use of certain fundamental intuitions, at least at the starting point.

Three different levels or layers may be distinguished in these fundamental intuitions. The first level is constituted by the *most general intuitions* underlying *all* forms of scientific pursuit. We may repeat here that, by stating that these intuitions underlie the pursuit of any science, we do, of course, not want to claim that their contents have to be examined in the science in question. It is the task of the *philosopher* to clarify and describe these primary intuitions in a systematic fashion, to determine their order and their interconnection. Phenomenological philosophers will point out with great emphasis that the systematic unfolding of experience in concepts and categories relies on prescientific familiarity. Man possesses, for instance "understanding of being" before he rises to ontological knowledge. He has experiences of time and space before he begins to philosophize about them. He tends in freedom to certain goals before he selects scientific truth, as such, as his purpose. It is to this prescientific familiarity, and to it alone, that applies Sartre's concept of "pre-ontological comprehension."[135] Later we will have an opportunity to revert to this point.

The second layer of intuitive knowledge is constituted by the understanding of *certain forms of behavior*. MacIver's oft-quoted example may again serve to illustrate this point. Let us assume that we are witnesses of the scene described by him. We *see* that the man *flees* and that the crowd *pursues* him. Note that we do not first see a "locomotion" and then draw conclusions from it, but on the contrary we immediately see the "flight" as well as the

---

[134]Concerning this method, see pp. 266 ff.
[135]Cf. above, p. 47.

"pursuit." Higher animals, e.g., dogs, are likewise capable of this kind of "seeing."

We do not want to consider here the question of how such seeing is possible and will restrict ourselves to the following observation. Both the living being, that is intentionally connected with its environment, and its body movements attuned to its environment constitute meaningful wholes. Hence the living being and its environment are perceived and understood as a single "picture." "Grasping, fleeing, warding-off, seeking," Plessner emphasizes, "as well as the 'dispassionate' forms [of motion], such as going, flying, swimming, and also the forms derived from special instincts, such as the building of a nest, love-making, . . . represent such pictures of motion."[135a] However, to see such a picture, it is necessary to observe the living being in its natural environment. For as soon as the animal is taken out of the milieu to which it is naturally attuned, it no longer attacks, seeks, threatens or flees, but exhibits only reactions in the sense of behaviorism.[136] Its behavior ceases to be intuitively comprehensible. "Wherever," says Plessner, "the purely physiological or physicalistic viewpoint, which certainly is fully justified [in its own realm], becomes the only authoritative standpoint, the connections between body and environment which appear 'like a picture' . . . are replaced by the schematic relationship between stimulus and reaction which can be tested only indirectly in an experiment."[137] Accordingly, certain elementary forms of behavior can be understood intuitively within the framework of a situation that is meaningful for the living being. When they are perceived, they are also understood. In this case intuition and *"Verstehen"* constitute an unbreakable unity.

The third "layer" of phenomena which can be grasped intuitively are certain forms of mimetic expression. This point likewise cannot be denied. Even a little child is sensitive to the smile or the frown of its mother and reacts friendly to the smile

---

135a Helmuth Plessner, "Die Deutung des mimischen Ausdrucks," *Zwischen Philosophie und Gesellschaft*, Bern, 1953, p. 138.
136 Cf. above, pp. 22 ff.
137 *Op. cit.*, p. 139.

but anxiously or defensively to the frown. Here also there is ques.ion of a natural attunement to the surrounding world which, however, in the case of man is primarily a world of persons. Generally speaking, we may say that the expression of joy, agression, fear, sadness and cheerfulness is intuitively grasped and understood.

Reverting to the dispute between MacIver and Lundberg, we would like to remark that the terrified attitude of the fleeing man and the terrifying attitude of the pursuing crowd are "seen" and at the same time understood. A piece of paper, on the other hand, that is whirled around by the wind does not manifest any expression. Anyone who because of objectivistic prejudices does not want to make use of such intuitive data does not speak the language in which he can describe man and things human, for the most elementary relationships between man and man are based on the mutual understanding of attitude and expression. A sociologist who refuses to take these elementary relationships into consideration is not an "understanding witness" with respect to human society.

We want to emphasize that only certain elementary forms of mimetic expression are immediately understood. Others require to be interpreted. While it is true that even in this interpretation intuitive elements play a role, we would like to see an essential difference between these interpretations and immediate intuitive understanding. For an interpretation is always made on the basis of knowledge, experience, and sometimes even of scientific experience, as we will see more in detail later. For this reason it appears desirable to us to make a more careful distinction between immediate intuitive understanding and interpretation than is made by Plessner.

To Understand and to Misunderstand. An important remark, however, needs to be added. We do not at all want to assert that intuitive knowledge of behavior and expression leads infallibly to true results. In this respect our concept of intuition differs from that of Bergson. For Bergson, it is true that intuition means coinciding with that which is most intimate and unique in the

165

other person. In our conception, intuition means the confident attitude of a knower for whom things are as he sees them. It is of intuition conceived in this way that we want to make the following assertions:

1. It is the necessary starting point of all sciences of experience.

2. Every science of experience is a critical selection, complementation and elaboration of the intuitive data; hence its terminus does not at all coincide with its starting point.

3. When those who pursue the human sciences proceed with their critique, they should positively take into consideration the possibility that the behavior and the expression of persons are as they are "seen."

The first two of these points have already been sufficiently illustrated. Regarding the last point, some may think that its formulation is somewhat too prudent. Yet, phenomenologists point out that in the intuitive understanding on the level of behavior and mimetic expression there can be question also of an *intuitive misunderstanding*. Plessner, for example, speaks of the "layer of conduct" in which "strictly speaking, intuitibility and intelligibility are inseparably given together, so that the conduct cannot be perceived without being at least first interpreted, respectively, *misinterpreted*.[138] And with respect to mimetic expression the same author says, "In making their experiments, the authors have observed that the interpretations are subject to considerable variations because the mimetic pictures are subject to several spheres of expression."[139] Accordingly, both behavior and expression may have two or even more meanings. For this reason to understand may indeed contain the danger of misunderstanding.

Some sociologists and psychologists conclude therefore that intuitive understanding must be wholly rejected as a source of

---

[138] *Op. cit.*, p. 142, author's italics.

[139] *Op. cit.*, p. 176. Plessner uses the plural because the experiments in question were made in collaboration with Buytendijk.

knowledge.[140] We are unable to share this view, for what has more than one meaning may certainly not be considered to be meaningless. On the contrary, naive prescientific understanding is a source of knowledge which must be used, but *critically,* in the pursuit of human science.

How is such a critical use possible? Plessner provides us with a valuable indication when he states emphatically: "The question whether someone is angry, jealous, sad, happy, jovial, whether he is ashamed, whether he is sorry or merely acts as if he is really filled with this affection, this question is settled within the framework of the actual *situation* by a consideration of the holistic characteristics of the behavior."[141] Accordingly, the critical examination of intuitive knowledge will have to be made in situations, more specifically, in situations or series of situations which within the framework of a given science can be considered comparable situations.

Let us assume, for example, that we have spontaneously conceived someone's smile as an expression of derision. In the course, however, of systematic observation the person in question reveals himself as rather uncertain, hesitant and clumsy, smiling whenever he comes face to face with difficulties. In such a case we will conclude from the holistic character of his behavior that his smile is an expression of embarrassment and not of derision.

To give another example, we see someone laugh and suspect that the laugh is "hysterical." Something in the behavior and in the expression of the person, something that is difficult to put into words, tells us that his laugh has to be *interpreted*. This impression may be true or false. To solve the doubt, it is necessary to make a long clinical observation and to compare the person's behavior with normal behavior in known situations. In this way it is possible to determine whether or not the sensory, intellectual and moral symptoms occur which together constitute the, admittedly ambiguous, picture of the illness called "hysteria." There

---

[140]Cf., e.g., Th. Abel, The Operation Called "Verstehen," *American Journal of Sociology,* vol. 54 (1948-49), pp. 221 ff.; Lundberg, *Foundations of Sociology,* pp. 51 ff.

[141]*Op. cit.,* p. 176.

exist empirical methods allowing the psychiatrist to verify the diagnosis "hysteria." The reason for applying this medical apparatus usually lies in an intuitive impression. The patient's expression reveals something, even though that which he expresses can be explained in many different ways.

Accordingly, within the framework of our view conduct remains conduct, it is not empiristically reduced to a series of "reactions to stimuli." Mimetic action likewise remains mimetic and is not reduced to muscular and glandular processes. Conduct and mimetic action differ essentially from the "behavior" of the behaviorists because they have a meaning that can be understood or misunderstood. Whether or not prescientific understanding has seen the true meaning is something that can be determined only on the level of scientific research.

Detour or Starting Point? A difficulty makes itself felt here. If ultimately scientific research has to decide, the objection can be made that the only crucial point is precisely this scientific investigation. The only thing that counts will be the scientific observation, the experiment, the inquiry, the study of documents, combined with the correct and, if possible, mathematico-s.atistical interpretation of the obtained results. Thus it will be useless to take into account an intuitive understanding which can very well be nothing but a misunderstanding. A neopositivist or representative of the Vienna Circle could appeal here to "Occam's razor," for the detour by way of *"Verstehen"* would appear to him to be merely a "multiplication of beings without necessity."

In reply, we may point out that this objection contains a faulty way of putting the problem. Every investigation is the investigation of something. Prior to scientific knowledge, this "something" consists necessarily of data known only through intuition. As we have shown above, this assertion applies also to the physical sciences.[142] The only disputed point is whether or not the human sciences must begin with the same "something" as their starting point. Do they have to take into consideration only those phenomena which appear in the "universe of discourse" of the physical

---

[142]Cf. above, pp. 109 ff.

6. Prescientific Intuition

sciences (including biology and physiology) or is there also something else that exists for them? This question amounts to asking whether or not Carnap's theory of science is acceptable. Our reply has been in the negative. The specific task of human science is the investigation of the typically human aspect of man. But *the human element is human only because it can be understood or misunderstood by human beings.* Accordingly, anyone who wants to abstract completely from *"Verstehen"* simply deprives human science of its object and changes it into physical science.

To illustrate the point by means of a different metaphor, the human element, as understood or misunderstood by human beings, constitutes the raw material of the human sciences. It may be compared with iron ore containing phosphorus. One who does not want to use this ore because it is impure neglects a rich source of wealth, and one who uses it, as it is found in nature, will produce only an inferior kind of iron. There is, however, a third possibility—namely, to subject the ore to a process of refining.

Reverting to our starting point, we may offer the following conclusion. Prescientific understanding of conduct does not offer any guarantee for the correctness and truth of this understanding. It contains merely an indication guiding the student of man with respect to the question of the direction in which the truth may be found. For this reason he will not consider the data of prescientific intuition as a detour but as a starting point.

169

7. THE PROBLEMS OF "VERSTEHEN": HYPOTHESIS AND INTERPRETATION

Intuition and Interpretation. The question may be asked of how every form of interpretation differs from naive intuition. The reply to this question has been prepared in the preceding pages. It may perhaps be summarized by saying that we always interpret on the basis of "something." This "something" is known through perception, memory, experience, etc. We think that we know it certainly—so certainly that we are willing to use it as a springboard for guesses, interpretations and conjectures. In other words, we make a clear-cut, albeit only implicit, distinction between facts of which we are certain, and that which we merely surmise. Consequently, interpretation is not at all a naive act.

There is, for example, a great difference between the "seeing" of aggressive behavior and the interpretation of an action as aggressive. In the first case I cannot do otherwise than conceive the behavior spontaneously as aggressive; in the second I compare several experiences, take the circumstances into account and arrive at the conclusion that I can understand the holistic character of this behavior only by conceiving it as the expression of aggressive intentions. In making this interpretation, I realize that I cannot wholly abstract from the fact that I am a European or American, an adult, a man and not a woman, etc., and that the experience on which I rely is therefore one-sided and limited. For this reason I present my opinion only as a provisional interpretation. I remain constantly ready to revise my interpretation in the light of new facts.

Precisely because of the careful fashion in which it weighs everything, interpretation plays an important role in science. The empirical sciences know two very different forms of interpretation, viz., anticipating interpretation and interpretation in the strict sense of the term.

Hypothesis. The anticipating interpretation is usually called *hypothesis.* It plays an extremely important role in some human sciences, such as psychology and sociology. Progress in these disciplines is accomplished largely by investigating whether a par-

170

ticular hypothesis should be retained or rejected. If the results are in favor of the hypothesis, its content may be incorporated into science as a provisionally justified conclusion.

The formulation of an hypothesis is, of course, not the first step of research, but has to be preceded by a first examination of the realm under investigation. Once, however, the man of research has become somewhat orientated, it becomes meaningful and useful for him to guide and direct his work by raising a specific question. Because asking a question implies some kind of foreknowledge of what the question means, any attempt to raise a problem always goes beyond the purely factual. The hypothesis, however, has the form of an accurately formulated assertion and even *has to* have this form since it is to be either established or refuted.

We consider it justified to call the hypothesis an *anticipating interpretation*. It runs ahead of the results to be achieved by the research, the experiment, the inquiry or the observation, and for this reason we call it "anticipating." It is based on a certain orientation in a given realm, on the knowledge of a number of facts, but it goes beyond these facts, and for this reason we may call it an "interpretation." Immediately, however, the question arises of *how an hypothesis is arrived at*.

The various scientific and popular text books say very little about this question. They concentrate on the preparatory activities, such as the defining of fundamental concepts, the first orientation in the realm of inquiry, and the formulation of provisional questions. They speak also extensively about the demands to be met by a good hypothesis. The various authors, moreover, are fairly unanimous with respect to these phases of the empirical inquiry. However, they say little or nothing about the question of how the hypothesis arises, and the little said by one author is more often than not flatly contradicted by the other.

Two extreme examples may serve to illustrate the point. According to Karl Popper, one has to derive from an existing axiomatic system judgments that are subject to falsification. Such empirically falsifiable judgments are hypotheses, which are assumed to be valid as long as they cannot be replaced by better

controllable hypotheses or falsified by experience.[143]   According
to G. J. Kruyer, on the other hand, the formulation of an hypothesis is "an exciting adventure beyond the boundaries of the
known." Although this adventure is aided by all kinds of means,
such as comparisons with other sciences and the search for
analogies, ultimately the hypothesis arises through intuition, i.e.,
"through a sudden illumination of the mind."[144]

We would like to point out that in reality the development of
science, at least in the realm of empirical human science, is simpler
than these two authors assume. A concrete example may serve
to support this assertion. Two educationists, M. Mathijssen and
G. Sonnemans, a few years ago conducted an inquiry about
"scholastic choice and scholastic success on the 'preparatory higher
education' level and the 'advanced lower' level in the [Dutch]
Province of North Brabant." The work in which they published
the results of their research begins with the following two main
hypotheses: 1) "The potential of intelligence of North Brabant's
children does not permit them to share more widely in 'preparatory higher education' or 'advanced lower education'." 2) "North
Brabant possesses a reservoir of intelligence which cannot be
developed by the type of education given in 'preparatory higher'
or 'advanced lower' schools."[145]   Nothing in their book suggests
that these two hypotheses have been deduced from an axiomatic
system, and the Preface makes it extremely improbable that the
hypotheses in question have resulted from a sudden illumination
of the authors. On the contrary, this kind of hypotheses arises
from an understanding interpretation of a set of problems that
is still prescientific. The term "prescientific," however, needs
to be rendered more precise here. For obvious reasons the set
of problems, as it presented itself to the educational authorities
of North Brabant, can be called "prescientific" only in a restricted
sense. It does not mean "naive," "intuitive," or "uncritical." The

---

143*Logik der Forschung,* sect. 11, pp. 22 f. Cf. *Logic of Scientific Research,* pp. 49 f.

144*Observeren en redeneren. Een inleiding tot kennisvorming in de
sociologie,* Meppel, 1959, pp. 148 f.

145*Schoolkeuze en schoolsucces by V. H. M. O. en U. L. O. in Noord-
Brabant,* Tilburg, n. d., p. 10.

educationists in question were experienced, in some cases even very experienced. Nonetheless, the result of their experiences had not yet been scientifically organized, compared, complemented and critically verified.

The hypotheses, moreover, were formulated by the authors partly on the basis of their own "prescientific" experiences or those of others. In reference to the investigators, then, the term "prescientific experiences" means *"pre-experimental"* or *"pre-research"* experiences. For the hypothesis goes beyond the scientific data known to them. And as Kruyer correctly remarks, imagination is needed to transcend these data. This need, however, should not be interpreted in the sense that the man of research gives free rein to his imagination. One who formulates hypotheses is not given to fancies but allows his imagination to be guided by a kind of *"Verstehen."* There is question here of "understanding" what is possible in a given realm and what is impossible. It is because of this pre-experimental understanding that the man of research is able to select "plausible" hypotheses from a large number of possible hypotheses, which may include also fantastic suppositions.

This prescientific or pre-experimental understanding likewise contains a danger of misunderstanding. However, the result of the research provides an opportunity to test the hypothesis and to reveal whether or not the prescientific interpretation was correct.

The Understanding Interpretation. In the realm of the historical sciences the *understanding interpretation* corresponds to the hypothesis of the psychologists and the sociologists. At first, this correspondence may seem surprising. Nevertheless, the divergence of the two methods is not as great as may appear at first. There exists definite points of agreement. The historian has to begin with a first orientation in the realm which he wishes to study, such as the history of a period, a people, an institution or a group of persons. He already knows many facts, sometimes even a superabundance of facts. The important point for him is to discover a connection that appears "plausible," and this plausibility is present when the connection makes the "meaning" of the historical events intelligible. The discovery of such a connection demands that the historian transcend the level of the purely factual. In doing this, he too will reveal that he is possessed of a constructive or reconstructive imagination. In a sense the picture he draws of the events may be considered an hypothesis. True, an historical interpretation cannot be tested as rigorously as an experimental hypothesis, in the broad sense of the term "experimental." Nevertheless, it is not correct to think that no verification is possible in the realm of the historical sciences. Historians also constitute a "research society," and those of them who are equally or even more familiar with the historical data in question will criticize the proposed interpretation and consider it either justified or unjustified. They will examine whether the interpretation does not do violence to known facts, whether it does not disregard certain data, and above all, whether the proposed interconnection makes the historical events more intelligible than other interpretations.

A previously mentioned example may serve to clarify this point. Theoretically it is possible to write the history of France at the end of the eighteenth and the beginning of the nineteenth centuries by starting with the hypothesis that Napoleon was nothing else than a base criminal. A number of facts could be adduced that can be interpreted in this way. However, there are also other data which contradict such an interpretation. The result is that the total picture of the historical events presented on the basis of this hypothesis will be distorted. It does not enable us to understand the period any better. For this reason the majority of historians will undoubtedly make the judgment that the hypothesis, "Napoleon was a criminal and nothing else," cannot withstand the test of critique. In this way the interpretation in question will then have shown itself useless, it will not have been confirmed.

Explicit and Implicit Empathy (*Nachfühlen*). There is one point in which the historian's approach differs from the methods attuned to experiments, viz., the fact that he deals explicitly with human purposes and values. We must therefore attempt to determine the typical attitude of the historian which enables him to understand the feelings, strivings, projects and ideals of historical persons without making them his own. How is it possible for him to "feel with" these persons without becoming partial, without giving in to passions and emotions, without sacrificing his scientific superiority?

The term "sympathy," in its broad sense, suggests itself spontaneously here. There is indeed question of a kind of *pathos,* i.e., the historian's understanding interpretation involves him with his entire humanity, *including his emotional life.* No matter how one looks at it, his emotional sympathy is not an obstacle but a condition for the understanding of man as man. On the other hand, this emotional involvement should not be misunderstood. Let us render the expression more precise. Max Scheler's careful analyses have taught us to distinguish many forms of sympathy and two of these need to be considered here. They are *"Mitfühlen"* and *"Nachfühlen."* As Scheler remarks, "From sympathy in the proper sense we must first of all distinguish every relationship which serves only to grasp, understand, and possibly to consider with empathy *("Nachfühlen")* the experiences of the other."[146] For instance, we are able to understand with a feeling of empathy that a child cries because it is hungry, without "sharing the feeling" of hunger. While sympathy has many grades, going as far as emotional identification *("echte Einsfühlung"),* empathy "always remains within the sphere of a cognitive relationship and is not an act implying moral relevance. The reputable historian, the novelist, the dramatist have to possess the gift of empathy on a very high level, but they do not need to have any sympathy for their objects or persons."[147]

Accordingly, empathy is not at all a mysterious or mystical act. It is something which we constantly practice and have to practice in daily life, viz., the emotional or co-emotional grasping of values and aims which are decisive for *others.* Although this act is personal, it is not arbitrary. It enables us to understand the conduct of our fellow men. For this reason the ability to have empathy is an indispensable instrument of the historian. By making use of it he does not become a novelist, for the results of his

---

[146]*Wesen und Formen der Sympathie,* Frankfort a.M., 5th ed., 1948, pp. 3f.
[147]*Ibid.*

emotional understanding are exposed to the critique of a "research society," they are judged by certain criteria which, despite the lack of their exactness, are nonetheless rigorous.

It is not only for the historian that the ability to understand human strivings, emotions and passions with empathy is indispensable. Take, for example, the case of a psychologist-psychiatrist who has to deal with a paranoiac. So far as diagnosis and therapy are concerned, it is, of course, not at all desirable that the psychiatrist share the feelings of his patient. The greater his tranquility, the better he will work. However, let us make the unrealistic assumption that our psychiatrist does not at all know what anxiety is and especially not the anxiety of one who feels himself persecuted. In such a case he would be unable to make an adequate diagnosis and to apply an effective therapy. An anthropologist, likewise, will not share in the magic beliefs of primitive tribes. For instance, he will not believe in the real influence of a fertility rite. Nevertheless, if he cannot understand emphatically the value which fertility plays in the lives of these people, he will not be able to present a correct picture of these lives.

One would look in vain for empathic understanding in the empirical research which tests the truth of an hypothesis. Yet the seeming absence of affectivity in the man of research should not deceive us. The *emotional understanding* of the experimentalist (in the broadest sense of the term) *precedes the formulation of the hypothesis.* It is *implicitly* contained in his prescientific experience, his prescientific exploration of his research area, and his prescientific formulation of the problem. It is there implicitly, even when it is not mentioned at all explicitly. Obviously, a sociologist, for instance, would not be able to formulate any important hypothesis if he did not understand the meaning of "need," "sexuality," "conflict," "power," "oppression," and "prestige," if he did not understand the emotional echoes which these terms evoke in individuals and groups. Yet this empathic understanding remains, as it were "frozen" in his work of research. The sociologist does not have to manifest his sympathy. On the contrary, a certain absence of affectivity is expected of him. It is

7. Hypothesis and Interpretation

here that lies the difference between the description of experimental investigation and the writing of history. The historian has to depict the past, to evoke it and to make it visible again. In doing so, he cannot *completely* hide his own inner state of affectivity, even though it is true that in this realm certain temperamental differences manifest themselves. He has, as it were, to "live-with" his characters both positively and negatively, to make them live again for us with him. Briefly, he is obliged to *express* his empathic understanding, while one who pursues experimental research in a human science does not have this obligation.

8. THE PROBLEMS OF "VERSTEHEN": VISION

The Indispensable Character of "Vision." Another important phenomenon needs to be distinguished from prescientific intuition, hypothesis and interpretation—namely, so-called *vision*. Naive intuition precedes any form of science and, consequently, is the necessary starting point of scientific research. Hypothesis and interpretation play a role in this research itself; hence they contribute to the formation of science in general and of human science in particular. *Vision,* on the other hand, presupposes that a science exists already. Its possibility is not conditioned by an integral knowledge but by a general grasp of all known facts, hypotheses, and plausible interpretations which refer to a given realm or a given set of problems. Accordingly, vision is not created from a vacuum, but flows from knowledge, orderly knowledge, lucid knowledge. Yet it goes beyond the well-trodden paths of scientific pursuits. For this reason the term "vision" is very appropriate. He who has it "sees" something, a new relationship, a new meaning, a new method to discover interconnections and meanings. The known facts arrange themselves, as it were, spontaneously and show forth a new "meaning." Or the old means of research seem unsatisfactory and the man of research begins to see how they can be improved, perfected or replaced. In this way a new methodic idea is born, an existing scientific apparatus is changed or a new branch of science is brought to life.

Accordingly, it is not correct to say that the development of science is exclusively dependent on the careful and conscientious examination of details. This detailed research is, of course, indispensable, but the intellectual mastery of the entire research area gives rise to an understanding of a higher order. Albert Einstein speaks in this context about "the search for those highly universal . . . laws from which a picture of the world can be obtained by pure deduction. There is no logical path leading to these . . . laws. They can only be reached by intuition based on something like an intellectual love (*Einfühlung*) of the objects of experience."[148] And Karl Mannheim emphasizes, "In order to know social reality one must have imagination, a particular brand of imagination I

---

[148]*Mein Weltbild,* 1934, p. 168, quoted by K. Popper, *Logik der Forschung,* p. 5, and *Logic of Scientific Research,* p. 32.

should like to call 'realistic' because it does not create fiction but exerts itself in binding together apparently unrelated facts by means of a vision of structural correlation which alone enables us to see the framework into which every fact, even the most casual one, is fitted."[149]

The framework of concepts into which, according to Mannheim, every fact, even the most casual one, must be fitted is, of course, the same as that which we have called above "universe of discourse" and "methodic idea." As an example of how on the basis of an ingenious vision a new branch of science is found as well as a new form of scientific discourse and a new methodic idea, we would like to refer to the discovery of psychoanalysis by Sigmund Freud. From his autobiographical writings it is evident that at first he could rely only on conjectures which he knew to be out of harmony with the current scientific opinions, and that, moreover, the facts brought to his attention by his professors and colleagues did not become significant for him before he had discovered a new connection between these facts. "Breuer," he writes, "[gave preference to] a kind of physiological theory . . . , but I *suspected* rather that there was question of an interplay of forces, of the working of intentions and tendencies."[150] "I had explained the matter *less scientifically,* and *suspected* everywhere tendencies and inclinations."[151] Freud adds, "What I had heard from them [Breuer, Charcot and Chrobak] remained dormant and inactive in me until on the occasion of the cathartic investigations it broke through as a seemingly original perception."[152] The methodic principle discovered in this fashion in its turn becomes a firm foundation, and on its basis new psychiatric and psychological facts can and must be "established." In this sense Freud wrote, "I would be very energetically opposed to it if anyone would want to place the theory of suppression and of resistance among the presuppositions of psychoanalysis instead of among its results."[153]

---

[149] *Essays on Sociology and Social Psychology,* New York, 1953, p. 190.
[150] *Gesammelte Werke,* London, 1940, vol. XIV, "Selbstdarstellung," p. 47.
[151] *Op. cit.,* vol. X, "Zur Geschichte der psychoanalytischen Bewegung," p. 49. Italics of the author.
[152] *Op. cit.,* "Selbstdarstellung," pp. 48 f.
[153] *Op. cit., "Zur Geschichte . . .,"* p. 54.

Three Forms of "Verstehen." In the preceding pages we have made a clear distinction between three forms of understanding, all of which go beyond discursive knowledge. Since the time of Dilthey, however, these three forms have been indiscriminately characterized as "intuition," "vision" or *"Verstehen,"* thus giving rise to a dangerous confusion. For this reason it appears doubly necessary to summarize and complement here the distinctions made in the preceding considerations.

The first kind of *"Verstehen,"* which we have called *prescientific intuition,* refers exclusively to the most elementary data without which man's existence would not be a human existence. It is in this sense that we have called it "fundamental." Because anyone who pursues a science is a human being, no one can begin his research by making abstraction from all elementary evidences. More specifically, in pursuing human science, one cannot abstract from the original understanding of certain forms of conduct and expression. We do not mean, of course, that whatever is naively understood, as it is understood, is also scientifically true. All we want to say is that the content of what is understood constitutes the starting point of a scientific inquiry.

Secondly, in the realm of human science there exists a *"Verstehen"* of certain human situations. This kind of understanding is historically and socially conditioned. It may be implicit in an understanding anticipation, in which case we call it an *hypothesis;* it may also be expressed in a description, and then we speak of an *interpretation.* In any case it has to be tested by means of scientific methods."[154]

Finally, there is a kind of *"Verstehen"* with respect to a scientifically investigated realm, scientific methods and their sets of problems. This kind of *"Verstehen"* we have described as *vision.* The characteristic feature of a vision is that *it cannot be unqualifiedly* tested through facts. For a vision is often accompanied by the discovery of a new methodic idea and this idea is the matrix from which originates an entire series of new facts. It should be evident that these facts therefore cannot constitute

---

[154]In this point we agree with Vercruysse, *op. cit.,* pp. 11-20. However, we do not want to go so far as to characterize *"Verstehen"* as an "independent method."

the touchstone of the vision which has led to their discovery. The above-mentioned example of psychoanalysis is very instructive here. If Freud's vision is correct, "suppression" and "resistance" actually exist but, if his vision is not justified, then "suppression" and "resistance" are mere figments of the imagination.

The criterion, therefore, for the evaluation of a "vision" lies in another and higher order. We have mentioned it before in a different context and may call it the *fruitfulness* of the new vision. This notion of fruitfulness has a very special meaning with respect to the realm of human science. *A vision is fruitful if it gives us a better understanding of man and things human.* It is not always immediately clear whether this fruitfulness is really present or merely apparently so. Sometimes it may happen that the fruitfulness of a new vision reveals itself only after decades of scientific work inspired by it. Only the history of a science, therefore, makes it possible for us to make a *definitive* judgment about the fruitfulness of a vision.

To Understand Understanding. When above we pointed out that a vision of the realm of human science makes us better understand everything human, we implicitly indicated also the second characteristic of this kind of understanding. For it is typical of things human that they are understood or misunderstood by human beings. Hence to understand the human element as such means to understand also the ways in which human beings conceive everything human. Briefly put, all more or less naive ways of judging, evaluating, interpreting and taking a position with respect to human relations, situations, activities, products, artistic creations, etc. in their turn have to be opened up to understanding by means of a vision. It is only in this way that the vision rises to the dignity of being a theory in the realm of human science.

A few examples may serve to illustrate this point. Let us take the phenomenon of "nagualism," which differs from totemism in this that not an entire tribe but an individual person believes that he has a kind of social relationship to a particular animal.[155] The

---

[155]Cf. G. van der Leeuw, *De primitieve mens en de religie,* pp. 18 ff.

external facts connected with this kind of mythical conviction may be described by anyone who happens to come into contact with primitive natives possessing a "nagual." Yet this does not mean that he has reached the level of human science. The question which the cultural anthropologist will have to ask himself is, How does it happen that the primitive person "conceives" his relationship to this particular animal in this way?

An analogous situation exists in the realm of psychology. A pubescent girl, for example, writes in her diary that her father is a tyrant. The investigating psychologist finds that he is just an ordinary family man to whom one can hardly ascribe any authoritarian inclinations. This finding, however, merely supplies the terms of the problems. The real task of the psychologist consists in making it intelligible why pubescent girls can possibly "see" their fathers in this fashion.

On this level elementary understanding is just as much a problem as elementary misunderstanding. We have mentioned, for example, how little children react friendly to a smile and anxiously to a frown. One does not have to be a psychologist to observe these reactions and to draw up statistics about them. The proper character of human psychology consists in providing us with an insight into the ability of babies to understand certain elementary forms of human expression. This task requires a theoretical vision of the essence of child existence, the essence of mimetics, the essence of human relationships, etc. The same applies to the problems of puberty, of "nagualism," and totemism.

We would like to add another remark. There is no doubt about the necessity and the usefulness of knowledge of the facts and understanding of statistically elaborated and scientifically utilizable data pertaining to the various realms of human science. This knowledge may not be undervaluated or overestimated. We may compare it to a springboard. The springboard has no reason for existence unless someone is ready to make a jump. This means that at a given moment someone will have to say what the facts mean, to what extent they express man's understanding or misunderstanding of everything human. In other words, naive understanding and misunderstanding themselves have to be understood in their turn.

8. Vision

From being an *id quo*, a means, they have to become an *id quod*, that which is understood, and this requires a scientific vision.

The Language of Facts. To clarify what we mean by a scientific vision, we may approach the matter from a third angle. In daily life one may sometimes hear the remark that a particular version of an event does not square with the "language of the facts." Strictly speaking, this expression is not correct, for facts do not say anything unless one makes them say something. No matter how plausible the connection of facts may appear, there has to be someone to conceive their connection and to express his thought. Only then does the interconnection exist as an intersubjective datum.

Before, however, one can make the facts speak, he has to be fully familiar with them. If this familiarity is present, if, for example, a man of research has a complete grasp of the facts in a particular empirical realm, then these facts become for him, as it were, "words." In this case the comparison with language is fully applicable. It should be kept in mind, of course, that not everything can be expressed in any language and that no language is the mere sum of all its words. To be able to speak a language, one has to know its structural laws, the way in which its words can be interconnected. To pursue our comparison, our man of research does not merely dominate the vocabulary of his science, but knows also which combinations of words are possible and impossible. He knows also that there are things for which his language does not have any words. Because of this intellectual control, he is able to speak in the language of facts. He is able to express something that itself is not a fact, something that transcends the level of facts. Because of the meaning which can be expressed in the language of facts, the facts themselves also receive meaning. They become meaningful facts. When we speak of vision with respect to a realm of science, we are referring to that which our man of research expresses by means of the facts.

How does a new vision arise? In reply we may point out that the analogy with a literary work of art is very illuminating here. A new scientific vision is born when an ingenious man of science makes the facts say something which hitherto they have

183

not said. The facts, for example, cited by Max Weber in his *Religionssoziologie* were known to the historians, economists and theologians of his time. However, he saw a connection which had escaped his contemporaries and in this way he gave rise to a new vision. It is true, of course, that the successful pursuit of a science leads also to the discoveries of new facts. But a new vision arises only when the man of science brings these new facts into connection with the older facts. To do so, he needs a new synthetizing thought. Just as a poet or litterateur enriches the language to make it say something which hitherto it did not say, so also does the discoverer of new facts enrich the "vocabulary" of the facts. But he becomes an ingenious man of science, comparable to a great poet, only when he uses this enriched vocabulary to express something which hitherto was not expressed—namely, a new vision of the realm of scientific research.

At the Boundary of the "Second Objectivity." The truly great man of science, we have pointed out, says in the language of facts something which itself is no longer a fact. He intentionally aims at something which lies above the level of the "second objectivity." It does not seem too difficult to show the truth of this assertion. An anthropologist who formulates a theory about the nature of totemism, "nagualism," or mythical mentality cannot do so without saying at least implicitly something about what man is, what human consciousness is or how man is related to nature. A psychologist who develops a theoretical vision regarding puberty bases himself on a certain conception of the essence of human existence, of human development and of the culture in which the pubescent human being has to grow up and find his place. An historian who proposes a certain vision of an era has to tell us about the decisive value and aims pursued by the human beings of that era. He cannot do so if he functions merely as a registrar of historical facts, but has to determine his attitude toward these aims and values. We do not mean to say that he has to speak explicitly about his attitude but only that at least his implicit attitude will reveal itself in the way in which he gives expression to the meaning of the historical events in the language of facts. The historian cannot even determine the meaning of a

8. Vision

single historical event without holding at least implicitly a certain view regarding the meaning of the state, rights, economy, religion or similar human values.

All this implies that the objectification making the fact a fact is abolished. As we have pointed out before, it is true that the fact as fact does not say anything about the free human aim and evaluation which gave rise to the fact.[156] Facts may be, as it were, "frozen" in the second objectivity. Ultimately, however, the one who pursues human science will interpret the meaning of the facts in the form of a vision. In this vision there must be at least implicitly question of man's use of his freedom, i.e., to continue our metaphor, the free aims and value judgments which the second objectivity had frozen into facts have to be thawed out.

With the consideration of the vision which is needed in the pursuit of a human science we have reached the boundaries of the second objectivity. The reason why is not difficult to see. In man everything is interconnected with everything. As the old Aristotelian-Scholastic saying goes, "the human soul in a way is everything." As soon as one makes any form of human understanding the object of a human discourse, he has to introduce also other forms. Man's surrounding world is composed of realities as he conceives them theoretically and as he uses or influences them practically. But man's surrounding world constitutes a unity in which everything is connected with everything. It is the whole of all realities existing for him. It is intentionally that we use here the term "realities" and not "things." For invisible realities also codetermine the character of his existence. Mythical, religious, philosophical convictions, political, social, cultural aims, collective, familial and personal ideals and norms influence the way in which man creates and modifies his surrounding world. It would be impossible to pursue human science without taking these realities into account, at least in a implicit fashion.

It is possible, of course, that the cultural anthropologist will speak about myths in such a way that anyone understands at once that for him myths are simply superstitions. The sociologist of religion may be able to see religion as pure "opium for the

---

[156]Cf. above, pp. 14 f.

185

people." The student of man may reject all ideals as metaphysical nonsense. All this, however, does not take away from the fact that these implicitly or explicitly determined attitudes go beyond the level of the second objectivity. In other words, judgments such as "myth is superstition," "religion is opium for the people," and "ideals are metaphysical fancies," may be true or false, but in neither case are they judgments of facts. They are always philosophical or even metaphysical judgments. Even the resolve to call all such judgments meaningless itself is the metaphysical statement of an attitude. Whether one admits this metaphysical character or rejects it with passionate abhorrence does not make the slightest change in its status.

Accordingly, our conclusion may be expressed in the form of a simple dilemma. Either the pursuit of human science is limited to the level of physical science or it is based on the philosophical determination of an attitude. There is no other possibility.

The "Tree of Science." If the question is asked of how our view differs from that of many other theories of science, the reply should be clear. Positivistic, neo-positivistic, logical-positivistic, operationalistic and behavioristic authors endeavor to characterize science as self-contained in a watertight compartment. According to them, science does not owe anything to prescientific experience and, on the other hand, is sharply divided from anything tainted by philosophy or metaphysics. The boundary problem of drawing these dividing lines is the issue which has fascinated all thinkers pertaining to the above-mentioned trends from David Hume to Karl Popper.[157]

We do not believe in the possibility of erecting such watertight compartments, but prefer to compare the life of science to that of other forms of life. Science is, as it were, a tree. It draws its strength from the dark soil of prescientific life and pushes its branches up into the air currents caused by philosophical problems. If it refuses to face these currents, it condemns itself to remain stunted undergrowth.

---

[157]Cf *Logik der Forschung,* pp. 7 ff. or *Logic of Scientific Research,* pp. 34 ff.

C. SCIENCE AND WISDOM

1. CRITICAL CONSIDERATION OF THE SCIENTIFIC ILLUMINATION: FAILING UNIVERSALITY

Community of Specialists. The scientific illumination constitutes the greatest effort of mankind to overcome the limitation, the intellectual immaturity and the narrowness of the everyday worlds. Its purpose is to construct one universal truth destined to replace the many mutually contradictory, ethnic, local and national myths. By eliminating superstitions and prejudices, it aims at making all nations collaborate without hindrance in the further development of the universal scientific doctrine. This doctrine or theory is to be the basis of a universal purposive praxis, viz., technology. Together, these two, science and technology, are to guarantee absolutely that mankind will irresistibly continue its progress.

Now that the era of scientific illumination has gone beyond its culminating point, it may perhaps be possible to present a provisional evaluation of the results attained by it. However, we will prudently restrict ourselves to a single aspect whose evaluation is relatively easy. We mean the question regarding the universality of scientific truth. Has mankind succeeded in finding a "universe of discourse," endowed with binding force for all its members? Has it managed to create a bond, called "science," which unites peoples and nations just as solidly as the myth used to do with respect to individuals belonging to a single world of archaic life?

In reply we may say that one thing is certain—namely, that the negative aim of the scientific illumination has been reached. The phenomenology of an international scientific congress provides us with the proof. In such a congress a theoretical physicist, for example, is able to lecture undisturbedly about the quantum theory. Even if his audience is composed of physicists from the most divergent nations, races and cultural backgrounds, they are able to follow the process of his very abstract thought. For the methodic ideas underlying his explanations are the common intellectual treasure of all specialists in the realm of theoretical

187

physics. For this reason they are able to proceed beyond the boundaries encountered in non-scientific life. The ethnical, religious and national divisions of non-scientific life are at least temporarily replaced by a new unifying bond, viz., the community of specialists.

The remark could be made that this international harmony is found only among those who pursue mathematics and physical science and that the situation is different in the realm of the human sciences. We readily admit that in this realm difficulties accompany the formation of international communities of specialists. Nevertheless, even here it is possible to form harmonious communities. It may be difficult, for example, for a Japanese who has grown up in Shintoism to understand what is meant by Max Weber's "asceticism pursued in the world" of a European Protestant. Nevertheless, by studying the relevant culture and literature for many years and through a certain empathic ability, he will succeed to some extent in understanding this religious attitude of man. The opposite is likewise possible. After many years of study and sojourn in Japan, a Western Protestant may attain a certain understanding of the spirit of the Shintoist tradition. The facts prove this possibility. International congresses are held in which German, Russian, American and Japanese specialists discuss problems of Japanese culture. Accordingly, even in the realm of human science it is possible to overcome the strictures of millenial traditions and to probe the mysteries of a foreign world of life. Here, too, there is question of international societies of specialists and of a discourse that is internationally intelligible.

A "Tower of Babel." There are, however, also other results that become manifest from a phenomenological analysis of the events ocurring at an international scientific congress. True, in the different sections of such a congress there exists in principle a possibility of orienting oneself and of understanding one another within the framework of an internationally established scientific discourse. Within the walls of one and the same room fruitful discussions are possible between men of learning whose nationalities, religions and political convictions are different. But the greatest difficulties arise when any of these specialists goes from

1. Failing Universality

one room to another. It may happen, for example, that an anatomist who strays into a room where certain psychiatrists are lecturing will have the impression of listening to a kind of lyric poetry. The classical philologist does not understand the linguistic problems, which Japanologists are trying to solve. The animal psychologist hardly understands the technical jargon of the clinical psychologists. This difficulty exists even with respect to such a fundamental and apparently simple psychological notion as that of "perception." As F. H. Allport expresses it, "Perception is really in danger of becoming a word with two meanings. The laboratory specialist and the social psychologist scarcely speak the same language.[158] For this reason John Cohen calls psychology "a Tower of Babel for every known and unknown tongue."[159]

Fragmentation is, indeed, a characteristic of scientific life in our time. Gabriel Marcel calls it a Babel-like situation and says, "The thorough specialists hardly enters into communication with anyone except those who pursue the same kind of research, and his work tends to become a closed book for other learned men who specialize in different works of research."[160]

The Origin of this Tower of Babel Situation. If the question is asked of how this situation could arise, the characterization of the "second objectivity" offers us a measure of understanding.

First of all, as we have seen, scientific research is possible through the discovery and application of methodic ideas. At first, these ideas were relatively simple and based on a single fundamental thought. At present, however, we have to deal with series of methodic principles based on one another in such a way that understanding the second series presupposes familiarity with the first. For this reason only specialists are able to dominate these complex methodic ideas and to apply them correctly.

Secondly, as we have seen, the usefulness of an empirical method has to become evident from its applicability. As a result, the methods used are devised and carefully attuned in reference

---

[158]*Theories of Perception and the Concept of Structure,* New York, 1955, p. 368.
[159]*Humanistic Psychology,* London, 1958.
[160]*Le déclin de la sagesse,* pp. 105 f.

to certain research situations. Some of these situations are of a very special nature, so that only a specialist who has spent many years studying such a special situation can claim that the methodic idea in question forms part and parcel of the scientific apparatus which he fully dominates. A psychologist, for instance, must have spent much time in experimenting with animals before he is able critically to evaluate the experiments of other animal psychologists.

Accordingly, the ever-increasing specialization is not a purely concomitant phenomenon of modern scientific life, but rather flows from the very essence of the "second objectivity." In many cases the man of science cannot be anything else than a specialist who has acquired a thorough experience in a determined category of research situations. The inevitable result is that his scientific horizon becomes more and more restricted. His "universe of discourse" expands in the ever-growing number of specialistic concepts and at the same time shrinks with respect to the realm covered by his scientific knowledge. He gradually becomes more and more a "scientific barbarian."

Thirdly, the development in question is not restricted to scientific *thought*. Not only the ideas and concepts are complex and exceedingly specialized, but the same is true of the language in which these ideas are embodied. All kinds of technical jargons arise which mean nothing at all to any outsider. Marcel speaks in this context about a "multiplication of hermetic languages."[161]

Finally, the scientist is not only a human being but also *one* human being. In the individual the sphere of scientific thought and action is not hermetically separated from the sphere of will and emotions. The latter will sooner or later be influenced by the former, and this influence makes itself felt in the contemporary life of science. For one specialist not merely fails to understand the language of the other but will sometimes also be inclined to call the other's language "unscientific nonsense." The concerns, for example, of the clinical psychologist and the psychotherapist are usually without interest for the animal psychologist and he will be inclined to view their activities as a kind of magic, unworthy of modern scientific pursuits. Many an anthropologist

---

[161] *Ibid.*

with a positive orientation, likewise, assumes a sceptical attitude in regard to the results attained by the interpretation of myths, and numerous demographers are barely able to conceal their scorn for the endeavors of a sociologist who seeks his orientation in the sciences of the mind.

In this way one can understand that different communities of researchers do not understand one another because they *do not want* to understand one another. They are unable to reconcile what the other specialists are doing with their own idea of science. The various groups of theorists are often suffering from prejudices, they fall apart into all kinds of clans which live in an atmosphere of mutual distrust, aversion and scorn.

Shattered Truth. But, one may object, was not the scientific illumination originally a movement to eradicate all prejudices? Did it not aim at breaking away the narrow horizons of the old worlds of clan-like life? Was not universal truth supposed to become the bond uniting all men and thus safeguarding progress? What has happened to the "republic of letters," spoken of by the ancient humanists? Where is the much-vaunted "brotherhood" of the men of science?

With these critical questions we return to our starting point. As we have seen, the scientific illumination has succeeded in stripping the old worlds in which men lived of their intellectual value. It did not succeed, however, in discovering a universal truth capable of binding rational beings together in a human way. The old communities, based on familial, ethnical, mythical and magical traditions, have been replaced by new communities founded on scientific visions, but the latter show no more mutual understanding than the former. Each of the various research societies is proud of the limited truth aspect revealed in its own perspective, but unable to situate this truth with respect to the truth of a different research society. It is for this reason that the insights gained through specialistic investigations lack the power to found the one truth of science. It is as if the "priests of positive science" belong to different sects which despise and excommunicate one another. Thus the one "religion" of mankind, based on scientific understanding, of which Auguste Comte had such great expectations, has remained a mere dream.

Accordingly, the universal validity of insights gained by objective science is in a precarious position. Even the purest representatives of the illumination disagree about the extent to which this validity should be admitted or rejected. Thus the scientific insights reveal themselves bereft of absolutely binding power. The result of this disagreement manifests itself with abundant clarity: *truth is shattered and mankind with it.*

The question which imposes itself here is whether this failure of the scientific illumination is not connected with a certain degeneration of scientific thought, known as "scientism."

2. CRITICAL CONSIDERATION OF THE SCIENTIFIC ILLUMINATION: THE NAIVE CHARACTER OF SCIENTISM

Scientism. By the term *scientism* we indicate here the conviction that science as a theory would be capable of solving all riddles of human existence and in the practical realm would be able to guarantee man's unlimited control of nature. We may note at once that this conviction is not indissolubly connected with the serious pursuit of science and that it may not even be considered a characteristic of the scientific illumination. It was unknown to such prominent men of science as Kepler, Linnaeus and Newton. In our time, likewise, and perhaps even especially in our time, there are many outstanding scientists who eschew the scientistic attitude. Scientism is not the essence of the scientific illumination but a degenerative phenomenon.

Historically speaking, the nineteenth century was the era of scientism. It was the century in which Karl Marx' "scientific" socialism thought itself called to offer a definitive solution for the economic, political and social problems of entire mankind, the century in which Ernst Meumann did not hesitate to claim that his "scientific" pedagogy could answer all educational questions on the basis of his experiments. In that century the learned biologist Ernst Haeckel seriously thought that he had solved *the* riddles of the world by means of a few popular-scientific considerations. His work, *The Riddles of the Universe*,[162] sold 400,000 copies in its German editions and appeared also in many translations. Apparently there was a widespread conviction that for a philosopher-scientist, famous for the latest scientific discoveries, there could not be any secrets.

In the following critique we intend to show that the scientistic viewpoint about the nature of science is fundamentally naïve. This expression does not mean that the scientistic man of science is gullible. It may very well happen that in the work he does in his laboratory, clinic, museum or study he is exceptionally prudent, exact and critical. But in that case his fundamentally naïve atti-

---

[162]*Die Welträtsel. Gemeinverstandliche Studien über monistische Philosophie*, 1st ed., Bonn, 1899. English ed., New York, 1900.

tude will reveal itself even more strongly, for with him there is, of course, no question of the trusting attitude of a primitive who in a wholly uncritical fashion assumes that things are as he sees them. Our learned man of science is high above such a naïve attitude—so high even that he unwittingly falls into another self-deception—namely, a *naïve attitude of a higher order.*

The "Second Naïve Attitude." What is this fundamentally naïve attitude of the scientist? It consists in this that *he forgets to take into consideration that his entire scientific discourse is based on idealizing presuppositions.* Whether these presuppositions are of a material or formal nature, their result is that his discourse is artificially circumscribed and limited. While this idealization makes it possible to describe systematically those aspects of reality which can be grasped by this idealization, it implies also that it is impossible even to speak of the other aspects of reality within the framework of the idealization. This is the price to be paid for the artificial restriction.

The more exact a science is and the more abstract its idealizations are, the more restricting also are its boundaries. Those who pursue it have to accept that many important things escape them. The partisan of scientism, in the pejorative sense of the term, however, reverses this relationship. He is convinced that nothing of importance escapes him, for whatever escapes him is "unimportant," "meaningless," "purely subjective," "emotional," or "metaphysical." (Note that, strictly speaking, he cannot even call anything "unimportant" in the discourse of his own science.)

The English physicist and astronomer Arthur Eddington criticizes the typically naïve attitude of the scientistic man of research in his well-known humorous illustration. He compares him with a zoologist who investigates how many fishes there are in a lake. Having only a net with two inch openings, he begins his work by formulating the axiom: "A fish is an animal with a diameter of more than two inches." If anyone interrupts his work by pointing out this definition simply begs the issue, his typical reply is, "Are you by any chance a metaphysician?"[163]

---

[163]*The Philosophy of Physical Science,* New York, 1949, p. 16. We have modified Eddington's example somewhat.

2. The Naive Character of Scientism

A similar ostrich-like attitude exists in the realm of human science. Kurt Lewin, for instance, gives the following advice: "Only ask the questions in your research that you can answer with the techniques you can use. If you can't learn to ignore the questions you are not prepared to answer definitely, you will never answer any."[164] The similarity of the attitude recommended by Lewin with that of Eddington's zoologist is very striking. Both ignore "uncatchable fishes." The characteristics of the scientistic self-deception contained in this attitude reveal themselves very clearly. Those who suffer from it do not hesitate to adapt their methodic ideas to the available scientific apparatus and they are blind with respect to the fragmentary character of knowledge gained in this fashion. The scientist, in the pejorative sense, does not accept that the truth discovered by him is only a particle of truth, and he forgets how misleading it can be to offer such a particle of truth as *the* truth unqualified.

This self-deception may assume extreme forms. Some of these scientists experiment with rats and think that they acquire thereby understanding of behavior as such. They observe how a few animals learn in an artificial environment and then formulate laws about learning *as such*. Others investigate the way of life of a few primitive tribes and draw conclusions about human nature in *general*. However, we are not especially concerned with such obvious derailments, for they are outgrowths, albeit typical outgrowths. What concerns us here is the naïve attitude which characterizes the scientistic pursuit of research *as such*. In the following pages we will present *three typical forms of this naïve attitude*—namely, *axiological, existential, and metaphysical naïveness*.

Axiological Naïveness. As we have seen before, anthropological research is of necessity entangled in the problems of values and purposes. This assertion applies, for example, to the historical sciences in the broadest sense of the term. The historian endeavors to describe an event with the same rigorous objectivity as the astronomer uses in relating an eclipse of the sun. A famous

---

[164]"Field Theory in Social Sciences," *Theoretical Papers,* New York, 1951.

saying of Tacitus, for instance, indicates that he wanted to write the annals of the Roman Empire *sine ira et studio,* "without rancor and prejudice." The modern demand of demonstrability and verifiability has given new luster to the historian's ideal of remaining emotionally aloof. Scientific objectivity, it is said, may not be jeopardized by sympathy.

On the other hand, however, the historian wants to make the events comprehensible by laying bare the motives and purposes of the persons and groups who played a role in them. He will speak therefore about economic, social, political and religious convictions. In doing so, he cannot avoid speaking of real or assumed impoverishment, real or assumed oppression, real or assumed religious ideals. He will have to make a decision regarding their real or assumed character. He will have to speak about the various positive and negative values in such a way that their meaning for the people of the era described becomes clear to all. For otherwise the historical figures become like schizophrenes whose actions, in the words of Karl Jaspers, are "incomprehensible."[165]

A strict positivist could, of course, make the firm resolution to abstain from making any decision. Without assuming any attitude at all, he may want to merely describe the events as they have happened and in the order in which they have happened. He wants to restrict his role to that of a chronicler. Even then, however, he cannot avoid, e.g., to devote 100 pages to Napoleon and only two to Marshal Ney, or he will consecrate an entire chapter to the socio-economic causes of the French Revolution and only a paragraph or two to the personal career of Mirabeau. This difference is enough to reveal the preference of the historian in question and to manifest implicitly his vision of history. In other words, in the realm of history there is no such thing as a "viewpointless" viewpoint.

Here lies the difficulty encountered by anyone who pursues a "boundary science." The axiological question is inherent in any form of history writing.[166] In this respect every historian

---

[165]*Allgemeine Psychopathologie,* Berlin, 5th ed., 1948, pp. 651 and 691.

[166]We do not mean to say that the axiological question plays a role only in the historical sciences. On the contrary, to a greater or lesser extent it is inherent in any human science.

has his own "style," his own way of solving the difficulties. If, however, the historian proceeds scientistically, he fosters the illusion that he is able to reach two contradictory ends at the same time. On the one hand, he wants to function only as the detached registrar of human behavior but, on the other, he thinks that he knows the meaning of human history. This is being naïve.

Existential Naïveness. This kind of naïve attitude is found especially among certain psychologists. Every psychologist ultimately shares Sartre's ambition perfectly to understand the individual man in his totality, and this means that all his concrete ways of acting, desires, aims, emotions, and value determinations have to be made comprehensible as flowing from a single fundamental choice[167] (or, if anyone prefers, a fundamental conflict, a disposition, etc.). Every psychologist dreams of obtaining a crystal-clear picture of this unique person in all his manifestations and in the most hidden recesses of his mind.

On the other hand, the psychologist wants to proceed empirically. He has, for example, a reliable method to "measure" intelligence, he knows how to go to the bottom of an emotional conflict, he possesses a typology of dispositions. Briefly put, he disposes of a veritable arsenal of methodic ideas. All these ideas, however, are based on the principle of the "twofold track." Intelligence, emotional conflict and disposition can be empirically determined only insofar as they can be systematically compared. Whether the comparison is made concretely, as in an intelligence test, or abstractly, as in classifying a disposition in a certain typological category, it should be evident that the two aims cannot go together. Their opposition may be expressed very succinctly by saying that the empirical psychologist tries to grasp the incomparable by means of systematic comparisons.

No psychologist can escape from this inner tension, but not all meet it in the same way. The careful psychologist is aware of the difficulty. He knows that in the language of facts he aims at something which is no longer a fact—namely, individual existence in its unicity or, in more scholastic terms, the person in

---

[167]Cf. above, pp. 36 f.

his incommunicability. The psychologist who adheres to scientism, however, does not see any difficulty here. He thinks that by mere skill in handling certain methods he will succeed also in fathoming the mysteries of human existence. This is being naïve.

Metaphysical Naïveness. All these illusions have their ultimate source in one fundamental naïveness, the *natural cognitive attitude,* so often described by Husserl. However, we do not wish to make here simply an appeal to Husserl, for we do not think that his phenomenological reduction and transcendental idealism offer a solution to the problems facing us.[168] Our critique of the natural cognitive attitude will be simpler but no less radical.

Let us begin with a few of the sensational scientific discoveries made in the past few decades. It is undeniably true that entire sectors of reality whose very existence was not even suspected by the past generation have now become the subject matter of scientific inquiry and discussion. Our scientists are rightly proud of these successes. However, let us ask one of these specialists how the various newly discovered sectors of reality are interconnected. What, for instance, is the relationship between the atoms of Bohr and Heisenberg and the realm of unconscious drives described by Freud? What is the connection of these drives with the genes spoken of by the specialists in the theory of heredity, such as T. H. Morgan? Very likely the man of science who is questioned in this way will reply by shrugging his shoulders. He does not know the answer and is not even interested in it. He is a specialist, interested in what happens in his laboratory, during his consultation hours or in his clinic. He is interested also in the laboratories, office hours and clinics of his fellow specialists and of representatives of allied disciplines. But he does not know relationships that are broader, and in his capacity as a specialist he does not have to know them.

Nevertheless, everything is not said with the mere observation that our man of science does not know the answer and is not even interested in it. He does not know it if by knowing is meant to know things in an objectively "observable" relationship. Yet

---

[168]Cf. our critique of Husserl in *The Soul of Metaphysical and Empirical Psychology,* 2nd impr., Pittsburgh, 1961, pp. 47-55.

2. The Naïve Character of Scientism

he is *confident* that the sectors of reality which are investigated by wholly different kinds of specialists are interconnected with his own sector in one way or another. For, that which our specialist calls "his field" is, at it were, surrounded by "bordering fields." These bordering fields, he trusts, will be connected again to other realms of reality through objectively observable relationships (in the sense of "second objectivity"), and so on. Note this "and so on." It expresses an "empty" anticipation—empty because it does not have any content. As Husserl says it, the *"fundamental form of the 'and so on,'* . . . which has its subjective correlate in *'one can always again,'*. . .is clearly an idealization, for *de facto* no one 'can always again'."[169] Nevertheless, our man of science cannot avoid making such an idealizing assumption which runs ahead of the "facts." The "realm," therefore, with which he is familiar is ultimately surrounded by "a dimly conscious horizon of undetermined reality."[170] This horizon appears to include also all those strange realities spoken of by his colleagues in other faculties or departments of the university. It is *the universal horizon of the world.* "Atoms," so we may interpret the scientist's shrug, "are atoms in the world, the unconsciously psychical is psyche in the world, the genes are genes in the world. This is the mutual interconnection of all the material and formal objects of the sciences. I do not understand what the other specialists are doing. But, if they are able to prove that the things of which they speak are really in the world, their research at any rate will be meaningful." The world is simply there, it is one and it contains everything that is meaningful for us. One is entitled to shrug his shoulders before a strange question, for everyone "naturally" trusts in the being and the meaningfulness of the world.[171]

This cognitive attitude is typical of what Husserl calls the *natural attitude.* The natural attitude and its naïve presuppositions

---

[169]*Formale und transzendentale Logik,* Halle a.S., 1929, p. 167.
[170]Husserl, *Ideen,* I, p. 49.
[171]The concept of the world used here is the phenomenological world concept. This world should not be confused with the created reality of theology, with the "whole of things" of scholasticism, with the "collection of all things" of Leibniz, or with the material cosmos of the physicist. It is not at all the all-embracing synthesis spoken of by criticist and idealistic philosophers. We speak of world in reference to the ultimate horizon which contains everything that is-for-me or is-for-us. By *Umwelt,* the surrounding world, we mean the world-for-us when the we-concept refers to a concrete human group.

199

lie at the basis of all the learned constructions raised by the second objectivity. For this reason there is not the slightest doubt about what our man of science would reply if his interviewer would dare to persist in asking further questions, such as: But what, then, *is* this world? Whence comes its *unity?* Why does everyone *"naturally"* trust it? Why does everyone experience its being as *meaningful?* His reply would be the classical parry: Are you by any chance a metaphysician?

The specialist's irritation is easily understood. The metaphysician, the philosopher who raises the question of being, is, indeed, the great spoilsport. For he sees the ivory towers of the specialized sciences not only from within but also from without, he sees several of them at the same time, he sees their relativity and their deficiency. For this reason he is able to ask questions that sound queer within the walls of any such ivory tower. The question about the being of the world is such a queer question. Yet, can the question be avoided? Is it not provoked by the modern pursuit of science with its numerous closed idealizing systems? When one listens to the Babel-like confusion of tongues, is he not compelled to exclaim: "You all speak different languages. What is it that all of you are talking about? Is it by any chance something that is in the world?" Would not, we may ask, reflection on this question perhaps be the first step in the right direction to overcome the Babel-like confusion?

To revert to our starting point, let us assume that the scientist whom we have interrogated in this strange fashion, simply refuses to reply. He *does not want* to be anything else than a specialist in a particular realm and refuses to make any assertion regarding the being of the world. He trusts the world, and that is all. *That* he trusts it so blindly is an enigma for him, but, being discrete, he does not dare to make an attempt to solve this metaphysical puzzle. To one so resigned our critique does not apply, for it is directed only against persons assuming a scientific attitude. Such people have more ambitious intentions. He is, e.g., a specialist in biology and thinks that *therefore* he knows what the world is. He is an excellent logician and thinks that *therefore* he is able to form a conception of the world. Such a claim is a sign of naïveness.

3. CRITICAL CONSIDERATIONS OF THE SCIENTIFIC ILLUMINATION: THE CRISIS OF THE "SECOND OBJECTIVITY"

The Specialists' Resignation. The resigned attitude of the specialists does not solve the above-mentioned dilemma. Like scientism, it leads to a degeneration of the life of science, albeit a different kind of degeneration. The man of science who, because of an ill-conceived modesty, restricts himself to the manipulation of certain techniques of research, gradually sinks to the level of a mere technician. The walls of his laboratory, experimental garden, museum, archives or library become the boundaries of his field of vision. He is no longer able to find a connection between what he thinks and does and the activities of other specialists of entirely different orientations. The end result is that he no longer knows exactly what he is supposed to be doing, for understanding what his special science really is requires a standpoint lying above this special science itself.

This situation reveals itself very strikingly in the realm of psychology. Binet's typical statement about the measurement of intelligence[172] may serve as a first example. It has its counterpart in James McK. Cattel's reply to the question of what psychology really is: "Psychology is what psychologists do." Such an attitude is no longer a question of scientific restraint and modesty, but rather a sign that through the resigned attitude of the specialists scientific activity is losing its character of intelligibility.

The Functional Loss of Modern Science. There exists, moreover, a third danger that has to be considered. The one-sided devotion to specialization could easily lead to a diminishing importance of science for man's life. One who is merely a specialist knows only a few atoms of truth, but he does not know how the structure of these atoms fits in with that of other atoms and, to continue our metaphor, how they can be used to form molecules and crystals of truth. He resembles a diamond-polisher who works his rough stone so thoroughly that nothing remains but dust. It certainly

---

[172]Cf. p. 10.

is no mere coincidence that working and thinking along the line laid down by specialized science is beginning to appear less and less satisfying to gifted young minds. There is a danger that sooner or later they will begin *really* to think and will become aware of the meaninglessness of their feverish activity.

The functional loss of modern science does not even wholly escape the ordinary citizen. He "feels" that science literally "cannot tell him anything." True, he remains interested in the results of empirical research insofar as they can lead to useful products. But the search for scientific truth for the sake of truth does not stir him. He has even a vague suspicion that the specialist knows everything except the main thing. The specialist cannot tell him how he ought to live, what the meaning is of his working and caring, what the sense is of the historical events in which he, the ordinary citizen, is directly involved. The specialized scientist cannot even tell him which aspects of these events are good or bad, useful or harmful, beneficial or dangerous. The political agitator "knows" all this but not the specialized scientist. The specialist cannot speak about these things, not in spite of but precisely because of his objectivity.

Thus, it is not surprising that many are convinced of the failure of the scientific illumination. The optimism and great expectations which it engendered at the beginning of the modern era have been succeeded by a wave of disenchantment, skepticism and even cynicism since the two world wars. The result of the second objectivity is that science as science has suffered a loss of its existential meaning for both the elite of its pursuers and the masses. The thesis of naïve confidence is being transformed into the antithesis of naïve distrust. The big question is whether there remains a possibility to overcome the "second naïveness" in its positive as well as its negative form.

Indigent Science. The conviction that, if the man of science wants to fulfill the task belonging to him in modern society, his knowledge and ability have to be supplemented by something that is lacking in contemporary science is rapidly gaining ground. The "disinterested spectator" has become rather unpopular, for he has failed not only in the realm of applied human science but

3. The Crisis of the "Second Objectivity"

even in that of its theory. *Integral theoretical knowledge of man as man requires in its very theory an addition that no longer lies on the level of the second objectivity.* Many contemporary university professors have come to accept this view. They know that the mask of scientific impartiality all too often conceals fear, sterility and a kind of intellectual psychasthenia. They are tired of the specialist's anxiously "noncommittal attitude." They expect something of him, something that goes beyond the limits of mere facts—a choice, decision, a profession. From the university professor in particular they expect a "profession," a declaration of faith, of purpose, of commitment, of allegiance.

In a broad sense there is unanimity on this point among many representatives of the human sciences. However, this agreement is more appearance than reality. As soon as anyone makes a statement about the way in which the rigorous pursuit of science has to be complemented, two diametrically opposed views make themselves felt.

The Free Play of "World Views." Among those who are dissatisfied with the modern pursuit of science one may often hear the opinion that there is no such thing as objectivity in the realm of human science. For this reason, it is said, those who study man as man should simply renounce the pretense of being impartial and disinterested. They should openly proclaim that their views in the realms of anthropology, psychology, sociology, economics, history and other human sciences are determined by their particular world view. What exactly is mean by "world view" in this context is not always very clear, but the term is used to characterize all convictions that are not motivated by science. Contemporaries speak about "world view" with reference to, e. g., belonging to a church, a nation, a people, an ethnical group, a political party, as well as to a social group or a common interest group, insofar as belonging to them expresses itself in a certain style of thinking. In this sense they speak, for instance, of the world view of the laborer, the manufacturer, the government employee and the middle class.

This mere enumeration shows what is to be expected of the unrestricted play of world views. It would amount to the death of science as such, for the various divergent views about man, his culture and his essential aims would flow from extra-theoretical motives. These views would be determined by national prejudices, political interests, economical aspirations. A few examples may serve to illustrate the point. Cultural anthropology would be differently conceived according as its authors belong to an ethnical group which feels oppressed or a group which feels itself called to leadership. Economic theory would depend on the question whether its creator has interest in free trade or in protectionism.

Such examples unfortunately are not purely imaginary. There always is an undeniable tension between the passionate policy of self-interest proper to prescientific life and the austere *ethos* of the life of science. If the postulate of objectivity would be relaxed in favor of the unbridled play of world views, this tension would simply disappear and the end result would be to make our civilization slide back to a primitive level. For in the primitive world of life the group interest expressed itself in the generally accepted convictions. The view, for example, that strangers are to be distrusted was useful for the preservation of the group. Modern analogies of such useful prejudices may be found in the national history textbooks of the various nations.

Moreover, dropping the postulate of objectivity would eliminate any discussion with at least a theoretical possibility of arriving at an agreement. For conflicting interest would make the different opinions irreconcilable. A higher synthesis would not be possible. Briefly put, the Babel-like situation would not be eliminated but become even worse and permanent. Those who favor a "free play of world views" in the human sciences do not seem to realize these consequences.

The Activity Neurosis of Science. As has been sufficiently shown in the preceding pages, our time is characterized by a crisis of science in general and of the human sciences in particular. However, this observation does not induce us to sing an elegy, for we see this crisis as a phenomenon of growth and development. It may be compared with a development crisis such as often occurs in man's psychological maturation.

3. The Crisis of the "Second Objectivity"

In the process of maturation it may happen that a youth, in passing from one phase to another, stands on a "threshold." He would have to adopt a new form of life but he does not dare. He would have to accept a new responsibility but is afraid of it. He would have to seek contact with new persons, who appear strange and dangerous to him. Note that the youth is not aware of his dread. He refuses to reflect on his situation. In order to escape from this reflection, he displays a feverish activity. No one can accuse him of not doing anything; on the contrary, he works under high pressure. Only the expert notices that despite all his external activity he does not make any inner progress. Psychologists refer to this condition as an *activity neurosis*. The unconscious dread may evoke also other phenomena, such as reverting to a preceding phase of development. A seventeen year old girl, for example, who cannot cope with the sexual condition of the adult may revert to sucking her thumb. The psychiatrist speaks in such a case of regression.

The developmental phenomena described above may serve as a metaphor for the problems facing us here with respect to the crisis of science. Modern science stands on a threshold which it cannot pass. It refuses to reflect on the "main issues." It is afraid of them and sees no possibility to accomplish the task facing it through "the trusted old means." It does not want to grow up in the new forms. As a result, modern scientific life resembles a river blocked by an obstruction: it expands and becomes shallow. New refined research methods are discovered; new specializations constantly increase; there is a tremendous pseudo-activity in congresses; new periodicals keep appearing; there is a veritable flood of popularizing works, but all these phenomena cannot hide the fact that depth is lacking. Especially in the realm of human science the problems are systematically avoided. There cannot be any doubt about the psycho-diagnosis of this condition, for it displays all the symptoms of an activity neurosis.

On the other hand, there is also an unmistakable tendency to regression. A symptom of it is the naïve opinion that all the ills of modern intellectual life can be cured by abandoning scientific objectivity. This pseudo-naïveness conceals the secret desire to

205

get rid of scientific responsibility. The idea is to escape from a set of problems one is unable to cope with and to silence the voice of scientific conscience. This is the reason also why the worlds of everyday life in the pre-scientific period are depicted in such idyllic colors. The slogan "back to nature" is interpreted in the sense of "let's undo the scientific illumination." "Let's throw overboard the results attained by one thousand years of intellectual efforts" is the cry for the new cure-all. Adults hope to become like little children by behaving in an infantile fashion. It suffices to call the phenomenon by its proper name to disclose its neurotic character.

An existential psychoanalysis of the life of science would have to consist of making the man of science aware of his hidden anxieties. While much more could be added, it has been sufficiently shown here, we think, that all the hesitations, all the fear and dread flow from a single primordial anxiety. The specialist sees how all problems of science in general and of human science in particular become metaphysical problems when one really wants to think them over thoroughly. At the same time he realizes that empirical and formal-logical methods offer little aid in approaching the realm of metaphysical problems. The average man of science feels himself faced here with an abyss and he acts like anyone who is seized with acrophobia—*he makes a desperate effort not to see the abyss confronting him.*

4. THE POSSIBILITY AND NECESSITY OF A THIRD FORM OF OBJECTIVITY

The Threshold Situation of Modern Science. We see a possibility of providing scientific thinking about man and his world with the complement it needs. This complement, we are convinced, has to be constructive. As we have already asserted, it is not possible to discard the achievements of the scientific illumination and to revert to the mentality of the world of everyday life. For this reason only he who has made his way through the scientific illumination is able to rise above it. For him there is no question of a disillusioned "back to," but only of a productive "forward." The present time gives rise to certain hopeful expectations in this respect. All signs indicate that we stand at the threshold of *a new phase in Western thought.* Standing on this threshold, one may discern two essential traits of this future phase. First, the new era will bring a *rapprochement of the empirical sciences and philosophy;* secondly, this philosophy will be also and even primarily a *metaphysical philosophy.*

At present this assertion is already losing the character of a prophecy and becoming the statement of an actual fact. The human sciences and metaphysical philosophy are gradually getting closer, although those who pursue the human sciences usually are not aware of it and sometimes even willy-nilly come closer to philosophy. For this reason it will be useful to illustrate the *rapprochement* in question from the standpoint of empirical science and specifically from that of empirical human science.

Metaphysical Implications of the "Vision." Let us assume that a cultural anthropologist writes a comparative study about the myths of a few primitive tribes and that, moreover, he proceeds in a strictly empirical fashion. This procedure means that he limits himself to recording the myths and to comparing them without making any statement regarding their possible deeper meaning. Being a very "positive" anthropologist, he deliberately and gladly leaves the interpretation of the myths to others.

In spite of the "positivism" of his approach, there is no escape from the act that he records the myths of certain tribes which he

considers to be "primitive." He, therefore, possesses a scientifically justified concept of primitivity. He has criteria to distinguish
primitivity from non-primitivity and the way in which he handles
these criteria are inevitably based on a certain theory. He will
view as primitive, e.g., the "savage" described by certain evolu-
tionists or he will characterize him as a man with a certain typical
mentality, as is done by Lévy-Bruhl and Van der Leeuw, or he
will consider certain external characteristics, such as the absence
of writing and technical culture, as essentials of primitivity. Whatever criterion he uses, in one way or in another our anthropologist
has to make a decision as to which groups of people are primitive
and which are not.

Moreover, our anthropologist studies certain human ideas,
convictions and ways of thinking as they find expression in the
customs, morals, stories and artifacts of the primitives. He calls
these ideas and convictions "mythical," and thus implies that he
knows what is mythical and what is not mythical. This distinction
likewise has to be based on a theory. The myth, for instance,
could be the invention of medicine men and shamans, aimed at
securing the control of the entire tribe by a small privileged class;
it could correspond to innate archtypes in the sense of Carl Jung;
it could be a consequence of a "biocultural dynamism" and be useful
insofar as it adds force to the solidarity of the group; it could be
considered as an expression of man's awareness of his dependence
on "numinal" forces and powers, in which case the myth could be
compared with religion. At any rate our positive anthropologist
will *actually* have to make a decision. If he does not make it
explicitly, his comparative study will show how he distinguishes
between the mythical and the non-mythical and therefore will
reveal what decision he has made.

The questions, however, of what primitivity and myth are
cannot at all be answered in an empirical way. While it may be
true that whoever busies himself with this problem will have to
speak the "language of facts," it is equally true that in this language
he will speak about something which no longer is a mere fact.

Similar considerations impose themselves with respect to
psychology, psychiatry, sociology and history. Is an emotion some-

4. *Necessity of a Third Form of Objectivity*

thing like a fit of coughing or does it reveal something about the being of man? Is an economic crisis to be compared with an earthquake or does it tell us something about the concrete way in which a group of men have used their freedom? The results of such considerations will always be the same—viz., the psychologist, psychiatrist, sociologist or historian will have to make a choice between several possible visions. The correctness of his choice cannot be controlled through experiment, inquiry, statistics, observation, study of documents, etc., for his choice is a supra-empirical decision. Briefly put, as we have shown above,[173] it is impossible to pursue human science without a *vision*. However, an important addition has to be made to this statement—namely, that *every vision is connected with other supra-empirical convictions*. Whoever choses one vision in preference to another makes a decision not in one but in many respects. The fact that the empirical investigator usually is not aware of this does not in any way diminish the elementary truth of this connection.

An analysis may serve to illustrate this point. Let us assume that our anthropologist views the myth as the invention of a priestly class for the purpose of justifying and continuing the traditional oppression of the other classes of the people. This view implicitly contains the idea that there exists no mythical-religious reality, that it is deceitful to speak of the invisible and supernatural, and that only the material is real. The view likewise implies that the socio-economic struggle of classes for material goods is the all-important event expressing itself in the fabrication of ideologies. In other words, the anthropologist in question will not merely develop an idea about the essence of the myth, but will present an idea that is indissolubly connected with a vision about the nature of man, of human society, human history and, last but not least, an idea about the essence of reality as such. We do not mean that every vision is necessarily a vision of "the whole," but that every vision has the immanent tendency to develop into a vision of "the whole." In other words, *in the realm of human science any vision contains a metaphysical vision.*

---

[173]Cf. pp. 178 ff.

The Question About the Meaning of the World. The question as to what extent the empirical man of science is willing to follow this tendency toward metaphysical growth depends on his temperament, inclinations, education, intellectual attitude and similar factors. He certainly has the right and in many cases even the duty to declare at a given moment: "This is as far as I want to go; I draw the line here, for beyond it I would get involved in a set of problems which are no longer directly connected with my special science." Nevertheless, this right does not take away from the fact that the first decision which he cannot at all avoid has already a certain metaphysical implication. Anyone who professes a conviction with respect to such questions as the nature of primitivity, of myth, human emotion, mental illness, history, language, society and similar human manifestations philosophizes as soon as he tries to give reasons for his conviction. This philosophy is metaphysical philosophy. As Gustav Kafka expressed it very clearly, "He does not have a choice between psychology with metaphysical content and psychology free from metaphysics, but every psychology contains metaphysical presuppositions."[174] Kafka's assertion applies not only to psychology but to empirical human science in general. Whether one finds this truth palatable or not is wholly irrelevant to its validity.

Thus, the man who pursues human science is faced with a difficult choice. On the one hand, he may limit himself to investigating details, collecting little facts and assembling them into groups, without ever making an effort to comprehend a broader realm and to pronounce himself about it. Aside from the question whether such a voluntary restriction is even possible, there is an obvious danger that his work will remain insignificant. On the other hand, the student of man as man will aim at a certain synthesis. As an historian, for example, he will evaluate the spirit of an era; as an anthropologist, he will pronounce a judgment about the customs of primitive tribes; as a sociologist, he will state his view about certain social phenomena. Let us assume that these men of science formulate their findings with the greatest pos-

---

[174]*Proceedings of the Tenth International Congress of Philosophy,* Amsterdam, 1948, p. 243.

4. Necessity of a Third Form of Objectivity

sible prudence. Even then the work of the historian who characterizes the spirit of an era makes a contribution to the question of what human history *is;* the anthropologist's systematic description of primitive customs and morals contributes something to the question of what morality *is;* and the sociologist who typifies social phenomena helps us understand to some extent what human society *is.* In all these cases there is always question of the *meaning* of certain phenomena and specifically, as we will see, of their ontological meaning.

How, we must ask next, are all these specialists' "givings of meaning" connected? In what consists the profound unity of all the different insights gained from scientific experience? What are we to call the whole to which every vision, no matter how limited it be, contributes something? The reply has already been given above.[175] The ultimate connection of all human experiences and of all the insights flowing from these experiences is constituted by the horizon of the world. The ultimate question aimed at in the empirical sciences is *the question regarding the meaning of the world.* And with this meaning is connected the great enigma faced by anyone who pursues a human science—namely, *the meaning which man's being-in-the-world has for man.* It is this meaning which is actually spoken of by the anthropologist, the psychologist, the psychiatrist, the sociologist, the historian, etc., even when they make desperate efforts not to speak of it.

What is Meaning? The introduction of the concept "meaning" shows that our view differs essentially from any type of positivistic, neo-positivistic or logico-positivistic conception. For someone like Ayer, for example, all our judgments referring to meaning are pseudo-judgments, for, so he would say, no observation could possibly be made that would prove the truth or falsity of these judgments. While we are quite willing to concede this impossibility, we would like to point out that neither observations nor any other forms of scientific research would take place, if the man of science did not think that such activities are meaningful. In other words, *knowledge of meaning is always presupposed.*

---

[175]Cf. pp. 198 f.

Accordingly, we could easily dispose of the whole objection by drawing attention to the fact that meaning is something ultimate which cannot be explained and does not need to be explained. However, such a reply could result in misunderstandings. For instance, it could be taken to mean that being-meaningful is a property of certain logical judgments, while what we mean by it here is something more fundamental. For this reason it will not be superfluous to situate the concept "meaning" in reference to more traditional notions. Certain well-known old theses and concepts of Aristotelian-Thomistic philosophy provide us with the necessary connection.

In this traditional philosophy of being the focal point is the being of all that is. Being is, first of all, *true*: as the old adage says, "being and true are convertible." Being, next, is *good*. To be is better than not to be; the being, therefore, of anything that is, is its first perfection. Thirdly, Neoscholasticism has added,[176] being is *beautiful*, esthetic. Thus, there arises the need of a concept capable of expressing at the same time and equally well these three aspects of the ontological perfection of being. Only the concept "meaning" can function as such. *That which truth, goodness and beauty have in common is their meaningfulness.* For this reason a philosopher with an ontological orientation will not hesitate to say that being as being is meaningful.

This statement, however, as well as the assertion that the being of anything which is may be called its first perfection, may be misunderstood. One could think, for example, that this being is a general fundamental property on which the other properties are based. This would be a mistake. The first perfection is not merely a condition and basis of possible further perfections, for these other perfections also *are*. A judgment, e.g., "this flower is beautiful," cannot be divided into two layers, first, "the flower is" as the first layer and, then, the flower is "beautiful" as the second layer. We should rather say that the being of the flower is a being-beautiful. As a matter of fact, its being in the form of being-

---

[176]Cf. John A. Peters, *Metaphysics*, No. 44 (to be published in the *Philosophical Series* of DUQUESNE STUDIES).

4. *Necessity of a Third Form of Objectivity*

beautiful is seized in a single act of esthetic appreciation. Meaning, therefore, even in the sense of practical, axiological and esthetic meaning, *is always meaning of being.* Negatively expressed, *outside the meaning of being there is no meaning.*

Meaning, Nonsense, Meaninglessness. This ontological insight, however, needs to be complemented from the phenomenological standpoint. The general proposition, "being as being is true," remains unsatisfactory, at least if we abstract from a possible theological foundation. It is not pure coincidence that in daily life we do not think of saying, "this thing is true." A thing is true only when someone, i.e., a conscious being or a community of conscious beings, dis-covers its truth. This dis-covery may be made by means of a gesture or a spoken word but also through a symbol or an artistic giving of form. Whatever may be the case, the thing has to be taken out of its unknownness-to-me, its concealedness-for-us. Only then will it *be* true for me and for us, only then will its being be the "ground" of its being-true-for me and for-us.

There is question here of an intentional achievement. I have made being visible by "dis-covering" it. Note that it does not owe its existence to my intentions, for my intentions are not creative.[177] Nevertheless, it owes its being-for-me or its being-for-us, its being-true-for-me and for-us to my, to our, dis-covering acts.[178] If my intentions would be contradictory, if, for example, I would make contradictory judgments concerning this single being or if I would perform self-contradictory acts with respect to it, there would be question of *nonsense.* Nonsense is the result of my defective intentional achievements. While this point does not cause any difficulty, one may ask what is to be said in this respect about things which I have not yet in any way noticed. Some philosophers restrict themselves to replying that such an objection ignores the issue. It cannot be made, they say, for what is not noticed *is* not for me, does not give me reason to ask any questions. This reply is acceptable if it is taken in reference to *definite* things, for such things are, of course, defined, determined by me in an active and passive

[177]Cf. above, pp. 44 ff.
[178]See above, p. 81.

213

interplay with them.[179] However, must the same be said with respect to the undiscovered, the unknown, the unattainable *in general,* i.e., the unnoticed that is not "this" or "that"? Is it impossible to speak of it?

The World as Horizon of Meaning. The dialectics of the horizon plays its typical role here. Let us begin with the horizon of visual perception. As long as we are unconscious, sleeping or keeping our eyes closed, no field of vision exists for us. The phenomenon of the "visual horizon" presents itself only on the occasion of an act of seeing. I have to perceive a thing or group of things visually and, in doing so, I become aware also of the fact that I do not see everything. I fix my sight on an object, seizing perhaps also a few details of its immediate surroundings, but I have only a vague impression of distant objects. Far away I do not perceive anything and this absence of perception gives rise to the phenomenon of the horizon. In other words, the visual horizon arises from the transition from that which I see to that which I no longer see. What I see has, of course, a certain meaning for me, at least the meaning of being and of being-true. As to what I no longer see, it certainly is not "nonsense," i.e., incapable of having a meaning, but provisionally it is still "meaningless" and I do not know whether I will ever be able to give it any meaning. Accordingly, every horizon is an horizon of meaning. It indicates the zone in which the meaningful-for-me changes into the meaningless-for-me.

The same considerations apply to practical and pragmatic relationships. Let us assume that a student is firmly resolved to become a Ph.D. He reveals great scientific ambition. The successful defense of a dissertation appears to him as the absolute goal to be attained. It is this goal which confers a relative goodness on certain things and acts that contribute to the attainment of the goal. Following courses, studying for and passing examinations are simply considered "means" to the realization of his ambitious plan. Paying tuition, commuting to and from the university, and buying books are viewed as means of second rank. To be able,

---

[179]Cf. above, p. 75.

4. *Necessity of a Third Form of Objectivity*

however, to obtain the doctoral degree, the student has also to rent a room, buy food, procure clothing. He has, moreover, to live, move around, see and breathe. Can he conscientiously claim that he is really breathing for the sake of the dissertation to be defended five, six or seven years from now? Would such a claim not be unrealistic? Is not the truth of the matter rather that the explicitly aimed-at goal is surrounded by concentric circles of means that are less and less explicitly wanted, and that finally a point is reached at which one can no longer exactly say what has to be considered a means and what not? With Künkel one may, therefore, speak here of an "aim-pyramid," to be understood in the sense that the apex of the pyramid is clear in the mind of the tending man while its basis is lost in vagueness. The thesis of the pragmatically meaningful and usefully ordered appears to change into the antithesis of the pragmatically meaningless, useless and chaotic. The "zone" in which this transition takes place is the horizon, in this specific case the pragmatic horizon. What has been said here with respect to a particular aim may be stated also of the complex of human aims and means: it, too, is surrounded by an "empty horizon of a known unknownness."[180]

A final example is supplied by esthetic apperception. In front of me there is a bouquet of flowers which simply strikes me as "beautiful." It stands in a vase which perhaps has also a certain gracefulness. The flowers and the vase are delineated against the background of a study which is esthetically neutral. The book case and the books, the desk and other furniture are neither ugly nor beautiful. The thesis of my esthetic emotion changes into the antithesis of esthetic indifference as soon as this background is co-intended. But it is impossible for me not to do so: I do it willy-nilly. Accordingly, here also there is question of an horizon. Like all other particular horizons, this one also is contained in the universal horizon of the world. The world, therefore, is the whole of the esthetically meaningful, indissolubly connected with the esthetically meaningless. For this reason a special work is required to express the esthetic meaning-for-us of the world— namely, the work of art.

---

[180]Husserl, *Erfahrung und Urteil,* p. 35.

The horizon of the world arises at the same time as the awakening of my consciousness. This horizon corresponds to my way of seizing the universe of being as a finite consciousness. I call forth this horizon as soon as I perform conscious acts. As soon as I conceive something as real, good or esthetic, I place it in a universal context, and this context debouches into the no-longer-real, no-longer-good or no-longer-beautiful for me. I cannot claim that I do not have any knowledge of these horizons, for the world is for me an unmistakable phenomenon. It is the horizon of everything that is meaningful for me.

The Ambivalence of Being-in-the-World. The *world is the horizon of everything that is meaningful for me.* This statement has two senses which are dialectically interrelated. It contains the thesis that everything contained within the horizon of the world has at least a minimum of meaning for me. But it implies also the antithesis that everything lying beyond the horizon is not yet meaningful and therefore meaningless. It is to be noted, however, that the meaningless is not the same as the absurd, the nonsensical, the incapable of meaning. Nonsense presupposes the activity of a faulty intentionality whose theoretical, practical or esthetic intentions are self-contradictory. Such intentions are necessarily explicit intentions and therefore intentions in the world. Here, however, we are concerned with the wholly anonymous of which I can affirm merely the indefinite and undetermined character. The unknown, that which in no way is determined, obviously has no explicit meaning for me. I cannot even say that it is *this* or *that*. We may add that the undetermined which lies beyond my horizon can never be fully explored by me. I "know" this without knowing it explicitly. Somehow I am conscious that I am finite and that mankind likewise constitutes a finite we-society. I "know" that I and this society will never succeed in exploring the infinite horizons of the non-worldly, in dis-covering everything concealed as being, as good or as esthetic. The meaningless is not only real but is even an overpowering reality for me.

For this reason *the phenomenon "world" is ambivalent.* The world is, on the one hand, the trusted dwelling in which, at least in principle, everything is theoretically, practically or esthetically well-ordered. On the other hand, the world is the boundary of everything that is true, good and beautiful for us—a boundary beyond which lurks a meaningless infinity. In the natural cognitive attitude I am oriented solely to the beings-for-me in the world. I stare myself blind at the familiar objects—or perhaps at scientific objects—and do not gaze into the distance. Wittgenstein's saying that "the world is the totality of facts" is typical of this attitude.[181] The picture, however, changes when we assume the metaphysical cognitive attitude or, as we will say later, the *transcendent cognitive attitude*. If we do so, we become aware of it that the whole of the meaningful-for-me and for-us may be compared with a tiny boat floating in an ocean of meaninglessness. The world in which there is a place for everything and in which everything can occupy its place is a mere nutshell compared with the fathomless and tumultuous sea surrounding and threatening it on all sides.

Undoubtedly, this awareness is an alarming experience for anyone and especially for one who pursues an empirical science. He suddenly realizes that the interconnection of beings, which he had so trustingly accepted as obvious in his naive confidence in the meaningfulness of the world, has literally no foundation at all. *Reality*, as it is described in the empirical sciences, even the part that is exactly described, *is a mystery*. This truth has to be understood, reflected upon and lived with in all its awe-inspiring consequences. One must have the courage to call this experience fearful and to endure its terrifying truth. The "one" in question here refers also to the man of science, of whom we have said above that he behaves like a novice in the mountains: he makes a desperate effort not to see the abyss yawning before him.

All this shows the importance of the dialog between the scientist and the metaphysician. Whatever turn this dialog may take, whatever the way in which both searchers for truth will ultimately interpret the mystery of the world, one thing at least is certain— the metaphysician will teach the experimental scientist to gaze

---

[181]Cf. above, p. 121. This critical remark does not prevent us from considering the author of the *Tractatus* a metaphysical thinker in a different respect.

into the abyss without becoming panic-stricken, and this will be the beginning of his wisdom.

Pre-Meaning and Signified Meaning. We have now reached the point of critical reflection. The descriptions given above are sound but, one may ask, are they exhaustive? Can they lay claim to completeness? Is man's anxious care for his being-in-the-world (Heidegger), is his experience of the utter meaninglessness of existence in the world (Sartre) the final word of philosophy? While it appears certain to us that this experience is an indispensable expression of the human situation, it could very well be true that the analyses leading to it have overlooked an unobtrusive but nonetheless important phenomenon.

To clarify this statement we may again take up the metaphor used above. The orderly whole of worldly beings-for-me was compared with a tiny boat floating on an ocean of meaninglessness. However, to use again the same image, is it not the sea which keeps the boat floating and is it not the sea which makes the boat and its motion possible? In other words, is not the horizon of the world the condition of the being-ordered and being-meaningful of the beings for me? If the reply is in the affirmative, do I have the right simply to call *empty of meaning* that which constitutes this horizon, that which limits and finitizes my intentions? To abandon all metaphor, do I not need for my givings of meaning something that is capable of meaning and that therefore is more correctly described as not-yet-meaningful than as meaningless? And is it not true that I always and of necessity feel called to make actually meaningful that which is capable of meaning?

Thus, it becomes apparent that the preceding analyses need to be made more complete. Let us start with a series of theoretical acts. These acts may be very simple from the logical viewpoint and concerned with the most trivial realities. For instance: the ink is blue; the pen is black; the office is well-lighted. I cannot avoid attributing these predicates to the objects in question, for they do possess the qualities mentioned above. Within the framework of the expressive means of which I dispose in English, I cannot avoid the use of the words "blue," "black" and "well-lighted." To unveil the truth of *this* office, I simply have to use *these* symbols.

4. Necessity of a Third Form of Objectivity

The situation is similar with respect to a practical action. Let us say that I consider it my duty to work now. By working I bring to light a possible goodness of a determined concrete situation. I realize something of the goodness which lies hidden here and now in these circumstances. I would likewise unveil hidden beauty if I were able to paint the light of the sun as it penetrates into my study and endows all objects in it with a luminous glow.

The question to be raised in connection with these examples is the following. When we say, "This predicate *belongs* to this reality," "I simply *have to* use these symbols," and "I unveil *hidden* ethical and esthetic values," are we using mere expressions devoid of sense? Are they sheer poetic flights of fancy? Or are these words the expression of unmistakable phenomena?

To find the answer, let us suppose that I assume an entirely different attitude. I tell others that my office is badly lighted. In that case I deceive them deliberately. But deception is possible only on the basis of a kind of primary "knowing." For I know that this thing which is my office possesses a possible truth and that I dispose of signs to disclose this "not-yet truth" to myself and to others in the form of explicit meanings. More generally expressed, there is something that primarily moves me to uncover hidden meaning, realize possible goodness, bring to light unnoticed esthetic values. Another question is, of course, whether I will give in to this primary impulse.

What right, therefore, do I have to say that what is not-yet-this, that the anonymous, the unknown, the unattainable is *empty, of meaning* for me? True, there is no aprioristic law which guarantees that endless progress will be made on the road of human giving-of-meaning. It is quite possible that something which now is concealed from us will forever remain hidden. But even that which will remain concealed forever is not simply empty of meaning. An important distinction has to be made here.

Of themselves, the unknown and the unattainable do not have any explicit meaning. The unknown does not mean anything because I cannot interpret it. It is not "significant" because I am unable to express its meaning in signs. Nevertheless, it is not empty of meaning. The proof is that the unknown being would reply to my questions if I could interrogate it correctly. It would communicate with me if I would approach it in a suitable fashion.[182] *It lets itself be discovered* and consequently it was already there, it possessed already an ontological meaning, although no one had as yet understood this meaning. From now on we will refer to this hidden and unspoken meaning as *pre-meaning* or *fundamental meaning*.

The meaning, on the other hand, which manifests itself only through my dis-closing acts we will call now the *signified meaning*. Through this terminology we want to draw attention to the fact that only by means of *signs* and *symbols* am I able to express what being is for me and for us. In this connection the terms "sign" and "symbol" are to be understood in a broad sense. They refer not only to words and concepts ("mental words") but also to gestures, expressive mimetics and artistic representations, for all of these are full of signified meanings. Moreover, a moral deed, a wise law, a beneficial political regime, likewise, can serve to manifest the hidden goodness of a concrete situation. Accordingly, in the broad sense in which the terms are used here, anything containing an explicit meaning for me and for us is a "sign" or a "symbol." For this reason all specifically human intentions may be conceived as attempts to discover the pre-meaning of beings, to express what the world is and what the being of man in the world implies. The search of science for truth is merely a single aspect of this giant effort of man.[183]

The above-formulated neo-scholastic thesis, "being, as being, is true, good, and beautiful,"[184] needs, therefore, to be complemented in a phenomenological fashion. We will say from now on that *every being as being contains a "pre-meaning."* I do not know

---

[182]Cf. above, pp. 81 ff.

[183]In a more profound analysis a distinction would have to be made between "symbol" in the narrow sense and "sign" and between immanent meaning and explicit "signified meaning." The body, mimetics, elementary forms of behavior as well as a work of art have an immanent meaning. By means of something pertaining to themselves they refer to something pertaining to themselves. Attention to this distinction has been drawn by the Gestalt psychologists and depth psychologists and also by phenomenological thinkers, such as Eugène Minkowski, Paul Ricoeur and Merleau-Ponty. We ourselves will speak later about "embodied dialectics" (see also p. 257).

[184]Cf. above, p. 212.

beforehand in what these pre-meanings consist and I cannot simply "read" them in being. I know only that I am called to unfold something of this meaningfulness in signified meanings. It is perhaps in this call, in this vocation that lies the meaning of my being in the world.

Why Metaphysics? Whence comes this original meaning of being? This is a crucial question of metaphysical philosophy, a question that can hardly be avoided. Two points are certain with respect to this question—namely, there is a hidden meaning (we have called it the "pre-meaning" or the "fundamental" meaning), and this meaning comes neither from me nor from us. Both of these points have been sufficiently shown in the preceding pages. As soon as I perform conscious acts, I am already caught in a network of relationships capable of meaningful interpretations. They are already "pre-meaningful." I know that I am not the origin of this pre-meaning and merely bear witness to it. Making use of an age-old comparison, one could speak here also of a light which makes the beings knowable and permits us to discover their goodness and beauty. Everything I see, I see in this light, but I myself am not this light. The question that imposes itself here irresistibly is, what is this light, stripped of all figures of speech? *Who or what is the ground of this fundamental meaning, this pre-meaning?*

As soon as this question is formulated, we are in the realm of pure metaphysics. The greatest of metaphysical thinkers have tried to penetrate into the darkness of this mystery, but the fundamental intuitions underlying their ideas differ from one another. A few of them may be mentioned here. The light which makes material beings knowable is a reflexion of eternal and immutable ideas (Plato). The pre-meaning of things owes its source to God, the Creator, to whose ideas the being and essence of things corresponds (Thomas Aquinas). The meaningfulness of nature is the expression of a self-thinking Consciousness (Spinoza). The pre-meaning arises from aprioristic forms of the human intellect and from necessary ideas governing the use of human reason (Kant). The Absolute Mind, estranged from itself becomes itself again because in the course of history it explains its own pre-meaning

221

in constantly clearer meanings (Hegel). The light is the Truth of Being which alone makes it possible to understand being as being (Heidegger).

It is beyond our task to compare the various profound attempts to grasp the mystery of ontological truth and even more to present a comparative critique of them. Nevertheless, we may point out that all these great metaphysicians share two convictions. First, they all admit that, if we call "worldly" everything appearing within the horizon of the world, then the "light" which makes worldly beings appear is *transcendent*[185] with respect to all worldly beings. Secondly, all these great thinkers are conscious of *their utter dependence on this transcendent reality*. Transcendence is the ground on which every thing is built, but it itself can no longer be given a foundation. It is the hidden treasure from which all riches flow but itself incapable of enrichment. It is the measure by which everything is measured but itself beyond measurement. From this consciousness that, with respect to all knowing, acting and representing, we are absolutely dependent upon a source of meaningfulness which is no longer human and no longer wordly, general categories and concepts flow of necessity. We mean philosophical, ethical and esthetic categories and ideas which in their innermost essence have to lay claim to universal validity.

Accordingly, on this level also there is question of *objectivity*. What has been described above positively as a peculiar consciousness of obligation and negatively as unwillingness to ascribe to things signified meanings that go against their pre-meaning finds its explanation in this *third form of objectivity*. The awareness of obligation on which this objectivity is based may be described also as a transcendent conscience with respect to truth. As Eduard Spranger expresses it, "The 'incorruptible conscience of truth' is a starting point beyond which no further inquiry can be made. As is the case with every conscience, it is concerned with me in my thinking. The important point is not that I do not become involved in logical contradictions, but that I personally receive before my mind's eye the content to be known in my thinking.

---

[185]It is to be noted that this concept of transcendence is broader than the specifically religious idea of transcendence.

4. Necessity of a Third Form of Objectivity

An element of 'revelation' is always implied in this. But all revelation overwhelms its recipient and opens new vistas to him. Man has to obey what thus is revealed to him."[186]

All this will appear a paradox to anyone who is accustomed to consider objectivity unqualifiedly in relationship with the principle of verifiability. Nevertheless, the consciousness of having to serve a transcendent reality imposes higher and more stringent demands on man's search for truth than any research society could ever require. For this consciousness may at a given moment demand that the controlling principles of the research community be rejected, that the criticism of this community be defied and new pathways blazed. Contemporaries like to speak of "revolutionary discoveries." An essentially new discovery will inevitably have to be expressed in a new "language" and embodied in a new scientific apparatus. Consequently, it cannot be verified through the existing scientific methods. The intellectual emancipation of the authentic discoverer and trailblazer is possible only because ultimately this man knows that he does not have to justify himself before human beings and their worldly institutions. The necessity and universality of his thinking is no longer based on the agreement of a society but on a *transcendent vision*. For this reason his attitude may be characterized as the *transcendent cognitive attitude*.

Three Levels of Objectivity. The question may be asked of how the three levels of objectivity described in the preceding investigations are related to one another. Despite their mutual differences, all three are historical phenomena, flowing from one and the same dialectics. They correspond to three phases in the "process" of man's growing self-consciousness and liberation.

On the level of primitive culture man breaks with the perspectivism of perception. He knows that other members of the we-community see beings differently and see also other beings, concrete beings as well as magical and mythical beings. The result is the formation of a "language," a first mutual understanding, tradition and norms which no longer cling to perceptible things.

---

[186]*Gedanken zur Daseinsgestaltung,* ed. by H. W. Bähr, München, 1955, p. 158.

On the level of the second objectivity thinking man is emancipated from the fortuitous relationships prevailing in a concrete cultural milieu. He breaks with the limitation of the we-community and constructs a theory that is valid for the whole of mankind. He abandons the solidity of the familiar milieu and boldly plunges into the restlessly moving sea of universal thought.

In the third objectivity man slips away from everything tangible—from mankind, its accepted "languages," its scientific apparatus, its verification through research communities. As a metaphysical philosopher he exposes himself to the dread of meaninglessness while he passionately affirms a meaning that is still hidden for all others. Nevertheless, his confidence in the universal validity of the glimpse of truth seen by him is based on the same primary experience which underlies even the objectivity of the archaic world. For he knows that he is seeing something which the others do not see, and it is this which gives him the right to speak.

Freedom and Bondage of Philosophical Thought. Numerous objections may be raised against the way in which we have justified the postulate of a third objectivity. Among scientists the complaints will probably assume more or less the following form. Both formal-logical and empirical sciences, they will say, dispose of well-established methods of demonstration. If the metaphysician considers these methods below his dignity, is it not obvious that he proceeds in an unscientific fashion? Will he not be able to make all kinds of assertions most arbitrarily? Does not the lack of solid arguments tempt him to make eloquence a substitute for solidity? May the fact that he thinks himself to "see" something be offered as a proof? Isn't it true that drunkards and the insane sometimes also think that they have discovered profound intuitions? These and other objections may be aptly summarized in a single critical question: *How can the validity of philosophical insights be established?*

In reply we must frankly point out that the truth of a philosophical insight can be proved neither after the example of a logistico-mathematical judgment nor after that of a judgment belonging to empirical science. The reasons have been given above. The proofs of logistico-mathematical and empirical sciences are valid within an artificial "universe of discourse." They apply only to carefully defined realms of knowledge. The circumscription, however, of these realms cannot be justified in a logico-mathematical or empirical fashion but ultimately depends on philosophy. Philosophy itself is essentially opposed to such artificial restrictions, for metaphysical philosophy claims to contain a vision of "the whole." For this reason it can be pursued only in freedom and not on the basis of methodic conventions.

Freedom, on the other hand, is not arbitrariness. To philosophize is not to hallucinate. Even the formation of a new philosophical vision does not have the extravagant character that the non-philosopher likes to ascribe to it. A new philosophy is not a mere cerebration. It may be useful in this connection to draw attention to three phenomena.

First of all, every philosophical insight flows from the dialog of the "lovers of wisdom," from their "philosophizing together," and the new insight is not an exception to this rule. One who really loves truth will propose more independent views only when necessity compels him. He becomes aware of this necessity when he cannot express his vision in the "language" hitherto used in the philosophers' dialog. This statement indicates the peculiar character of every metaphysical philosophy—such a philosophy is *at the same time a fragment of truth and a "language" to express this truth.* What is meant here by "language" should be sufficiently clear from the preceding pages. The philosopher's language is his discourse, i.e., it is an orderly whole of worded concepts and categories and at the same time a methodic idea that is the matrix of these concepts, categories and "vocables." The new language of the metaphysician sprouts from the old idioms. Accordingly, a metaphysical philosophy is never entirely new or wholly unintelligible; it may introduce surprising and difficult "words" in the dialog of wisdom's lovers; it may sometimes cause hesitations and cause the dialog to falter, but it does not put an end to it.

The second point to which we would like to draw attention is the dialectic relationship between the method and the content of metaphysical philosophy, which the non-philosopher usually does not understand. In philosophy the method is not a question of secondary importance nor can one method be replaced by another. *A fortiori* it would be impossible to evaluate the thoughts of a philosopher on the basis of the "well-established method" of an empirical or formal-deductive science. On the contrary any new philosophy *is* at the same time a new method. *It is a fragment of truth and simultaneously a pathway to this truth* in such a way that the one cannot be considered without the other. Descartes' philosophy, for example, is indissolubly connected with his critical-reflective method, that of Spinoza with his deduction "in geometrical form," and that of Hegel with his typical dialectic way of thinking.

If, therefore, one wants to investigate the truth content of a philosophy, the only possible approach is the unprejudiced and sympathetic following of the trail blazed by the philosopher in question. If at the end of the path we find a fragment of truth which throws light on the things around us and on ourselves, then we have to do with a genuine philosophy, with an authentic contribution to the philosophical dialog of the centuries. The idea, however, that a philosophical truth can be verified in the sense of checking it by "counting" or "measuring" flows from the thought patterns of the "second objectivity" and obviously is inadequate here.

The third phenomenon that should draw the criticist's attention is the *fruitfulness* of a truly philosophical thought. As we have pointed out before,[187] a scientific vision is fruitful because it makes us better understand man. The same applies *a fortiori* to a philosophico-metaphysical vision. For such a vision does not refer only to a limited set of problems connected with a realm of experience, but rather is a vision of "the whole." It lays claim to being fundamental. That it really is fundamental appears from the fact that it is possible to "build on" it. We mean a single metaphysical interpretation of the being of man and the world, if it is convincing, makes us at the same time understand better numerous forms of human existence, human history, human views of nature, etc. It opens new perspectives and is the fertile soil of new visions. For this reason a genuine philosophy stimulates the intellectual life from which it has arisen. It will be sufficient to enumerate in this

---

187. Cf. pp. 180 f.

4. Necessity of a Third Form of Objectivity

connection the names of Plato, Aristotle, Saint Augustine, Abelard, Thomas Aquinas, Nicolas of Cusa, Descartes, Leibniz, Kant, Hegel and Husserl. Concretely speaking, this stimulation means that *a new philosophical vision, born from the dialog of searchers for truth, itself again gives rise to continued dialog.* True, sometimes it may happen that a philosophical genius turns away from his fellow philosophers, opens his own "school" and sharply criticizes the thought of others. Historically speaking, however, such a secession is neither total nor lasting; moreover, even the most severe criticism is ultimately a contribution to the dialog of the searchers for truth.

The search for truth is not limited to philosophers, but undertaken also by those who pursue the sciences. The question therefore arises whether or not the specialists in empirical human science are capable of giving rise to important visions on the foundation of a *particular* philosophy. For instance, has the existential philosophy of our time exercised a stimulating influence on the sciences of man? The history of thought teaches us that it may take decades and even centuries before such a question can be answered satisfactorily. But it teaches us also that the answer will eventually be given.

Precarious Dialog. We have now returned to our starting point. Our inquiry has confirmed our view that the empirical scientist and the metaphysical philosopher have to collaborate. This collaboration is necessary to prevent the "second naiveness" in its positive or negative form. By means of the dialog between the empirical scientist and the metaphysician modern scientific life may be able to pass the "threshold" described above.

Serious objections, however, arise here. Is all this not merely wishful thinking? Do not the scientist and the philosopher speak different languages? Are their attitudes not different? Does not history show us many examples of mutual misunderstanding? Briefly, while collaboration may be desirable, is it really possible? This is the question to be examined now.

5. HUMAN SCIENCE AND PHILOSOPHY

Old Prejudices. If it is true that in the realm of human science every great synthesis implies a metaphysical vision, then those who pursue the study of man as man may draw several conclusions from it. They may be led to reject empirical human science as "non-scientific"; they may endeavor to pursue metaphysical philosophy on their own, even though they are aware of the fact that they are insufficiently prepared for it; or, they may seek the collaboration of one philosopher or of a group of philosophers.

From the preceding considerations it should be evident that we consider collaboration the only correct solution. In practice, however, collaboration between the student of empirical human science, on the one hand, and the philosopher of metaphysical orientation, on the other, usually runs into difficulties. There are many old misunderstandings and stubborn prejudices among both philosophers and empirical scientists.

The first of these to come to our mind is the positivistic conception of the supremacy to be attributed to logico-mathematical and empirical sciences. Auguste Comte's historical vision regarding the future development of scientific life directly contradicts the convictions defended in this book. Comte's idea about the three phases of man's intellectual progress is too well known to be repeated here in detail. His prediction is that the theological thinking of the first phase and the metaphysical thinking of the second phase will be definitively overcome by the "positive" thought of the third phase. The last-named phase, he claims, will be characterized by this that man will no longer seek religious or metaphysical explanations for natural phenomena, but will exclusively rely on observation and experiment to discover the connection of phenomena, formulate laws and predict future events. Empirical sciences will solve all problems regarding nature and man in a satisfactory way.

If we look at the course of history over the past 130 years, we see that it constantly has shown the nineteenth century philosopher's daring prophecy to be a lie. The facts confirm this statement, even if we abstract from the eloquent data that have reference to man's religious life. True, the enthusiasm for empirical research has not abated but continues to be as intense as ever. However, this undiminished interest does not take away from the fact that at present more metaphysical works are published than ever before, that metaphysical thinkers are studied, commented upon and reprinted in new editions more than at any other time in the past, and that there is a new, intense and widespread interest in the philosophies of Plato, Aristotle, the Scholastics, Malebranche, Schelling and Hegel. Moreover, a renewed need of metaphysical insights makes itself felt not only among the "common man" but also among the very "priests of science."

This need is connected with a fact overlooked by Comte— namely, that *neither the formal nor the empirical sciences are capable of constructing an ontology.* If the scientific illumination had given a conclusive system of explanations, albeit limited only to visible reality, "positive" thought would have satisfied the large majority of men. However, as the history of the past two centuries shows, this is not the case. Several reasons could be adduced to explain why. One of these has been mentioned already. Visible reality is a reality formed, modified and arranged by man, which constitutes also and even primarily man's surrounding world. If we do not know the mystery of human existence, these human surroundings likewise remain ultimately without any explanation. Existing man, however, is a "metaphysical animal." He is essentially oriented toward Transcendence, and this orientation cannot be explained by means of the empirical sciences. Here lies the innermost reason why the pursuit of the positive sciences cannot give a satisfactory interpretation of reality, yet such an hermeneutic ontology is desired by contemporary man.

"Discretion" Instead of "Resignation." In our conviction our time offers a greater philosophy than former eras for a *rapprochement* between the philosopher and the student of empirical science, because on both sides there is now greater discretion. Both apply themselves more zealously to the "art of discernment." While they are more aware of their competence than before, they also realize its limitations. For this reason their claims present themselves with greater modesty.

Phenomenology and the Human Sciences

This statement applies first of all to the empirical scientists. Relatively few of them continue to adhere to rigid scientism. Most scientists are aware of it that they question reality in a definite way and that the determined character of their questions amounts to a self-imposed limitation of their "universe of discourse." Modern physicists are no strangers to this awareness of limitation. Werner Heisenberg, for example, writes: "Even in physical science, therefore, the object of research is no longer nature in itself but nature as exposed to man's questioning, and to this extent man here also encounters himself again."[188] Heisenberg does not hesitate to add that "therefore the world view of physical science ceases to be, strictly speaking, a world view of physical science."[189] How, then, we may ask, does the world view of physical science arise? The reply will have to be that inevitably it cannot be formed without either explicit or implicit use of philosophical ideas. For this reason the physicist needs the collaboration of the philosopher, even if he wants to limit himself to presenting a connected view of material reality. If he realizes this, he will undoubtedly show the necessary discretion.[190]

The modern philosopher, likewise, will proceed with more circumspection than some of his predecessors. The "imperialism of speculative thought," which seemed quite natural in the era of the great philosophical systems, is hardly possible in our time. For Hegel it may still have been possible to proclaim in his "inaugural dissertation" of 1801 that there could be no planet between Mars and Jupiter, even though in the same year Piazzi had already discovered the planet Ceres. Now, however, the time is past in which the philosopher can make the bona fide claim that, by virtue of his philosophical insights, he is capable of

---

[188]"Das Naturbild der heutigen Physik," *Deutsche Enzyclopädie,* Hamburg, 1955, vol. VIII, p. 18.

[189]*Op. cit.,* p. 21.

[190]"Physics passes today through a fundamental change, the most characteristic feature of which appears to be the return to its original discretion wi'h respect to its own value." And, "only by leaving open the question of what bodies, matter, energy, etc. ultimately are, does physics attain knowledge . . . which may be able to lead to genuine philosophical insights." Heisenberg, *op. cit.,* p. 132.

fulfilling the function of the physicist, the psychologist or the sociologist. Such flagrant transgressions need hardly to be feared in our era.

Universal Theory or Hermeneutics? Besides the preceding kind of discretion, common to the philosopher and the scientist, another and higher type of discretion is expected of the philosopher. He has to realize that his philosophy possesses only a *hermeneutic* value. No matter how systematically and rigorously he may proceed in his thinking about the meaning of history, the destiny of man, the being of the world and similar topics, the result can never be more than an interpretation. For the philosopher is not an acosmic spirit, hovering above the course of history and raised above social reality, who is capable of comprehending the universe of being in a single glance. No matter how painful it may seem to him, he has to recognize that it is possible to attempt different philosophical interpretations, flowing from different historical situations, different existential experiences, different philosophical temperaments. Even if he wants to hold fast to a single philosophical tradition, he will have to permit fellow philosophers of the same "school" to interpret and apply the fundamental ideas of "his" tradition in different ways. Negatively expressed, we have to abandon the dream that all philosophers would work together in building up one and the same immutable system in the same way as many skilled technicians work together to construct the various parts of one perfect machine. This dream was a typical manifestation of the optimism which animated the era of scientific illumination and expressed itself in the ideal of a single encyclopedic theory, such as the *Encyclopédie, ou Dictionnaire raisonné des arts et des métiers* of Diderot and d'Alembert (1751 ff.), Herbert Spencer's *System of Synthetic Philosophy* (1860-1896), and the *Encyclopedia of Unified Sciences* (1938 ff.).[191] This dream is based on the illusion that a single group of thinkers is in possession of an infallible method for the discovery of truth. Such an infallible method is actually conceived either in an empiricist fashion, after the model of the experimental sciences, or rational-

---

[191]Cf. above, pp. 19 f.

istically, after the model of the logico-mathematical sciences. In this way science becomes the norm of philosophy, and the "second objectivity" is viewed as the criterion of the "third objectivity." This illusion moved the "illuminated" thinkers of the eighteenth, nineteenth and twentieth centuries to impose their empiricist or rationalistic way of thinking as obligatory for all philosophers and to brand as "unscientific" any assertion which disagrees with their own views. As we have seen above, none of the historical attempts to impose a rationalistic or empiricist standard of uniformity on all intellectual discipline has produced the desired unity or unanimity, not even among the leading protagonists themselves.

We would like to replace the imperialism of "the system" by the view of philosophy which has gained widespread adhesion in Europe since the appearance of Martin Heidegger's work *Sein und Zeit*.[192] According to this view, philosophy is an interpretation of some everyday aspect known by all at least implicitly. It is a dis-covery of that which is concealed behind the apparently familiar. To understand *ontologically* what is *ontically* experienced, is the task of philosophy.[192a] When we speak hereafter of the hermeneutic conception of philosophy, we refer to this conception of philosophy as a systematic interpretation of the familiar and yet unknown.[193]

The Necessity of Philosophical Pluralism. If every philosophical system, no matter how many-sided and extensive it be, is nothing but the hermeneutic interpretation of certain fundamental experiences, then there is nothing absurd about the existence of many philosophical systems. For in that case this plurality merely shows that no thinker possesses a method through which he can fully conquer the whole of truth. If any thinker had discovered such a method, he or his successors would have been in possession of the whole truth, so that nothing would have been left for others to add

---

[192]Cf. *Sein und Zeit*, p. 37; *Being and Time*, pp. 61f.

[192a]Regarding the distinction between "ontological" and "ontic," cf. Heidegger, *Sein und Zeit*, p. 63: "Die Beschreibung bleibt am Seienden haften. Sie ist ontisch. Gesucht wird aber [in der Ontologie] das Sein [des Seienden]." English ed.: "Such a description is always confined to entities. It is ontical. But what we are seeking is Being" (p. 91).

[193]See below, pp. 235 ff.

for, as Hegel expresses it very profoundly, "truth is the whole." "Philosophizing together" would have come to an end, because there would be nothing left to question. The holistic character of the whole truth would not even have left any room for doubt. Everyone would have reached the state of perfect intellectual rest in the joyful contemplation of the one and only truth.

As a matter of fact, it is not possible to point to a single moment in the history of mankind at which such a situation has ever existed. True, there have been periods of petrified thinking and spiritually indigent eras in which intellectual life came to a relative standstill. To the extent, however, that man continued to think, he always did so in a realm of tension between "the known" and "the unknown." To think is to seek for the unknown-known or, in our terminology, to reflect on the pre-meaning. Every philosophy is a hermeneutics of the world's pre-meaning and, because all human interpretations cannot exhaust the riches of its hidden meaning, a plurality of philosophical visions is inevitable. Even the most universal system contains, let us repeat it, only a *part* of truth and an approach to this partial truth. There is, therefore, room for thinkers who proceed from other fundamental experiences, who draw attention to other aspects of the experienced reality, or who give different foundations, interpretations and applications of known principles.

"Loving Contest." This situation is painful, yet also consoling. It is painful because it shows man that it is impossible for him to see the whole of truth within the horizon of a world. At the same time, it is consoling because it shows that divergent philosophical theses do not have to be contradictory in the sense in which this term is used in logic. For every philosophical statement has to be considered within the framework of a philosophical vision. When the apparently contradictory judgments are understood in this way, it becomes evident that each of them corresponds to an entirely different intellectual perspective. For this reason such judgments cannot be reduced to logical contradictions by means of formal thought processes. At least, the reduction will be only apparently successful, and a more profound interpretation will

usually show that the two supposedly contradictory judgments do not refer to exactly the same thing.

Accordingly, the history of philosophy is neither a series of mistakes nor a continuous progress of knowledge based on essentially the same method, but it is a struggle for light, a searching for ever new ways of grasping "the whole." And because the light is immeasurable and the whole infinitely rich, more may be expected from several divergent attempts to discover something of the whole than from a single continuous endeavor which always proceeds in the same stereotyped fashion. No matter how strange it may appear, on the level of the third objectivity the most severe "ethics" of truth is quite compatible with sympathy for a certain philosophical pluralism.

This defense, however, of pluralism in philosophy should not be misunderstood. We do not at all claim that truth is manifold, that all philosophical theses are only relatively true, or that all are equally false. Such skeptical and relativistic claims are utterly foreign to us, for we are convinced that every genuine philosopher has seized something of the truth.[194] This implies that he does not have the whole truth, for if he did, he would cease to philosophize, to strive for wisdom. Our willingness to leave room for modern philosophical pluralism likewise does not mean that we consider all philosophical systems equally valuable. As a matter of fact, in the third study of this book we will manifest a definite preference for a particular philosophical approach. What the value of a system is will reveal itself ultimately in the greater or lesser contribution it is capable of making to the dialog of the searchers for truth, as this dialog is conducted throughout the course of centuries within a given culture or between different cultures. A single philosophical system, however, can never supply the norm by which to judge another system in a definitive and fully justified way.

It may be clear now why genuine philosophers never assume the mutual relationship of "research fellows" as is done by biologists, physicists and chemists. Inevitably every philosopher will

---

[194]As Paul Ricoeur expressed it to us in a conversation, "il [le philosophe] a de la vérité."

consider the partial truth he has discovered as *the* truth and the pathway he has cleared to truth as *the* approach. This situation is, so to speak, a kind of "transcendental illusion," an "inevitable albeit not insoluble illusion." Because of this "illusion," the dialog of philosophers always assumes the character of a dispute: it is essentially kept going through greater or lesser differences of opinion. The outsider, who merely understands the all too human forms of this passionate clash of opinions, has the impression of witnessing an endless and hopeless debate. The insider, on the other hand, knows that philosophers "naturally" constitute a militant *community*: they simply cannot go on without one another; the critique of one leads the other to a more refined insight into his own vision, and even the most obstinate opponents are fundamentally fellow proponents. Briefly put, the internal struggle of philosophers is a "struggle of love." True philosophers are not primarily united by personal affection but by their common desire of wisdom, as the very definition of philosophy implies. While it may be deplored that this common love does not always express itself in the form of personal good-will, sympathy, understanding, loyalty and fair play, this situation does not take away from the fact that, despite their striking contrasts, true philosophers are united by a common intellectual bond.

Philosophical Pluralism and Hermeneutic Horizon. The outsider who is repelled rather than attracted by the dialectic altercations of the philosopher is primarily the specialist in empirical human science. He would like to keep out of the dispute and to remain neutral. He is able to maintain this aloofness until he discovers that he actually has already chosen sides in the discussion. To his dismay he discovers that he has opted for a certain metaphysical vision, not explicitly and verbally but implicitly by the way in which he describes man and his surrounding world. He suddenly becomes aware of the fact that he has shown preference for one party without even taking note of the arguments of its opponents. As soon as he realizes this, he understands that it is *impossible* for him to remain neutral. He begins to see that the philosophers' dialog concerns *him also* and that he has to learn their language if he wants to follow their discourse.

As soon as the specialist in human science begins actively to participate in the dialog of the searchers of truth, this dialog appears to him in a new light. He begins to realize that the divergent views of true philosophers do not arise from defective concepts or logical mistakes, but flow from their different attitudes with respect to the "ultimate realities." Once he has understood this, he realizes also that he is not called to "verify" the arguments of the philosophers in the sense of having to "control," "check" or "correct" them. He cannot be the referee of this philosophical dispute but has the more simple and more agreeable role of *being entitled and obliged to choose.*

What is the basis on which the specialist in empirical human science has the right to choose? Two elementary conditions give rise to it. First of all, he is in the possession of knowledge. He has had experiences and he has established these experiences in the sense of the "second objectivity." He understands also the meaning of these experiences within the framework of an artificially organized realm of experience. He knows, as it were, their technical meaning, but their *ultimate meaning* escapes him. His knowledge remains on an ontic level.

It is the task of the philosopher to *offer* the empirical scientist a meaningful vision of the facts of experience. This is the second above-mentioned condition on which the scientist's right is based, for to the philosopher's obligation there corresponds a right on the side of the scientist. One who pursues an empirical science and especially an empirical human science has the right, after listening to the philosophers' discussion, to choose the particular heremeneutics which enables him to organize his factual knowledge in a responsible synthesis. In other words, he will choose a vision which attributes to his experimental data an intelligibility that goes beyond the purely technical grasp. In this way it is possible for him to say in the language of facts something that transcends the level of mere facts, without having to take the risk of plunging into metaphysical adventures for which he is ill-prepared. Because of this collaboration of philosopher and empirical scientist, the latter's ontic experience is changed into an ontological insight. And this insight may correctly be considered a contribution to the interpretation of the meaning of the world and of human existence in the world.

Briefly put, what the philosopher offers the empirical scientist is an *horizon of higher intelligibility.* Because this higher intelligibility always contains also a justified—even from the philosophical standpoint—interpretation, we will refer to this horizon as an *hermeneutic horizon.*

The Importance of the Hermeneutic Horizon. Our statement regarding "higher intelligibility" should not be misunderstood. We do not at all want to deny that the empirical notions as such are already endowed with a certain intelligibility. They are interconnected with other notions and together with them constitute the "universe of discourse" of the pertinent science. Within this discourse knowledge of the research techniques may serve to determine the functional interrelationship of the terms. Binet, for instance, has a certain right to declare that intelligence is that which is measured by his tests. Such a description even fits in very conveniently with the operationalistic approach.

As the reader will recall, the leading ideas of this approach have been described and criticized in the preceding pages.[194] However, let us illustrate the unsatisfactory character of the way in which operationalism determines its concepts by means of a single example. If anyone had asked Binet a second question— namely, what the tests are with which he experimented—his only reply could have been that they are means to measure intelligence. The two replies show both the strong and the weak sides of this kind of rigorous empiricism. At first its closed "universe of discourse" makes a strong impression because all its terms are clearly defined. On closer inspection, however, it appears that the empiricist relies on the content of notion *B* to determine that of notion *A* and then refers back to *A* to determine *B*. In other words, the intelligibility of the entire empiricist-operationalistic discourse does not go beyond the level of a " 'technified' knowledge" (Marcel).

One who wants to overcome the lure of empiricism has to try to arrive at a genuine justification of scientific concepts and

---

[194]See p. 159.

especially of the fundamental concepts of the sciences. New elements have to be introduced into the scientific discourse. These elements, however, cannot be borrowed from a different realm of scientific experience. No one, for instance, will think of introducing the concepts used in esthetic literature into economics or economic concepts into psychology. The new terms, therefore, will be derived at first from a more profound hermeneutics of the old terms. Such an interpretation, however, can be made only by one who is able to rise intellectually above the experiences that are to be interpreted. Eduard Spranger explicitly formulates this requirement with respect to psychology when he says: "Genuine understanding requires knowledge which goes beyond the standpoint of the immediate experience of life and aims at objective-spiritual interconnections of the greatest variety."[196]

Similar methodic demands apply to all other human sciences. They may be expressed as follows. To formulate a hermeneutics it is necessary, on the one hand, to rise above the type of knowledge attained in empirical science and, on the other, to keep constantly in touch with the problems of this science. Only in this way will it be possible to elevate the empirical insights and make them play a role in a dialectics that is essentially no longer empirical. If this is done, what other name should be given to such a consideration of "physics" than that of "metaphysics"? Isn't it true that a metaphysical philosophy which is aware of its responsibilities is called to safeguard the intelligibility of empirical research on the highest level?

Two examples may serve to illustrate the importance of the hermeneutic horizon for the study of a human science. The first of these refers to historical research. Very divergent visions are possible with respect to what we currently call "human history." That of Saint Augustine, for instance, is diametrically opposed to the Marxian view. Hegel does not see history in the same way as Spencer, and Comte views it differently from Dilthey. It is up to the historian, of course, either to follow the conception of a great thinker or to create his own hermeneutics. There is an almost endless number of ways in which he can determine his attitude.

---

[196]*Psychologie des Jugendalters,* Heidelberg, 23rd impr., 1953, p. 5.

5. Human Science and Philosophy

But in all this diversity one thing is certain—namely, that the way in which he interprets the meaning of history will express a metaphysical conviction. If the historian does not adduce reasons for his vision, if he does not explicitly speak of his vision, then his metaphysics remains implicit and literally un-justified. On the other hand, if he gives reasons, he pursues metaphysical philosophy. In this case he is faced with a new choice. Either he philosophizes "on his own" as an amateur or he begins by becoming acquainted with a few outstanding philosophers of history. Only in the last case, however, will his choice assume the character of a fully justified deed.

Similar conclusions apply to the realm of psychology. The existence of human groups and individual persons is open to very divergent interpretations. For instance, Goethe, Napoleon and Beaudelaire permit widely different psychological characterizations. Everyone of the psychological biographists will be able to appeal to the facts, but on the basis of the facts alone the specialist will usually not be able to say that this characterization is "correct" and that one "incorrect." The facts are grouped; they are shown in a typical fashion, but they are not forged, at least not when the author is a bona fide biographer. The only remark which the criticist can make sometimes is that the hermeneutic horizon in which the facts are placed has not been well-chosen, so that the characterization appears one-sided, forced and unbalanced. It does not enable us to obtain a better understanding of the concrete existence proper to this unique individual.

Whatever may be the case, it is beyond doubt that the psychologist's hermeneutic horizon is connected with a philosophical-metaphysical view of man. As Buytendijk remarks, the "orientation of psychology toward existence has . . . made the bond of this science with philosophy more intimate."[197] However, even he who does not use the term "existence" or sees man's existence as nothing else than a series of meaningless reactions, thinks from the standpoint of a particular metaphysical conviction, no matter how primitive and uncritical this conviction may be.

---

[197]*De vrouw*, p. 24.

Accordingly, is it asking too much that the psychologist become acquainted with the visions of a few outstanding philosophical anthropologists as they have manifested themselves in the course of history? Isn't it a question of direct concern to him how man has viewed himself and what typical possibilities and difficulties revealed themselves in these self-interpretations? Isn't a certain knowledge of philosophy simply indispensable for him? As Gusdorf writes: "There is no question of imposing again a philosophical imperialism under the guise of any doctrine. Scientists, scholars and technicians must continue to work in their own domain and in accord with their particular methodology. They are only asked to become acquainted with the horizon within which they pursue their research and to acknowledge the idea that they are not masters of an autonomous mental realm. The dense and manifold character of human reality is accessible only to a broadened and comprehensive intelligence, for which the technical questions and the technical solutions, instead of being self-contained, are merely stages in an immense inquiry into man, no matter what kind of apparatus is used."[198]

Empirical Scientists with Philosophical Interest and Philosophers Trained in Empirical Knowledge. Two conditions must be fulfilled if the dialog of the philosophers and the specialists in the human sciences is to be satisfactory. These two conditions should be formulated as clearly as possible. On the one hand, the *philosopher* must be willing to make a thorough study of the realm of experience proper to the specialist in the empirical human sciences; he has to know his main methods and fundamental concepts as well as the technical meaning which these basic concepts possess for the specialist. His "third objectivity" has to be based on familiarity with certain sectors of the "second objectivity." The *specialist,* on the other hand, must be willing to become acquainted with the "languages" of the philosophers who are important for him; he has to become familiar with their methods and systems of concepts. Briefly put, the specialist will have to be more than a

---

[198]"Sur l'ambiguité des sciences humaines," *Diogène,* no. 26 (avril-juin), 1959, p. 73.

mere specialist, and the metaphysical "dreamer" will have to be more than just a dreamer. Only then will the two be able to collaborate fruitfully.

This demand is not at all unrealistic, as may appear from the fact that, especially in the boundary region between empirical human science and philosophy, there exist special branches of philosophy, some of which are even of great antiquity. For example, the ancients possessed philosophies of life, of law, of moral and esthetic consciousness, and of politics. For centuries likewise there has been question of philosophy of language, culture, religion, history, society, economy and psychology. Philosophical anthropology, in the broadest sense, may perhaps be called to become the central discipline around which all these "special metaphysics" can be gathered together.

While it is true that most of these branches of philosophy have existed for centuries, living contact between philosopher and specialist was often absent or insufficient. The speculative thinker thought that he could comprehend the manifold realms of experience without have to resort to systematic experiences. The specialist, on the other hand, considered himself able to build an ontology without a thorough study of philosophy. The idea did not arise in him that, to be integral, his theory needed a prolongation in the philosophical dimension of metaphysics. Positivism, neopositivism and logical positivism zealously endeavored to drive a wedge between thinking on the technical-empirical level and metaphysical thought. The new element, characteristic of intellectual life in our time, is the widespread desire for broader and more profound knowledge. Great expectations are based on a new contact between science and wisdom, since "unwise" science has led to an impasse.

A Glance into the Future. These desires and expectations may be viewed as symptomatic of the contemporary intellectual situation. They show that metaphysical aspirations continue to live in modern man. However, the return to the metaphysical dimension may not be equated with a return to primitivity, myth and magic. Anyone who would seriously advocate such a return would brush up against the fact that modern man has intellectually come of age. The scien.ific illumination, then, cannot be undone but can only be raised to a higher level. The road to a metaphysics that can pass muster as a twentieth century metaphysics, therefore, leads by way of the "second objectivity" to the realm of the "third objectivity."

This assertion is in harmony with the historical vision explained in this study. Briefly summarized, this vision claims that in the past Western thought has ascended from the "natural" uniformity of archaic culture to the artificial uniformity of a universal scientific culture. From this artificial uniformity Western thought will have to risk the leap toward the free multiformity of a great metaphysical vision. The leap has to be made, for there is no other way up.

THIRD STUDY
PHENOMENOLOGY AND EMPIRICAL HUMAN SCIENCE

1. DIALECTICAL PHENOMENOLOGY

Historical Introduction to the Problem. Many contemporary authors do not hesitate to speak of "phenomenological psychology," "phenomenological anthropology," "phenomenological psychiatry," and similar topics, but the fact that they use these modern terms does not always guarantee that they understand exactly what these expressions mean. Even among those who collaborate to some extent in a scientific realm there often are considerable differences of opinion on the matter. When the subject comes up for discussion, each one appeals to a particular author whom he considers to be a phenomenologist, without being able to situate him historically within the whole of the phenomenological movement.

We may add, moreover, that becoming acquainted with the pre-history of phenomenology would be likely to confuse one who dedicates himself to the pursuit of a human science. He would notice that many great phenomenologists went so far in their critique of empiricism that they rejected the whole of the empirical human science existing in their time, and that they condemned scientific objectivism so strongly that they did not want to tolerate objectivity any longer. His first impression would be that these phenomenologists were simply anti-scientists.

A few historical considerations may serve to illustrate this point. At least three phases can be distinguished in the development of Edmund Husserl's anti-empiricism. In his *Logische Untersuchungen* (first ed., 1900-01), he penetratingly showed the impossibility to derive the laws of logic from the results of the empirical sciences. In his *Ideen zu einer reinen Phänomenologie und phänomenologischen Philosophie* (first ed., 1913), he defended the rights of the "sciences of essence" (*Wesenswissenschaften*)[1] against the domineering influence of the "sciences of

---

[1]See also *Ideas: General Introduction to Pure Phenomenology*, tr. by W. R. Boyce Gibson, Library of Philosophy, London and New York, [1931].

Phenomenology and the Human Sciences

facts" (*Tatsachenwissenschaften*). This critique found its culminating point in the above-mentioned work, *Die Krisis der europäischen Wissenschaften und die transzendentale Phänomenologie* (first published in part in 1936). This crisis, Husserl argued, is caused by the metaphysical blindness of those who pursue the "sciences." His critique, then, seems general and sharp.

Max Scheler inherited his anti-empiricist feelings from both Kant and Husserl. He was at once convinced that the laws governing moral value judgments had to be aprioristic.[1a] Ethics, he held, had to be conceived not as a science of experience but as an eidetic science studying the content of moral consciousness.

The rejection of the "sciences" assumed a more general character in the next generation among what we may call with some qualifications "the phenomenological philosophers of existence." Martin Heidegger significantly wanted to stay away from all anthropology, psychology and biology in his analysis of *Dasein*.[2] Gabriel Marcel's anti-scientism manifested itself already in his *Journal métaphysique* (1927), but never became as militant as that of his fellow Frenchmen Jean-Paul Sartre, Simone de Beauvoir and Francis Jeanson. This group raised a new battle cry. They combat no longer primarily scientism, positivism and naturalism, but direct their most passionate attacks against "objective thought." This new aim implies that these authors reject the attitude of the man of science as such. For Jeanson, for example, the whole of psychology is nothing else than a system of moral excuses. The scientific psychologist favors "bad faith," for he "contributes through his method to comfort man in his denial of everything human."[3]

In view of such statements it is wholly legitimate to ask what possible meaning could be attributed to "phenomenological psychology" or to "phenomenological psychiatry." Isn't the very concept of "empirical human science on the basis of phenomenology" a contradiction?

[1a] Cf. his main work, *Der Formalismus in der Ethik und die materiale Wertethik*, Halle a S., 1913.
[2] Cf. *Sein und Zeit*, pp. 45-52; *Being and Time*, pp. 70-77.
[3] *Signification humaine du rire*, Paris, 1950, p. 196.

246

1. Dialectical Phenomenology

On the other hand, the opposite question is also justified. Does the phenomenological attitude of necessity imply the rejection of scientific thought as such and of "objective thought"? What gives rise to confusion is that the attitude of certain prominent phenomenologists is ambiguous in this respect. We may point to Scheler and Merleau-Ponty as examples. In the writings of both something strange occurs. Scheler rejects induction as a method and seeks to find material a priori laws, yet he does not hesitate to make use of the results attained by inductive experience in his arguments. For instance, to prove the existence of an undifferentiated empathy *(Einfühlung)* in children and primitives, Scheler appeals to the investigations of Jaensch. He "refutes" Darwinism by referring to Hertwig, Driesch and Rädl.[4] This tendency to utilize inductively attained results manifests itself even more strongly in his later work, *Die Stellung des Menschen im Kosmos.*[5] Here he "solves" among others the problem of the phylogenesis of instincts, arguing against Loeb, Jennings, Spencer and Wundt on the basis of arguments borrowed from Alverdes and other unnamed "more recent research."[6]

The point becomes even more striking in Merleau-Ponty. He simply supports his views by a host of empirical facts. In his description, for instance, of the higher forms of behavior he constantly refers to the research of Kafka, Revesz, Buytendijk, Fischel, Koehler and other animal psychologists.[7] His descriptions of pathological behavior are almost wholly based on Goldstein, Grünbaum, Gelb, Head, Van Woerkom and others. It is hardly necessary to point out that these psychiatrists had reached their results through empirical methods. Of course, Merleau-Ponty is not ignorant of this fact. His aim appears to be to show that the results of empirical research contradict the world view of empiricism. But this aim implies that Merleau-Ponty takes empirical research seriously. The results of empirical human science are so important in his eyes that they can serve as arguments against

---

[4]*Wesen und Formen der Sympathie,* Frankfurt a.M., 5th ed., 1948, p. 31, note 2 and p. 138, note 1.
[5]München, 1949.
[6]p. 23.
[7]*La structure du comportement,* Paris, 1942, ch.II, pp. 65-171.

the philosophy of empiricism. The crucial question, then, which Merleau-Ponty himself does not clearly raise is this, *Is an empirical human science possible without empiricism?*

This, however, is not all. The same Merleau-Ponty who, judging from his battle cries, rejects all objectivity,[8] does not hesitate to appeal in his concrete analyses to the category of objectivity. Describing, for instance, a case of color amnesia, he writes, "When two *objectively similar* colors are presented to the sick person. . ."[9] Thus we face the following alternative: either Merleau-Ponty just talks without knowing what he is saying or what he means by "objective thought" does not correspond with what we call "objectivity," but refers to "objectivistic thought." If this is so, a second embarrassing question arises—namely, *Is objective science possible without objectivism?*

Accordingly, thoughtless talk about "*the* phenomenological psychology" or "*the* phenomenological psychiatry" is possible only for one who is utterly unaware of the fundamental difficulties. Such a person does not ask himself how an essentially anti-empirical philosophy can provide guidance to essentially empirical research. Meanwhile, however, one point should be clear from the preceding considerations—namely, that the possibility or impossibility of an empirical human science on a phenomenological basis depends on the reply to the preliminary question: *What is phenomenology?* Only when we have arrived at clarity on this point will it be possible to return to the problem under scrutiny here.

What is Phenomenology? In principle, there are three ways of replying to this question, which we have been asked repeatedly. First, one could describe the views and systems of all thinkers who have written about phenomenology or who call themselves phenomenologists. This procedure would force him to analyze the most divergent views from Johann Heinrich Lambert[10] to Nikolai Hartmann, from Martin Heidegger, as author of *Sein und Zeit*,

---

[8]He ask us, e.g., to believe in the "radical subjectivity of our entire experience and its truth value." *Sens et non-sens*, Paris, 1948, p. 187.

[9]*Phénoménologie de la perception*, p. 223. Italics of the author.

[10]*Neues Organon oder Gedanken über die Erforschung und Bezeichnung des Wahren und dessen Unterschiedung vom Irrtum und Schein*, Part IV, *Phänomenologie*, Leipzig, 1762.

1. Dialectical Phenomenology

to Alfred E. Kuenzli and his collaborators.[11] Whether a systematic analysis and comparison of the various publications would lead to the discovery of a common element is not certain.

A second possibility would be to write a history of the phenomenological movement.[12] This historical approach would have the advantage of making it easier to understand the origin of the various trends from a single stream of thought. Obviously, however, such an approach would be beyond the scope of this book.

The third possibility is to indicate as succinctly as possible what *we* ourselves mean here by the term "phenomenology." The emphasis lies here on *succinctly*. In the future we hope to have an opportunity to consider this question in a different work and to approach it from a purely philosophical standpoint. Within the framework of this book we will merely clarify the nature of phenomenology insofar as it is required for considering the possibility of a human science on a phenomenological basis.

A second argument could be adduced in favor of this third procedure. The history of human thought has become so complex that even a simple interpretative description implies the taking of a philosophical position. Leaving, then, the historical approach to others, we will present our view. We prefer quickly to cut through the Gordian knot rather than patiently disentangle the confused lines of historical development.

The Hermeneutic Character of Phenomenological Philosophy. The phenomenological philosophy of which there is question here is characterized by three features: it is *hermeneutic, intuitive* and *dialectic*. Let us briefly indicate what is meant by each of these three characteristics, beginning with the first, the *hermeneutic postulate*.

Post-war phenomenology has the distinguishing feature that it no longer adheres to the Cartesian ideal of removing all presuppositions. In this sense it has abandoned certain beloved themes of Husserl's thought. The past few decades have subjected this ideal of knowledge to relentless criticism. The question has

---

[11]*The Phenomenological Problem*, New York, 1959.
[12]This has been done by H. Spiegelberg, *The Phenomenological Movement*, The Hague, 1960.

249

been raised whether Descartes really proceeded without presuppositions and whether his requirement does not lead to infinite regress. The most serious objection, however, is that the Cartesian demand does not agree with the phenomenological situation. The philosopher's thinking is always already situated, it is a "committed thought," an "embodied thought."[13] Something is always presupposed when I begin to philosophize—namely, my existence. Note that we do not say "my being" in an abstract fashion, as was thought by Descartes, but my existence here and now. This has important consequences for my thinking. I philosophize, for example, as someone who has grown up in western culture, as someone who possesses habitually a certain spiritual inheritance. Even if I were to imitate Descartes and lock myself in my room to meditate in solitude, I would not be able to forget how other philosophers have tried to solve the difficulty I am facing. Plato, Aristotle, Thomas, Kant, Hegel and Husserl are present in my room even if I would maintain a careful silence about their presence. I always philosophize together because my concrete existence is a co-existence; as such, it is always situated from the historical and social points of view. Accordingly, it is useless for me to try to build a system in a vacuum.

What, then, is expected of philosophy now? Something far greater than a system built in a vacuum, no less than an interpretation of the mystery of my existence.[14] Such an interpreting explicitation of something which is not transparent in itself the Greeks used to call *"to hermēneuma,"* and for this reason we speak now of a *hermeneutic attitude of mind.* Negatively this hermeneutic attitude consists in this that the philosopher does not claim the ability to begin his work as an acosmic, unhistorical and socially unconnected consciousness. Positively it is characterized by this that the philosopher considers his own existence with all its essential features to be pre-given. He will endeavor to discover the essential structures of this existence and to understand their metaphysical meaning.[14a]

---

[13]See, e.g., Merleau-Ponty's fascinating critique, "Le cogito," in *Phénoménologie de la perception*, pp. 423-68.
[14]We have mentioned this point above, see pp. 230 f.
[14a]Cf. above, p. 233.

1. Dialectical Phenomenology

Since Martin Heidegger this view, we may repeat it, has become common to a large number of philosophers. Only one question remains to be answered, what are the essential structures of human existence? What are "existentialia" and what are not "existentialia"? This question contains a difficulty that is often underestimated, and the lack of clarity concerning the relationship between philosophy and empirical human science is connected with this thorny problem. We will revert to this point later.

The Intuitive Character of Phenomenological Philosophy. The term "phenomenological" is derived from "phenomenon," but it is extremely important to realize that "phenomenon" does not mean the same for the phenomenologist as for the pursuer of natural science. We may even say that the two meanings are diametrically opposed. An example again may serve to clarify this assertion.

When the physicist calls the light which I perceive a "phenomenon," he wants to say that it is "merely a subjective appearance." Light is not really the phenomenon that I perceive. This phenomenon is an indication of real light, but at the same time conceals it. If the physicist is asked what light really is, he will first have recourse to models, such as waves and particles, but because these models fall short of what he wants to say, he will ultimately refer us to certain mathematical ideas. To know what light really is, we have to perform a number of mathematical operations. The result is, as Louis Rougier remarks, that what we know about real light is something which even the blind can know.[15]

The phenomenologist, on the other hand, will remark that light is primarily what I perceive visually. All further judgments about light, whether they are of an esthetic, psychological or physical nature, are based on this one fundamental event, viz., my experience of light. All series of mediate experimental evidences presuppose the first immediate evidence, which is that the phenomenon "light" exists for me.

It should be evident that the term "phenomenon" is used here is a wholly different sense. In Greek *phainesthai* means "to show

---

[15]*Traité de la connaissance*, Paris, 1955, p. 298.

itself," to become visible, to appear. Heidegger translates *phainomenon* as *"das-Sich-an-ihm-selbst-zeigende,"* the *"Offenbare,"*[16] i.e., that which of itself is manifest. The phenomenon, then, is not a smoke screen, concealing the "thing-in-itself," on the contrary, I am in contact with the thing itself when and to the extent that it becomes a phenomenon for me. It was this that Edmund Husserl had in mind when he launched his famous appeal: "Back to the things themselves." His maxim meant an appeal addressed to the philosophers to get away from constructions, theories and hypotheses, even so-called "scientific" theories, from traditional concepts not corresponding with any phenomenon, and from pseudo-problems, which sometimes had occupied the attention for genetrations, e.g., the question whether or not there exists an "external world."

Husserl made a distinction between *evidence* and "opinion out of touch with the things" (*sachferne Meinen*). Husserl speaks of "evidence" when the intended reality is present to the knowing mind immediately, i.e., without the intermediary of signs, symbols, causal or final series. The reality in question manifests itself with the entire wealth of its content. He speaks in such a case of "self-givenness" (*Selbstgegebenheit*), and French phenomenologists express the same when they say that the thing is "given in person." When the reality in question is not self-given and has never been self-given, its presence is suspected or anticipated in an empty, i.e., vague and contentless, way. The hypothetical cancer virus, for example, is "merely suspected" (*vermeint*) but not intuited or seen. That which can be immediately seen, intuited, is evident, and this being-evident is the ultimate, unsurpassable aim of every cognitive intention.[17]

Intuition is the cognitive act corresponding to the being-evident of real being. Note that intuition is not synonymous with sense perception. When, e.g., I make the judgment: "No one can tend to his unhappiness as unhappiness," the content of this judgment is immediately clear, yet there is no question of perception. True, the most original intuition is the perceptive intui-

---

[16]*Sein und Zeit*, p. 28.
[17]See, e.g., *Logische Untersuchungen*, Halle a.S., 4th ed., 1928, pp. 121 f.

1. Dialectical Phenomenology

tion, and *ultimately* all intuition is based on it. Nevertheless, perceptive intuition can serve as the basis of an intuitive grasping of relationships. The intuition, spoken of by the phenomenologist encompasses both "sight" and "insight."

For the philosopher an important consequence flows from this concept of intuition. This consequence has both a negative and a positive aspect. Negatively formulated, it means: *what is evident cannot be demonstrated.* The corresponding positive principle is: *what is evident does not need to be demonstrated.* For to demonstrate means to make "visible," open to insight. All demonstrations, deductions, arguments and the like ultimately have to lead to insights, whether direct or indirect insights. Accordingly, what can be directly intuited cannot be deduced from anything else.

In this sense phenomenology is a philosophy of intuition. According to Husserl, the principle of intuition is "the principle of all principles." He formulated it as follows. "Concerning the principle of all principles, no conceivable theory can make us doubt that every intuition, which lets us see something in its original way of being, is a legitimate source of knowledge, that whatever presents itself to us by intuition in its originality (as it were, in its bodily reality) has to be simply accepted as it presents itself, but only within the limits within which it presents itself."[18]

Accordingly, for phenomenological philosophy evidence is the same as truth which affirms itself, which "makes itself true." To prove, therefore, within the framework of phenomenological philosophy means primarily to discover evidences or to reduce to evidences, for the intuiting of the evident is the apex of the cognitive act. Intuiting is, as it were, what "beatific vision" is in the scholastic theory of the human act, the final perfection and ultimate satisfaction.[19] Precisely these terms, all of which indi-

---

[18]*Ideen zur einer reinen Phänomenologie* . . ., ed. by M. and W. Biemel, The Hague, 1950, vol. 1, p. 52.

[19]The reader will realize that the term "intuition" does not refer to a kind of inspirational knowledge or instinctive understanding, but to the direct gaze (*Anschauung*) at what presents itself to us. It does not at all exclude an active search for the essence presenting itself. Tr.

cate something absolute, give rise to reflection. The comparison with "beatific vision," likewise, may serve as a warning, for no Christian theologian ascribes this vision to any mortal man. Thus we cannot escape from asking the question, *What in our wordly existence is evident in this eminent sense?*

The Limits of Intuition. In our opinion, the principle of intuition is not subject to doubt. Nevertheless, its value for the concrete pursuit of philosophy may not be as great as appears at first. As soon as one wants to apply it, he is beset by a number of typical difficulties. To clarify this point, let us consider the realm in which Husserl himself liked to dwell, the realm of perception. The thing is the most simple object, and perception is the most elementary mode of intuiting. Yet even here certain problems arise. There are impeding factors, of which it would be vain to assert that they are "merely accidental."

The thing appears of necessity in perspectives.[20] He gives the example of a cube, which allows me to see only three sides at the same time. I suspect the existence of the three other sides, but I do not see them. If I turn the cube around, the three other sides escape me. While I look at the thing as a whole, I do not know anything about its details, and if I pay attention to the details, the whole escapes me. Briefly, perceptive intuiting is not a cognitive act definitively satisfying me. It consists of a series of acts which, in principle, is endless, without ever grasping its object in a definitive and integral fashion.

The thing may also be covered and concealed by other things. That which I intend may not be that which presents itself. This situation may lead to typical consequences. That which is in the foreground is not the thing I intend and for which I have already a name, but I consider it as the thing intended and give it the corresponding name. Columbus, for example, went to look for the Indies. After a long voyage, he perceives land and does not doubt that this land is the Indies. The real Indies, however, are, as it were, "covered" and what lies in the foreground is Central

---

[20] As Husserl expresses it, "Es schattet sich ab," an expression that defies translation. Tr.

1. *Dialectical Phenomenology*

America. Phenomenologically speaking, it is in this way that the opposition arises between "appearance" and "reality" between "appearance" and "being." Yet appearance itself also *is*. But it is not the cognitive object which, running ahead of my experiences, I anticipated. Such mistakes are not "purely accidental." I anticipate of necessity what I will perceive, experience or discover. By anticipation I assign to that which I expect a place within the framework of my conceptual systems.

We may refer here also to the phenomenon of horizon, already mentioned several times in this book. "I fix my sight on an object, seizing perhaps also a few details of its immediate surroundings, but have only a vague impression of distant objects."[21] This statement regarding the visual horizon may be applied, with due changes, of course, also to cultural and pragmatic horizons. For instance, I see a table as a thing to put something on, a child sees a table as a possible place to play hide and seek, and, as we have repeatedly emphasized, "to see" and "to see as" constitute one and the same concrete intuitive act.

From all this we may draw the conclusion that the usefulness of the principle of intuition has been overrated by some phenomenologists. Even Husserl himself in his younger years expected too much of it. The perfect integral "self-givenness," described in his *Logische Untersuchungen,* does not correspond with the experience which a finite subject among finite subjects has of a finite object among finite objects. In other words, the grasping of a concrete object in a single act of intuiting is not a human experience. This assertion applies specifically to perceptive experience. Human perception has the character of an endless (in principle) series of acts rather than of a definitive, absolutely satisfying intuition. We may add that Husserl himself later became less enthusiastic about his intuitionistic optimism. Writing thirty years after his *Logische Untersuchungen,* he says, "Evidence is first of all a naively handled method, whose meaning remains concealed. One has to consider what it can accomplish to know . . . what its value is and within which horizons"[22] it can be used. Accordingly, for Husserl

---

[21]Cf. p. 214.
[22]*Formale und transzendentale Logik,* Halle, 1929, p. 177.

phenomenology was not simply identified with intuitionism. Thus it is necessary critically to reflect on phenomenology.

The Dialectic Character of Phenomenological Philosophy. While the hermeneutic and intuitive character of phenomenology are readily acknowledged by many phenomenologists, they hardly pay attention to dialectics. On the other hand, however, we find that all prominent phenomenological philosophers practice a certain dialectics.[23]

Within the context of this book we may be satisfied with the remark that *the dialectical principle is the indispensable complement of the principle of intuition.* Hitherto no one has seen this, save Martin Heidegger. In his programmatic introduction to *Sein und Zeit* he emphasizes: " 'Behind' the phenomena of phenomenology there is essentially nothing else; on the other hand, what is to become a phenomenon can be hidden. And just because the phenomena are proximally and for the most part *not* given, there is need for phenomenology. Covered-up-ness is the counter-concept to 'phenomenon.' "[24] Now the method to "unveil" systematically that which at first is "covered up" is the dialectic method. Let us try to make this clear.

Following Husserl's example, we may begin with an act of perception. As we have just indicated, perceptive evidences have a precarious character. They usually show us a fortuitous fragment of reality in a fortuitous perspective dimly defined with respect to a fortuitous horizon. What do we do in daily life, to complement these imperfections of perception? What do I do, for example, when I compare the different perspectives of a spatially extended thing with one another and make corrections through these comparisons? How can I neutralize the impeding action of covering and concealing objects? The reply is that I change position in such a way that they are no longer in my way, and to accomplish this I endeavor to look at the thing from opposite viewpoints. What do I do to correct my anticipations, which are

---

[23]It would lead us too far afield to prove this point. So far as Husserl is concerned, we may refer to our sketch, "Intuition und Dialektik in der Philosophie Edmund Husserls," *Edmund Husserl, 1859-1959,* The Hague, 1959, pp. 148-153.

[24]*Sein und Zeit,* p. 36; *Being and Time,* p. 60.

1. Dialectical Phenomenology

perhaps unjustified? I compare my "pre-view" (*Vormeinung*) with the experiences of others. How can I understand the pragmatic and cultural apperceptions of other human beings? By placing myself to the best of my ability in their surrounding world; for instance, I try to see the table as a small child sees it.

If the question is asked of what all these prescientific methods to correct the imperfection of experience have in common, the reply is that all of them are based on a change of standpoint for the purpose of overcoming the limitation proper to fortuitous perspectives. This change of standpoint does not take place in an arbitrary fashion. There is always a principle of order present; for instance, a spatial, temporal or pragmatic principle. And within a given order placing oneself on two opposite standpoints appears to be the most fruitful thing to do. There is question here of an embodied logic.

Accordingly, the dialectics with which we are concerned here is not a "phenomenology of mind." Contrary to what happens in Hegel, it is not the self-realization of Thought which, by thinking, "itself brings about the solution of its own contradictions."[25] In our rejection of "inhuman consciousness" we have already indicated in a passing way the reasons for this difference.[26] Our concept of dialectics differs from that of Hegel. For us, dialectics is not, as it is for Hegel, "the course of the Subject or Spirit, who begets himself, guides himself and reverts to himself."[27] On the contrary, by *dialectics* we mean *every orderly change of standpoint which allows man in his striving for meaning to neutralize systematically one-sided perspectives and limiting horizons.*

Dialectics as Dialog. It goes without saying that terms such as "standpoint," "orderly change," and "perspectives," used in the

---

[25]Cf. Hegel, *Enzyclopädie der philosophischen Wissenschaften im Grundrisz*, 1830, ed. by F. Nicolin and O. Pöggeler, 6th ed., Hamburg, 1959, § 11, p. 44. What we are saying here should not be viewed as a critique of Hegel, but as the determination of an attitude with respect to Hegel's style of thinking. We wish to make this restriction here because, as appears from various passages of this work, the author himself is greatly indebted to Hegel.

[26]Cf. pp. 51 ff.

[27]*Phänomenologie des Geistes,* ed. by G. Lasson, Leipzig, 3rd ed., p. 44.

preceding pages, have an analogous meaning. This point becomes evident as soon as we pass from speechless experience as embodied dialog to dialog as explicit dialectics. Previously, in speaking about the first objectivity, we have already stressed the importance of language for the human we-community.[28] We may now apply what was said there to the problem of dialectics.

Language may at first seem to be a means to eliminate once and for all the limitation of sense perception.[29] As soon as I explicitly assert that something is true, I think that I can transcend all horizons and perspectives. I think in good conscience that my judgment is true for all the members of my we-community. The judgment is evident or can be reduced to an evidence. There is no question here, so it seems at first, of perspectives, horizons and modes of appearing; at least, that is the naive claim of me, the speaker.

As we know, however, from the preceding studies,[30] horizons of a higher order begin to play a restricting and confusing role here—namely, the horizons of the various prescientific and primitive worlds. Nevertheless, this does not take away from the fact that the use of speech characterizes a level which is unmistakably different from that of speechless dealing with things. The first descriptions referred to a *pre-predicative dialectics*. This dialectics is characterized by this that it is one with the situation itself. A spatial change of place, for example, belongs to looking at a thing; the removal of concealing obstacles belongs to the unveiling of a hidden object. Within the framework of such a dialectics no truth can ever be expressed about the situation because in such a case dialectics is not distinct from the situation. It is a wordless dialectics because on this level there is no need of words.

The "word," however, introduces a new element into this interplay. For the "word" is a sign which points to that which it signifies but is not the signified itself. The relationship between the sign and the signified is an intentional relationship. The Stars and

---

[28]Cf. pp. 81 ff.

[29]"Die Sprache," says Hegel, "aber ist, wie wir sehen, das wahrhaftere: in ihr widerlegen wir selbst unmittelbar unsere Meinung." *Phänomenologie des Geistes*, p. 68.

[30]Cf. pp. 88 ff.

1. Dialectical Phenomenology

Stripes, for example, are a sign of the U. S. A., but they are not this country. By pointing to something that is not concretely present, the flag transcends the concreteness of the situation. In other words, the sign renders it possible to make the absent spiritually present. The word, as sign and as sound symbol, is eminently suitable for this purpose.[31]

Accordingly, the endeavor to make being present, by means of words, as being-true, being-beautiful, being-good, is characteristic of a special level of dialectics and especially of *predicative dialectics*. There is no question here of a perceiving or acting subject dealing with one or more objects, but rather of a mutual communion of subjects. The attempt of a "we" to show the true (respectively, the good or the beautiful) by means of language is what we have called repeatedly *dialog*. In the dialog or colloquy a plurality of subjects plays an active part. They depend on one another in their bold undertaking, for, as we have pointed out before, in his innermost essence each of them is "needy."[32]

Note that we deliberately used the terms "endeavor" or "attempt." "Attempt" points to the purely contingent character of mankind's dialectic-dialogical endeavor. The community of "needy cogito's" may be able to arrive at a clear understanding in a certain realm or on a certain level, but the attempt may also fail and the endeavor become less concerted. It is exposed to all the vicissitudes of the human community. On the purely philosophical level we have to admit that nothing and no one can safeguard the development of dialectics either as "leading forward" or as "reverting to itself." Mankind stands alone here with its freedom and its responsibility.

---

[31]It is beyond our scope to consider here the problems connected with the twofold character of the word as sign and as symbol.

[32]Cf. pp. 84 f.

2. THE CRISIS OF EVIDENCE

Merleau-Ponty's Doubt. In the second study we have sketched the development of human thought in three phases, corresponding to three essentially different forms of objectivity.[33] In a first phase man's speech made dialog possible for him and thus emancipated him from the concreteness of his situations. In the second phase the construction of a universal theory gave him victory over the limitation of the prescientific discourse with its everyday, national, mythical and cultural horizons. Through artificial restriction of the realm of experience pathways were made to scientific evidences, evidences which within the realm of experience in question have a compelling character. A consequence of this artificial restriction was the fragmentation of mankind's thinking into specialized modes of thought, whose mutual connection we are no longer able to encompass. Inevitably, dialog between various searchers for truth became very difficult.

This state of affairs made a third great effort necessary—the search for evidences on the philosophical level. Philosophical evidences, unlike the evidences of the special sciences, would not be made possible by the "poverty of their aim" and the "defectiveness of their subject matter,"[34] but rather would encompass and unify all special realms of knowledge. True, there are philosophers who reject the idea of "evidence." In practice, however, they also appeal to such philosophical evidences, even though they avoid the use of the term. But no other modern philosophical trend has placed so much emphasis on the idea "evidence" as phenomenology. The classical phenomenologists especially considered "evidence" a fundamental notion. Considering the intuitive character of phenomenological philosophy, this emphasis is hardly surprising.

Thus, it is all the more remarkable that the idea "evidence," so central in Husserl's phenomenology, has lost much of its value in the post-war years. This devaluation is due largely to Merleau-Ponty's critique of the Cartesian and Husserlian viewpoint. Merleau-Ponty's main objection against the central position of the idea "evidence" is this that an evidence, even a philosophical evidence,

---

[33]Cf. pp. 65-243.
[34]Hegel, *Phänomenologie des Geistes,* p. 29.

is valid only within a determined realm of thought. The most rigorous and methodic reflection in the style of Descartes and Husserl, he argues, cannot prevent this restriction, for even such a reflection implies entire fields of experience,[35] although the meditating philosopher is not aware of it. Undoubtedly, it is true that, as soon as I enter a certain realm of thought, I have to make the rules of this realm mine; consequently, the evidences flowing from them appear compelling to me. A clear example is offered by mathematics. The theorems of Euclidian geometry, for instance, are evident when I study the Euclidean system. But as soon as I begin to analyze the presuppositions of this system, I realize that these presuppositions could also be replaced by others, and in that case the "evident" conclusions would be different.

In the realm of human existence the limited character of evidence does not manifest itself with equal clarity. Precisely in this realm man is inclined to speak of philosophical evidence. For example, the validity of a certain social norm may be considered unqualifiedly evident. One who has grown up within the framework of western culture, for instance, will find it evident that the father is "naturally" the head of the family. But if later he comes into contact with a matriarchal culture, this evidence becomes shaky. The history of thought offers examples of what one could almost call a "breach of evidence." For the cultured Europeans of the second half of the nineteenth century, for instance, the steady progress of mankind through scientific discoveries and technical advances constituted an indubitable fact. "Progress" with a capital was an "evident fact" even for the most learned among them. The experience of two world wars, however, has swept away this evidence. "Once I get into it, once I enter into a certain order of thinking," says Merleau-Ponty, "whether, e.g., Euclidean space or the existential conditions of this or that society, I find evidences. Yet these evidences are not irrevocable, for this space and this society are not the only ones possible. Certitude, then, is established only 'until further notice'."[36] In other words, evidence is

---

[35]"des plans entiers d'experience." *Sens et non-sens, Paris,* 1948, p. 195.
[36]*Phénoménologie de la perception,* p. 454. The examples used above have been borrowed from Merleau-Ponty.

valid only when I open myself to it, and the "I" here does not mean "I, this thinking thing," or "this pure consciousness," but "I, this concrete human being with my historical, social and cultural horizons." The evidences are not, so to speak, truths which make themselves true, but *we* make them true. "The laws of our thinking and of our evidences are facts, indeed, but not separable from us."[37] This thesis of Merleau-Ponty is rich in consequences. One would have to conclude from it that, when the social and cultural climate changes and when we as concrete human beings become different, our evidences likewise cease to be evident.

One may ask whether this conclusion applies unconditionally and in reference to all evidences. Does Merleau-Ponty want to say that there are no truths which are valid independently of the historical, social and cultural context in which they were first formulated? Is his last word in the realm of theory of knowledge really a kind of phenomenological relativism and historicism?

A profound study would be needed to reply to this question. Specifically, it would be necessary to give a better foundation to Merleau-Ponty's important thought and at the same time to express it in a more radical fashion. We would have to examine what his doubt means when it is driven to its extreme consequences.

Formal and Intuitive Evidences. Let us begin by asking ourselves whether and to what extent the formal evidences of thinking constitute a special group with respect to the "intuitive" evidences in the narrow sense. Purely formal evidences play an important role in the life of science. We see without any special effort that, e.g., $a + b = b + a$, and this insight is important for algebraic thinking. To grasp this evidence, the mathematician does not have to perceive or to imagine anything. When d'Alembert says, "Evidence pertains properly to ideas whose connection is perceived at once by the mind,"[38] the question that remains unanswered here is, How does it happen that our mind spontaneously and without difficulty seizes the connection between certain ideas?

With respect to mathematical evidences the principle governing the answer has already been given in Section B of the Second

---

[37] Merleau-Ponty, *op. cit.*, p. 455.
[38] *Discours préliminaire de l'Encyclopédie*, ed. by Wieleitner, Heidelberg, 1912, p. 51.

2. The Crisis of Evidence

Study.[39] The fundamental concepts of geometry are indeed "ideas" in the narrow sense. They have originated through the idealization of certain features of spatial reality. For this reason it is true to a certain extent that in nature there are no points, lines or surfaces in the geometric sense. On the other hand, however, this does not take away from the fact that without the experience of spatially extended and localized things it would have been impossible to form mathematical concepts, such as point, line, surface, body, point of intersection, and congruence. Without this experience no connection would have been discovered between these "ideas" and our intellect would not find any opportunity to seize immediately anything whatsoever.

Analogous connections may be pointed out with respect to arithmetical evidences. Undoubtedly, it is true that in reality nothing corresponds to a numeral concept, such as "three." Nevertheless, the formation of arithmetical concepts presupposes experiences concerning unity and plurality, whole and part, equality and inequality, as well as the performance of certain activities, such as arranging in orderly fashion, combining, taking-away and dividing. Note that the level of arithmetical thinking differs essentially from that of all conceivable concrete experiences, yet arithmetical thinking cannot exist without these experiences.

We would like to include also logic in these considerations. Logical concepts, such as "something," "identity," "non-identity," "agreement," "disagreement," "characteristic," "relation," and "connection," are rooted in our concrete dealings with beings. The elementary rules of logic owe their compelling force to our habitual knowledge about the identity, unity, inner indivision of being and its difference from other beings. In other words, the logical evidences are based on a certain experience of being as being.[40]

It is, moreover, impossible to draw a sharp dividing line between formal evidences of thinking and intuitive evidences (whence

---

[39]Cf. pp. 109 ff.

[40]Cf. Husserl, *Formale und transzendentale Logik*, Halle, 1929, Ch. IV, "Rückführung der Evidenzkritik der logischen Prinzipien auf die Evidenzkritik der Erfahrung," pp. 179 ff.

Husserl's theory of non-sensuous intuiting, *"kategoriale Anschauung"*).[41] The element of experience plays a role also in the first-named type of evidence. Why is it that we understand at once that of two moments one is earlier and the other later? Or that of three different intensities, one lies between the other two? Why do we understand at once that the father-son relationship is asymmetrical but the brother-brother relationship is symmetrical? Unlike what happens in most mathematical insights, the apparent reason is that these evidences are more directly connected with experience.

An additional remark may be made here. Our argument appears nonsensical if the phenomenological concept of experience is replaced by the empiricist concept. According to empiricism, experience consists in this that the sense organs of a living being are acted upon. Experience is a series of sense impressions which, as sense impressions, are essentially alike and all equally bereft of meaning. The experience spoken of by the empricist is a special kind of mechanism, through which the "external world" acts on an organism. As phenomenologists, however, we speak of experience in reference to our original orientation to beings insofar as it leads to knowledge. For us, experience is the necessary beginning of consciousness, and we consider thinking in concepts and categories as the continuation of the same primordial orientation on an essentially higher level. Experience, therefore, is not a meaningless event. For it safeguards the first orientation of the knowing being in its surrounding world, it constitutes on a higher level the foundation on which the world is thoughtfully interpreted. If one starts with *this* concept of experience, it becomes possible to see the connection between experience and evidence. Provisionally we may observe that every evidence corresponds to the result of certain experiences: formal-logical and mathematical evidences indirectly by means of idealizing thought, and intuitive evidences in the most direct fashion.

If this is the case, we are justified in concentrating our attention hereafter on the intuitive evidences, for they are the soil from which the formal evidences spring. If it is true that the supra-

---

[41]Cf. *Logische Untersuchungen,* vol. II/2, Halle a.S., 3rd ed., 1922, pp. 128-203.

temporal validity of all intuitive evidences has to be doubted, then it is true also that the very foundation on which the formal evidences are based has been shaken.

The question that remains is, *What is an intuitive evidence?* In the preceding pages we have criticized the exaggerated idea of it proposed by Husserl in his *Logische Untersuchungen*. In our view, there is no integral intuitive "self-givenness" for man.[42] The important point now is to describe the content of the concept "evidence" in such a way that it can be reconciled with the dialectic character of human experience.

Experience, Intuition, Evidence. "Every evidence," we have just said, "corresponds to the result of certain experiences." This statement implies that not every experience leads to evident knowledge. For instance, while I get acquainted with a landscape, a social condition or a language, I gather experiences. I proceed gropingly from one partial perception to another, from one partial insight to another. Only under the most favorable circumstances will my exploration lead to the acquisition of an evident insight. It is for this reason that above we spoke of the "result" of certain experiences. There is question of result in the realm of knowledge only when the various cognitive intentions lead to the same synthesis. As long, for instance, as I am not certain whether an excavated object is a weapon or an ornament, my urge to know is not satisfied, no matter how certain I may be about the form or shape of the object. In such a case I will weigh the pros and cons and will not claim that I now know "what the thing is."

In addition, before we can speak of a cognitive result, the exploration must have come to a relatively definitive end, it must have led to a clear and unhampered insight. Only then the phenomenon of "consciousness of fulfilled expectation" (*Erfüllungsbewusztsein*—Husserl) will occur. Accordingly, we may call the result an intuition where the data of the particular experiences are in agreement so that they can be united into a single immediate insight, where, moreover, all cognitive intentions have been satisfied in a relatively definitive way, so that the exploring activity

---

[42]Cf. above, pp. **254** ff.

has come to a relative standstill, to rest. Thus in our terminology intuition can be the result of seeing (perceiving) as well as of an immediate insight. The intuitive insight, for example, that the excavated object is a weapon is based *inter alia* on perceptions, but it is not a perception. The typical element here is that the knower is convinced that the object is what he takes it for. For this reason he does not critically reflect on the result obtained.[43]

Is Intuiting Already an Evidence? According to Husserl, evidence is "the complete agreement between the intended and the given, as such."[44] However, how can a man know what his fellow-man intends? How can he know even exactly what he himself intends? To realize Husserl's required agreement, the "intended" has to be made manifest. This can be done only by means of *language.* The expression in words, therefore, of the intuitive insight is not a mere addition. What has been intuited must be expressed by means of signs, otherwise there can be no question of evidence. Modern philosophical anthropology agrees with this idea. On the specifically human level exploration terminates and finds its apex in the typical judgment: "It is so." In this way man's "consciousness of fulfilled expectation" differs essentially from the "aha experience" (*Aha-Erlebnis*) observed in higher animals.[45] On the human level the identification of the "given" with the "intended" is brought about through an identification of the intuited with that which speech has revealed. Only after this identification is made are we able to speak with Husserl about an "experience of truth."

Radicalization of, and Victory over the Relativistic Doubt. There are two ways in which the "evident datum" can cease to be evident. First of all, the collapse may take place on the level of perceptive life. Our preceding analyses have shown how this is possible. Man's knowing and acting have a dialectic character, human experience is essentially unfinished. Thus the result of our experience is always and of necessity incomplete. At a given

---

[43]Cf. pp. 156 f.
[44]*Logische Untersuchungen,* II/2. p. 122.
[45]By "aha experience" Wolfgang Köhler means the psychical state of an animal which finds the sought solution.

moment partial data of experience, which seemed to be relatively complete, may reveal a gap, and this gap is later filled in the most unexpected way. Everyone is acquainted with such unexpected turns, which degrade the supposed cognitive result to being merely the starting point of new explorations. The things appears to have literally and figuratively many "sides" whose existence we did not even suspect. Something, for instance, that appeared to be a bay now shows itself as a firth, the mainland is really only an island, the color which after due scrutiny we pronounced to be green now appears to be blue. No naive intuiting can sustain the claim of being complete and perfect.

The second possibility which may cause an evidence to become shaky is connected with the necessity of expressing the intuited in language. The perceiver has to indicate the perceived by means of intersubjectively intelligible sound symbols corresponding with intersubjectively valid concepts. This act of naming then enters into the dialog of the searchers for truth and is submitted to an intersubjective critique. Once again we may refer here to the case of Columbus. From the dialog of seafarers, discoverers and geographers it became clear that what Columbus kept calling the "West Indies" was really Central or South America. This did not mean, of course, that Columbus had not seen or discovered anything. Yet it meant that the agreement of the intended with the intuited had not been reached. What was an evidence for Columbus revealed itself to be the mistake of a genius.

The two indicated possibilities by virtue of which the evident insight, formulated on the basis of an intuiting, can later become doubtful are always and everywhere present. Every description of man's cognitive life has to take the possible failure of intuition into consideration. With respect to philosophy this means that we can no longer rely on any philosophy of truth that is exclusively based on intuition. Either we have to cease speaking of supra-temporal truth—which is the road to historicism-relativism—or we have to give up naive intuitionism. This is the true dilemma raised by Merleau-Ponty's critique.

On closer inspection, however, relativism reveals itself un-phenomenological. Certain phenomena can be indicated which cannot be explained on a relativistic basis. For, despite all kinds of historical, cultural and social differences, human beings understand one another when they speak of their most fundamental experiences, such as their experiences of time, space, body, sexuality, death and morality. They understand one another, even though there are secondary differences with respect to the particular way in which, e. g., the body, time or death are experienced.[46] Accordingly, evidences concerning fundamental experiences can be discovered and formulated, even though it is true that it is not sufficient "to have a close look."

Thus we think that we have to opt for the second horn of the dilemma. It seems possible to us to divest the theory of evidences from its, philosophically speaking, simplistic character. For the same dialectic principle which has such a destructive influence on all naive evidences, itself can become a source of evidences pertaining to a higher level.

The way in which the relativistic impasse can be overcome may be provisionally indicated as follows. *Every evidence can be changed into a non-evidence in the course of speechless or spoken dialectics, save those evidences which are immediately concerned with the being of the dialectics itself.* For, no matter what course the dialectics takes, it remains dialectics. The evidences directly involved in this point are evidences of a higher order. The results of intuitive experience are not destroyed in them but elevated. We will call them "primary evidences." In our view, phenomenological philosophy has to rely essentially on these primary evidences.

Primary Evidences. All this, however, does not mean very much unless we can reply to the question, *Which evidences are primary?* What do we mean by evidences which are directly concerned with the being of dialectics? Everything depends on the answer to this question.

Let us begin by recalling here what we have said with respect to the phenomenological concept of dialectics.[47] We indicated that

---

[46]Cf. above, pp. 79 f.
[47]Cf. pp. 251 f.

the "being of dialectics" does not mean for us the movement of Thought which, by thinking, overcomes its own oppositions. Such a movement is not a phenomenon for us. What we are speaking about here is the *concrete being of dialectics*. Because it is concrete, it encompasses my being and my experiencing-acting interplay with things and beings, it refers to Me and You and Our necessary dialog, it includes the efforts of a We to become oriented in an enigmatic world. In other words, for us dialectics is not the immanent development of an inhuman consciousness, but the effort of mutually connected existences to discover the meaning of their existence.

Everything, now, that is directly connected with this concrete dialectics is primarily evident. Primarily evident is my existence, which includes the existence of You and of Us; primarily evident is my openness to You and to Us and through You and Us to the things and beings of our surrounding world; primarily evident are the sign and the language through which I make my experience exist as experiences for You, for Us but first of all for myself. Among the primarily evident phenomena is my body, without which I am unable to discover any meaning and to project any values; likewise, space and time, as they are projected by my bodily and psychical being; my efforts to realize the meaningful in the realm of knowledge, morality, culture and religion; the specifically human emotions which come forth from the personal, ethical, esthetical and religious existence are intimately connected with this concrete dialectics. The world also, as horizon of everything that is meaningful-for-me, must be included in the concrete dialectics.

This quick and incomplete list of examples should not cause any surprise. The realms of human experience enumerated here under the title "primary evidences" have actually been the traditional object of phenomenological research. The recurrent themes among three generations of phenomenologists have always been and still are the phenomenology of personal existence and of co-existence, of sign and language, of the body, of perception and bodily movement in space, of the original "lived experience" of time as well as of the phenomenology of ethical, esthetical, mythical and religious experience. This constancy appears to us as an argument in favor of the considerations which lead us to admit primary evidences. The themes of phenomenology appear not to have been chosen fortuitously. Wherever primary evidences can be discovered, the phenomenological philosopher can do useful work, but where no such evidences can be found, he enters the realm of empirical knowledge. We will come back to this point later.

Meanwhile this much is certain—there is only a *limited number of primary evidences*. For primary evidences are insights into the elementary structure of existential dialectics insofar as this dialectics is always and everywhere the same, regardless of the historical, cultural and social situation. It goes without saying that such insights cannot be very numerous and have a rather general character. But that is the price which the phenomenological philosopher has to pay for the fundamental character of his insights.

The Elevation of Natural Evidences by Means of Dialectics. A serious objection against our view could be formulated as follows. I grant you that there is something like an elementary structure of existential dialectics. Because this structure is necessary and general, it can be found everywhere. Yet some evidences are directly connected with it and others only indirectly. Only the former are primary evidences. By means of what criterion can the primary evidences be distinguished from naïve evidences? How does the phenomenologist know which insights are fundamental from the philosophical point of view? He cannot appeal to "general consensus," "sound reason," or "invincible conviction," for all such "criteria" are caught in the naïveness of the so-called "natural attitude."[48]

Moreover, the objection continues, people are generally inclined to consider as fundamental either that which happens very frequently or experiences which impress them very much. As we ourselves have pointed out, in a society of a patriarchal structure the authority of the male and father is "evident," for that is what we constantly find to be the case. The unusual but impressive, likewise, may give rise to the appearance of an evidence. An

---

[48]Cf. pp. 199 f.

270

2. The Crisis of Evidence

example is provided by the way a person in love looks at the world. He will be very much inclined to apply the fashionable qualifier "existential" to his amorous experience. A spontaneous evidence is unbreakably connected with this experience—namely, the attractiveness of his beloved. All his other views are grouped in a natural way around this central evidence, for precisely this is characteristic of the "world view" of a person in love. How, then, is one to show that this emotional evidence is not a primary evidence?

In reply, we must admit that there is indeed a serious difficulty here. We have the impression that the phenomenologists, except Husserl in his later years, have underestimated this difficulty.[49] To overcome it, it is necessary systematically to eliminate the natural evidences. A special method is required for this and this method is of a philosophical nature.

There are two important preliminary questions that have to be raised first. They are: How can a philosopher discover universality and necessity? and, How are these two—universality and necessity—related to each other? Obviously, necessity cannot flow from universality, conceived in the empiricist sense, for neither pre-scientific nor scientific induction leads to compelling conclusions. Rather the opposite is true, i.e., *the universality, spoken of by the philosopher, is a consequence of the necessity.* Note that there is not question here of a pure necessity of thinking but of an "existential" necessity. How can the philosopher discover and show this necessity?

In principle, the reply is: by way of dialectics, i.e., by systematically choosing and eliminating limiting horizons. The limited validity of the spontaneous evidences cannot be shown through a single intellectual operation, the narrow-minded restricted character of the "natural attitude" cannot be eliminated in a single

---

[49]We cannot enter here into details about Husserl's theory of evidences and his concept of apodictic evidence, but provisionally refer the reader to our article, "Beschouwingen over het vraagstuk der apodicticiteit en de kritische verantwoording van de fenomenologie," *Tijdschrift v. Philosophie,* vol. 8 (1946), pp. 203 ff. See also the interesting critique of Alphons de Waehlens, *Phénoménologie et vérité,* Paris, 1953, pp. 28 ff. In our opinion no definitive conclusion has yet been reached with respect to the interpretation of Husserl on this point.

stroke. To be really fruitful, the method has to suspend the spontaneous assent with respect to every empirical evidence and formulate first the contradictorily opposite judgment. In other words, the validity of the natural thesis has to be checked through the validity of the "unnatural" antithesis. If the content of the thesis is not destroyed, limited or corrected by the antithesis but confirmed by it, then the thesis is valid of necessity. In such a case the thesis expresses a primary evidence. If, on the other hand, the antithesis can not only be thought but also lived and "existed," i.e., if I can exist and behave according to it, then the thesis is by the very fact of limited validity only. It cannot lay claim to necessary validity.

It should be noted that, logically speaking, the antithesis can always be thought whenever the thesis itself is meaningful. However, in the case of primary evidences the formulation of the antithesis leads to exactly the same evident content as the thesis. We say *content,* for there is no question of denying that progress is made by our knowledge. The thesis is a natural evidence. The antithesis is a deliberate effort to destroy the validity of this spontaneous evidence. This attempt results in an—usually implicit—affirmation of the thesis. The synthesis is equal to the thesis in content, but this content is purified of philosophical naïveness. In this sense we speak of an "elevation" of the thesis, for, as Hegel correctly said, the negation of the negation is not the same as the original affirmation.

Three examples may serve to illustrate the point. On the basis of a spontaneous intuition I assert that I have the power to reflect. The antithesis, "I do not have the power to reflect," is a meaningful logical judgment, for no one can say that this statement cannot be thought. However, while I concretely affirm the antithesis, I am reflecting on the contents of my cognitive acts. Thus I affirm in an implicit, non-expressive, fashion that which I wanted to deny. The antithesis can be thought, but it cannot be "lived." For this reason the evidence regarding my power of reflection is indeed connected with a structure of my experience; this evidence is true not only in fact but of necessity.

The world, as horizon of everything that is meaningful for me, may serve as the second example. The "unnatural" antithesis says

2. The Crisis of Evidence

that the phenomenon of the world is merely appearance. From a logical standpoint this antithesis can be accepted and defended, as is sufficiently evident from the history of philosophy. However, when I formulate two judgments, one after the other, I am performing acts in time. The one judgment is not the other, but the two co-exist, they have a certain relationship to each other. What do I call that "in which" my two acts of judging and the corresponding judgments exist and are related to each other? Wittgenstein's concept of "logical space" is evidently insufficient as an answer. Moreover, I have formed two opposite judgments and their contradiction seems absurd to me. I would like to relegate one of the two judgments from the world in order to arrive at a single meaningful statement. Why? Because the world is the horizon of the meaningful-for-me and because I tacitly take this horizon into account. The antithesis that the phenomenon of the world is mere appearance reveals itself against my concrete way of existing. It leads to the affirmation of the same evidence as contained in the thesis, but now this evidence is rendered philosophically more profound and capable of a metaphysical interpretation.

When the spontaneous evidence is not a primary evidence, the antithesis simply corrects it. Because, for example, the bay appears now to be a firth, the continent an island, the green shade blue, I change and modify my cognitive and operative dealings with the objects in question. But these dealings are not essentially modified and even less rendered impossible. The antithesis, therefore, can at least, be maintained in an existence. We say, "it can be maintained" and not "it is definitively true," for it is conceivable that the new empirical judgments in their turn may have to be modified. By means of our dialectical method we have shown only one thing—namely, that the above-mentioned spontaneous evidences are not primary evidences. While they flow from my dialectic dealings with other beings, they are not connected with this dialectics itself.

We may think here also of the "invincible conviction" of a person in love that his beloved is the summum of human beauty. Such an emotional conviction also is based on a spontaneous evidence.

The person in love sees the beloved immediately as attractive and charming. Again, all the distinctions that could be made between "to see" and "to see as," between "perception" and "apperception" do not correspond to his primary lived experience. Nevertheless, this spontaneous evidence is not universally and of necessity evident, not even for the person in love himself. The antithesis, according to which his beloved is not the most beautiful human being, is, as he knows, not only conceivable but also "liveable." For his fellow-subjects are quite capable of existing consistently in harmony with the antithesis.

We do not want to assert, let us stress it, that emotional views are valueless with respect to knowledge.[50] We demand, however, that *all* spontaneous evidences—and emotional evidences are spontaneous *par excellence*—be submitted to a dialectic critique to discover whether or not they are primarily evident. We think, moreover, that the first task of the phenomenological philosopher consists in laying bare the elementary structures of existence and co-existence on the basis of primarily evident insights.

An additional remark concerning our description of the systematic sifting of the natural evidence must be made here. The object of this critical inquiry is man's dealing with persons and things, in other words, his wordless or verbal dialectics. But we have used the same term "dialectical" also in reference to the method of our critical process of refinement. Is there question here of sheer co-incidence and consequently of a confusing terminology?

The reply is in the negative. Philosophy, as we have repeatedly emphasized is unthinkable without both inner and external dialog, without dialectics.[51] True, the philosopher's dialectics belongs to a very high level; it does not destroy man's cognitive and operative dealing with persons and things or his scientific dealing with them, but elevates it. But this difference of level does not take away from the fact that every concrete act of philosophizing is a part of *the* human dialectics. Because of this, every antithesis going counter to the being of dialectics is unmasked as non-"existable" by the concrete act of philosophizing. For the same

---

[50]Cf. our work, *Das Gemüt*, Utrecht, 1956, pp. 72-84.
[51]Cf. above, pp. 188 ff.

reason in the pursuit of philosophy itself it becomes clear which evidences are universal and of necessity connected with the being of dialectics and which evidences lack this character of necessity. It is here that the method sketched above for eliminating purely natural evidences from the philosophical discourse finds its strength.

Conclusion. We are now sufficiently prepared to reply to the question about the essence of phenomenology. By phenomenology we mean a philosophy which describes and interprets human existence in its dialectic bond with other beings. In other words, the phenomenological philosopher wants to present an analysis and a hermeneutics of his existence and of his original dependence upon other existences. Accordingly, his orientation to, and dealing with others constitute the starting point of his philosophy. The evidences referring to this starting point are, of course, spontaneous evidences of experience. Phenomenological philosophy is possible only when the philosopher succeeds in discovering general and necessary structures of experience which characterize his existence as human, conscious, free, personal and bodily. Only then do his descriptions in the I-form have philosophical importance. Thus the phenomenologist considers Merleau-Ponty's methodological demand justified that man be defined on the basis of his experiences.[52] This recognition, however, does not mean that the phenomenologist's descriptions of man's essence can be simply based on the natural evidences of experience.

The primary aim of phenomenology is to lay bare the general and necessary structures of experience. We see as the proper means to this goal the methodic-critical sifting of natural evidences. This refining leads to the discovery of primary evidences that are directly connected with such structures. The analyses of the phenomenological philosopher differ from empirical or artistic descriptions in this that they aim at the discovery of evidences which can be shown to have a necessary character. In this way the phenomenologist is led to describe the most general features of the interplay of existences on essentially different levels and in essentially different realms. Phenomenology, as we see it, is wisdom

---

[52]Cf. *Phénoménologie de la perception*, p. 498.

concerning the human existence. It is not a rigorous science but a rigorous philosophy.

The phenomenological philosopher elevates all natural evidences, even those concerning the "evident" being-there of the world. Because he changes this naïve evidence into a philosophical insight, he is obliged also to interpret it. The phenomenological philosopher raises the question concerning the meaning of the world and concerning the meaning of the being of the world. Because, by asking this question, he is thinking about the universal horizon, he is less restricted by this horizon than are other philosophers. His mental attitude may be characterized by the well-known expression of Ludwig Binswanger: "In the world—beyond the world" (*in der Welt—über die Welt hinaus*). In this way it happens that phenomenological philosophy *can,* as it were, spontaneously lead to a metaphysics.

3. ON THE BOUNDARY OF PHILOSOPHICAL ANTHRO-POLOGY AND EMPIRICAL HUMAN SCIENCE

Phenomenology's Contribution to Empirical Human Science. The preceding considerations suggest in what way the phenomenological philosopher can contribute to empirical human science. The phenomenologist starts with the idea that human experience contains a meaningful structure. He tries to disclose and describe this structure in the wealth and manifold forms of man's experiences. For this purpose he disposes of an analytic-explicitating method, which differs essentially from scientific induction. In dialectics he possesses a means to show the universal validity and necessity proper to his descriptions of essences. By laying bare a fundamental structure of human experience, he provides the framework for empirical research. He contributes to its comprehensibility. The phenomenological philosopher is able to say, albeit only in general terms, to which dimension of intelligibility the phenomena belong. For this reason he can be a suitable partner in the dialog with those who pursue empirical human science, such as, historians in general and the historians of culture and of religion in particular, anthropologists, sociologists, psychologists and psychiatrists. It is not *in spite of,* but precisely *because of* his independence as a thinker that he is able to play a complementary, orientating and interpretative role.

The principle which he follows in this has a negative as well as a positive aspect. The negative aspect may be formulated in this way. The phenomenological philosopher will not attempt to explain man and the world on the basis of the results obtained by scientific induction, for all scientific theories implicitly presuppose man and his world. On the positive side, the phenomenological philosopher will endeavor *philosophically to interpret all human forms of existence, including that of pursuing science, on the basis of man's being-in-the-world.* In this respect his attitude differs considerably from that of the representatives of most other philosophical trends.

Contribution of Empirical Human Science to Phenomenology. These remarks are far from exhausting the question of the relationship between phenomenology and empirical human science. As we have pointed out, because of his phenomenological methods, the phenomenologist is able to provide a framework for the empirical student of man who wants to know what it is that his facts point to. However, when we study the works of prominent phenomenologists, they do not at all impress us as describing merely frameworks. On the contrary, they discuss living groups and types as well as theoretical, ethical and artistic realities produced by human beings in certain situations. If the phenomenologist were really to limit himself to uncover primarily evident structures of experience, he would produce an extremely abstract philosophy which could hardly aspire to the title "philosophical anthropology."

As a matter of fact, none of the great phenomenologists can be reproached for limiting himself to such structures. This statement is obviously true with respect to Scheler, Merleau-Ponty, Buytendijk, Plessner or Ricoeur. Let us consider however, the case of the relatively abstract thinker Husserl. In his well-known Vienna lecture, *Die Krisis des europäischen Menschentums und die Philosophie,*[54] Husserl compares *inter alia* the spiritual ethos of Europe with that of India. One may ask how this is possible if phenomenology is *nothing else* than the discovery of the fundamental structures of intentionality. How does the philosopher Husserl even know about the existence of such a thing as an old Indian culture? By what right does he, the rigorously methodical philosopher, introduce such a notion in his philosophical discourse? Yet, on the other hand, it is obvious that these and other historical considerations give character and liveliness to Husserl's lecture.

One thing at least is certain—Husserl borrows the concept "old Indian culture" from the science of history, and he does so without the slightest hesitation. Without giving it a second thought, he makes use of established empirical data. Since Husserl is known for his conscientiousness, bordering or scrupulosity in methodological issues, there must be good reason for his seeming carelessness. This reason is not hard to find. Husserl gratefully uses the results of empirical research after he has scrutinized the essence of experience in a philosophical way. For Husserl, the

---

[54]*Die Krisis der europäischen Wissenschaften* . . . pp. 314 ff., see p. 320.

historical data are not "ultimate data," as Sartre could polemically remark,[55] but noemata of certain noetic achievements which he has analyzed elsewhere. They are not a starting point for him, not a basis or a presupposition, but serve only to differentiate, enrich and clarify his argument.

This point is not without importance even in the philosophical perspective. The primarily evident insight into the structures of experience would remain fruitless for the philosopher if he were not able to apply it to the data of history, sociology or anthropology, even though these data themselves are not primarily evident.

The objection can be made, of course, that such a procedure is dangerous. It may happen that the empirical datum, to which the philosopher applies his principles, may be shown to be incomplete and uncertain as a consequence of subsequent research. Yet we should not be too seriously concerned about this objection. The implied risk has been taken by all great thinkers from Aristotle to Bergson. The fact that we know how incomplete Aristotle's psychological insights were and how defective Bergson's biological insights does not diminish our esteem for their philosophical achievements. The philosopher is undoubtedly justified in applying his principles to the results of empiricial research which he in his time could and had to consider firmly established.

Accordingly, the insight into the primarily evident structures of experience is a *starting point* for the phenomenological philosopher. Nevertheless, it is obvious that, when he takes part in a dialog with other searchers for truth, he will have to address himself to those who pursue empirical science. It would be misjudging the laws of dialectics to think that the philosopher is immune to the consequences of this dialog. It is impossible for him not to go beyond his starting point. And it is only then that it will appear whether or not his fundamental insights are fruitful; only then his principles will be tested for their usefulness; only then a philosophical anthropology can be born in which living human beings and groups of men recognize themselves as in a mirror.

---

[55]Cf. above, p. 35.

What conclusion must be drawn from all this? A first conclusion presents itself in a very simple way. The philosopher cannot make use of the results obtained by the empirical sciences and at the same time ridicule scientific experience. Sartre, for example, who in his study of Baudelaire appeals to the objective data of the history of literature, has no right to declare war on "objective thought."[56] On the contrary, he should candidly admit that he makes generous use of the data supplied by the "second objectivity."

An Objection from the Viewpoint of Existential Philosophy. The same argument could easily be brought to bear against other antiscientistic writers. Like all other such arguments, however, this "appeal to the speaker" lacks the required philosophical scope. It does not clarify anything philosophically. For this reason it seems necessary to us to examine the further consequences of our view, especially because this view is exposed to fundamental criticism. Radical philosophers of existence will not fail to raise the following objection.

The fact as fact is not open to insight. It does not tell us anything about the existential orientation of a person or group. Man's exercise of freedom lies concealed *behind* the fact but, as we ourselves have admitted, does not reveal itself *in* the fact.[57] It follows, therefore, that we would have to admit that man cannot be described in the language of facts, for man is not a thing, not an object.[58] With respect to man, the empirical scientist cannot predicate anything, for man has already transcended all "data" while they are being established. This is connected with his free existence. Freedom is essentially transcendence of everything factual, observable. Consequently, a philosopher who appeals to the data of empirical human science implicitly denies human freedom.

Moreover, the objector continues, this statement applies not only to man himself but also to everything human, to the deeds,

---

[56]Cf. pp. 47 f.
[57]Cf. p. 8.
[58]"Anthropology studies only objects," says Sartre in his recent work, *Critique de la raison dialectique,* Part I, Paris, 1960, p. 107. What he means by "anthropology" is exactly the same as what we call "empirical human science."

the surrounding world, the situation of man. The situation also is nothing without man's free intention. Let us think, for example, of the typical situation arising from the fact that I encounter an obstacle. A huge rock lies across my path. Considered in itself, the rock is what it is. It receives the meaning of "obstacle" only from my intention to pass along this path. Only in this way does the situation arise which we call "path blocked by an obstacle."

The surrounding world likewise is a realization arising from man's free praxis. Despite Hyppolite Taine's stubborn defense, it is not true that every surrounding world is the product of a concurrence of conditions.[59] A totally different culture could have arisen on French soil if the intentions of its inhabitants had been orientated differently. The empirical scientist also either implicitly or explicitly presupposes in his descriptions that determining factors are at work, which he calls, e.g., "milieu," "race," "historic moment," "social structure," or "neurosis-creating situation." He makes use at least of a deterministic working hypothesis. He considers man, at least provisionally, as the result of endocrine secretions, drive mechanism or economic processes. This implicit determinism cannot be reconciled with a philosophy that recognizes the freedom of human existence. Consequently, the philosopher, and especially the phenomenological philosopher, will in principle have to remain aloof from any form of empirical human science. Such is the objection raised by certain existentialistic philosophers.

The Finite Aspect of Man's Exercise of Freedom. This objection makes us return to the problematics raised by "surrounding world" and "situation." A few critical remarks concerning this matter have already been made,[60] but they led to results that were mainly negative. We pointed out that for a creative freedom there is no situation, and that human freedom is not creative. Human freedom is finite, and this finiteness manifests itself negatively in its lack of absolute creativity and positively in its dependence on others. Consequently, it is just as incorrect to claim that man creates the situation as it is to assert that he is determined by the

---

[59] Taine, *Les origines de la France contemporaine*, 25-27th impr., 12 vols., Paris, 1906-09.
[60] Cf. pp. 42-55.

situation. To admit that he is determined would indeed amount to a denial of human freedom.

This critique may now be supplemented in a constructive fashion. We know now that the dependence implied in the dynamic unfolding of human existence assumes a dialectic form. It may be compared with a dialog in which the questioner and the questioned constantly appear to each other in a different light. This comparison applies equally to man's theorizing and his praxis. Thus it is an obvious procedure *to apply the dialectic principle to man's relationship with his situation.* A concrete analysis may serve to clarify the point.

In 1084 Saint Bruno went to establish himself as a hermit in a savage region of the French Alps. The term "environment" seems eminently suitable to indicate this inhospitable massif, which can be described only in terms borrowed from physical geography.[61] By the very fact, however, that Saint Bruno seeks a place where ne and his companions can devote themselves undisturbed to their pious meditations, the environment ceases to be environment. The saint asks the mountains and valleys a question: "Where can I establish myself as a hermit?" The mountains and valleys reply, albeit wordlessly. They reply by what they are. Thus there begins a dialectics, in which the things are involved negatively and positively. They are opposed to, or in favor of a certain human intention. They are "useful," "safe," "harmful," "unsuitable," "dangerous." Precisely because things arrange themselves, as it were, around an intention, a situation is born.

What, then, is the meaning of "environment"? It means that man addresses his question to *something,* that he speaks with *someone,* or negatively, that he does not call the situation into being from nothing. Thus the concept "environment" indicates a boundary of human freedom, it tells us that this freedom has to depend on other beings, which it is able to produce, elevate and ennoble but cannot create in the absolute sense. From this it follows also that what is called the "environment" cannot be wholly meaningless.

---

[61]As we have seen, Sartre makes a distinction between the "environment" (*milieu*), which is what it is, and "situation," which is meaningful because of a human intention. Cf. p. 43.

3. On Boundary of Philosophy and Human Science

However, there is more. Let us revert to the year 1084 in the French Alps and assume that Saint Bruno has found a place where he and his companions can establish themselves. Their first question has now been answered. The landscape of the Chartreuse massif has become again "environment," i.e., surrounding reality without explicit meaning. But it does not remain such very long. The first reply has affected the questioner. From a man looking for a place where he can establish himselves he has now become one looking for building materials. From the first reply there arises the second question: "Where do we find the materials for our cabins?" Thus the "environment" that had become situation Number One changes into situation Number Two. The Chartreuse landscape is no longer the same landscape, it is no longer a peaceful valley, suitable for hermits, but a landscape rich or poor in wood, it contains "useless" and "useful" wood, construction lumber or firewood.

In this way we could reconstruct the dialectic course of history from the year 1084 to the present time, in which an important intention of Saint Bruno's followers is to get rid of troublesome tourists. This intention, of course, gives rise to an entirely new situation. However, it is not necessary to reconstruct history in this way, for every part of it would merely reconfirm our above-expressed conviction. The possibility to "proceed in freedom from projected meaning to projected meaning" (Buytendijk) is not based on an absolute creative power but on a productive dialectics, which is typical of a finite existence.

The epistemological question to be raised in this connection is, *How can such a concrete dialetics be described?* A pointer to the reply may be found in our own analyses. Typical phases and stages have to be discovered in the dialectic communication of man with things and persons. In addition, for every phase one has to indicate the realities on which man or the group of men depend. In other words, the participants in his dialog have to be discovered, identified and characterized. They are the persons, things, conditions and relations which are indispensable for the actual pursuit of man's freedom. Thus, *the boundaries of his freedom have to be indicated,* and this task may very well be done by means of empirical science.

Such a groping search for and outlining of the limits pertaining to the concrete exercise of freedom does not mean a denial, not even an implicit denial, of freedom. Freedom is always presupposed, even though it cannot be described as freedom in the language of empirical science. Yet something is nonetheless said about this finite freedom—namely, what it is *not*. Thus the empirical scientist resembles the artist who makes a woodcut. Apparently he does nothing else than cut away parts of the wood. But it is precisely because of his cutting that something becomes visible on the wood—namely, a figure. The figure is that part of the surface which the artist's chisel does not touch. In an analogous way we may say that human freedom is that about which the empirical student of man says nothing but which he has always in mind and which he can concretely delineate by determining its boundary.

The remarks made here with respect to the situation apply also to the bodily and psychical "I" of man. Or more correctly expressed, the dialog with the situation contains also always a dialog with man's own bodily-psychical "I." A child, for instance, who learns to write asks certain questions of the pencil and paper, but in doing so, also questions his own motor mechanism ("How should I hold the pencil?") and memory ("How was that again?"). When the process of learning has reached a certain stage, the child is changed. The question of how the pencil is to be held is no longer in question, but there is now a dialog with recalcitrant muscles to produce a smooth motion of writing. The entire process of development can be described only through cross cuts, called "phases." The use of this term is not deceptive so long as the empirical student of man keeps in mind that *the "phase" is his own methodic idea.* Objectifications, likewise, are not harmful provided the psychologist knows that they are methodic auxiliary means. He may not forget here that "the" muscles, "the" motor mechanism, and "the" memory are also the child. They are the child insofar as in learning the child struggles with himself. They indicate a limit of his freedom, which lies within the child himself.

In the sociological realm the relationships are similar. If a sociologist, walking through a crowded quarter of a city, thinks that he can predict with a certain degree of accuracy the future social status of the children playing there,[62] his opinion does not necessarily include any determinism in the sense of Taine. All the sociologist claims is that he can determine with great probability the social conditions required for the exercise of freedom by human groups. This claim does not exclude that in principle there is a possibility for a Corsican lawyer's son to become a dictator or for an American newspaper boy to become a multimillionaire. The sociologist limits himself to observing the obstacles opposed to such a spectacular change of status. As George Gurwitsch emphasizes, "Sociology is the science of human freedom and of all the obstacles which this freedom encounters and overcomes in part. The other human sciences, whether they be called economics, law, moral sciences, anthropology, human geography, or demography etc., are distinct from sociology only through the limitation of the direction taken by the effort [to overcome the obstacles] and by the selection of the obstacle to overcome. The reality studied by all these sciences is the same—namely, the human condition, viewed in the particular light thrown upon it by a specific method."[63]

A few conclusions may be drawn from all this.

1. *The reality of human freedom can neither be disproved nor proved by empirical methods, for this freedom is the basis of all human activities,* including that of pursuing science. The freedom of the researcher is primarily evident, and the validity of this primary evidence is always implicitly presupposed.

2. Even though *empirical human science* works with exact, statistical methods, it *does not imply a deterministic philosophy.*

3. Man's freedom is presupposed in all human sciences. This freedom makes the scientific discourse in question possible; consequently, it cannot be a term of this discourse. In other words, freedom is not a "factor" in the empirical sense.

4. *Empirical human science is a complex of sciences, all of which throw light on the finite aspect of human existence.* They

---

[62]Cf. E. J. Leemans, *Op de drempel van de sociologie,* Nijmegen, 1960.
[63]"Réflexions sur les rapports entre philosophie et sociologie," *Cahiers internationaux de sociologie,* vol. 22 (1957), p. 10.

determine the boundaries and the condition of the concrete exercise of human freedom. Thus they tell us, albeit indirectly, in what concretely the freedom of individuals and groups consists.

The Orientation of Human Science to Itself. We are now sufficiently prepared to meet an especially difficult problem— namely, the fact that human science refers back to itself. The fact of this orientation to itself cannot be denied. A few examples will suffice to illustrate this.

As we have seen, archaic man lived in a "periodic time."[64] For his primitive mind the great events of primordial time kept repeating themselves. Thus the object of experience, for the individual as well as the group, was a fixed datum. This archaic mentality, however, did not last. Sometime, somewhere mankind began to think historically. The result was that time was no longer a circle but a line; history no longer repeated itself but became travelling along a road, which is inevitably supposed to lead somewhere.[65] Once man no longer believed that the same events come back again, he began to transmit what happened first orally and then by way of writing. Briefly put, mankind began actively to pay attention to history. Inevitably this pursuit exercised influence on the course of history itself. The fact that certain human groups knew about their own, real or imagined, past and that they knew or thought they knew the purpose of history has caused the greatest historical developments. In other words, *knowledge of history has made history.*

Similar remarks apply to other human sciences. Archaic mankind lived in the conviction that the social structure was the expression of the cosmic order. It made no distinction between nature and culture. According as this archaic mentality began to disappear, man began to make a distinction between the immutable cosmos and changeable society. The laws governing society now became an object in themselves. By assuming control of society, mankind began to pay attention to sociology, in the broad sense of the term. The awareness, however, of the fact that human society

---

[64]Cf. pp. 94 f.
[65]Cf. G. van der Leeuw, *De primitieve mens en de religie,* p. 107.

is perfectible exercises influence on the course of history. For, realizing the imperfect character of his society, man looks at his social destiny quite differently from the way in which he would consider it if he were not aware of its imperfectness. In other words, *sociological ideas have codetermined social development.*

Psychology provides us with a final example. It is a well-known fact that modern man has psychology on his mind. We mean that he is aware of the existence of psychological laws. A well-known phenomenon may serve to illustrate this. While the Middle Ages did not sufficiently distinguish between "unable to believe" and "unwilling to believe," this distinction is very much present in the mind of modern western man. For this reason religious tolerance is easier to achieve now, and man's behavior in this respect has become different. In other words, a *certain knowledge of psychology has modified the object of psychology.*[66]

The question now is *how this state of affairs has to be evaluated from the epistemological viewpoint.* How can the researcher as subject study himself as object? Has it not been stated quite clearly that we can establish facts only when we stand apart from and facing the whole in which facts are to be distinguished? Have we not claimed that this *standing-opposite-to,* at-a-distance-from is a condition required for the making of statements about facts? Where, then, is this inner distance needed for the attainment of the "second objectivity"?

Our reply to these objections is a simple denial of a presupposition contained in them. The well-known catch phrases, according to which the knowing subject cannot be at the same time the known object or the eye is unable to see itself, do not at all agree with the phenomenology of the pursuit of science. As soon as we reflect on the situation of encounter or on dialog as the fundamental situation of research about man as man,[67] important characteristics reveal themselves and make it clear that the way in which empirical human science refers back to itself is wholly different from a reflection in the sense in which this term is used

---

[66]Cf. p. 123 ff.
[67]Cf. pp. 156 f.

in speculative philosophy. These distinguishing characteristics may be briefly indicated in the following way.

1. Man asks himself a question, but he does not ask himself as total existence. He interrogates himself in a certain respect, e.g., the historical, sociological or psychological respect.

2. Man asks himself a question, but he does not ask himself as he is but as he was. For, by raising the scientific question, man's existence has entered a new phase. All his preceding phases have now become past phases.

3. Man questions himself not as an acosmic, unhistorical, non-social spirit. The question, "Why was I who I was?" implies other persons, things, conditions and social relationships.

Accordingly, the questioning man is not simply identical with questioned man. There is a certain distance between the two, a certain standing-opposite-to, limited though it be, and this distance suffices to give rise to the fundamental situation of a genuine encounter or an authentic dialog. In this way all the safeguards required by the "second objectivity" are present.

An analysis may serve to illustrate the point. A sociologist writing about the social conflict knows, of course, what a conflict is. He relies in this on a prescientific intuition, even though, as a sociologist, he never appeals to it in explicit fashion. Nevertheless, it is evident that without this prescientific experience he would never have thought of studying the problematics of the social conflict and of reporting about it in an understanding way.[68]

The evidence concerning the existence of human conflicts is merely the prescientific foundation. It permits the sociologist to consider reality from a formal viewpoint—viz., the viewpoint of conflict. The original choice of a formal object produces at the same time a first distance between man as questioning and man as questioned.

Secondly, the sociologist speaks about conflicts which, at the time of his research, are no longer his conflicts. For in his research he assumes the theoretical and not the practical attitude;

---

[68]Cf. pp. 156 f.

otherwise he would not be pursuing science. Even if he has ever been personally involved in a certain social opposition, this fact pertains to a past phase of his life while he is trying to arrive at truth. The new, truth-seeking phase of his existence situates his former ardent aims, born from the conflict, in a new and scientific context and thus eliminates them.

Thirdly, empirical research is not a meditation on ideas. Our sociologist will not look, as it were, in a mental mirror to see the image of man in a conflict situation. The conflict situation cannot be described without taking into account social, economic, ethnical and juridical relations, political, cultural and religious conditions, geographical, demographic and technical data. Here, too, one will have to admit that the conflict of the free individual existence can be delineated and made concrete by empirically determining what in this conflict the free individual existence is *not*. In doing this, the empirical researcher simply presupposes the dynamism of free existence.

Accordingly, the problem of objectivity, as raised by positivists and behaviorists is a pseudo-problem. The essential orientation of the human sciences to themselves is not an invincible obstacle for their pursuit in the spirit of the "second objectivity." One restriction, however, has to be made. The student of man as man has to be resigned to an immediate consequence of this reference to itself of human science—namely, the fact that *a human science is never finished*. This incompleteness is a result of its dialectic nature. Just as, e.g., Siegmund Freud could not foresee what character western culture would assume, as co-influenced by the dissemination and popularization of psychoanalysis, so likewise is the contemporary psychologist or sociologist unable to predict what effect his own theory will produce. The only thing certain is that every human deed—and to conceive an anthropological vision is a deed—opens a new phase in the dialectic course of history, so that every subsequent pursuer of the human science in qustion will have to take this phase into account.

Relative Universal Validity and Necessity. If the phenomenological philosopher is entitled to introduce the results of scientific experience in his considerations, this right will have far-reaching consequences for his discourse. On the one hand, his descriptions will become richer, more differentiated, better attuned to concrete reality, and closer to life. On the other hand, the entire theory of primary evidences, as developed above, will need to be complemented on an important point.

While it is true that phenomenal philosophy is primarily a systematic discovery of the dialectics of existence and has to rely primarily on the corresponding primary evidences, the phenomenologist cannot be satisfied with this. He will want to apply his insights here and now to reality. But this desire implies that he has to complement the evidences of universal and necessary validity with evidences that possess only a more restricted validity.

As we have indicated, there exist structures of experience which are characteristic of man as man. But human beings are either male or female. The question of how these structures vary within the framework of male or female existence is a legitimate question even from the philosophical point of view. At least since the time of Plato there has been a philosophy of the sexes. How, for instance, does the woman experience her body, her orientation to the other, her existence in a cultural world, etc.? Such questions have to be answered, starting with general existential insights, yet in such a way that one does not rigidly cling to their universality. Buytendijk's well-known book about the woman begins with the words, "The starting point of his study has been that the woman is a human being," and he quotes with approval Paul Häberlin's saying that "the particular features of man cannot be investigated without a 'general concept' of man."[69] He then applies this methodic principle to the woman. To characterize the woman's specific mode of existence, he analyzes human intentionality. Intentionality, so it appears, reveals itself in two forms, as breaking resistance and as being-together. Starting with these two variants of intentionality, Buytendijk builds up a phenomenology of the male and female modes of existence. No phenomenological philosopher will deny that these analyses have philosophical importance. Nevertheless, Buytendijk does not formulate

---

[69]Buytendijk, *De vrouw*, Utrecht, 1952, pp. 9 and 19. Published in German as *Die Frau*, Köln, 1953; in French as *La femme*, Bruges, 1954.

3. On Boundary of Philosophy and Human Science

any absolute "*a priori.*" There is question of universality and necessity, but only of the kind that is typical of male or female existence.

A second example may be borrowed from our own analyses. It is characteristic of man's mode of existing that the beings can be conceived as mutually connected. The whole of all meaningful connections gives rise, as we have seen, to the phenomenon of the world.[70] However, within the framework of this primary evience it is possible to introduce a further differentiation. The mutual interconnection of the beings, which is always and of necessity presupposed, may be seen as a magic bond, as is typically done in the mythical world view of the archaic cultures. It may happen also that exclusively causal relations are recognized as real, which view would correspond with a postulate of the scientific illumination or at least of one of its phases. The formulation of such a typology of world views is not possible without data borrowed from positive anthropology, general history and history of culture. But such empirical data enable the philosopher to give a richer content to a general and rather abstract primary evidence.

These two brief analyses should suffice. We think that they have sufficiently shown that *relative universality and relative necessity also may be meaningful* for the philosopher and especially for the philosophical anthropologist. Mikel Dufrenne formulates this insight very clearly when he says: "Briefly put, certain a priori's are more universal than others."[71] The relativity of this universality does not diminish its philosophical value so long as it remains related to something non-relative. This non-relative element, we may repeat it, is found in the primarily evident insights as they flow from existence itself. The phenomenologist may, as is done, e. g., by Scheler and Merleau-Ponty, enliven and enrich his descriptions by using empirical data without giving in to empiricsm. The philosopher may taken this course without exposing himself to the reproach of ambiguity, provided that he knows what he is doing.

---

[70]Cf. p. 199.

[71]*La notion d' 'a priori,'* Paris, 1959, p. 37. This shows how far the phenomenological *a priori* is removed from that of Kant. The many meanings attached to this technical term made us abstain from using it.

The Boundary Region. In the preceding pages we have marked a boundary between the form of objectivity proper to the sciences of experience and that proper to philosophy and metaphyiscs. Attempting to stress the contrast, we endeavored to describe as distinctly as possible the essence of certain attitudes of mind. The differences, characterized in this fashion, are indeed essential. However, this statement does not mean that the philosopher and the pursuer of a human science are concretely separated by a sharp boundary line. The very idea of relative universality, spoken of above, points in the opposite direction.

However, this is not all. As we have seen, the student of man as man is compelled to interpret the facts which he discovers. This interpretation, we said, will ultimately have to reach a supra-empirical level, and thus always requires an hermeneutic horizon.[72] Consequently, the empirical scientist will either have to make use of someone else's philosophical vision that is known to him or propose his own philosophical interpretation of his findings. This philosophical or also-philosophical interpretation may be prudent and modest, but it can also assume the form of a full-fledged philosophical meditation, for which the empirical data in question merely provided a suitable occasion.

On the other hand, philosophical investigations are possible which concentrate on a certain realm of human experience. Numerous examples to the point are provided by the philosophy of the sexes, of history, language, law and politics. As a rule, the philosophical insights acquired through these investigations have a less universal validity because the experiences in question are not universal. They are in fact limited, and this limitation is established by way of experience. For this reason we have given the philosopher the right to make use of those empirical data which he expertly can consider reliable.

When these conditions are taken into account, it becomes obvious that the study of man as man can be pursued also in these two forms: first, in the form of an empirical inquiry whose philosophical bearing is explicitly formulated, and secondly, in the form of a philosophical inquiry which is empirically enlightened and

---

[72]Cf. pp. 237 ff.

enriched. Concretely speaking, it may happen that the difference between the two types of anthropological studies will be very small. While such studies would actually be borderline cases, they are by no means rare. The value of such studies, likewise, should not be underestimated. There is no justification for denying that certain publications in the realm of the positive human sciences contain insights of great value for the philosophical anthropologist. On the other hand, there is no doubt that philosophical studies have been directly fruitful for the sciences of experience.

Accordingly, strictly speaking, there is no question of a boundary line separating philosophy from empirical human science. We come closer to the truth when we speak of a *boundary region*. By using this term, we convey the idea that, on the one hand, some pursuers of the empirical sciences, reflecting on the contents of their experience with man, have arrived at insights of philosophical importance, and on the other hand, that there are philosophers who have thrown light on the concrete existence of man in a way that has proved illuminating for the man of empirical research. Despite Comte's prophecies, there has been an encounter in this realm between the philosopher-metaphysician and the man of positive research.

Many prominent men of learning become somewhat nervous when they come within sight of the "boundary region." They would like to know "what they are supposed to be dealing with here," and ask themselves whether what is offered here is philosophy or empirical research. This dilemma is likely to lose some of its importance when it is approached from the standpoint of an hermeneutic concept of philosophy. The philosopher wants to interpret the riddle of human existence, and the student of a human science wants to make a contribution to this interpretation. The fact that the latter moves on an essentially different level and uses essentially different methods from the former does not jeopardize the identical orientation of their intentions. If the two methods are independent of each other, what is there to prevent a thinker from using both? If a philosopher throws light on the achievements of man as pursuer of science, why should he not make use of these achievements? Briefly, in itself, the external resemblance which may occur between empirical research that pays attention to philosophy and philosophical investigations that are empirically documented does not give rise to any alarm.

No *essential* objection can be raised against the close connection between philosophical anthropology and positive human science. However, this does not exclude that life in the "boundary region" has *de facto* to face certain dangers. It could even very well happen that an imperfect understanding of the nature of phenomenological philosophy would make these dangers even greater. Whether or not this is actually the case is a question that needs to be examined now explicitly.

4. THE DANGERS OF PHENOMENOLOGY

Lack of Ethos with Respect to Truth. What are the dangers threatening man when he enters the "boundary zone" between empirical approach and philosophy, positive human science and philosophical anthropology? We would like to compare the position of such a man with that of the captain of an ocean-going vessel. In the middle of the ocean, thousands of miles from both coasts, he has to keep his ship on the right course. In comparison with him, the captain of a coastal vessel has it easy. He knows the light beacons of the one coast that matters for him. Thus he has fixed points of orientation, by means of which he can quickly determine his course. The sailor on the ocean, however, has lost sight of the light beacons of one coast long before those of the other become visible. In a certain sense he is in a "no man's land." It could happen here that a strange illusion takes hold of him. After being out of contact for many days with the coast, he may imagine that light beacons do not exist. He no longer looks for orientation points, but thinks that he can determine his course "autonomously," relying on his feelings, impressions and "intuitions." It is conceivable that our captain would drift around aimlessly and fruitlessly, without anyone of the crew noticing it.

Dropping the metaphor, the aim pursued by all who study *theoria,* who try to arrive at understanding, is the truth. As we have seen, there are typical ways by which mankind has reached truth. In the realm of scientific experience there are certain rules guiding man in his search. These rules have not been arbitrarily imposed, but on the contrary have shown their usefulness during the course of many centuries. True, unlike the laws of the Medes and Persians, these rules are not irrevocable. They demand to be adapted to new realms of experience and, consequently, to be renewed. Every change, however, of the rules governing the empirical approach has to be empirically justified. In no conditions is anyone permitted simply to disregard these rules.

It is conceivable also that a philosopher is anti-scientistic. If so, he rejects scientific experience as a whole. He can do so, however, only on philosophical grounds. In other words, his rejection of scientific experience has to be philosophically justified. The point is that for such a philosophical justification other norms have to be observed. As we have seen, like the scientist, the philosopher may not proceed "autonomously," in the sense that he can go his way arbitrarily, capriciously, in a sovereign fashion. He who rejects the "second objectivity" has to philosophize ex professo, he has to encompass the entire problematics inherent in his rejection. But one who philosophizes in this way is no longer in the boundary area between science and philosophy.

What usually happens, however, is much more simple, at least from the psychological standpoint. The writer in question thinks himself above the rules of the "second objectivity," and does not even suspect that on the level of the "third objectivity" there are other and more rigorous rules to be followed. For this reason he chooses the easy way of relying on fancies. He lacks the necessary ethos for truth. For, one who wants to attain the truth must be willing to make the necessary effort and, reversely, where no serious effort is made, there is no question of seeking the truth but only of self-seeking.

Phenomenological Impressionism. Why is it that precisely the phenomenologist is tempted to put a premature end to his efforts to orientate himself in the "boundary region"? Two reasons may be given. First, as we have explained in the preceding pages,[73] some phenomenologists do not sufficiently distinguish between the tendency to objectivity (in the second sense) and the objectivistic attitude.

The second reason lies in a defective interpretation of the phenomenological principles. A future historian of philosophy will observe that an imperfect and one-sided knowledge of phenenological philosophy has given rise to a peculiar view. "Phenomenology" came to be viewed as a philosophy whose guiding light is contained in the two words, "I see." On the basis of this view, the naiveness of the natural attitude, which Husserl tried to eliminate, has been proclaimed the highest virtue of the phenomenologist. One may legitimately ask why there is need of a phenom-

---

[73]Cf. above, pp. 69 ff. and 201 ff.

4. The Dangers of Phenomenology

enological movement if man is able to read the essence of beings by looking at them. As early as 1927 Martin Heidegger protested against this short-sighted and superficial view. Precisely because the phenomena are usually *not* given, phenomenology is needed, Heidegger observed. And the conclusion he drew from this is: "Thus the very *point of departure* for our analysis requires that it be secured by the proper method, just as much as does our *access* to the phenomenon, or our *passage* through whatever is prevalently covering it up. The idea of grasping and explicating phenomena in a way which is 'original' and 'intuitive' is directly opposed to the *naïveté* of a haphazard, 'immediate,' and unreflective 'beholding'."[74]

Meanwhile thirty years have passed. The worship of "immediate and unreflective beholding," rejected by Heidegger in his junior years, has led in our days to a typical phenomenon of degeneration, which we may call "phenomenological impressionism." On the basis of belief in the natural evidences, "phenomenology" came to be considered as an uncritical intuitionism. No attention was paid to the fact that the naiveness of seeing, which received so much praise, could not even be genuine, for authentic naiveness is not aware of itself. This strange attitude of mind makes us think of a certain trend of literature and art, the trend of rendering impressions. To render things ingenuously, naively, and at the same time accurately as they appear, was the artistic slogan of the impressionistic painters, poets and litterateurs, and the title of the Austrian impressionist Peter Altenberg's bundle of poetry stated it very succinctly, "As I see it."[75] It goes without saying that this impressionistic art has nothing to do with either philosophy or science.

Suggestion as "Phenomenological Method." There is another danger to which certain phenomenologists are exposed. Because they cannot appeal to primary evidences whose truth imposes itself, they have to find their convincing power elsewhere. This requires that they be expert writers, capable of representing matter in a suggestive way. Not without reason does J. Th. Snijders

---

[74]*Sein und Zeit,* pp. 36 f.; *Being and Time,* p. 60. See also above, pp. 256 f.
[75]Peter Altenberg (pen name of R. Engländer), *Wie ich es sehe,* 1896.

complain about the "magic torrent of words"[76] that characterizes these phenomenologists.

Sartre's famous "dialectics of the stare" is a typical example of suggestion. With his remarkable art of writing he depicts a very special situation for our mind's eye. Less vividly expressed, this situation could be described as follows. Driven by unhealthy curiosity or envy, I look through the keyhole into a room. When I am caught, there occurs a radical change in the structures of my consciousness. I have to admit that I have really become an object looked at and judged by the other. The other's stare takes away from me the free disposal of all things which a moment ago I still considered my tools. I find myself in a world which the other has taken away from me.[77] From this description Sartre draws far-reaching metaphysical conclusions. They culminate in the assertion that "we can consider ourselves 'slaves' insofar as we appear to another."[78]

Let's now think of another situation. Suppose that a young man looks in through a window facing the street. A girl is reading in the room. He tries to draw her attention in many ways, but the girl does not see him or pretends not to see him. Next, we assume that the girl suddenly puts down her book and looks him in the eye. Will the young man be reduced to an object by his gaze? Will he feel that his world is alienated from him? That he has been degraded to a slave because he "appears" to the girl? Would not her gaze make him experience himself as a subject more than before? What, then, remains of the metaphysical conclusions which Sartre draws with respect to the I-You relationships?

This simple example proves, we think, one thing—the use of suggestion as a philosophical method does not lead to the discovery of truth. *A suggestive description does not show anything,* for the psychological effect of any suggestion can be neutralized by the opposite suggestion.

"Literary" Phenomenology. The phenomenologist who has lost his theoretical bearings is exposed also to the temptation of

---

[76]"Phaenomenologie een gewone psychologie?", *"Gewone Psychologie,"* *Gawein,* vol. 8 (1960), pp. 88 ff.

[77]Sartre, *L'être et le néant,* pp. 317 ff.

[78]*Op. cit.,* p. 326.

4. The Dangers of Phenomenology

taking refuge in the realm of the esthetical. To a certain extent it is easy to see why. The experiences which this phenomenologist describes in an impressionistic fashion are fortuitous snatches of reality. If he were to express them in dry and prosaic terms, their insignificant character would show itself most glaringly. Thus the desire arises in our phenomenologist, usually in an unconscious way, to embellish his descriptions by using an artistic style. The "well-written" work of such a phenomenologist assumes a literary character. He feels encouraged in this because precisely in our time prominent thinkers have drawn attention to the truth concealed in the work of art.

While one may agree with most of what Heidegger says about the revealing power of the work of art, which places us in the presence of truth,[79] he may, nonetheless, see *an essential difference between artistic truth and theoretical truth.* Much could be said about this distinction, but we will limit ourselves to a few brief remarks, which should be understood in the light of the views in this book. *Theory is an attempt to express the meaning of the world in the form of intellectual symbols.* Its expression symbols are "worded" concepts, categories and ideas. Its contribution to revealing the meaning of the world may be of a more or less general nature. Never, however, will theory as theory, by becoming more and more particularized, succeed in giving adequate and integral expression to the individual by means of intellectual symbols. Theory may try to approach the individual, and this approach is even one of its main purposes, but it cannot fully grasp the individual. The old scholastic saying, "the individual is ineffable," is fully applicable to theory as such. Its task, therefore is not to seize the individual but *to name and interpret the supra-individual meaning of the individual existence.*

What is the ultimate boundary attainable to the theorist is the starting point for the artist. His first and immediate act is to grasp the individual in its individuality. Through a few strokes with his brush, a few words or sounds, he manages to produce in our mind a living person, a unique event, a unique situation.

---

[79] See, e.g., "Der Ursprung des Kunstwerke," *Holzwege,* Frankfurt a.M., 2nd ed., 1952, pp. 7 ff.

As Pierre Godet expresses it, what he offers us is "an individual essence that is ideal even insofar as it is individual."[80] This assertion applies even to so-called "abstract" art. "The power of this kind of works of art can be enormous, for they lead us from the individual to the universal, but make the universal present to our esthetic regard in a sense-perceptive way through image and representation."[81] For *the artist works with intuitive symbols.* They permit him to show the universal in the individual and in this way to present a meaning or rather several meanings.

We may think here of the above-mentioned analyses of Heidegger. It is quite possible to meditate in the spirit of Heidegger's "metaphysics of the soil" on the occasion of Vincent Van Gogh's sketch representing the peasant's boots.[82] However, nothing prevents us from attaching another and negative meaning to the shapelessness of these peasant boots. A troubadour of the late Middle Ages, looking at these clumsy things would have spoken sarcastically about lack of courtliness, about vulgarity, boorishness and meanness. Thus it appears that the work of art as work of art may give rise to several very divergent givings of meaning. The artist shows us at the same time several meanings that are imminent in his concrete symbolism, but none of them is "the correct meaning." "All images [projected by the novelist]," says Buytendijk, "are symbols, without any necessary and purposive relationships." They form part of "the world of playful existence."[83] For this reason, we may add, the images have many meanings and do not have any absolutely binding character. Intellectual symbols, on the other hand, always have something purposive. In part, they are even invented or made for the purpose of expressing *this* determined shade of meaning, and of expressing it with necessity insofar as this is possible. If this necessity is actually never reached in a perfect way, the reason lies in the fact that language

---

[80]"Sujet et symbole," *Signe et symbole,* Neuchâtel, 1946, pp. 105 f. Quote on p. 128.
[81]J. A. Peters, *Het kunstwerk als verschijnend symbool.* Maastricht, 1961, p. 25.
[82]Cf. Heidegger, *op. cit.* (footnote 79), pp. 22 ff.
[83]"De waarde van de roman voor de psychologische kennis en de psychologische vorming," *Tijdschrift* v. *Philosophie,* vol. 11 (1949), pp. 351. Quote on page 365.

is not totally a system of intellectual signs. At any rate, every theorist aims at expressing a theory in words that have an absolutely binding power.

Accordingly, the truth of a work of art differs essentially from that of the theory. For this reason the man who wants to produce something has to make a choice, and this choice is an existential choice, preceding the various acts of choosing. A certain style of interpreting the meaning of the world has to become his form of life. The fundamental artistic attitude offers typical possibilities, and likewise the theoretical attitude. One, however, who tries to conceal his lack of thinking capacity behind a smokescreen of literary descriptions will miss his chances in both directions.

Justified Synthesis. The preceding pages have shown us some of the dangers which threaten anyone who enters the boundary region between philosophy and empirical human science. The danger, we may repeat, lies not in the mixed subject matter as such. No objections can be raised against either a philosophical interpretation of empirical data or philosophical considerations enriched and clarified by empirical facts. However, the man of learning who enters this realm has to know what he is doing. He has to remain on guard.

The positive student of man, for example, who on the occasion of a linguistic investigation attempts to say what language is, should realize that he is philosophizing. He has to take into account, moreover, that from the time of the Presocratics till the present many important ideas have been put forward concerning the nature of the *logos.* He has to realize that the vision of any great philosopher can be set aside only for solid reasons. If he is aware of all this and still has the courage to propose his own philosophy of language, then and only then has he every right to proceed. The empirical student of man who begins to philosophize without paying any attention to what has been achieved in this realm forgets that even in philosophy there are norms and that even in philosophy it is possible to make oneself ridiculous.

In a similar way the philosopher has to realize that he is literally "not at home" in certain realms of systematized expe-

rience. He is merely a guest in these realms and may borrow frag-
ments of truths from his hosts. He himself, however, is responsible for the choice of his hosts and for the quality of the selections
he borrows from them. For this reason he should have more than
a casual acquaintance with a certain realm of experience, a certain
familiarity with the problematics inherent in this realm, as well
as with the specific difficulties and possibilities encountered in this
kind of research.

In other words, what is needed is a sense of responsibility. It
is not possible and even undesirable that absolutely everything put
forward in a study be actually "demonstrated." In a synthetic
study, in which experimental science and philosophy intermingle,
it could not even be done. But the author has to ask himself in
what way his assertions *could be established.* If he knows to what
realm they belong, then be knows also how, in principle, they can
be established. Although such knowledge usually remains implicit,
it gives the necessary orientation to his synthetic dissertation, so
that there is no danger that the author in question will lose sight of
his course.

5. THE POSSIBILITY OF EMPIRICAL HUMAN SCIENCE

As Edmund Husserl has pointed out, the question of how science in general or any particular science is possible cannot be the first question of one who philosophizes in a radical way. Philosophy is more fundamental than science, philosophical insights are based on a special type of evidences, and philosophical objectivity cannot be simply compared with scientific objectivity. Thus it cannot be the principal task of the philosopher to conceive a theory of science. Nonetheless, it may be one of his undertakings. We have undertaken this task here with respect to a special pursuit of science, whose character is still under discussion.

One of the results of this extended and many-sided investigation may be expressed in these words: *empirical human science is possible.* It is possible not because it is actually pursued but because it *can* be pursued in a meaningful way. More specifically it can be pursued in such a way that it is empirically justified and at the same time remains human science. In other words, the terms "empirical" and "human" science do not constitute together a contradictory concept.

All the objections, raised against empirical human science from the standpoint of objectivism or from that of certain forms of existentialism, appeared to be ineffective. By way of conclusion, we may summarize here the three main objections.

The Anthropological Dilemma. There would really be a dilemma here if the situation were such as described by the imaginary objector.[84] True, one who pursues a human science considers human individuals and groups as founders and workers of their surrounding world. It is true also that the culture known as "science" is a part of this surrounding world. Thus it may happen, indeed, that the scientific study of the human condition results in a change in this condition itself.

This description, however, of anthropological inquiry does not take into account the laws of dialectics. The act of theoretical wonder itself constitutes a new phase in the dialectics of human

---

[84]Cf. pp. 7 f.

existence.[85]   The very act of asking a question creates a certain distance between the new phase and the preceding phases of the individual or collective existence. Thus *enough* distance is present to give rise to the situation of an encounter. *Too much* distance between the questioner and the questioned subject would deprive the anthropological inquiry of its human character. For encounter and dialog demand a situation that is meaningful for all the persons taking part in it.[86]   And *absolute* distance between two finite beings would make a cognitive act impossible in principle. Accordingly, no argument against the possibility of human science can be based on the fact that this science refers back to itself.

Man's Freedom. The difficulty drawn from man's freedom would be invincible if the description of freedom, presented by the objector, could pass as a phenomenological description. In reality, however, this description corresponds to the fancy image of freedom as ascribed by man to purely spiritual beings. With reference to these fanciful images we would like to make the following remarks. Let us assume that to be free means to be able to do whatever one wants. Since, however, human existence is a finite existence, it follows that *man cannot will everything.* He may will *this* or *that,* but he cannot will both if the one excludes the other. "To will this," moreover, means that he is willing to proceed in a certain way and to overcome an obstacle by making use of a certain means, so that he can attain *this.* In other words, willing a meaningful goal makes it appear to him as meaningful also to proceed in a certain way, to overcome a certain obstacle and to use a certain means, for otherwise he cannot will the goal.[87]   Thus free man is not as changeable as Proteus in the ancient Greek myth. On the contrary, his freedom is embedded in a whole of socially, economically and culturally determined ways, obstacles and means, which together constitute his *situation.* Thus it appears that *what free man tends to is that which is meaningful in a concrete situation.* Consequently, it is possible for one who knows the situ-

---

[85]Cf. pp. 288 f.

[86]Cf. pp. 144 f.

[87]Cf. the concept of "necessity of the end" in Thomas Aquinas, *Summa theol.,* p. I, q. 82, a. 1 c.

ation to construct a typology of his tendencies, of the typical obstacles he meets in his tendencies, and of the typical means he uses to overcome them. This typology may be constructed in an empirical way. By laying bare this aspect of unfreedom of the human situation, the pursuer of empirical human science makes a contribution to our knowledge of the concrete forms in which man exercises his freedom.

The objection could be raised that this aspect of unfreedom can be determined with great probability as soon as there is question of human *groups*. But what about the study of individual existences? Is it not true that here the most surprising value judgments and purposes play a role? Are not these purposes sometimes emotional and irrational? Are they not wholly unpredictable? Is not human existence capable of making true what is most improbable? These questions lead us to the third difficulty.

Purpose as a Problem. With respect to this difficulty, formulated at the beginning of this work,[88] we would like to make two remarks.

First of all, the individual existence cannot be compared with the existence of an acosmic, asocial and suprahistorical consciousness. Even the most eccentric individual person is involved in a concrete historical, social and cultural situation. He chooses, decides and acts within the framework of this situation. No matter how much his value judgments, purposes and projects deviate from those of the group, they are not entirely divorced from them. Even if a "revolutionary" individual would deliberately go counter to the norms of the group, his behavior could still be understood as a protest against the group. In this way knowledge of the historical, cultural and social situation as well as of the group contributes to our understanding of the individual purposes and value judgments. And this knowledge is knowledge of facts, gathered by way of experience.[89]

Secondly, and this is even more important, we have pointed out that it is necessary to arrange the mass of facts meaningfully, and we have emphasized that *Verstehen* may play a very definite

---

[88]Cf. pp. 8 f.
[89]Cf. pp. 45 f. and 48 ff.

role in this arrangement. We have studied it in its three forms, as *prescientific intuition*,[90] as *hypothesis* or respectively *interpretation*,[91] and as *vision*.[92] With respect to the first two forms of intuitive understanding, it has been pointed out that their results may not simply be considered as true. Prescientific understanding of elementary behavior and expressions does not absolutely safeguard the correctness of this understanding; hence it is merely a starting point and not the substance of research concerning man as man. As to an hypothesis or interpretation, its correctness has to be confirmed by confronting it with the facts. Thus, these two forms of intuitive understanding simply fall under the principle of verifiability as we have re-interpreted and formulated it.[93]

The vision also is exposed to the critique of the research society. But in this case the critique will not assume the form of a verification in the narrow sense of the term. There is no question here of being factually true or false—for by definition "vision" implies knowledge of and familiarity with the entire realm of facts—but of the usefulness, scientific fruitfulness and adequacy of a certain way of viewing the facts. If this critique functions in a normal way, then every attempt of a fanciful author to say in the "language of facts" something that goes counter to the spirit of this language will be rejected as unscientific.

In none of these three cases does man's intuitive understanding of man have the character of an illumination, a mystic inspiration, or an infallible revelation. On the contrary, in the discourse of the experts all insights into man as man, even those that have been gained intuitively, are communicated in humble awareness of the fact that they are subject to completion and correction. They are exposed to that form of critique which safeguards the continuity, discipline and self-control of any pursuit of science. It is in this sense that we consider ourselves entitled to conclude that human science can be pursued as an empirical science.

---

[90]Cf. pp. 152 f.
[91]Cf. pp. 170 ff.
[92]Cf. pp. 178 ff.
[93]Cf. p. 136.

6. THE POSSIBILITY OF EMPIRICAL HUMAN SCIENCE ON A PHENOMENOLOGICAL FOUNDATION

Purification of Experience. If a genuinely human science can be pursued on an empirical basis, then this possibility has to be used. In this case there is no reason to substitute for the integrity of empirical research the dishonesty of a pseudo-empirical attitude, and all that really matters is to keep the pursuit of the human sciences free from all kinds of philosophical prejudices which do not flow from the very essence of the empirical sciences themselves. These philosophical prejudices may be compared with weeds. The superficial watcher of the garden does not recognize them, but the expert will distinguish them immediately from the useful plants. We have mentioned three types of these prejudices—*empiricism,* which is based on a faulty conception of the essence of experience;[94] *objectivism,* which flows from a misconception concerning the partners playing a role in experience;[95] and *scientism,* which results from a metaphysical overvaluation of empirical insights.[96]

It is greatly desirable that the research concerned with man as man be purified from all distracting pseudo-philosophical accretions, for these accretions are irrelevant to the nature of the empirical sciences. This statement, it should be noted, is made in reference to the nature of these intellectual realities known as the "empirical sciences," it does not express a wish to have those who pursue these sciences perform this purification. Psychologically speaking, it would be very naive to assume that the empirical scientist himself would undertake this task. For the possibilities and difficulties contained in his research situation lead very easily to the birth of the above-mentioned prejudices. It is very tempting for the man of research to conceive experience as a stream of stimuli from which knowledge arises automatically. For the formation of his theory it is very easy to suppose that the object of his study does not "act" but merely "reacts" in function of a situation known to him in all details. And being justly proud of his discoveries, he

---

[94]Cf. pp. 263 f.
[95]Cf. pp. 18 f., 75 f.
[96]Cf. pp. 269 f.

is readily tempted to attribute to his discovery an incorrect metaphysical value.

The obvious conclusion, then, is that the purification of experience from empiricist, objectivistic and scientistic prejudices cannot be the task of the empirical scientist alone.

On the other hand, there cannot be any question of giving up the empirical approach. It is simply impossible for mankind to disregard the "second objectivity" and to return to the "first objectivity" of the archaic cultures. The reasons why such a return cannot come under serious discussion have already been indicated: a deliberate primitivity is not primitive; a deliberate naiveness is not naive; a deliberate non-critique is a critique that has been artificially silenced. More generally expressed, there is no turning back on the road of dialectic experience. Mankind, which thanks to the scientific illumination has reached the level of the "second objectivity" is unable and even less willing to forget this achievement. The imposing experience of the "second objectivity," gathered over the centuries, can be eliminated only through another experience, the experience of a new intellectual reality. As Hegel says, "This new object, which entails the voiding of the former object, is the experience gained from it," i.e., gained from the former object.[97] This new "object," discovered by mankind's dialectic experience in the course of the twentieth century, is *phenomenological philosophy.*

The purification of the human sciences from empiricist, objectivistic and scientistic prejudices is possible only through the close collaboration of those who pursue these human sciences with the phenomenological philosopher.

Limitation of Experience. In his philosophy Hegel often uses the technical term *"aufheben."* What is the meaning of this term and in what way is it connected with the problems discussed here? According to an interpretation based on Hegel himself,[98] three phases or moments should be distinguished in the act of *"aufheben,"*

---

[97]*Phänomenologie des Geistes,* p. 61.
[98]See, e.g., *Die Wissenschaft der Logik,* ed. by G. Lasson, Leipzig, 2nd ed., 1932-1934, vol. I, pp. 93-95, vol. II, pp. 494-500; *Phänomenologie des Geistes,* pp. 57 f., 76 f., 121 f., 123 f.; *Enzyclopädie,* par. 82.

which may be characterized as "denial," "preservation," and "eleva-tion." This means that the result of the former experience is, first, denied by the new experience and that its validity is corroded; that, secondly, this result is taken over and preserved; and that, thirdly, it is raised to a higher level through the new experience. When we demand here that phenomenological philosophy perform the act of *aufheben* with respect to empirical human science, we are thinking of these three "Hegelian" phases, albeit in a very special sense.

To begin with the first, what is the meaning of "denial" in con-nection with the problematics of this book? The "denial of the first [object is not its] destruction." The phenomenological phi-losopher will not destroy or eliminate the result of empirical ex-perience, but he will draw attention to the limitation of this "first" experience. He will limit its value. He is eminently qualified to do so, for he knows the essentially different forms of intentional acts and the corresponding noemata. He is capable also of analyz-ing the achievements of scientific intentionality and of evaluating their scope. In doing so, he will ask himself especially what really has been experienced in the course of an empirical inquiry and what has been introduced merely as an hypothetical concept. Con-cretely speaking, such a limiting critique will be concerned with two phases of the anthropological inquiry—namely, its *starting point* and the *development* of that which is contained in this starting point.

The *starting point* of the inquiry has to be a real experience concerning man and things human, even though the realm of pos-sible experiences is conventionally limited within the framework of the human science in question. Moreover, this experience must have led to an evidence, to a first and provisional expression in words of that which was experienced. Again, this first natural evidence is not "infallible." In the course of the inquiry it may become clear that the experience is incomplete, based on a mis-understanding, or incorrectly expressed. Nevertheless, it consti-tutes the indispensable starting point of further inquiry. From the negative viewpoint, theories, hypotheses, models, philosophical, social or political conceptions cannot form the basis of a human science. They belong to what Husserl calls "opinions unrelated to the matter" (*sachferne Meinen*). Such "opinions" are not suitable starting points from which the pursuer of a human science can undertake his explorations.

The *further development of the inquiry* has to contain all the time the explicitation of that which is contained in the experience. This explicitation may be performed by means of interpretations, hypotheses, models and theories. However, care must be taken lest the known is "explained" through the unknown, the familiar through the hypothetical, human reality through a model of human reality. For the danger is not at all imaginary that the explaining assumes the character of a forced interpretation. As J. Lindschoten points out, "Every reconstruction of the person by way of a *model* precedes the original givenness of the person."[99] We may point here to the behavioristic explanations of the phenomena "behavior," "living being" and "situation," which, as we have seen, do violence to these phenomena.[100] Briefly, what is experienced or known may never be submitted to the Procrustean torture of a theory "unrelated to the matter."

If the phenomenological principles regarding the choice of the starting point and the explicitation of the experiences are observed, no prejudices, such as empiricism, objectivism or scientism, will be able to exercise their confusing influence on the course of the research. In that case we can be certain that the above-demanded purification of empirical knowledge will be accomplished.

Preservation of Experience. If the validity of something is subject to corrosion and limitation, it has to be, and if it is, it has to be recognized as being. As soon as something is recognized as being, its validity is "made true" and therefore preserved.[101]

What does this statement mean in connection with the problems facing us? It means that empirical knowledge has to be preserved as empirical, that the scientific apparatus has to be kept as scientific. This preservation is fully justified also from the phe-

---

[99]*Das Experiment in der phänomenologischen Psychologie,* lecture delivered in Bonn, July, 1955, Ms. 1955, p. 13.
[100]See above, pp. 23 f.
[101]". . . das dies Aufheben sei, musz es dies Andere sein." Hegel, *Phänomenologie des Geistes,* p. 121.

nomenological standpoint because this empirical knowledge and its apparatus, *considered in themselves,* are neither antiphenomenological nor phenomenological.

Accordingly, the experiment remains experiment, the inquiry inquiry, the medical examination medical examination, and the study of documents remains the study of documents. All the technical rules that apply to the respective methods remain in force; for instance, the rules governing statistics, medical differential diagnosis, paleography, and the historical critique of sources.

The scientific apparatus likewise remains what it is. Yet there is something that changes—namely, the attitude of the researcher with respect to the human being which he investigates. For it makes a difference whether the psychologist proceeds according to the schema of a "rat in a maze" or according to the fundamental thought of encounter. It is not irrelevant whether the sociologist, in interviewing someone, thinks that by means of sounds he has to provoke reactions from a strange organism or believes that he should have a conversation which is meaningful both for him and for the interviewed person.

These critical remarks belong to what we have called "the purification of the human sciences from empiricist prejudices." Once more, however, considered in itself, the empirical apparatus has to remain empirical, i.e., changes and corrections in it may be demanded only on empirical grounds.

Elevation of Experience. The thesis which through the antithesis is affected in its validity but nonetheless preserved corresponds to what Hegel calls "the negation of the negation." It leads of necessity to a new unity on a higher level, i.e., to the elevation of the thesis and the antithesis to a level of higher intelligibility.

Within the scope of our inquiry the "elevation" in question refers to the last phase of research concerning man as man—the phase of *vision.*[102] It goes without saying that not every research project in the realm of human science has to culminate in a vision and even less in a relatively independent vision. What will usually happen is that most research projects are based on an *implicit*

---

[102]Cf. pp. 183 f. and 207 f.

vision. This, however, does not take away from the fact that the value of a human science stands or falls with *the possibility of arriving at a justified vision.* If this possibility does not exist, then the pursuer of a human science will have to limit himself, as it were, to collecting little stones for a mosaic without ever being able to arrange them into a picture. The result would be that his study does not reach the level of a human science.[103]

As we have indicated, in the vision objectification is eliminated. The pursuit of human freedom, the free choice of purposes, the free value judgments, which were, so to speak, "frozen" in the climate of the "second objectivity," thaw under the rays of the vision. Human individuals and groups appear again as human.[104] The question is how this result can be attained in a responsible way.

One thing is certain here. The formulation of a vision requires an hermeneutic horizon, an horizon which is always also of a philosophical metaphysical nature.[105] It is our contention that the hermeneutic horizon which phenomenological philosophy offers to the researcher concerned with man as man manifests itself as *essentially superior.* This contention admits that human science can be pursued also in a different philosophical perspective. For instance, it is possible to conceive a general psychological theory on the basis of a neo-Kantian,[106] neo-Hegelian[107] or personalistic[108] vision. Nevertheless, we insist that the hermeneutic horizon provided by phenomenology deserves preference. The reason why has already been indicated. It lies in the fact that *phenomenological philosophy,* and only phenomenological philosophy, *is a fundamental philosophy of human existence* and that this philosophy possesses a rigorous character. It contains in principle everything which in a universal and necessary way is

---

[103]Cf. p. 210.

[104]Cf. pp. 184 f. See also Hegel, *Die Wissenschaft der Logik,* vol. II, p. 499: "Dieses Resultat hat nun als das in sich gegangene . . . Ganze sich die Form der *Unmittelbarkeit* wieder gegeben."

[105]Cf. p. 186 and pp. 237 f.

[106]Cf., e.g., Paul Natorp, *Allgemeine Psychologie nach kritischer Methode,* I Buch, Tübingen, 1912.

[107]Cf., e.g., Eduard Spranger, *Psychologie des Jugendalters,* Heidelberg, 23rd ed., 1953.

[108]Cf., e.g., William Stern, *Allgemeine Psychologie auf personalistischer Grundlage,* The Hague, 2nd ed., 1950.

valid for human existence, whether individually or collectively. The phenomenological philosopher tells us what the essential character will be of man's seeking of meaning, his aiming at purposes and his value judgments. He tells us this, albeit in very general terms, with reference to all realms of specifically human activity. By doing so, he offers the researcher of human science guidance in his understanding of the human element as such. This guidance may be compared with a skeleton, offering support to a body. It is the task of those who pursue human science to cover this skeleton with the flesh of empirical data. In this way the phenomenologist sees to it that the empirical study of human science is raised to the level of the "third objectivity." He enables the empirical student of man as man to formulate a vision which can pass scrutiny from the standpoint of "wisdom."

Toward a New Ideal of Science. The light in which the phenomenological philosopher sees the phenomenon "science" differs from that of the nineteenth century scientistic thinkers. For him, scientific thinking is merely a phase in the process of mankind's growing consciousness. This thinking, moreover, is not essentially immutable, but develops dialectically and reveals alongside continuity also the discontinuity of typical phases.

It is possible that this dialectic-phenomenological view may exercise a fruitful influence at a turning point in the history of science. The turning point in question is historically characterized by this that a group of men of science more or less deliberately endeavors not to do violence to the human element when they try to determine and describe it empirically. For this endeavor implies that these pursuers of human science have de facto conceived a new norm governing the scientific character of human research. Meanwhile the theoretical justification of their new ideal of knowledge causes them great difficulties. These difficulties, however, cannot be overcome within the framework of the special human sciences. The phenomenological philosopher, who disposes of essential insights into human existence, may perhaps be able to make a contribution to the theoretical justification of the new form assumed by their scientific knowledge. Perhaps it is his role to act as "midwife" at the birth of *a new ideal of science.*

313

BIBLIOGRAPHY

T. Abel, "The Operation Called 'Verstehen,'" *American Journal of Sociology*, vol. 54 (1948-49), pp. 221 ff.

A. Adler, *Praxis und Theorie der Individualpsychologie*, 5th ed., München, 1930.
Menschenkenntnis, 6th ed., Zürich, 1954.

K. Ajdukiewicz, "Das Weltbild und die Begriffsapparatur," *Erkenntnis*, vol. 4 (1934).

H. Albrecht, *Über das Gemüt*, Stuttgart, 1961.

J. L. d'Alembert, *Discours préliminaire de l'Encyclopédie*, ed. by H. Wieleitner, Heidelberg, 1912.

F. Alexander and Th.M. French, *Studies in Psychosomatic Medicine*, New York, 1948.

F. H. Allport, *Theories of Perception and the Concept of Structure*, New York, 1955.

G. W. Allport, *Becoming. Basic Considerations for a Psychology of Personality*, New Haven, 1955.

Aristotle, *Opera Omnia*, Berlin, 1831-1870.

R. Aron, *Introduction à la philosophie de l'histoire. Essai sur les limites de l'objectivité historique*, Paris, 1933.

A. J. Ayer, *Language, Truth and Logic*, London, 2nd ed., 1948.
The Problem of Knowledge, London, 1956.

S. Bachelard, *La conscience de la réalité. Étude phénoménologique sur la physique mathématique*, Paris, 1958.

J. Barion, "Dialektik der Natur und Geschichte," *Erkenntnis und Verantwortung*, Düsseldorf, 1960, pp. 91 ff.

R. F. Beerling, *Moderne doodsproblematiek*, Delft, 1946.
Kratos. Studies over de macht, Antwerpen, 1956.

N. Beets, *Over lichaamsbeweging en sexualiteit in de puberteit*, Utrecht, 1959.

K. L. Bellon, *Inleiding tot de natuurlijke godsdienstwetenschap*, Antwerpen, 1948.
"Nieuwe wegen in de godsdienstwetenschappen," *Studia Catholica*, vol. 28 (1953), pp. 241 ff.

R. Benedict, *Patterns of Culture*, 18th impr., New York, 1960.

G. Berger, *Le cogito dans la philosophie de Husserl*, Paris, 1941.

E. Berghoff, *Entwicklungsgeschichte des Krankheitsbegriffes*, Vienna, 2nd ed., 1947.

H. Bergson, "Introduction à la métaphysique," *Revue de métaphysique et de morale*, Jan., 1903.

315

Phenomenology and the Human Sciences

Phenomenology and the Human Sciences

Phenomenology and the Human Sciences

R. Berlinger, "Der geschichtliche Augenblick," *Jahrbuch f. Psych. u. Psychother.*, 1958, pp. 20 ff.

C. Bernard, *Introduction à la médicine expérimentale*, Paris, 1900.

E. W. Beth, *De wijsbegeerte der wiskunde van Parmenides tot Bolzano,* Antwerpen, 1944.
Inleiding tot de wijsbegeerte der exacte wetenschappen, Antwerpen, 1953.
De weg der wetenschap. Inleiding tot de methodeleer der empirische wetenschappen, Haarlem, 1958.

D. Bidney, *Theoretical Anthropology,* New York, 2nd impr., 1954.

J. Bierens de Haan, *Sociologie, ontwikkeling en methode,* The Hague, 1946.

R. Bierstedt, *The Social Order. An Introduction to Sociology,* New York, 1957.

R. Biese, *Die Erkenntnislehre des Aristoteles und Kants in Vergleichung ihrer Grundprinzipien historisch-critisch dargestellt,* Berlin, 1877.

L. Binswanger, *Ausgewählte Vorträge und Aufsätze,* Bd. I, 2nd ed., Bern, 1961; Bd. II, Bern, 1955.

H. Birault, "L'onto-théo-logique hégelienne et la dialectique," *Tijdschrift v. Philosophie,* vol. 20 (1958), pp. 646 ff.

F. Boas, *The Mind of Primitive Man,* New York, 1913.

R. Boehm, "Husserl et l'idéalisme classique," *Revue philosophique de Louvain,* vol. 57 (1959), pp. 351 ff.
"Les ambiguités des concepts husserliens d' 'immanence' et de transcendance," *Revue philosophique,* vol. 149 (1959), pp. 481 ff.
"Pensée et technique," *Revue internationale de philosophie,* vol. 52 (1960), pp. 1 ff.

H. Boelaars, "Husserls reducties en haar betekenis voor het Thomisme," *Tijdschrift v. Philosophie,* vol. 6 (1944), pp. 333 ff.

O. F. Bollnow, *Neue Geborgenheit. Das Problem einer Überwindung des Existentialismus,* Stuttgart, 1955.
Existenzphilosophie, Stuttgart, 4th ed., 1955.

M. Bonaparte, *Psychoanalyse et anthropologie,* Paris, 1952.
Psychoanalyse et biologie, Paris, 1952.

E. G. Boring, *A History of Experimental Psychology,* 2nd ed., New York, 1957.

M. Boss, *Einführung in die psychosomatische Medizin,* Bern, 1954.

P. J. Bouman, *Sociologie. Begrippen en problemen,* Antwerpen, 6th ed., 1958.

G. Bouthoul, *Les mentalités,* Paris, 1952.

G. Brand, *Welt, Ich und Zeit,* The Hague, 1955.

F. Brentano, *Psychologie vom empirischen Standpunkt,* ed. by O. Kraus, 2nd ed., 2 vols., Hamburg, 1955 and 1959.
Versuch über die Erkenntnis, ed. by A. Kastil, Leipzig, 1925.
Wahrheit und Evidenz, ed. by O. Kraus, Leipzig, 1930.

Bibliography

S. Breton, *Intention et intentionnalité*, Paris, 1956.

P. W. Bridgman, "Operational Analysis," *Philosophy of Science*, vol. 5 (1948), pp. 114 ff.
The Logic of Modern Physics, New York, 7th impr., 1954.
The Way Things Are, Cambridge, Mass., 1959.

J. F. W. Brugmans, *Psychologische methoden en begrippen*, Haarlem, 4th ed., 1958.

A. Brunner, *La personne incarnée*, Paris, 1947.

E. Brunswik, "The Conceptual Framework of Psychology," *International Encyclopedia of Unified Sciences*, Chicago, 1952.

B. Th. Brus, "De taal by Merleau-Ponty," *Nederl. Tijdschr. v.d. Psych. en haar grensgebieden*, vol. 13 (1958), pp. 31 ff.

M. Buber, *Dialogisches Leben*, Zürich, 1947.
Das Problem des Menschen, Heidelberg, 1948.

Ch. Bühler, *Der menschliche Lebenslauf als psychologisches Problem*, Göttingen, 2nd ed., 1959.

A. Busemann, *Der Aufzähl-Test*, München, 1955.

F. J. J. Buytendijk, *De Vrouw*, Utrecht, 1952. German ed., *Die Frau*, Köln, 1953; French ed., *La Femme*, Bruges, 1954.
"Zur Phänomenologie der Begegnung," *Eranos-Jahrbuch*, vol. 19 (1951), pp. 431 ff.
"Vernieuwing in de wetenschap," *Annalen v.h. Thijmgenootschap*, vol. 42 (1954), pp. 230 ff.
Algemene theorie der menselijke houding en beweging, Utrecht, 2nd ed., 1957.
"Das Menschliche in der menschlichen Bewegung," *Der Nervenarzt*, vol. 28 (1957), pp. 1 ff.
Das Menschliche, Stuttgart, 1958.
"Wat is psychologisch kennen?" *Gawein*, vol. 9 (oct. 1960), pp. 2 ff.
"De waarde van de roman voor de psychologische kennis en de psychologische vorming," *Tijdschrift v. Philosophie*, vol. 11 (1949), pp. 351 ff.

R. Carnap, "Die physikalische Sprache als Universalsprache der Wissenschaft," *Erkenntnis*, vol. 2 (1931-32).
"Über Protokollsätze," *loc. cit.*, vol. 2 (1931-32) and 3 (1932-33).
"Psychologie in physikalischer Sprache," *loc. cit.*, vol. 3 (1932-33).
"Testability and Meaning," *Philosophy of Science*, vol. 3 (1936) and 4 (1937).
"Logical Foundations of the Unity of Science," *International Encyclopedia of Unified Sciences*, vol. 1, no. 1, Chicago, 1938.
Meaning and Necessity. A Study in Semantics and Modal Logic, Chicago, 2nd ed., 1958.

C. G. Carus, *Von den Naturreichen*, ed. by W. Keiszer, Berlin, 3rd ed., 1944.

I. Caruso, "Excerpta Anthropologica," *Jahrbuch f. Psych. u. Psychotherap.*, vol. 6 (1958), pp. 1 ff.

E. Cassirer, *Das Erkenntnisproblem in der Philosophie und Wissenschaft der neueren Zeit*, 4 vols., Berlin, 1906-1957.

Essay on Man. An Introduction to a Philosophy of Human Culture, New Haven, 3rd impr., 1945.
Philosophie der symbolischen Formen, 3 vols., Oxford, 2nd ed., 1954.
The Logic of the Humanities, New Haven, 1961.

R. B. Cattel, *Personality and Motivation Structure and Measurement,* New York, 1957.

D. Chantepie de la Saussaye, *Lehrbuch der Religionsgeschichte,* ed. by A. Bertholet and E. Lehmann, two vols., Tübingen, 1924-25.

A. M. J. Chorus, *Inleiding in de empirische karakterkunde,* Leiden, 1958.
Psychologie van de menselijke levensloop, Leiden, 1959.
"Wijsgerige en nationale krachtlijnen in de ontwikkeling der psychologie," *Ned. Tijdschrift v. d. Psych. en haar grensgebieden,* vol. 15 (1960), pp. 85 ff.

P. Christian, *Das Personenverständnis im modernen medizinischen Denken,* Tübingen, 1952.
"Möglichkeiten und Grenzen einer naturwissenschaftlichen Betrachtung der menschlichen Bewegung," *Jahrbuch f. Psych. u. Psychotherap.,* vol. 4 (1957), pp. 346 ff.
"Begegnen und Antreffen (Zur Problematik einer anthropologischen Psychologie)," *loc. cit.,* vol. 6 (1958), pp. 93 ff.

H. Cohen, *Logik der reinen Erkenntnis,* Berlin, 3rd ed., 1923.

J. Cohen, *Humanistic Psychology,* London, 1958.

A. Comte, *Principes de philosophie positive,* Paris, 1896.
Cours de philosophie positive, Paris, 5th ed., 1907.

B. Croce, *Die Geschichte als Gedanke und als Tat,* tr. by G. Bondy, Bern, 1944.

R. Dahrendorf, *Homo sociologicus,* Köln-Opladen, 1960.

A. de Coninck, *L'unité de la connaissance humaine et le fondement de sa valeur,* Louvain, 2nd ed., 1947.

B. Delfgaauw, *Beknopte geschiedenis der wijsbegeerte,* vol. 3, Baarn, 1952.

A. Dempf, *Einheit der Wissenschaft,* Stuttgart, 1955.
Kritik der historischer Vernunft, München, 1957.

A. de Muralt, *L'idée de la phénoménologie,* Paris, 1958.

D. M. de Petter, "Metaphysiek en phenomenologie," *Lezing v.d. Vereniging v. Thom. Wijsbegeerte,* 20 Nov., 1960.

F. Dessauer, *Naturwissenschaftliches Erkennen,* Frankfurt a.M., 1958.
Was ist der Mensch? Die vier Fragen des Im. Kant, ibid., 1959.

J. de Vries, *Denken und Sein,* Freiburg, 1937.

A. de Waehlens, *Une philosophie de la volonté,* Louvain, 1951.
Phénoménologie et vérité, Paris, 1953.
Existence et signification, Louvain, 1958.
"Réflexions sur une problématique de l'inconscient. Husserl et Hegel," *Edmund Husserl, 1859-1959,* The Hague, 1959, pp. 251 ff.

Bibliography

J. Dewey, *Encyclopedia of Social Sciences,* vol. 9, pp. 601 ff.
Reconstruction in Philosophy, Boston, 2nd ed., 1957.
Essays in Experimental Logic, New York, 1916.

A. de Wilde, *De persoon. Over de grondslagen van het personalistisch denken,* Assen, 1952.

E. J. Dijksterhuis, *Die Mechanisierung des Weltbildes,* Berlin, 1954.

W. Dilthey, "Ideen über eine beschreibende und zergliedernde Psychologie," *Sitzungsberichte der Berliner Akademie,* 1894.
"Studien zur Grundlegung der Geisteswissenschaften," *Gesammelte Schriften,* vol. 7, Göttingen, 2nd ed., 1958, pp. 3 ff.
"Der Aufbau der geschichtlichen Welt in den Geisteswissenschaften," *ibid.,* pp. 79 ff.
Einleitung in die Geisteswissenschaften, vol. 1, Stuttgart, 4th ed., 1959.

J. F. Donceel, "What Kind of Science is Psychology?" *"The New Scholasticism,* vol. 19 (1945), pp. 117 ff.

M. Dufrenne, *Phénoménologie de l'expérience esthétique,* Paris, 1953.
La personnalité de base, Paris, 1953.
La notion d'a priori, Paris, 1959.

F. Dunbar, *Emotions and Bodily Changes,* New York, 4th ed., 1954.

E. Durkheim, *Les règles de la méthode sociologique,* Paris, 13th ed., 1956.

H. C. J. Duyker, "Nomenclatuur en systematiek der psychologie," *Ned. Tijdschr. v. de Psych. en haar grensgebieden,* 1959, pp. 182 ff.

H. C. J. Duyker, B. G. Palland and R. J. Vuijk, *Leerboek der psychologie,* Groningen, 1958.

A. S. Eddington, *The Philosophy of Physical Science,* Cambridge, 1949.

W. Ehrlich, *Philosophische Anthropologie,* Tübingen, 1957.

A. Einstein, *Mein Weltbild,* 1934.

M. Eliade, *Le mythe de l'éternel retour,* Paris, 1949.
Traité de l'histoire des religions, Paris, 1949.
Das Heilige und das Profane, Hamburg, 1957.

Engländer (pen-name of Peter Altenberg), *Wie ich es sehe,* 1896.

H. J. Eysenck, *The Structure of Human Personality,* London, 1953.
and others, *Perspectives in Personality-Theory,* New York, 1957.
Sense and Nonsense in Psychology, Harmontsworth, 1957.

C. Fabro, "Controverse sul pensiero dei primitivi," *Euntes docete,* vol. 1, (1948), pp. 55 ff.

M. Farber, *The Foundation of Phenomenology,* Cambridge, Mass., 1943.
Naturalism and Subjectivism, Springfield, 1959.

J. Favez-Boutonier, "Psychologie clinique et phénoménologie," *Bulletin de Psychologie,* vol. 12 (1959), no. 163, pp. 569 ff.

J. K. Feibleman, *Inside the Great Mirror. A Critical Examination of the Philosophy of Russell, Wittgenstein and their Followers,* The Hague, 1958.

E. Fels, *Der wirtschaftende Mensch als Gestalter der Erde,* Stuttgart, 1954.

C. Fervers, "Psychologie als Grundlage der Psychotherapie," *Jahrbuch f. Psych. u. Psychother.,* vol. 1 (1953), pp. 58 ff.

L. Festinger and L. Katz, ed., *Research Methods in the Behavioral Sciences,* New York, 1953.

J. G. Fichte, *Grundlagen der gesammten Wissenschaftslehre,* 1794, Hamburg, 1956.

E. Fink, "L'analyse intentionelle et le problème de la pensée spéculative," *Problèmes actuels de la phénoménologie,* ed. by H. L. Van Breda, Paris, 1952.
Sein, Wahrheit, Welt, Vor-Fragen zum Problems des Phänomen-Begriffs, The Hague, 1958.
"Les concepts opératoires dans la phénoménologie de Husserl," *Husserl, Cahiers de Royaumont, Philosophie III,* Paris, 1959, pp. 214 ff.
Alles und Nichts. Ein Umweg zur Philosophie, The Hague, 1959.

R. Firth, ed., *Man and Culture. An Evaluation of the Work of B. Malinowski,* London, 1957.

J. C. Flugel, *A Hundred Years of Psychology,* Durkworth, 1945.

L. K. Frank, *Nature and Human Nature. Man's New Image of Himself,* New Brunswick, 1951.

V. E. Frankl, "Dimensionen des Menschseins," *Jahrbuch f. Psych. u. Psychother.* , vol. 1 (1953), pp. 186 ff.
Theorie und Therapie der Neurosen, Vienna, 1956.

S. Freud, *Gesammelte Werke,* ed. by A. Freud, 17 vols., London, 1940 ff.

H. Freyer, *Soziologie als Wirklichkeitswissenschaft,* Leipzig, 1930.
Einleitung in die Soziologie, Leipzig, 1931.

J. Fröbes, *Lehrbuch der experimentellen Psychologie,* Vol. 1, Freiburg, 1917.

G. Funke, "Phänomenologisches und dialektisches Bewusztsein," *Erkenntnis und Verantwortung,* Düsseldorf, 1960, pp. 63 ff.

L. Gabriel, "Die Einheit der Wissenschaften," *Wissenschaft und Weltbild,* vol. 7 (1954), pp. 48 ff.

H. G. Gadamer, *Wahrheit und Methode. Grundzüge einer philosophischen Hermeneutik,* Tübingen, 1960.

A. Ghelen, *Der Mensch, seine Natur und Stellung in der Welt,* Bonn, 1950.
Urmensch und Spätkultur, Bonn, 1956.

A. Gemelli and G. Zunini, *Introduzione alla Psicologia,* Milan, 1947.

J. J. Gielen, "Onbehagen rond de fenomenologische methode in de pedagogiek," *Opvoeding, Onderwijs, Gezondheidszorg,* vol. 12 (March, 1961), pp. 177 ff.

Bibliography

J. Gillin, ed., *For a Science of Social Man,* New York, 1954.

E. Gilson, *La philosophie et la théologie,* Paris, 1960.

L. Gilson, *Méthode et métaphysique selon Franz Brentano,* Paris, 1955.
La psychologie descriptive selon Franz Brentano, Paris, 1955.

F. J. Glastra van Loon, *Norm en handeling. Bijdrage tot een kentheoretische fundering der sociale wetenschappen,* Haarlem, 1957.

P. Godet, "Sujet et symbole," *Signe et symbole,* Neuchâtel, 1946, pp. 105 ff.

V. Goldschmidt, *Les dialogues de Platon. Structure et méthode dialectique,* Paris, 1947.

K. Goldstein, *Der Aufbau des Organismus,* The Hague, 1934.

V. Gorgé, *Philosophie und Physik,* Berlin, 1960.

H. Gouhier, *L'histoire et sa philosophie,* Paris, 1952.

R. F. Gräbner, *Methode der Ethnologie,* Heidelberg, 1911.

E. Grassi and T. von Uexküll, *Die Einheit unseres Wirklichkeitsbildes und die Grenzen der Einzelwissenschaften,* München, 1951.

E. B. Greene, *Measurement of Human Behavior,* New York, 1941.

F. Grégoire, *Etudes Hégeliennes,* Louvain, 1958.

J. Groen, J. J. G. Prick and H. Faber, *Psychosomatiek, geneeskunde en mensbeschouwing,* Amsterdam, 1953.

B. Groethuysen, *Philosophische Anthropologie,* München, 1928.

R. Guardini, *Freiheit, Gnade, Schicksal,* München, 1949.
Welt und Person, Würzburg, 3rd ed., 1950.
Das Ende der Neuzeit, Würzburg, 1951.
and O. F. Bollnow, *Begegnung und Bildung,* Würzburg, 1959.

P. Guillaume, *Introduction à la psychologie,* Paris, 1946.

G. Gurvitch, "Réflexions sur les rapports entre philosophie et sociologie," *Cahiers internationaux de sociologie,* vol. 22, 1955.

A. Gurwitch, *Théorie du champ de la conscience,* Bruges, 1957. To be published in this series as, *Field of Consciousness.*

G. Gusdorf, *La decouverte de soi,* Paris, 1948.
L'expérience humaine du sacrifice, Paris, 1948.
My·he et métaphysique, Paris, 1953.
"Sur l'ambiguité des sciences humaines," *Diogène,* vol. 26 (avril-juin 1959).

P. Häberlin, *Der Mensch,* Zürich, 1941.

A. E. Haeckel, *Die Welträtsel. Gemeinverständliche Studien über monistische Philosophie,* Bonn, 1899. Tr. as *The Riddles of the Universe,* New York, 1900.

H. Häfner, *Schulderleben und Gewissen,* Stuttgart, 1956.

Phenomenology and the Human Sciences

A. I. Hallowell, *Culture and Experience*, U. of Penna. Press, 2nd ed., 1955.

P. Halmos, *Towards a Measure of Man. The Frontiers of Normal Adjustment*, London, 1957.

G. Haring, ed., *Personal Character and Cultural Milieu*, Syracuse, 1956.

N. Hartmann, *Die Philosophie des deutschen Idealismus*, Leipzig, 1929. *Grundzüge einer Metaphysik der Erkenntnis*, Berlin, 3rd ed., 1941.

G. Heberer, G. Kurth and Schwidetzky-Roesingi, *Anthropologie*, Fischer-Lexikon no. 15, Frankfurt a.M., 1959.

G. W. F. Hegel, *Enzyclopädie der philosophischen Wissenschaften im Grundrisz*, ed. by F. Nicolin and O. Pöggeler, Hamburg, 6th ed., 1959. *Phänomenologie des Geistes*, ed. by G. Lasson, Leipzig, 2nd ed., 1921. *Die Wissenschaft der Logik*, ed. by G. Lasson, Leipzig, 2nd ed., 1932-34. *Vorlesungen über die Philosophie der Geschichte*, ed. by F. Brunstad, Reclam, 1925.

E. Heidbreder, *Seven Psychologies*, New York, 1933.

M. Heidegger, *Sein und Zeit*, 1st Part, Tübingen, 7th ed., 1953. Translated as *Being and Time*, New York, 1962. *Vom Wesen des Grundes*, Frankfurt a.M., 3rd ed., 1949. *Kant und das Problem der Metaphysik*, Frankfurt a.M., 2nd ed., 1951. Translated as *Kant and the Problem of Metaphysics*, Bloomington, Ind., 1962. *Was ist Metaphysik?*, Frankfurt a.M., 5th ed., 1949. Translation in *Existence and Being*, London, 2nd ed., pp. 353ff. *Über den Humanismus*, ibid., 1949. *Platons Lehre von der Wahrheit*, Bern, 2nd ed., 1954. *Vom Wesen der Wahrheit*, Frankfurt a.M., 3rd ed., 1954. Translation in *Existence and Being*, pp. 317ff. *Holzwege*, ibid., 2nd ed., 1952.

W. Heisenberg, *Das Naturbild der heutigen Physik*, Hamburg, 1955. *Physics and Philosophy. The Revolution in Modern Science*, London, 1958.

R. Heiss, *Wesen und Formen der Dialektik*, Köln, 1959. *Algemeine Tiefenpsychologie*, Bern, 1956.

H. E. Hengstenberg, *Philosophische Anthropologie*, Stuttgart, 1957.

P. Henle, ed., *Language, Thought and Culture*, Ann Arbor, 1958.

J. E. Heyde, *Entwertung der Kausalität. Für und wider den Positivismus*, Stuttgart, 1957.

E. R. Hilgard, *Theories of Learning*, New York, 2nd ed., 1956.

J. Hillman, *Emotion. A Comprehensive Phenomenology of Theories and Their Meaning for Therapy*, London, 1960.

P. R. Hofstätter, *Einführung in die Sozialpsychologie*, Vienna, 1954. "Behaviorismus als Anthropologie," *Jahrbuch f. Psych. u. Psychother.*, vol. 4 (1957), pp. 357 ff. "Die Sozialanpassung und die zweite Natur des Menschen," *op. cit.*, vol. 6 (1958), pp. 112 ff.

Bibliography

J. M. Hollenbach, *Der Mensch als Entwurf*, Frankfurt a.M., 1957.

G. Homans, *The Human Group*, London, 2nd ed., 1957.

J. Honigman, *Culture and Personality*, New York, 1956.

K. Horney, *New Ways in Psychoanalysis*, New York, 1939.

P. Th. Hugenholtz, *Tijd en creativiteit. Ontwerp von een structurele anthropologie*, Amsterdam, 1959.

C. L. Hull, *A Behavior System. An Introduction to Behavior Theory Concerning the Individual Organisms*, New Haven, 2nd ed., 1958.

E. Husserl, *Logische Untersuchungen*, 3 vols., Halle a.S., 4th ed., 1928.
Die Idee der Phänomenologie, ed. by W. Biemel, The Hague, 1950.
Ideen zu einer reinen Phäänomenologie und phänomenologischen Philosophie, ed. M. and W. Biemel, The Hague, 1950-52.
Cartesianische Meditationen und Pariser Vorträge, ed. by S. Strasser, The Hague, 1950.
Formale und Transszendentale Logik, Halle a.S., 1929.
Erfahrung und Urteil, ed. by L. Landgrebe, Hamburg, 1948.
Die Krisis der europäischen Wissenschaften und die transzendentale Phänomenologie, ed. by W. Biemel, The Hague, 1954.
Husserl. Troisiéme colloque philosophique de Royaumont, Paris, 1959.

J. Hyppolite, *Logique et existence. Essai sur la logique de Hegel*, Paris, 1953.

J. Jacobi, *De psychologie van C. G. Jung*, Amsterdam, 1949.

W. James, *Principles of Psychology*, New York, 1891.
The Will to Believe, London, 1897.
Varieties of Religious Experience, London, 1902.
Pragmatism; a New Name for Some Old Ways of Thinking, London, 1907.
The Meaning of Truth, London, 1909.
Some Problems of Philosophy, London, n. d.

A. L. Janse de Jonge, *De mens in zijn verhoudingen. Hoofdstukken uit de phaenomenologische psychologie*, Utrecht, 1956.

K. Jaspers, *Psychologie der Weltanschauungen*, Berlin, 1919.
Die geistige Situation der Zeit, Berlin, 1931.
Philosophie, Berlin, 1932.
Vernunft und Existenz, Groningen, 1935.
Der philosophische Glaube, München, 1948.
Allgemeine Psychopathologie, Berlin, 5th ed., 1948.
and A. Poortmann, *Wahrheit und Wissenschaft. Naturwissenschaft und Humanismus*, Zwei Reden, München, 1960.

F. Jeanson, *La phénoménologie*, Paris, n. d.
Signification humaine du rire, Paris, 1950.

E. Jensen, ed., *Mythe, Mensch und Umwelt*, Bamberg, 1950.
Mythos und Kult bei den Naturvölkern, Wiesbaden, 1951.

C. G. Jung, *Psychologische Typen,* Zürich, 4th ed., 1942.
Die Beziehung zwischen dem Ich und dem Unbewuszten, Zürich, 4th ed., 1945.
Seelenprobleme der Gegenwart, Zürich, 1931.

G. Kafka, "Die metaphysischen Voraussetzungen der Psychologie," *Actes du Xme Congrès International de Philosophie,* Amsterdam, 1949, pp. 918 ff.

J. Kälin, "Neue Aspekte der menschlichen Stammesgeschichte," *Annalen v.h. Thijmgenootschap,* vol. 47 (Sept., 1959), pp. 132 ff.
"Das Menschenbild der neuen Anthropologie," *Jahresbericht der Görresgesellschaft 1956,* Köln, 1957, pp. 5 ff.

H. M. Kallen, ed., *The Philosophy of William James,* New York, n. d.

I. Kant, *Werke,* ed. by A. Buchenau and E. Cassirer.

A. Kardiner, *The Individual and His Society,* New York, 1939.
The Psychological Frontier of Society, New York, 6th impr., 1956.

D. Katz, *Mensch und Tier, Studien zur vergleichenden Psychologie,* Zürich, 1948.

L. Klages, *Zur Ausdruckslehre und Characterkunde,* Heidelberg, 1926.

O. Klemm, *Geschichte der Psychologie,* Leipzig, 1911.

G. P. Klubertanz, *The Philosophy of Human Nature,* New York, 1953.

C. Kluckhohn, *Mirror for Man,* New York, 1949.
and H. A. Murphy, *Personality in Nature, Society and Culture,* New York, 2nd ed., 1955.

A. Kockelmans, "Eenheid en verscheidenheid in de wetenschap volgens het standpunt der phaenomenologie," *Tijdschrift v. Philosophie,* vol. 22 1960), pp. 331 ff.

K. Koffka, *Principles of Gestalt Psychology,* London, 4th impr., 1955.

Ph. Kohnstamm, *Persoonlijkheid in wording,* Haarlem, 1929.

W. Koppers, *Urmensch und Urreligion,* Olten, 2nd ed., 1946.

J. Kraft, *Von Husserl zu Heidegger. Kritik der phänomenologischen Philosophie,* Frankfurt a.M., 2nd ed., 1957.

D. Krech and R. S. Crutchfield, *Theory and Problems of Social Psychology,* New York, 1948.

A. L. Kroeber, ed., *Anthropology Today. An Encyclopedic Inventory,* Chicago, 1953.

F. Krueger, *Der Strukturbegriff in der Psychologie,* Jena, 2nd ed., 1931.

G. J. Kruyer, *Observeren en redeneren. Een inleiding tot de kennisvorming in de sociologie,* Meppel, 1959.

J. P. Kruyt, *Onkerkelijkheid in Nederland. Haar verbreiding en haar oorzaken,* Groningen, 1933.

Bibliography

A. E. Kuenzli, ed., *The Phenomenological Problem,* New York, 1959.

H. Kuhn, "Die Liebe zum Sein und die Verlockung des Nichts," *Jahrbuch f. Psych. u. Psychother.,* vol. 6 (1958), pp. 41 ff.

F. Künkel, *Grundzüge der praktischen Seelenheilkunde,* Stuttgart, 1935.
Einführung in die Charakterkunde, Leipzig, 1935.

H. Kunz, Über Sinn und Grenzen psychologischen Erkennens," Beiheft zu *Psyche,* Stuttgart, 1957.

R. C. Kwant, "Menselijke existentie en geschiedenis volgens het wijsgerig denken van M. Merleau-Ponty," *Alg. Ned. Tijdschr. v. Wijsb. en Psych.,* vol. 46 (1953-54), pp. 231 ff.
"Transcendeert Merleau-Ponty het realisme?" *Tijdschrift v. Philosophie,* vol. 16 (1954), pp. 236 ff.
"De historie en het Absolute," *op. cit.,* vol. 17 (1955), pp. 264 ff.
"Het phenomenologisch wetenschapsideaal," *Tijdschrift v. Zielkunde en Opvoedingsleer,* vol. 41 (1955), pp. 20 ff.
"De zingedachte van M. Merleau-Ponty," *Bijdragen,* vol. 16 (1955), pp. 1 ff.
The Phenomenological Philosophy of Merleau-Ponty, to be published in DUQUESNE STUDIES, *Philosophical Series.*

D. Lagache, *L'unité de la psychologie,* Paris, 1949.

B. Lakebrink, *Hegels dialektische Ontologie und die thomistische Analektik,* Köln, 1955.

A. Lalande, *Vocabulaire technique et critique de la philosophie,* Paris 7th ed., 1956.

J. H. Lambert, *Neues Organon oder Gedanken über die Erforschung und Bezeichnung des Wahren und dessen Unterscheidung vom Irrtum und Schein.* Part IV, *Phänomenologie,* Leipzig, 1762.

L. Landgrebe, *Phänomenologie und Metaphysik,* Hamburg, 1949.

M. Landmann, *Erkenntnis und Erlebnis,* Berlin, 1951.
Philosophische Anthropologie, Sammlung Göschen, Bd. 156/156a, Berlin, 1955.
Der Mensch als Schöpfer und Geschöpf der Kultur. Geschichts- und Sozialanthropologie, München, 1961.

M. J. Langeveld, *Studien zur Anthropologie des Kindes,* Tübingen, 1956.
ed., *Inleiding in de psychologie,* Groningen, 2nd ed., 1957.

G. Lauer, *La phénoméologie de Husserl. Essai sur la génèse de l'intentionnalité,* Paris, 1955.

L. Lavelle, *De l'aete,* Paris, 1945.

P. F. Lazarsfeld, ed., *Mathematical Thinking in the Social Sciences,* Glencoe, Ill., 1954.

E. J. Leemans, *Op de drempel van de sociologie,* Nijmegen, 1960.

M. Leenhardt, "Quelques éléments communs aux formes inférieures de la religion," *Histoire des religions,* ed. by M. Brillant and R. Agrain, Part I, Paris, 1953.

W. Leibbrand, *Heilkunde. Eine Problemgeschichte der Medizin,* Freiburg, 1953.

Ph. Lersch, *Aufbau der Person,* 6th ed., München, 1954.

E. Lévinas, La théorie de l'intuition dans la phénoménologie de Husserl, Paris, 1930.
En découvrant l'existence avec Husserl et Heidegger, Paris, n. d.

L. Lévy-Bruhl, *Les fonctions mentales dans les sociétés inférieures,* Paris, 9th ed., 1928.
Le surnaturel et la nature dans la mentalité primitive, Paris 2nd ed. 1931.
La mythologie primitive. Le monde antique des Australiens et des Papous, Paris, 1935.
Carnets, Paris, 1949.

K. Lewin, "The Conflict Between Aristotelian and Galilean Modes of Thought in Contemporary Psychology," *A Dynamic Theory of Personality. Selected Papers,* New York, 1935, pp. 1 ff.
Principles of Topological Psychology, New York, 1936.
Field Theory in Social Science. Theoretical Papers, New York, 1951.

J. Lindworsky, *Experimentelle Psychology,* 5th ed., München, 1931.

J. Linschoten, *Op weg naar een fenomenologische psychologie. De psychology van William James,* Utrecht, 1959.
Das Experiment in der phänomenologischen Psychologie, lecture delivered at Bonn, July, 1955. Ms. 1955, p. 13.

R. Linton, *The Study of Man,* New York, 1936.
The Tree of Culture, New York, 1959.

Th. Litt, *Das Allgemeine im Aufbau der geisteswissenschaftlichen Erkenntnis,* Leipzig, 1941.
Denken und Sein, Stuttgart, 1948.
Mensch und Welt, München, 1948.
Hegel, Versuch einer kritischer Erneuerung, Heidelberg, 1953.

J. H. Loenen, *Over het onderscheid tussen een wetenschappelijk en een niet-wetenschappelijk doel der wijsbegeerte,* Assen, 1959.

B. Lorscheid, *Max Schelers Phänomenologie des Psychischen,* Bonn, 1957.

K. Löwith, *Das Individuum in der Rolle des Mitmenschen,* München, 1928.

H. Lübbe, "Positivismus und Phänomenologie (Mach und Husserl)," *Beiträge zur Philosophie und Wissenschaft U. Szilasi zum 70 Geburtstag,* München, 1960, pp. 161 ff.

W. A. Luijpen, *Existential Phenomenology,* 2nd impr., Pittsburgh, 1962.

G. A. Lundberg, *Foundations of Sociology,* 2nd ed., New York, 1953.
"The Natural Science Trend in Sociology," *American Journal of Sociology,* vol. 61 (1955), pp. 91 ff.

N. R. F. Maier and T. C. Schneierla, *Principles of Animal Psychology,* New York, 1935.

B. Malinowsky, *Sex and Repression in Savage Society,* London, 1926.
Argonauts of the Western Pacific, 2nd ed., London, 1932.

Bibliography

K. Mannheim, *Man and Society in an Age of Reconstruction,* London, 1940.
Essays on Sociology and Social Psychology, London, 1953.

G. Marcel, *Journal métaphysique,* Paris, 1927.
Être et Avoir, Paris, 1935.
Du refus à l'invocation, Paris, 1940.
Homo Viator, Paris, 1944.
Positions et approches du mystère ontologique, Louvain, 1953.
Le mystere de l'être, Paris, 1951.
Les hommes contre l'humain, Paris, 1951.
Le déclin de la sagesse, Paris, 1954.
L'homme problématique, Paris, 1955.

J. Maréchal, *Le point de départ de la métaphysique,* 5 vols., Paris, 1922-26.

J. Maritain, *The Degrees of Knowledge,* New York, 1959.

H. I. Marrou, *De la connaissance historique,* Louvain, 1954.

M. Mauss, *Sociologie et anthropologie,* Paris, 1950.

R. May, *Man's Search for Himself,* London, 1953.

W. McDougall, *An Introduction to Social Psychology,* London, 29th impr., 1948.

M. Mead, *Coming of Age in Samoa,* 2nd ed., New York, 1952.
Growing up in New Guinea, London, 1930.
and M. Wolfenstein, *Childhood in Contemporary Cultures,* Chicago, 1955.

J. Meinertz, *Psychotherapie als Wissenschaft,* 2nd ed., Stuttgart, 1952.

C. A. Mennicke, *Moderne psychologie,* 2nd ed., Amsterdam, 1946.
Mensch und Menschlichkeit, ed. by Althans, Barth, Buber and others, Stuttgart, 1956.

D. Mercier, *Critériologie générale,* 8th ed., Louvain, 1923.

M. Merleau-Ponty, "Le primat de la perception et ses conséquences philosophiques," *Bulletin de la Société Française de Philosophie,* Oct.-Dec., 1939.
La structure du comportement, Paris, 1942.
Phénoménologie de la perception, Paris, 2nd ed., 1945.
Sens et non-sens, Paris, 1948.
"La philosophie et la sociologie," *Cahiers internationaux de sociologie,* vol. 10 (1951), pp. 55 ff.
"Les sciences de l'homme et la phénoménologie," *Cours de Sorbonne,* 1951-52, Paris, n.d.
"Les relations avec autrui chez l'enfant," *Cours de Sorbonne, n.d.*
"Sur la phénoménologie du language," *Problémes actuels de la phénoménologie,* 1952, pp. 92 ff.
Eloge de la philosophie, Paris, 1952.
Les aventures de la dialectique, Paris, 10th ed., 1955.
Signes, Paris, 1960.

R. K. Merton, *Social Theory and Social Structure,* Glencoe, 1949.

J. S. Mill, *A System of Logic,* London, 1843.

R. Mohr, *Die christliche Ethik im Lichte der Ethnologie,* München, 1954.

R. Müller-Freienfels, *De voornaamste richtingen in de hedendaagse psychologie,* Utrecht, 1938.

G. E. Müller, *Hegel, Denkgeschichte eines Lebendigen,* Bern, 1959.

G. R. G. Mure, *A Study of Hegel's Logic,* Oxford, 1950.

E. Nagel, *Sovereign Reason and Other Studies in the Philosophy of Science,* Glencoe, 1954.

P. Natorp, *Allgemeine Psychologie nach kritischer Methode.* I Buch, Tübingen , 1912.

O. Neurath, "Soziologie im Physikalismus," *"Erkenntnis,"* vol. 2, 1931.
"Protokollsätze," *op. cit.,* vol. 3, 1932.
"Radikaler Physikalismus und 'wirkliche Welt,'" *op. cit.,* vol. 4, 1934.

R. Niebuhr, *Glaube und Geschichte,* München, 1951.

L. Noël, *Le réalisme immédiat,* Louvain, 1939.

J. Nogué, *Esquisse d'un système des qualités sensibles,* Paris, 1943.

J. Nota, *Max Scheler. Een worstelen om het wezen van den mens,* Utrecht, 1947.

J. Nuttin, *Psychoanalyse en spiritualistische opvatting van de mens,* Antwerpen, 1949.
"Consciousness, Behavior and Personality," *Psychological Review,* vol. 65 (1955), pp. 349 ff.
"Les lois du comportement et la liberté. Une psychologie de l'activité libre de l'homme est-elle possible?" *Jahrbuch f. Psych. u. Psychother.,* vol. 6 (1958), pp. 119 ff.

A. Oldendorff, *De psychologie van het sociale leven,* Utrecht, 1953.

C. E. Osgood, *Method and Theory on Experimental Psychology,* New York, 1954.

R. Otto, *Das Heilige,* 2nd ed., München, 1947.

T. Parsons, *The Structure of Social Action,* 2nd ed., Glencoe, 1949.
and E. A. Shills, ed., *Toward a General Theory of Action,* Cambridge, Mass., 1954.

C. S. Peirce, *Collected Papers,* Cambridge, Mass., 1931 ff.

C. Perelman and L. Olbrechts-Tyteca, *La nouvelle rhétorique. Traité de l'argumentation,* Paris, 1958.

J. A. Peters, "Over den oorsprong van het woord," *Tijdschrift v. Philosophie,* vol. 13 (1951), pp. 163 ff.
Metaphysics, to be published in DUQUESNE STUDIES, *Philosophical Series.*
"Aristoteles over de tijd," *Studia Catholica,* vol. 33 (1958), pp. 286 ff.

G. Pfahler, *Der Mensch und sein Lebenswerkzeug,* Stuttgart, 1955.

R. Pierloot, *Algemene problemen van de klinische psychosomatiek,* Utrecht, 1954.

J. Pieper, *Grundformen sozialer Spielregel,* 3rd ed., Frankfurt a.M., 1955.

Bibliography

H. Plessner, *Die Stufen des Organischen und der Mensch. Einleitung in die philosophische Anthropologie,* Berlin, 1928.
"Sociologie en anthropologie," *Mens en Maatschappij,* vol. 25, 1950, pp. 276 ff.
Zwischen Philosophie und Gesellschaft, Bern, 1953.

A. Podlech, *Der Leib als Weise des In-der-Welt-seins,* Bonn, 1955.

H. Poincaré, *La valeur de la science,* Paris, 1929.

F. L. Polak, *Kennen en keuren in de sociale wetenschappen,* Leiden, 1948.

G. Politzer, *Critique des fondements de la psychologie,* Paris, 1928.

L. J. Pongratz, *Psychologie menschlicher Konflikte. Phänomenologie und Theorie,* Göttingen, 1961.

J. A. Ponsione, "Typen van stratificatie," *Soc. Gids,* vol. 2, 1955, pp. 82ff.

K. R. Popper, *The Logic of Scientific Discovery,* London, 2nd ed., 1960.
Logik der Forschung, Vienna, 1935.

A. Portmann, *Vom Bild der Natur,* Basel, 1947.
Biologische Fragmente einer Lehre vom Menschen, 2nd ed., Basel, 1951.
Zoologie und das neue Bild vom Menschen. Fragmente zu einer Lehre vom Menschen, 2nd ed., Hamburg, 1956.

H. J. Pos, *Filosofie der wetenschappen,* 4th ed., Arnhem, 1953.
"Valeur et limites de la phénoménologie," *Problèmes actuels de la phénoménologie,* pp. 31 ff.

M. Pradines, *Traité de psychologie générale,* Paris, 2nd ed., 1946.

J. J. Prick and H. G. van der Waals, *Nederlands handboek der psychiatrie,* vol. I, Arnhem, 1957.

H. Prinzhorn, *Leib-Seele-Einheit,* Zürich, 1927.

E. Przywara, *Mensch, Typologische Anthropologie,* Neurenberg, 1959.

A. R. Radcliff-Brown, *Tabu,* Cambridge, 1940.

H. Reichenbach, *The Rise of Scientific Philosophy,* Los Angeles, 1958.

P. Ricoeur, "Husserl et le sens de l'histoire," *Revue de métaphysique et de morale,* vol. 54, 1949, pp. 230 ff.
Philosophie de la volonté, Paris, 1950.
"Etudes sur les 'Méditations Cartésiennes' de Husserl," *Revue philosophique de Louvain,* vol. 52 (1954), pp. 75 ff.
"Sympathie et respect," *Revue de la métaphysique et de morale,* vol. 59 (1954), pp. 380 ff.
"Kant et Husserl," *Kantstudien,* vol. 46, 1954, pp. 44 ff.
"Le symbole donne à penser," *Esprit,* vol. 27, 1954, pp. 60 ff.
Histoire et vérité, Paris, 1955.

H. Rickert, *Die Grenzen der naturwissenschaflichen Begriffsbildung. Eine logische Einleitung in die historischen Wissenschaften,* 3rd ed., Tübingen, 1921.

W. Riese, *The Conception of Disease,* New York, 1953.

A. Roe and G. G. Simpson, *Behavior and Evolution,* New Haven, 1958.

M. D. Roland-Gosselin, *Essai d'une critique de la connaissance,* Paris, 1932.

H. Rorschach, *Psychodiagnostik,* 6th ed., Bern, 1948.

E. Rothacker, *Einleitung in die Geisteswissenchaften,* 2nd ed., Tübingen, 1930.
Logik und Systematik der Geisteswissenschaften, Bonn, 1948.
Probleme der Kulturanthropologie, Bonn, 1948.

L. Rougier, *Traité de la connaissance,* Paris, 1955.

B. Russell, *Philosophy,* New York, 1927.
Our Knowledge of the External World, 2nd ed., New York, 1929.
An Inquiry into Meaning and Truth, New York, 1940.

J. P. Sartre, *L'imaginaire. Psychologie phénoménologique de l'imagination,*
Paris, 1940
Esquisse d'une théorie des émotions, Paris, 2nd ed., 1948.
L'être et le néant, 36th ed., Paris, 1950.
L'existentialisme est un humanisme, Paris, 1954.
Saint Genet, comédien et martyr, Paris, 15th ed., 1952.
Baudelaire, 22nd ed., Paris, 1947.
Critique de la raison dialectique. Vol. I, *Theorie des ensembles practiques,*
Paris, 1960.

F. Sassen and B. Delfgaauw, *Wijsbegeerte van onze tijd,,* Antwerpen, 4th
ed., 1957.

M. Scheler, *Die transzendentale und die psychologische Methode,* Leipzig
1900.
Von Umsturz der Werte, 2 vols., Leipzig, 1919.
Vom Ewigen im menschen, 4th ed., Bern, 1954.
Schriften zur Soziologie und Weltanschauungslehre, 3 vols., Leipzig, 1924.
Die Wissensformen und die Gesellschaft, Leipzig, 1926.
Philosophische Weltanschauung, Bonn, 1929.
Der Formalismus in der Ethik und die materiale Wertethik, Halle a.S.,
3rd ed., 1930.
Nachlassband I. Zur Erkenntnislehre und Ethik, Berlin, 1933.
Wesen und Formen der Sympathie, Frankfurt a.M., 5th ed., 1948.
Die Stellung des Menschen im Kosmos, München, 1949.

F. Schelling, *Werke,* ed. by M. Schröter, München, 1927 ff.

K. Schilling, *Geschichte der sozialen Ideen: Individuum, Gemeinschaft, Gesellschaft,* Stuttgart, 1957.

M. Schlick, "Über das Fundament der Erkenntnis," *Erkenntnis,* vol. 4 (1934).

W. Schmidt, *Der Ursprung der Gottesidee,* 6 vols., Münster, 1926-35.
*Handbuch der vergleichenden Religionsgeschichte. Ursprung und Wesen
der Religion,* Münster, 1930.

K. Schneider, *Psychiatrie heute,* 2nd ed., Heidelberg, 1955.

H. Schoeck, *Soziologie; Geschichte ihrer Probleme,* München, 1952.

C. Schoonbrood, "Engelse analytische filosofie vóór en na 1940," *Studia
Catholica,* vol. 33 (1958), pp. 47 ff., 113 ff.

Bibliography

A. Schuetz, "Le problème de l'intersubjectivité chez Husserl," *Husserl, Cahiers de Royaumont,* Paris, 1959, pp. 334 ff.
Der sinnhafte Aufbau der sozialen Welt. Eine Einleitung in die verstehende Soziologie, 2nd ed., Vienna, 1960.

O. Schwarz, *Medizinische Anthropologie,* Leipzig, 1929.

R. Siebeck, *Medizin in Bewegung,* 2nd ed., Stuttgart, 1953.

G. Siegmund, *Der kranke Mensch. Medizinische Anthropologie,* Fulda, 1951.
Tier und Mensch. Beitrag zur Wesensbestimmung des Menschen, Frankfurt a.M., 1958.

F. Sierksma, *De religieuse projectie,* Delft, 1956.

H. Sigerist, *Geschichte der Heilkunde,* München, 1932.

B. F. Skinner, *Science and Human Behavior,* 3rd ed., New York, 1956.

H. Skjervheim, "Objectivism and the Study of Man," *Filosofiske Problemer,* no. 23, Oslo, 1959.

J. Smedslund, "The Epistemological foundations of Behaviorism. A Critique," *Acta Psychologica,* vol. 11, 1955, no. 3.

A. Snijders, "Gnoseologie van het mythische denken," *Tijdschrift v. Philosophie,* vol. 23 (1961), pp. 477 ff.

J. Th. Snijders, "Phaenomenologie een gewone psychologie?" *Gawein,* vol. 8, 1960, pp. 88 ff.

G. Söhngen, *Sein und Gegenstand,* Münster, 1930.

P. Sorokin, *Contemporary Sociological Theories,* New York, 1928.

K. W. Spence, *Behavior Theory of Learning,* New York, 1960.

H. Spiegelberg, *The Phenomenological Movement. A Historical Introduction,* The Hague, 1960.

E. Spranger, *Psychologie des Jugendalters,* 23rd ed., Heidelberg, 1953.
Gedanken zur Daseinsgestaltung, München, 1955.

W. Stern, *Allgemeine Psychologie auf personalistischer Grundlage,* The Hague, 2nd ed., 1950.

S. S. Stevens, "Operational Definitions of Psychological Concepts," *Psychological Review,* vol. 42, 1935, pp. 517 ff.

S. Strasser, "Beschouwingen over het vraagstuk van de apodicticiteit en de critische verantwoording van de phaenomenologie," *Tijdschrift v. Philosophie,* vol 8 (1946), pp. 203 ff.
Objectiviteit en objectivisme, Nijmegen, 1947.
"Het gedrag als metaphysisch probleem," *Alg. Ned. Tijdschr. v. Wijsb. en Psych.,* vol 42 (1949), pp. 1 ff.
The Soul in Metaphysical and Empirical Psychology, 2nd impr., Pittsburgh, 1961.
Das Gemüt, Utrecht, 1956.
"Phenomenological Trends in European Psychology," *Philosophy and Phenomenological Research,* vol. 18 (1957), pp. 8 ff.

"Het wezen van de mensch," *Annalen v.h. Thijmgenootschap,* vol. 46, 1958, pp. 1 ff.
"Das Gottesproblem in der Spätphilosophie Edmund Husserls," *Philos. Jahrbuch der Görresgesellschaft,* vol. 67 (1959), pp. 130 ff.
"Intuition und Dialektik in der Philosophie Edmund Husserls," *Edmund Husserl,* 1859-1959, The Hague, 1959, pp. 148 ff.
"Misère et grandeur du fait," *Husserl, 3e colloque philosophique de Royaumont,* Paris, 1959, pp. 170 ff.
"Beschouwingen over natuur en cultuur naar aanleiding van het vraagstuk der menselijke sexualiteit," *Huwelijk en sexualiteit,* Utrecht, 1961, pp. 1 ff.

E. Straus, *Psychologie der menschlichen Welt. Gesammelte Schriften,* Berlin, 1960.

H. Taine, *Les origines de la France contemporaine,* 27th ed., Paris, 1906-09.

P. Teilhard de Chardin, *Le phénomène humain,* Paris, 1955.
L'apparition de l'homme, Paris, 1956.

A. A. Terruwe, *De neurose in het licht der rationele psychologie,* Roermond, 1949.

P. Thévenaz, "La question du point de départ chez Descartes et Husserl," *Problèmes actuels de la phénoménologie,* pp. 11 ff.

Thomas Aquinas, *Summa theologica,* Paris, 1939.
Qaestiones disputatae, 6th ed., Turin, 1931.
Quaestio disputata De anima, ed. by F. Hedde, Paris, 1912.

M. Titiev, *Introduction to Cultural Anthropology, New York,* 1959.

E. C. Tolman, *Purposive Behavior in Animals* and Men, New York, 1932.
"An Operational Analysis of Demands," *Erkenntnis,* vol. 6 (1936).

E. Troeltsch, *Der Historismus und seine Probleme,* Tübingen, 1922.

S. Ullmann, *The Principles of Semantics,* 2nd ed., New York, 1957.

J. O. Urmson, *Philosophical Analysis. Its Development Between the Two World Wars,* Oxford, 1958.

Utrechts Universiteitsfonds, ed., *De evolutieleer na honderd jaar,* Haarlem, 1959.

Th. van Baaren, *Wij mensen. Religie en wereldbeschouwing by schriftloze volkeren,* Utrecht, 1960.

H. L. Van Breda, *De transcendentaalphenomenologische reductie in Husserl's laatste periode 1928-38.* Ms, Louvain, 1941.
"Phenomenologische Methode," *Katholieke Encyclopedie voor Opvoeding en Onderwijs,* vol. 3, The Hague, 1954, pp. 351 ff.
and J. Taminiaux, ed., *Husserl et la pensée moderne. Actes du deuxième colloque international de phénoménologie,* The Hague, 1959.
, ed., *Edmund Husserl 1859-1959,* The Hague, 1959.

T. P. van de Geer, "Psychologische toepassingen van de informatietheorie," *Ned. Tijdschr. v.d. Psych. en haar grensgebieden,* vol. 12 (1957), pp. 295 ff. and 332 ff.

Bibliography

J. H. van den Berg, *Kroniek der psychologie,* The Hague, 1954.
The Phenomenological Approach to Psychopathology. An Introduction to Recent Phenomenological Psychopathology, Springfield, 1955.
and J. Linschoten, ed., *Persoon en wereld,* Utrecht, 1953.

L. van der Horst, *Anthropologische psychiatrie,* Amsterdam, 1945.
"De zieke mens en de geneeskunde," *Ned. Tijdschr. v.d. Psych. en haar grensgebieden,* vol. 12 (1957), pp. 278 ff.

G. van der Leeuw, *Inleiding tot de phaenomenologie van den godsdienst,* Haarlem, 1924, 2nd ed., 1948.
De primitieve mens en de religie, 2nd ed., Groningen, 1952.
Phänomenologie der Religion, 2nd ed., Tübingen, 1956. Tr. as *Religion in Essence and Manifestation,* New York, 1962.
ed., *De godsdiensten van de wereld,* Amsterdam, 1941.

K. van der Loo, B. Kouwer and W. Bladergroen, "Tests," *Ned. Tijdschr. v.d. Psych. en haar grensgebieden,* vol. 12 (1957), pp. 237 ff.

J. van der Meulen, *Heidegger und Hegel oder Widerstreit und Widerspruch,* Meisenheim, 1953.

A. L. van Kaam, "The Impact of Existential Phenomenology on the Psychological Literature of Western Europe," *Review of Existential Psychology and Psychiatry,* vol. 1 (1961), pp. 63 ff.
The Third Force in European Psychology, Greenville, Del., 1960.

P. H. van Laer, *Philosophico-Scientific Problems,* Pittsburgh, 1953.

J. A. van Leent, *Sociale psychologie in drie dimensies,* Utrecht, 1961.

D. J. van Lennep, *Gewogen—bekeken—ontmoet in het psychologisch onderzoek,* The Hague, 1949.

A. G. van Melsen, *Science and Technology,* Pittsburgh, 1961.

C. A. van Peursen, "Functioneel," *Ned. Tijdschr. v.d. Psych. en haar grensgebieden,* vol. 14 (1959), pp. 341 ff.

G. Van Riet, *L'épistémologie thomiste,* Louvain, 1946.
"Mythe et vérité, *Revue philosophique de Louvain,* vol. 58 (1960), pp. 15 ff.
Problème d'épistémologie, Louvain, 1960, pp. 345 ff.

F. Van Steenberghen, *Epistemology,* New York, 1949.

E. V. Vercruysse, *Het ontwerpen van een sociologisch onderzoek, Uitgangspunten en richtlijnen,* Assen, 1960.

A. Vetter, *Natur und Person,* Stuttgart, 1949

B. von Brandenstein, *Der Mensch und seine Stellung im Allg. philosophische Anthropologie,* Einsiedeln, 1947.

V. E. von Gebsattel, *Prolegomena einer medizinischen Anthropologie,* Berlin, 1954.

V. von Weiszäcker, *Der Gestaltkreis. Theorie einer Einheit von Wahrnehmen und Bewegen,* Stuttgart, 3rd ed., 1947.
Fälle und Probleme. Anthropologische Vorlesungen in der medizinischer Klinik, Stuttgart, 1947.

333

Körpergeschehen und Neurose. Analytische Studie über somatische Symptombildung, Stuttgart, 1947.
Der kranke Mensch. Eine Einführung in die medizinische Anthropologie, Stuttgart, 1951.

L. von Wiese, *Philosophie und Soziologie,* Berlin, 1959.

J. Wach, *Das Verstehen,* 3 vols., Tübingen, 1926-33.

J. Wahl, "Sur l'interprétation de l'histoire de la métaphysique d'après Heidegger," *Les cours de Sorbonne,* Paris, 1956.

J. B. Watson, *Psychology from the Standpoint of a Behaviorist,* Philadelphia, 1919.

M. Weber, *Gesammelte Aufsätze zur Wissenschaftslehre,* Tübingen, 2nd ed., 1951. Tr. as *The Methodology of the Social Sciences,* Glencoe, Ill., 1949. *Gesammelte Aufsätze zur Religionssoziologie,* Tübingen, 4th ed., 1947. Translated in part as *The Protestant Ethic and the Spirit of Capitalism,* New York, 1930.

H. Wein, *Realdialektik. Von Hegelscher Dialektik zu dialektischer Anthropologie,* München, 1957.

A. Wellek, *Ganzheitpsychologie und Strukturtheorie. 10 Abhandlungen zur Psychologie und philosophischen Anthropologie,* Bern, 1953.
"Die Entwicklung der Grundannahmen der Psychologie und die Überwindung des Phänomenalismus und Psychologismus," *Jahrbuch f. Psychol. u. Psychother.,* vol. 4, Heft 3/4, 1956.

H. Werner, *Einführung in die Entwicklungspsychologie,* 3rd ed., München, 1953. Tr. as *Comparative Psychology of Mental Development,* New York, 1940.

L. White, *The Evolution of Culture,* New York, 1959.

L. Wittgenstein, *Schriften,* vol. 1, Oxford, 1960; vol. 2, Oxford, 1958; vol. 3, Frankfurt a.M., 1960.
Tractatus logico-philosophicus, 3rd ed., London, 1947.

W. Wundt, *Grundzüge der physiologischen Psychologie,* vol. 1, Leipzig, 6th ed., 1908. Tr. as *Principles of Physiological Psychology,* New York, 1904.

A. Wylleman, "L'homme et la création des valeurs," *Revue philosophique de Louvain,* vol. 58 (1960), pp. 88 ff.

P. T. Young, *Motivation of Behaviour. The Fundamental Determinants of Human and Animal Activities,* New York, 3rd ed., 1946.

H. L. Zetterberg, *On Theory and Verification in Sociology,* New York, 1954.

INDEX OF NAMES

335

336

INDEX OF SUBJECT MATTER